Anti-Leftist Politics in Modern World History

Anti-Leftist Politics in Modern World History

Avoiding "Socialism" at All Costs

Philip B. Minehan

BLOOMSBURY ACADEMIC
LONDON • NEW YORK • OXFORD • NEW DELHI • SYDNEY

BLOOMSBURY ACADEMIC
Bloomsbury Publishing Plc
50 Bedford Square, London, WC1B 3DP, UK
1385 Broadway, New York, NY 10018, USA
29 Earlsfort Terrace, Dublin 2, Ireland

BLOOMSBURY, BLOOMSBURY ACADEMIC and the Diana logo are
trademarks of Bloomsbury Publishing Plc

First published in Great Britain 2022
This paperback edition published 2023

Cover design: Terry Woodley
Cover image © *Ruins* (Detail) by Fernando Velazquez. Oil on canvas, 100 x 160cm, 2020

Library of Congress Cataloging-in-Publication Data
Names: Minehan, Philip B., author.
Title: Anti-leftist politics in modern world history : avoiding "socialism"
at all costs / Philip B. Minehan.
Description: London ; New York : Bloomsbury Academic, 2021. |
Includes bibliographical references and index.
Identifiers: LCCN 2021025431 (print) | LCCN 2021025432 (ebook) |
ISBN 9781350170643 (hardback) | ISBN 9781350170650 (ebook) |
ISBN 9781350170667 (epub)
Subjects: LCSH: History, Modern–20th century. | History, Modern–19th
century. | Right and left (Political science)–History. |
Socialism–History. | Liberalism–History. | Imperialism–History. |
Communism–History. | Fascism–History. | Neoliberalism–History.
Classification: LCC D445 .M56 201 (print) |
LCC D445 (ebook) | DDC 909.82–dc23
LC record available at https://lccn.loc.gov/2021025431
LC ebook record available at https://lccn.loc.gov/2021025432

ISBN: HB: 978-1-3501-7064-3
PB: 978-1-3502-2979-2
ePDF: 978-1-3501-7065-0
eBook: 978-1-3501-7066-7

Typeset by Newgen KnowledgeWorks Pvt. Ltd., Chennai, India

To find out more about our authors and books visit www.bloomsbury.com
and sign up for our newsletters.

For Ángeles and Miranda

Contents

Figures

Preface

A troubling insight emerged for me out of a close comparative study of the civil wars in Southern Europe of the 1930–40s, namely, that Adolf Hitler and Nazism were and are a distraction from the *even* more fundamental problem of politics against the left that actually combined in a complex of ways to finally make the Second World War unavoidable. This ran counter to the view across much of the political spectrum of historians that the Second World War was "Hitler's War," that Hitler led the way to war in the mid-to-late 1930s, while the leading figures of the Soviet Union and the liberal capitalist states did not want it, until it was too late to avoid it.[1] That view is only partly true. Though Hitler and Nazi Germany led the way, the march to war could have been stopped had it not been for Britain's policy of appeasement. Though this is not necessarily anything new, it becomes another proposition altogether when appeasement is seen in the context of the fundamental anti-Communism and anti-leftist tendencies that Hitler and Nazi Germany shared—not completely, but to a crucial extent—with Britain, as well as with many of their French and US counterparts at the time. This overlap continued not just up to the Munich Agreement of September 1938 but right up to mid-August 1939. For Britain, which was the leading state in foreign policy for the liberal capitalist world at the time, such politics brought on appeasement, led to the abandonment of the democratic Spanish Republic to a fascist onslaught, and gave rise to the refusal to work with the Soviet Union in any way against fascism and Nazism—until the war was in full force. Though the British foreign policy makers at the time apparently did not realize it, these were also the signs that showed Hitler he could take a shot at world domination. Those signs cannot be understood without factoring in the complex web of anti-leftist politics of the time, against varieties of communism, mainly the Soviet type, but also against varieties of socialism and anarchism, either domestically or internationally. That hostility was a central part of the fundamental political drive of the great power states outside of the Soviet Union and functioned most tragically in favor of the Nazi drive for power and war. This is not to deny that a whole host of other forces were embedded in Germany's aggressive drive and Britain's appeasement of it. There were Germany's pre 1914 imperialist gambles, its defeat in 1918, the harsh punishment meted out to it by the victorious states at the Versailles Conference, the weaknesses of the Weimar Republic, the Nazi racialist ideology, and the Great Depression; for its part, Britain in the mid-1930s was militarily unready for war, and politically it was not exactly a popular option. But these forces combined do not sufficiently explain Britain's perceptions, misperceptions, and final political decisions of 1935–9.

The genocidal horrors of the Second World War and the slaughter of innocents throughout occupied Europe, China, and across Southeast Asia took a death toll of fifty to sixty million people. If anti-leftist politics were a crucial part of what brought on such horrors, they needed to be seriously explored and addressed. The earlier origins and consequences of the problem, as well as how they persisted into the post–Second World War era, including up to the present, increasingly appeared to be necessary parts of the project. Once I began the research into places and times worldwide, I saw the problem just about everywhere in modern capitalist societies and situations of imperialism and colonial rule. Of course, it was varied and often extremely complex, yet it was, and remains to this day, a recognizable pattern. The way it played out in the interwar years and the 1940s was only the most widespread, vicious, and violent example to date. The overall problem I was therefore compelled to bring into relief was that of anti-leftist, or anti-"socialist" politics in modern world history, from the early 1800s to the present.

What clinched my resolve to write the book was the political drama in the United States surrounding the financial crisis of 2008–9 that brought on the Great Recession. At that time, even Alan "Ayn Rand" Greenspan, "for decades … regarded as the high priest of *laissez-faire* capitalism," was advising that American banks would have to be nationalized.[2] Out of perceived practical and even national self-interest, we were witnessing the possible shift toward government ownership and control of large portions of American capitalism's financial and manufacturing sectors. There's no telling where that would have gone—chances are it would have been temporary, yet it would have been an important development and precedent. In any case, after decades of neoliberalism, it was a breathtaking spectacle with astounding implications. Many of the reflexive critics of anything deemed "leftwing" in the United States would have derided it as a "socialist" solution to the crisis. However, in the end, there was a crucial and conspicuous pullback by the newly elected president, Barack Obama, who, despite being ridiculously maligned no matter what by Rush Limbaugh-type conservatives as a "socialist," insisted that the US government should not be in the business of banking or manufacturing, yet it should provide massive subsidies to save them from collapsing, because they were "too big to fail."[3] The supremely contradictory proposition and reality was that of "free market capitalism," in which the US government was not taking over big banks and businesses, yet sustaining them with massive government subsidies. This is often referred to as "socialism for the rich," which, of course, is no socialism at all. It is plutocracy—the rule of the rich—along with callousness toward the needs of the working and lower middle classes that had been ravaged by decades of neoliberal capitalist economic globalization and financial trickery. I saw a hidden parallel between this US government bailout of the crisis-ridden banks and the road to the Second World War. Despite the vast differences between the two situations and their outcomes, it was striking that they were both crucially shaped by the determination to avoid something called "socialism," whether real, fictional, or a combination of the two, when *perhaps* it was somehow lurking. This was about avoiding socialism at all costs, which challenges the conventional notion among historians of the interwar years that Neville Chamberlain's and Britain's policy of appeasement toward Nazi Germany in the later the later 1930s was about "avoiding war at all costs." Instead, certain variations on anti-leftist politics converged in the great power states outside of the Soviet Union in a way that brought the world into another war, the worst yet in human history, which otherwise could have been avoided. Britain's anti-Bolshevism blinded it to the dangers of Nazism. Decades later and quite removed from the 1940s, Obama's "too big to fail" policy reinforced the tendencies within the United States toward plutocracy and oligarchy; it also may have offered a political opportunity for the plutocratic, oligarchical, fascistic, and cynical Donald Trump in 2016.

Going for a comprehensive view of the problem also meant exploring the ways that "socialism" was received in early-nineteenth-century France and Britain, when the term first appeared in political discourse. The animus against it as a new political form was rhetorically violent. Socialism was bestial, insane, sexually perverted, and the end of civilization. It was the kind of dehumanizing language that would and did help justify the later physical violence inflicted upon the proto-socialists in Paris of 1848 as well as the leftists of the Commune of 1871. On a very practical and self-interested level, Alexis de Tocqueville, the famous French aristocrat, politician and author—in particular of *Democracy in America*—was highly attuned to what he saw as the threat of socialism in 1847–8. In speeches to parliament, he warned his bourgeois colleagues that they were "sleeping on a volcano" of social revolutionary ferment. At least he saw the value of granting broader voting rights for French men in 1848, so as to pacify radicals and preserve what he believed were the precious property rights that had been gained out of the French Revolution. But his aim was to gain allies on the somewhat more popular level for the new liberal bourgeois constituency, not to surrender to any new model of social and economic organization that would involve a qualitatively more expanded democracy. He was vehemently opposed to the emergent socialism of the times and condemned the workers' uprising of June of 1848, which was ruthlessly crushed by the French National Guard. Four to five thousand demonstrators were killed in the streets—many thrown into the River Seine, thousands more imprisoned and forced into exile. They had risen up because state support for their employment was suddenly to be terminated, and they wanted it reinstated.

These were just some of the treacherous politics of early capitalist production and market liberalization in Paris and beyond. It was the beginning of an exceedingly rough historical dynamic that expanded worldwide and continues to this day. This book presents a historical account and analysis of many major examples of the problem. It starts in certain parts of Europe, where the problem was first fully evident. Exploring representative examples, it then follows the expanding pattern across the rest of the world. The book seeks a comprehensive and global perspective, though not an exhaustive one—which would be virtually impossible—on the problem of political hostility against the left, including the disasters and the systematic inequalities and injustices, which, in tight conjunction with capitalism, extreme nationalism, racism and patriarchy, it continues to reproduce in the present.

Some will immediately raise certain objections to the book's argument, two in particular: first, the murderous records of Stalin, Mao Zedong, and Pol Pot—the purges, the Gulag, the Kulaks; the Cultural Revolution and the Killing Fields—show that anti-leftist politics have not been aggressive enough in the past two hundred years. If that were my line of research and analysis, I would most likely suggest that a full-on anti-Communist invasion of the Soviet Union at any point in its existence, or such an action against Communist China, or even perhaps against the regime of Pol Pot in Kampuchea, would have added to the most horrific disasters of modern history and in some cases could have led, in effect, to humanity's nuclear self-annihilation. But another kind of argument, one both methodological and historical, which I pursue off and on throughout the book, is that aggressive anti-Communism had a tendency to produce monstrosities, not as anything separate from capitalism and liberalism, but as bastardized offspring of the forces of capitalist production, market liberalization, and their attendant political pathologies. By structural-economic necessity, those forces constantly create political oppositions, some of them deranged, but most of them, despite their flaws, inclined toward protection of labor and the more common good. Yet all of them, for purposes of market expansion in the service of capitalist production and rates of return on investments, if at all possible, must be maligned, neutralized, and undermined, if not destroyed. The second objection to the book's interpretive angle may be that it is overly one-sided. It mainly deals with politics against the left for the past two hundred years—not leftwing fanaticism, not the failures of actually existing socialism, and so forth. This is true, but the purpose of the book is to draw attention to the very serious and under-recognized problem of the systemic and political syndrome of hostility against the left. The book sheds light on the very one-sided distribution of economic and political power in modern history, and the tensions, conflicts, and periodic catastrophes that it engenders.

Notes

1. See, e.g., Jackson Speilvogel, *Hitler and Nazi Germany: A History* (New Jersey: Prentice Hall, 2001), Chapter Seven, "Hitler's War," pp. 192–231; Eric Hobsbawm, *The Age of Extremes: A History of the World, 1914–1991* (New York: Vintage, 1996) pp. 141–7. The study of the civil wars of the 1930s–40s referred to is my own, *Civil War and World War in Europe: Spain, Yugoslavia and Greece, 1936–1949* (New York: Palgrave Macmillan, 2006).
2. Krishna Guha and Edward Luce, "Greenspan Backs Bank Nationalization," *Financial Times*, February 17, 2009. Available online: https://www.ft.com/content/e310cbf6-fd4e-11dd-a103-000077b07658.
3. Brian Beutler, "Obama: Nationalization Would Be More Expensive Than Our Plan," *Talking Points Memo*, April 14, 2009. Available online: https://talkingpointsmemo.com/dc/obama-nationalization-would-be-i-more-i-expensive-than-our-plan.

Acknowledgments

I have many people to thank for their inspiration, encouragement, and support over the years while this book gestated and finally took shape. Number one has to be Angeles Sancho-Velázquez, my partner and colleague, whose interest, patience, and critical support for my efforts, from the beginning, have been invaluable. Certain professors, friends, and students I have had over the years in various institutions and social settings have been highly influential, sometimes more than they could ever realize. These include Ed Segel and the late John Pock of Reed College, who introduced me to serious history and sociology. Procopis Papastratis of the Panteion University in Athens, along with his wife and colleague, Aspasia, have always been vitally supportive. They introduced me to Manolis Glezos, whom I was fortunate to interview at his bookstore on Ippokratous Street Athens in 1981. Each in his own different way, Phillip Shashko and Richard Clogg were steady supporters in those years and remained so ever since. The Vergos and Angelidaki families have always been endlessly generous towards me. This means the late Costas Vergos, his wife Keti, and their sons, Yiorgos and Kiriakos, and Yiorgos's wife Lizabetta. Irini Angelidaki is perhaps the most generous and spirited person I have ever known. From the UCLA Department of History, Professors Ivan Berend, Robert Brenner, and Perry Anderson have all been profound, lasting, and ever-present intellectual influences and inspirations. Special thanks and gratitude also go to numerous friends and colleagues from UW-Milwaukee, among them Carolyn Eichner, Kennan Ferguson, Rachel Buff, Joe Austin, Aims McGuinness, Tami Williams, Margot Anderson, Steve Meyer, Neal Pease, Merry Wiesner-Hanks, Kris Ruggiero, Jasmine Alinder, Marcus Filipello, Christine Evans, Nicholas Fleischer, Lex Renda, Joe Rodriguez, Winson Chu, and Karolina May. Other close and vitally supportive friends at far-flung universities include Stergios Skaperdas, Dave Arnold, Stephen Miller, Tom Mertes, Lissa Wadewitz, Louise Zamparutti, Michael Wintroub, Elen Miele, Claudio Fogu, Wülf Kansteiner, Vinayak Chaturvedi, Jennifer Jordan, Henry Wend, Sue Giaimo, and Marina Iossifides. My gratitude and warm regards go to students I have been fortunate to have in my classes over the years, all of whom have challenged and inspired me. They are too many to name, but top among them are Kalani Inoa, Michael Payne, Timothy Melgard, Amaya Gregory, Cossette Asenjo, Christopher Quintana, and Samantha Nambu.

Very special thanks and gratitude go to Fernando Velázquez for allowing me to use a part of one of his fabulous paintings for the cover of this book. This is an honor. I would also like to express my love and gratitude to Agrippina Velázquez, as well as to Mariló, Jesús, and Javier Sancho-Velázquez, and to Miguel and Vadic Sancho-Velázquez. They have all always been very loving and supportive of my efforts.

My present colleagues and friends that I am so fortunate to have at or through California State University at Fullerton include Professor Andrea Patterson, who offered very helpful critiques of my chapter drafts, as well as her partner Marlowe, who has always been interested in and supportive of my work. Warms thanks to Joe Gonzales, David Kropf, Sandra Perez, Kevin Lambert, Margaret and Steve Garber, Saul Tobias, Craig McConnell, April Bullock, and, perhaps most importantly, the late Nancy Fitch. Amazing friends and intellectual comrades include Eric Schantz, Lucia Aviles, Patrick and Cheryl Cleary, and Phil Blumenfeld. Deep and warm regards and thanks go to my always-supportive sister, Florence Minehan, brother-in-law Marko Tubic, and my nieces, Madeleine and Lydia Minehan-Tubic. Other indispensable friends include Shelly and Indie Lalonde, Bill Meier, Sam Breidenbach, Jeannine Ramsey, Jim Erickson, Philip von Mehren, and Martha Bache-Wiig.

The fact that this book will see the light of day is due to the interest and institutional support of Bloomsbury Academic, specifically the editors Faye Robinson, Maddie Holder, and Abigail Lane, who have been enthusiastically, consistently, and professionally supportive from the start. I will remain very appreciative of what they have done for me. Thanks also to Terry Woodley of Bloomsbury Academic for the book cover design, and to the people at Newgen, especially Shyam Sunder, for their work in the book's production.

Lastly, but most fundamentally and importantly, I thank my late parents, William B. Minehan and Mary Castle Minehan, for their sustained and courageous commitments to a better world.

Introduction and Historical Background

Introduction

In December 1838, a Philadelphia, Pennsylvania, newspaper republished the following item under the title "SOCIALISM," authored by "An Anti Socialist":

> I do most solemnly aver, from evidence of their own showing, with inconvertible facts before me, that these doctrines and sentiments are a sin-loving, soul destroying, Providence condemning, holy spirit denying, Saviour rejecting, God-hating, law abandoning, rulers despising, authority condemning, virtue-destroying, vice advancing, youth corrupting, polygamy-encouraging, adultery-enforcing, accountability refuting, conscience stifling, murder cloaking, property depreciating, community debasing, infidelity introducing, rebellion making, infernal machine, – a family's misery, and progeny's curse.

This was over the top, no doubt, yet only a bit more so than the standard anti-socialist tirades of the times, and since. Its source was in the free-market maximalist *Preston Chronicle* based in Lancashire, England, and was reprinted in the budding textile-manufacturing areas in and around Philadelphia. In all its excess, the passage is emblematic of the overarching systemic and political problem addressed in this book, namely, that the system of capitalist production, coupled with the policies and politics of market liberalization, creates great varieties of leftwing oppositions. First and foremost, these are matters of self-protection, but mainly, because they tend to threaten profit margins, but also often seem to threaten social, cultural, and religious norms, they are then attacked, virulently and hysterically. To the rhetorical violence was soon added the option of physical violence. The book argues that this is one of the fundamental and problematic syndromes of modern history. Capitalist societies and states, in their liberal and authoritarian forms, because of their exploitative character, lay the necessary grounds for leftwing politics; those politics emerge as they do—again, mainly for self-protection—and come under rhetorical and physical fire. This is even true in the realm of falsehoods, that is, on the level of demonization and the "specter" of the left. But, with or without any strong dose of fiction, or propaganda, it adds up to a very powerful and often destructive pattern that has been evident over the past two hundred years.

Indeed, intermixed with the violent rhetoric of the earlier 1800s, extreme physical violence was soon deployed against much of the left, beginning most dramatically with the massacres of thousands of working people and their supporters in Paris in 1848 and again in 1871. Capitalist industrial society was beginning its uneven spread across parts of Europe, the United States, and Japan, leaving the rest of the world vulnerable to their predations. By the actions of those few rival great power industrial states, imperialism and colonialism spread across Africa, Asia, the Middle East, and South America. Where those historical impositions took place, and their inherent injustices became evident, varieties of leftwing politics emerged. People began to think about, seek, and organize for liberation from colonial rule. In turn, a discernable pattern of aggressive anti-leftist politics followed. The syndrome established in the original liberal capitalist societies and states was then introduced to peoples across the colonized worlds, with problems and consequences that were quite distinct from those experienced in the "core" countries.

What later became known as Third World anti-colonialist nationalism, such as that of the pre–First World War *Ghadar* movement that developed in the South Asian diaspora for Indian independence from Britain, became the target of British and other states' colonial authorities worldwide. Meanwhile, the xenophobic nationalists of the pre–First World War era in Europe rhetorically attacked the socialist and internationalist left, with successes sufficient to seriously contribute to the collapse of the Second International and therefore help pave the way for the First World War. In their real and contrived anti-"bolshevism"—intertwined with virulent Nazi anti-Semitism—Fascism and Nazism then led the march to the Second World War, bringing on the dynamics of occupation, collaboration, and leftwing anti-fascist resistance during the war. The imperialist maneuvers against Third World national liberation movements during the Cold War, as well as the weaponization of finance and free-market extremism in the era of neoliberalism, continue to exemplify the problem, as have crucial aspects of the "war on terror" and the recent creep of neo-fascism. Most recently, the COVID-19 pandemic has ripped the cover off the increased inequalities promoted by neoliberal policies since around 1980, amounting to a veritable change in consciousness and awareness of the magnitude of the problem. But, as transparent as the problem has become under the pandemic, inequality has only continued to worsen.[1] This book provides a sweeping look at this series of topics, arguing that they constitute a highly and predictably conflicted and destructive unity, from which, for the sake of self-preservation, humanity ought to exit.

For better and for worse, the system of capitalist production has been spectacular in terms of its material output and the extent to which it has transformed the world. The way the system combines with the policies and politics of market liberalization are complex and dynamic, but, to an extent that at least matches its productivity, it is also mightily prone toward destruction. Capitalist production and market liberalization are driven to destroy the social and political oppositions for which they lay the groundwork; they also destroy other social formations previously outside of their reach, as well as the natural environment. However, as important as this problem is of the destructive side of capitalism, its recognition is nothing new.

It has been seen since the mid-nineteenth century, most famously by Karl Marx, though the extent of its production and destruction has obviously been beyond what he was able to observe. In updated form, this recognition is a part of the central argument of this book, which is that, by necessity, the forces of capitalist production and market liberalization establish the necessities for two things: first, the creation of varieties of "socialist" oppositions against them as political-economic systems; second, that the oppositions must be outmaneuvered and, when deemed necessary, destroyed. This pattern is closely tied to the imperatives of profitability, but by no means exclusively so; it is also bound up with matters of religion, ideology, politics, gender, race, and identity. Plenty of aggressive politics against "socialism" predated the hostility against "communism" that was of particular concern for Marx as expressed in his and Engel's *Communist Manifesto*. Overall, the consequences of such politics against the left, however they are differentiated or combined, have been periodically abysmal.

Opposition against leftwing or "socialist" politics is not a particularly discreet object of analysis. It is as tricky as the social positions, mentalities, and interests of its extremely wide-ranging agents, as well as those of its changing targets. For that matter, speaking of the "specter"—considering the opening line of Marx's *Communist Manifesto*—"A specter is haunting Europe – the specter of communism"[2]—this, again, may be a most unoriginal study. Yet Marx used that observation and phrase mainly to present his *Manifesto*, to clarify matters, present his theory of history that he considered to be scientific, and to therefore dispel the specter. With some outstanding exceptions, such as *The Eighteenth Brumaire of Louis Bonaparte*, Marx mainly ventured into political economy, leaving an invaluable legacy of something more concrete and measurable than what happens on the territory of mass political mobilization, which all too often involves deception, hyperbole, fear, and manipulation. He was not in a position to sufficiently recognize the importance and potentially destructive force of those politics, which ended up permeating Europe and—by way of imperialism, colonialism, and the basic uneven development of capitalism—much of the rest of the world, to this day. It is those politics that have only expanded on the world stage against real and alleged forms of "socialism" that comprise the main subject matter of this book.

The likeliest targets for anti-leftist politics have included a wide variety of actual socialists, anarchists, communists, Bolsheviks, Maoists, and Third World nationalists, among others. However, one has to be cautious in treating any of the targets as "actual" ones, because they are typically made out to be villains and demons in order to mobilize constituencies, as well as to spotlight the targets for attack, as in Ronald Reagan's description of the Soviet Union as the "evil empire." Some of the targets, one way or another, were self-identified as leftist. But then there are cases where it appears that there is no justifiable ground whatsoever for attacking some individuals, groups, or organizations as "socialist," "leftist," "bolshevik," or what have you, depending on the circumstances. Making these matters into the metaphysics of good versus evil has been standard practice since the early 1800s, and it has never advanced the historical understanding, let alone a rational solution, of the problems. General Franco and his co-conspirators in mid-1936, for example, absurdly branded Spain's Second Republic of 1931–6 as "Bolshevik." Hitler targeted the "Jewish Bolsheviks"; even Barack Obama as US president was slammed as a "socialist" by influential figures on the American right. Liberals, conservatives, religious ideologues, xenophobic nationalists, imperialists, fascists, neoliberals, and neoconservatives have all eventually come aggressively into action against various forms of "socialism," with the intended or unintended effects of advancing capitalism and market liberalizations in their liberal, corporate, and authoritarian forms. The attacks have functioned to sustain and advance societal systems of injustice. The drives behind these politics are about class and institutional interests, reinforced and defended by people who either believe, or cynically claim, that they are guarding their cultural identities, often associated with their "freedom," against alien threats. Combined with the other major forces of modern history—state power, race, class, nationalism—aggressive politics against the left over the past two hundred years have an intense pattern of tension, conflict, and warfare within and between societies and states.

As destructive as such politics have been, in combination with the boom-and-bust tendencies of capitalism, they also trend toward self-destruction. While so far they have pulled back from the brink, reconstituted and redeployed, the threat to life on the planet—the natural intertwined with the human—which has been brewing and expanding exponentially for at least two hundred years, has brought us onto manifestly and immediately dangerous territory. Figuratively, it's been about playing with fire; mythologically, it's about Icarus flying too close to the sun, burning and crashing; literally, it's gigafires in California, the melting of the polar ice caps with catastrophic consequences for coastal areas worldwide, India "set to become the world's flood capital," and the acceleration of all of the above by the thawing of the permafrost of far northern global territories that are releasing massive amounts of methane gas.[3] Capitalist production and free-market policy extremism encourage a myopia whose systemically destructive character can no longer be accepted.

While human-made climate change has been in the works for these two hundred years and more, and environmentalism more generally had serious local attention from forest conservationists, ornithologists, and naturalists across the world for hundreds of years, global climate change only became a more popular issue in the latter decades of the twentieth century. Not all environmentalists are on the political left; hunters and sport fishermen who wish to preserve and protect nature for their purposes trend toward conservatism; "eco-fascists" acknowledge the problem of climate change but want to solve it by means nothing less than genocidal—radical reductions in human populations worldwide, especially those with darker skin. But all the while, much of the weaponry of the shortsighted drive for profit within the capitalist system has been pointed at the moving and changing target of "socialism." Liberal and leftist environmentalists have now been conveniently packed into the "socialist" or "radical left" category. For those that really belong in such categories, it is a matter of intelligence and pride to be protective of the planet and its people. But this book is very much about the problem of the recurrent and often deadly demonization of such people and politics.

Historical Background in Europe to 1871: The Problem of the Left and the Liberal Solutions

Early anti-socialist rhetoric and politics belong in the broad and enduring context of elite versus popular conflict that originally occurred through the Liberal and Industrial Revolutions. The French Revolution pitted new versus old elites but, with critical timing and consequences, also involved relatively spontaneous popular interventions on the parts of peasants and poorer Parisian artisans and *sans-culotte* laborers. The Storming of the Bastille, the peasant uprisings associated with the "Great Fear" and the Women's March on Versailles in 1789 were classic examples of popular elements, in effect providing an indispensable push for the advancement of the new, liberally minded elites' interests against those of the old regime. After 1789, popular interventions continued, with significant impacts, as in the establishment of price controls on essential goods in 1793, described as "the law of the maximum." But such interventions diminished for the remainder of the revolution and would not be seen in force again until the 1830s. Even given the fractured and vulnerable character of state power at the time, poorer urban and agrarian people's politics were not sustainable, because lower-middle- and working-class people had no broad, self-protective political organizations or ideology nor any reliable representative force advocating for them at the state level. Their gains in legal and civil rights were relatively significant, but spotty and tenuous, and their social and economic interests remained entirely subordinated to those of well-heeled elites of the old regime and the new wealthy liberal elements.

Britain was also clearly on a path to modernity, but in contrast to France's mostly liberal political revolution, its transformation was characterized and sustained by what became the original case and model of capitalist development, first in agriculture, then, through the Industrial Revolution, in manufacturing. This change in Britain had major political consequences as well, but they were far less explosive in terms of sheer violence. Under the constitutional monarchy, the political changes were more long term and incremental, while the society's socioeconomic changes were as profound and influential as anything anywhere in terms of modern historical change as well as state power on the world stage. While these processes differed significantly between England and France, they still gave rise to two modern great power states. The German confederation, dominated by the Prussian monarchical and imperial state, was slower in terms of the emergence of bourgeoisie, a middle-class, liberal politics, as well as state unification, but even there, as well as in England and France, society and politics were in an unprecedented type of flux that opened fantastic new vistas for social thought and practice. Yet, it is still important to realize that the era of "utopian" socialism came in a relatively quiet political period. In the recent past were the convulsions of the liberal revolutions—the American, French, and Haitian—and the Napoleonic era just after them, while close on the horizon was the new radicalism of the industrial proletariat, those claiming to represent them, and those trying to keep them subjugated.

It was a crossroads moment, an open-ended political-cultural space for visionary reformist politics or, as literary critic Marc Angenot calls it, "romantic" socialism.[4] The lives of the major early reform socialists—Robert Owen in Britain and the Frenchmen Charles Fourier and Henri de Saint-Simon—illustrate the situation well. They were born in the 1760s–70s and grew up in a world whose air was thick with liberal and radical republican politics, revolution, and war. But industrialization and its working classes that were very soon to comprise the basis of the "social problem" that concerned observers of all sorts were only just beginning. Despite their serious support from some intellectual and sociopolitical sectors of French society, Fourier and Saint-Simon in the early 1830s were as castigated and ridiculed by the French establishment as Owen was by its British counterpart. They were presented as sexual perverts, posers, cultists, corrupters, religious heretics, and destroyers of civilization. Theirs were the arguments "of a demented sect, for the new 'social science.'" For the *Times of London*, Owen, Owenism, and its "beastly paganism" typified "the obscenities and orgies of the Socialists."[5] Such arguments that were so common in Britain and France suggest that the perceptions of and the perceived threat from the reform socialist tendency, only in its infancy, was license for political and rhetorical hysteria.

Regarding again the "sin-loving, soul destroying … murder cloaking" view of "socialism" presented at the outset of this introduction, it is instructive to consider Owen in the setting of early 1800s' manufacturing in Britain. He argued that social compassion and cooperation could and should be built into the organization of manufacturing. At his factory in New Lanark, Scotland, which he managed since 1800 and owned since 1813, he showed how to do it and make it profitable. Employees there were treated with a dignity and respect for their health, education, and well-being that contrasted sharply with the abusiveness and hyper-exploitation of men, women, and children characteristic of most factories of the era. Those conditions only got worse and were documented in the "Sadler Report" that was presented to the British parliament in 1832, which led to the somewhat lessened exploitation of child labor through the Factory Acts of 1833.[6] But, save for Owen's precious few collaborators, including the liberal philosopher Jeremy Bentham, the world beyond of relative superprofits was a magnet for the vast majority of the small population of entrepreneurs. One would think that high profits must have been the core force against Owenist socialism, yet it was more than that. There was also a complex, self-interested, fear-based, as well as religious, determination, all arguably verging on the crypto-socialist, that such a system was indeed superior precisely because it was both practicable and more humane—even, that is, more Christian. No doubt, Owen drew tremendous fire for his unapologetic rationalist and atheistic view of life and the cosmos. But his French counterparts, Charles Fourier and Henri de Saint-Simon, were religious, as well as socially and historically visionary, to the point where both were completely shunned by the Catholic Church, with Saint-Simon excommunicated for proposing a "new Christianity" based on practical notions of the common good. All three "utopians" were essentially attacked as religious, political, and economic heretics. But their distinctive commitments to more humane systems of political economy and the common good only grew with time. They were fed in a contradictory and dialectical manner by continued expansion of the very system of capitalism and market liberalization that necessitated such commitments for purposes of self-protection in the first place.

Glossing over for the moment the differences within each of the sides of this debate—the "socialists" versus the "anti-socialists"—these were two basic political-economic and cultural models, one respecting labor in idea and practice, and the other advocating for capital and liberalized markets. On the social and cultural level, they barely interacted, while on the political-economic level they were mutually locked in an uneven battle through the new urban factory system. The side that featured concern for labor's well-being usually fought uphill. "Owenism" and socialism had its supporters, but the demonizers won the day then, as they tended to do, with important variations, up to our neoliberal era, beginning with Margaret Thatcher and Ronald Reagan famously leading the charge in the late 1970s–80s, which created powerful repercussions into the present. However, in view of what was to come in the late 1830s–40s—revolutionary socialist ideas and programs, as well as the spontaneous radical left politics of the Revolutions of 1848—figures such as Owen, Saint-Simon, and Fourier advocated for only a limited form of social reformism. As capitalist industrial society expanded robustly and almost exponentially, in turn, its socialist oppositions proliferated and intensified.

Those that sustained, but also advanced the reformism toward more revolutionary ideas in France in the 1830s and early 1840s, included the Saint-Simonian women, inspired by their namesake's proto-feminism. A figure that was sympathetic with the Saint-Simonians was the feminist author and activist, Flora Tristan, who argued that only gender equality on all fronts would ensure genuine democracy.[7] In terms of the advance of mass politics in relationship to the state, the radical republican Auguste Blanqui clamored since late 1830s–40s for the seizure of the state on behalf of "the people." The proto-anarchist Pierre Proudhon famously argued that "property is theft," by which he meant big property. Louis Blanc proposed a possible socialist workers' economy through a system of "social workshops" that would mitigate the harshness of competitive labor markets. A version of his idea was applied in the economic crisis that hit Paris particularly hard in 1848, though the "national workshops," as they were called, ran up against major and violent obstacles.

In England, Radicals, Chartists, and Owenists in the 1840s merged the struggle for voting rights with those of economic and social justice in and around the workplace, though the vile caricatures, mentioned above, of the internal enemy in England did not turn out to be an actual prelude to systematic violent physical attacks on them. This was clearly not the case in France, which had its violent legacies out of the Revolution of 1789 that set precedents for spasms of more of the same throughout the nineteenth century. French politics and rhetoric were heated and polarized, but it got a lot worse. The conservative French press declared all the leftists to be perverted and monstrous. But by 1847, a wrenching economic crisis had pushed a third of Parisians into unemployment, making radical socialist ideas all the more attractive. On the side of the established order, and perhaps going to the heart of the matter, the liberal Alexis de Tocqueville sounded the alarm very clearly to his colleagues in the French Chamber of Deputies in late 1847, warning them not to fall asleep over the "active volcano" of revolutionary socialism, which, he argued in no uncertain terms, threatened the individual property rights gained through the French Revolution.

De Toqueville was right about the potentials for revolutionary upheaval. Yet it happened not just in Paris, not just in proto-socialist ways, but also in broader leftist ways across Europe in a spate of uprisings summarized in two famous phrases: first, it was the "springtime of the peoples"; second, "history reached its turning-point and failed to turn."[8] It started in Paris in February, when liberals and workers joined together in protest against extremely restrictive voting and other civil rights. They overthrew King Louis-Philippe, and a provisional government was established that declared the Second Republic. In rapid succession in the coming months, liberals, left-leaning workers, and liberal nationalists from the Italian peninsula to the Austrian Empire, the German Confederation, and Ireland were all inspired to join together to rise up for progress on their respective political fronts. In the first place, they all appeared victorious, until they broke ranks over questions of the social good versus liberal individualist rights. In the second place, because of that exposed vulnerability, the reactionary authorities of the old regimes smashed them all. In Paris, Frankfurt, Vienna, and Milan, the division made them all vulnerable to attack; the workers paid the worst price in terms of the loss of life. That was the overall pattern—major lurches forward, but in the end all beaten back and defeated.

In Paris, on the anti-leftist side, the iron police and military fist was added in 1848 to the biting rhetorical ridicule of the 1820s–30s. It was an instructive example of the realities of liberal middle- and upper-class aversion to, and active hostility against, anything that smacked of socialist politics. After the tacit February alliance with the proto-socialists in the quest for universal male suffrage, the liberals backpedaled politically and turned right. They dreaded the consequences of socialism's popular momentum, particularly as it was reinforced through the national workshops that now employed upwards of a hundred thousand people. Low taxes, unregulated markets, and individual rights to amass major private property holdings were clearly paramount for the liberals. They agreed to the government's declaration made on June 23 that the national workshops would be shut down in three days. That was the trigger for the workers' uprising. The liberals then opened the way for the old-regime conservatives, the army, and the National Guard to launch a violent crackdown on the socialists and radical republicans. Two to three thousand people were killed, over four thousand exiled to colonies, mostly to Algeria, and tens of thousands were imprisoned. The battle lines of the liberal revolution were now more clearly redrawn for the conflict between the liberals and conservatives, on the one side, and the socialists of various sorts, on the other. Had the Revolutions of 1848 not ended in the conservative reaction as they did, European history heading into the late nineteenth and early twentieth centuries would have been different. German unification would still have gone forward, but had it been under a liberal-leftist dominated republican program, the Prussian mark on the new state would have been significantly weaker. Likewise, the dissolution of the Austrian Empire would likely have occurred sooner, which probably would have meant a less predatory inclination of the state of Austria vis-à-vis the Balkans. As opposed to the mark of Cavour and the Kingdom of Piedmont-Sardinia, the influences of Mazzini and Garibaldi would have been more prominent in the political complexion of the Italian state. But this is not what happened.

Following upon the vicious, but temporary, chastening of labor in Paris and elsewhere in Europe, the French and broader European economies began an upturn, which rendered the political scene relatively quiet for the following fifteen to twenty years. In that period, the bourgeoisie, big and small, which in 1848 still had radical elements seeking greater electoral political representation, turned fully conservative, choosing to protect their gains against the threat of the new working classes, which remained in a growing ferment of leftwing politics. What became an inspiration for large portions of the growing working classes and their potential leaders was the historical, political, and economic thought of Karl Marx. Amid the upheavals of 1848, though without impacting them, came the publication of the *Communist Manifesto*. It got attention because it offered a bold, provocative, and plausible historical perspective on capitalism and the destiny of the working class, as well as a persuasive call to action. Its opening line about the specter of communism haunting Europe involved some exaggeration and did not acknowledge the fact that the specter of socialism had already been a problem for its opponents for some decades. But the argument and its implications resonated well in working-class and some political intellectual circles, while they also shocked, far and wide. Adding to the tension, and probably most importantly in the long run, Marx and Engels claimed to have developed a new science of human history. Socialism and communism, they argued, were the waves of the future that would emerge out of class struggle—the motor force of human history. Just when the socialist versus anti-socialist politics had become severely polarized and bloody, there came a grand and durable historical and theoretical lens through which to strategically evaluate those politics, yet then proceed to change the world for the better, or attempt to do so, through socially revolutionary political organization and action. In Paris and throughout Europe, while the socialists and radical republicans had been dealt a very hard blow, the growth of industrial society, early forms of labor unionism, and expanded voting rights—always uneven from one country to the next— helped them all to become more popular and powerful.

However, the unifications of Italy and Germany into nation-states—as they actually took place—from the 1850s to 1871, which were seen as strategic and political imperatives by all the leading forces involved, also threw up countervailing forces against the strengthening left. Italy united in 1861 under the leadership of three distinct figures that represented the demographic and political diversity of the Italian peninsula, which was mostly under Austrian dominance up to the 1850s. Count Camillo Cavour of the Kingdom of Piedmont-Sardinia, the radical liberal nationalist Giusseppe Mazzini, and the radical left populist Giuseppe Garibaldi all needed one another's influence and leadership qualities to achieve unification. But in the end, Cavour, the monarchy, and the Piedmont region made the major marks on the new Italian state. Cavour's background was aristocratic and military; his political inclinations were toward constitutional monarchy with a strong attraction to liberal British elitism. He was also able to maneuver very pragmatically and effectively on the great power political scene of the time, as he did by sending military forces to help Britain, France, and Turkey against Russia in the Crimean War in 1854. For that, he expected and got returns. Five years later, France supported Piedmont-Sardinia and its allied regions in the war that drove the Austrians out of most of northern Italy.

Cavour had clearly seen Mazzini, the leftwing republican nationalist, as a top political rival, outing him to the Austrian authorities for a planned insurrection in Lombardy in the 1850s. Mazzini was the consummate revolutionary liberal and moral nationalist democrat, moved by the vision of a united Italy in harmony with the rest of Europe's liberal, republican, and democratic trends. His inspiration was immeasurable, and his sympathy was with Garibaldi, though at that point of unification Mazzini was on the sidelines. He had opposed Cavour's amoral strategic maneuvering. For his part, Garibaldi was a phenomenally charismatic and popular radical republican figure. After fighting alongside radical republican guerilla forces in South America for independence from Spain, Garibaldi landed in Sicily in 1859 to lead a band of "red shirts" to liberate the island, then sail to the mainland and help unify the Italian south with the north, which was being liberated and unified under Cavour's forces. His popular army, growing dramatically in size and morale, defeated the Spanish and French forces that had controlled the southern areas up to that point. The final goal was to take Rome, which remained under the control of the Pope's military. Cavour's and Garibaldi's armies met there in 1861, neutralized the Papal forces, and completed the unification of the new state as a constitutional monarchy under King Victor Emmanuel II. Garibaldi detested Cavour as much as Mazzini did, but he deferred to the new Kingdom of Italy. Cavour outmaneuvered his popular leftwing rivals as he made the monarchy and the Piedmont the lead forces in the country's unification. While the influences of Mazzini and Garibaldi remained vital and durable within Italian, European, and later Third World anti-colonialist politics, the divisions that those three figures represented on the Italian political scene helped to make for a structurally shaky "Liberal State," as it was called, on the way to the First World War.

In contrast to the relatively lively and diverse politics on the Italian scene, the brightest liberal and leftist hopes of the German Confederation were quashed in the outlawing of the Frankfurt Assembly of 1848–9. What predominated in the balance of forces within the Confederation was the Kingdom of Prussia, soon under the Chancellorship of Otto von Bismarck, who made Cavour, his Italian counterpart, look like a liberal radical. Bismarck had utter contempt for anything but the land-owning Prussian *Junker* elite class from which he originated. Given the pressures inherent in European great power state competition, German unification was, by some means, a highly likely development. The Prussians under Bismarck were in the best position to lead the way, just as Cavour and the Piedmontese led the way to a united Italy. From 1864 to 1871, Bismarck directed the three wars that culminated in German unification. First came the incorporation of the northern principality of Schleswig-Holstein, which was virtually uncontested; second came against the Austrian Empire as a potential rival to Prussia in the drive to unify and dominate the new Germany. Prussia defeated Austria in seven weeks in mid-1866. The last step was to persuade and cajole the rest of the southern German principalities to join with the nationalist unification effort. The Franco-Prussian War of 1870–1 did just that, and more.

The way that Bismarck conducted the unification of Germany created four major historical consequences: an extremely bitter relationship with France, a precedent for extremely xenophobic nationalism, a unified and powerful new German state that changed the balance of power in Europe and caused global repercussions, and a blow against the French state and ruling classes that virtually necessitated the establishment of the Paris Commune of 1871. The war severely fractured French and especially Parisian socioeconomic and political structures, creating a power vacuum that compelled those left behind—Parisian elites fled the city in droves as the Prussian forces converged upon it—to fend for themselves. Short-lived though the Commune was—from March 18 to May 28—it was and is recognized as history's first socialist revolution. Its loose leadership and sympathetic popular base included representatives of all of the left-leaning political tendencies that had taken shape in the city since the Revolution of 1789. Once the French state and Parisian political, governmental, and military elites began to regroup, they attacked the Communards ruthlessly, executing twenty to twenty five thousand of them. The fact was on full display that a large and powerful swathe of France's elites feared and hated the Parisian left more than the remaining Prussian military occupiers of the city. This type of elite collaboration with enemy occupiers against leftwing resistance became a pattern repeated in numerous subsequent civil wars in the twentieth century, including those in Russia, Spain, China, Greece, and Yugoslavia. There have also been striking parallels between the patterns seen in those conflicts with the patterns seen, for example, in Indochina and Korea, though one must tread carefully with such comparisons. Synghman Rhee of South Korea and Ngo Dinh Diem of South Vietnam were both heads of American anti-Communist client states in the 1950s–60s; both countries were in long-standing states of devastating warfare that were inseparable from the legacies of French and Japanese colonialism that combined with the major dislocations of the Second World War. Though the courses and consequences of all of the above conflicts were dramatically variable, the core similarity between them was the hard drive of anti-leftist politics, from France in 1871 to Vietnam and Korea nearly one hundred years later.

The following seven chapters of this book track the volatile history of anti-leftist and anti-"socialist" politics in Europe, Africa, Asia, and the Americas, from 1871 to the present. The book has three parts and seven chapters, whose headings tend to be organized around the sharply critical idea of the series of "solutions" to the "social problem" as it first appeared and was recognized in nineteenth-century industrial society. The social problem is mainly treated as the problem of the left that is created by the system of capitalist production combined with the policies of market liberalization. Part I begins with the chapter on the "The Imperial Solution" to the social problem, which was a catastrophe for most of the world; the "Fascist Solution" followed and brought on another horrific war. In Part II of the book, "The US-led Global Anti-Communist Solution" was extremely harsh, sometimes unspeakably so; it also nearly brought the world to self-destruction. Part III of the book, entitled "The Neoliberal Solution," has only one chapter, "The Overkill," which deals with the failures of the neoliberal solution to the problems of global economic development and environmental degradation. The conclusion of the book goes for a large synthesis, and the epilogue mainly addresses the years 2016 to early 2021, including the COVID-19 pandemic. The large scope of the book means it necessarily presents a very selective look at the problem. More examples could have helped, but hopefully the study will stimulate further critical discussion and research.

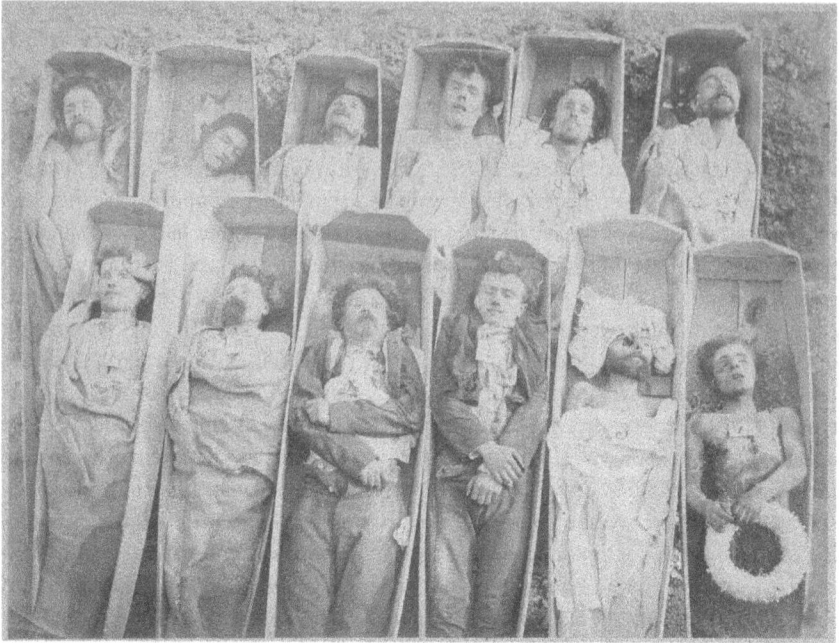

Figure 1 Communards in their coffins. Paris, May 1871. These men had just been shot and killed by the Versailles army. Medium: daguerreotype. Collection: Musée Carnavalet. https://www.parismuseescollections.paris.fr/fr/musee-carnavalet/oeuvres/cercueils-contenant-des-morts-commune-de-paris-1871-paris.

Credit: Photograph taken by André-Adolphe-Eugène Disdéri, May 1871. Permission: public domain, commons.wikimedia.org.

Notes

1. See the Fall 2020 article by Joseph Stiglitz, "Conquering the Great Divide," International Monetary Fund. Available online: https://www.imf.org/external/pubs/ft/fandd/2020/09/COVID19-and-global-inequality-joseph-stiglitz.htm.
2. Karl Marx and Friedrich Engels, *The Communist Manifesto*, ed. Samuel H. Beer (Wheeling, IL: Harlan Davidson, 1955), p. 8.
3. https://www.theguardian.com/environment/2020/mar/11/polar-ice-caps-melting-six-times-faster-than-in-1990s; "Many Indian Districts 'Hotspots' of Climate Change," *The Hindu*, December 11, 2020. Available online: https://www.thehindu.com/news/national/many-indian-districts-hotspots-of-climate-change/article33303346.ece.
4. Marc Angenot, *Rhétorique de l'anti – socialisme – Essai d'histoire discursive 1830–1917* (Québec: Les Presses de l'Université Laval, 2004).
5. Ibid., pp. 19–21. Angenot makes very good use of Albert O. Hirschman's argument in *The Rhetoric of Reaction: Perversity, Futility, Jeopardy* (Cambridge, MA: Harvard Belknap, 1991). The "new social science" was the work of Auguste Comte, seen by many as the founder of the field of sociology, as he took up the study of the "social

problem." Prior to striking out on his own, he was an assistant to Saint-Simon. For just a few of the numerous examples of the vitriolic commentaries in Britain, see *Times of London*, February 7, 1840, p. 5, column C: "Leading Articles—Socialism"; also, February 20, 1840, p. 6, column D: "Socialism, and the New Poor Law."

6. See the "Sadler Report" of 1832 on the website "Project Gutenburg Self-Publishing Press," which includes an explication of its surrounding controversies: http://self. gutenberg.org/articles/sadler_report.

7. For an elaborate and longer-term contextualization of the Saint-Simonian Women, of Flora Tristan's writing and politics, and more, see Carolyn Eichner, *Surmounting the Barricades: Women in the Paris Commune* (Bloomington: Indiana University Press, 2004), pp. 42, 172.

8. The first phrase seems to be of indeterminate provenance. For a dispute about its broad applicability, see Jean-Claude Caron, "The 'Printemps des peuples' (Springtime of the Peoples): For Another Understanding of the 1848 Revolutions," Revue d'histoire du XIXe siècle, vol. 52, no. 1 (January 2016), pp. 31–45; the latter phrase is from A. J. P. Taylor, *The Course of German History* (London: Hamish Hamilton, 1945). He applied it specifically to German Confederation at that time, but it has often been used aptly to describe the broader significance of the Revolutions of 1848 in Europe.

Part One

The Failed Solutions: Imperialism, the Great War, Fascism, Anti-Bolshevism, and the Second World War

Introduction

The proposed so lutions to the problem of the left from the 1870s to the end of the Second World War not only mostly failed but also backfired spectacularly. Imperialism and colonialism were systems of abuse and exploitation that also brought on the Great War, out of which leftwing politics surged in Europe and left-oriented anti-colonialist revolutionary movements developed worldwide, including, of course, in Russia. The Great War also brought on fascism, Nazism, and a worldwide counterrevolutionary trend that ultimately posed a threat to the liberal capitalist states. Fascism was the lead force that brought on the Second World War, though its rise was crucially facilitated by the anti-Communist tendencies of the liberal capitalist states. The result of the Second World War was the ultra-dangerous and often extremely brutal Cold War between the United States and the Soviet Union, as well a phenomenal proliferation of leftist politics across the world, including Communism, as in China; Communist and nationalist anti-colonialism, as in Indochina; and socialist anti-colonialist movements in Asia and Africa. The Cold War imposed a zero-sum-game type of strategic framework in most of the world, including Latin America, with violent consequences. The crises of the 1930–40s turned Britain firmly toward social democracy, which, while it lasted, actually did help alleviate the domestic social problem. In the United States, the New Deal—a very mild version of Britain's social democracy—was at least sustained after the war, but the country got afflicted with extreme and insidious anti-Communism, on the one hand, and a broad civil rights and anti-war movement significantly inspired by Third World anti-colonialist politics, on the other hand. But, aside from civil rights, social democracy and their late-nineteenth-century precursors in some European states, most of the major, large-scale events and developments in this era were not primarily meant to be solutions for the myriad manifestations of the "social problem"; instead, they were mainly the complex results of the self-interested strategic courses of action chosen by the dominant classes of the advanced industrial states, both domestically and internationally.

1

The Imperial Solution, 1871–1917

The underlying and combined brutalities of extreme nationalism and imperialism were fully unmasked beginning in August 1914, as the great power states collapsed into the Great War. The quests for power and glory through territorial conquest, control over resources, trade routes, exploitations of peoples deemed to be inferior, and the co-optations of domestic populations—all of which appeared to be succeeding—were, finally, either extremely destabilized or destroyed. The war heaved up vast fatalities: approximately twenty-two million in total, military and civilian, in Europe, Russia, the Middle East, Africa, and Asia. Particularly from 1916 onward, the result was a worldwide surge of a wide spectrum of leftwing politics variously targeting war, nationalist aggression, imperialism and colonialism, and capitalism. In its geographical extent, at least, it was beyond anything the world had yet seen, surpassing even the wave of revolutionary liberal politics of the 1770s to the 1850s in Europe and the Americas. It involved a stunning range of the world's peoples, cultures, and religions of the time: socialist-oriented reformists and revolutionaries across Europe and the Americas, including anarchists and communists, as well as socialist-inspired anti-colonial nationalists in the colonized worlds of Africa, the Middle East, and Asia. In Europe, the surge of wartime and postwar leftist politics was the great backfire against prewar inculcations of nationalist ideology, the rallying of support for the "civilizing missions" of imperialism, and the incorporations of the new working classes into the societies and political systems of the time. The leftwing surge was against all these things and what they led up to, namely, the war itself in all of its wanton self-destruction whose fallout has kept coming ever since. In much of the rest of the world less affected by the fighting, the backfire was against the deepening entrenchments of European, Japanese, and American colonial power.

In the late nineteenth century, figures such as Britain's Cecil Rhodes famously declared imperialism to be necessary and desirable for resolving the "social question" at home. In fact, imperialism had been presented by its supporters as the premier solution to all sorts of problems within the great power states of the time. But, for the ultra-imperialist Rhodes, it was "a solution for the social problem" in the home country—the problem posed by the growing industrial working class, which was harshly exploited in terms of low wages and inhumane working conditions, if not simply unemployed and desperate. In mid-1895, fresh from attending a series of "wild speeches" to the unemployed in London's working-class East End, Rhodes proposed that

> in order to save the 40,000,000 of the United Kingdom from a bloody civil war, we colonial statesmen must acquire new lands to settle the surplus population, to provide new markets for the goods produced in the factories and mines. The Empire, as I have always said, is a bread and butter question. If you want to avoid civil war, you must become imperialists.[1]

Looking back at any point from a few months into the First World War and onward, the inseparably self-serving and self-destructive character of Rhodes's "solution" is obvious. But this is exactly how it reflected the profound contradictions of *The Age of Empire*, as Eric Hobsbawm described the period: "Its basic pattern ... is of the society and world of bourgeois liberalism advancing towards what has been called its 'strange death', as it reaches its apogee, victim of the very contradictions inherent in its advance."[2] In certain ways Rhodes epitomized and even heightened the contradictions, but no doubt he was also a creature of them, and on the international strategic level he was proposing nothing new. At least since the seventeenth century the competitive great power European scene featured especially British, French, Dutch, and Belgian rivals, mercantile operators that had extremely unusual combinations of state, commercial, technological, military, manufacturing, and financial power. Britain's model of agrarian capitalism then got transplanted to the towns and cities to bring on the Industrial Revolution from the late eighteenth century onward, giving it an undeniable edge on the world stage. Britain's early modern rivals also later developed versions of that capitalist productive power, as did the United States, Germany, and Japan, even though Britain's status as "the workshop of the world" persisted to the early twentieth century. In other words, while those states had their differences, many distant parts of the world were relatively vulnerable enough for all of them to stake their claims and impose their particular regimes of trade, exploitation, and eventual colonization. Still, these powers were highly inclined toward periodic catastrophic war with one another, as attested to by the Seven Years' War (1754–63), as well as the ominous developments of the Franco-Prussian War and the unification of Germany in 1870–1.

Rhodes was already in 1895 a gold and diamond magnate, prime minister of Britain's Cape colony in South Africa, and soon to be a top advocate for the Second Boer War of 1899–1902 that saw British imperial forces defeat and incorporate the Dutch Afrikaners in that territory. Clearly, the system of imperialism that would supposedly solve the "social problem" was already well established, but its development was being accelerated by the second Industrial Revolution—steamships, vast extensions of railways, steel production, internal combustion engines, telephones, electricity, and chemicals—which enabled Britain, France, Germany, Holland, and Belgium to increase their imperial holdings to one-quarter of the world's territory. Perhaps most centrally, the "scramble for Africa" was taking its infamously bloody toll under King Leopold of Belgium in the Congo Free State, where viciously coercive local labor systems had already killed millions and promised more of the same into the early 1900s.[3] While the social problem largely persisted within the imperialist states, with some amelioration, a new, particularly transparent, and often vicious problem was being created between those states and their foreign territories and colonies.

On the matter of domestic social pacification and stability, there may have been short-term advantages to Rhodes's proposition that redoubling empire building would alleviate the social problem and essentially avoid social revolution, though this is very difficult to demonstrate conclusively. Rhodes actually had some cryptic common ground with the moral and political critic of imperialism John Hobson who, in *Imperialism: A Study* (1902), argued that the system involved greedy and cynical efforts to gain outlets for commodities and maximum profits abroad, with the effect, to some minimal extent, of buying off the working classes. Rhodes did not exactly express it that way, but he believed imperialism would help to avoid social revolution by providing "bread and butter" to the working classes. Even Lenin's observations and arguments about the "aristocracy of labor" that he believed had emerged in the socialist labor movements and parties were, in effect, endorsements from the nominal enemy for Rhodes's call for greater colonial expansion for the sake of the home front.[4] Imperialists were proving very effective in co-opting reformist labor leaders to their cause. However, imperialism was as much about the seductions of nationalist chauvinism as it was about economic gain. Peoples elsewhere now under European colonial rule could indeed be uplifted by German, French, American, or English culture—or so went the thinking under the increasing ideological hegemony of the "civilizing mission" and the emotional hegemony of nationalist glory.

In the most minimal sense and in the short run—saying nothing yet about the war on the unseen horizon—imperialism within its states of origin did not worsen labor conditions or push workers toward more revolutionary politics. If anything, it did the opposite. But there is no doubt that capitalist industrial society and productive power expanded in the period before the First World War beyond anything seen to date, despite the Long Depression of the 1870s–90s. With its deflationary pressures, that slump helped accelerate imperialism worldwide, with each state recklessly seeking to fuel its own advancements and outperform its rivals. However, imperialism as it was characterized at the time presupposed the fundamentals of capitalism and industrialization, not the other way around. Imperialism was an expression of increasing capitalist productive power in a few states. Needless to say, the benefits of the new industrial society were distributed extremely unevenly. And where standards of living did increase somewhat for industrial workers, who in Germany and Britain, for example, saw their wages double from the 1870s to 1913, this was more clearly attributable to robust capitalist development domestically than it was to imperialism. As a projection of the political, economic, technological, and military power of the capitalist states, and as a means of gaining greater resources and markets, imperialism helped sustain the new industrial societies as it also subjugated peoples and territories throughout the world. Through those combined systems or not, there was definitely no "immiseration of labor," which was Marx's phrase that suggested increasingly vast impoverishment was inevitable and imminent under capitalism; nor was there any *ultimate* crisis, which would have manifested politically by way of the social problem in the economically advanced states. The social problem continued to be endemic, but so far manageable, in the model of capitalist industrialization and imperialism of the era.

The strongest claim that people like Rhodes could make was "success by association," in the sense that the British Empire was a prominent dimension of the British state and industrial society. Sensational claims about empire were easy to make, and some believed them to be true. It is clear that Rhodes had a business interest in making such a general pitch. In the end, imperialism may have alleviated some of the tensions in the advanced states, but it was marginal. For those subjected to colonial rule, it was often deadly. Yet, also on the deep downside of this ledger, within the powerful states as well as beyond them, capitalist industrialization and imperialism combined to result in the annihilation of millions in the Great War, and it did not stop there.

In hindsight and in the longer run, at least into the middle of the Great War, it is evident that imperialism was not the solution to what Rhodes, unintentionally and all but explicitly, described as a system of grave social injustice. In the shorter run, however, up to 1914, the expansion and the material gains of capitalism and imperialism—aside from whether the latter was the "highest stage" of the former or not—were critical and indispensable in isolating labor radicalism. They convinced large swathes of industrial laborers and their political leaders to resign themselves to, if not cooperate with, the imperialist politics of the leading states. Such combinations of structural reality and political pressure were difficult to resist. What prevailed in early-twentieth-century Europe was no exception; it goes far in explaining the infamous *de facto* collapse of the Second Socialist International, when it dropped its anti-war stance and its socialist internationalism in the face of the impending war in 1914. While Lenin ceaselessly assailed European labor's increasing tendencies toward reformism and its compromises with imperialism, calling it all sheer "opportunism," a number of factors gave him a position of tremendous personal power and relative maneuverability in Russia. The imperial state was undeniably shaky, nor could it promote to its budding working class the seductive sort of "civilizing mission" claimed by the French and the British; its police forces were repressive, often brutal, but inefficient on the broad and lively fronts of Russian radicalism. Lenin's strategic intelligence was remarkable, which was reflected in his political and economic analyses as well as in the organizational model and power of his Bolshevik faction within the Russian Social Democratic party. For a brief, rare, and crucial moment, the devastating dislocations of the war allowed Lenin, his party, and the soviet organizations within Russia to evade the normally extreme and varied hostilities against the revolutionary leftwing politics of the era.[5]

With his notions that imperialism would pacify the working classes, Rhodes had plenty of company within the British establishment and among their counterparts in other great power states when it came to domestic and colonial policies. The arguments and justifications ran the gamut from cultural and political to demographic and economic. There were also many prominent and self-proclaimed "reluctant" imperialists, such as Disraeli's rival Gladstone, as well as Germany's Bismarck, but the trend of increasing support for empire was largely the same. Underlying Disraeli's influential "one nation conservatism" was the assumption that the social problem in Britain was composed of the rich versus the poor—the "two nations"—and the only way to unite them and achieve the greatest glory for Britain was through a common imperial mission. This would instill a cosmopolitan dignity into the working classes that would raise their self-esteem, bond them to the aristocracy, and reveal the crass and callous character of the liberal middle classes and the Liberal Party. In this political-cultural pitch from the elites to the masses, Disraeli oversaw the expansion of voting rights, state-sponsored social welfare legislation, and the legalization of trade unions. In a speech in Manchester in 1872, he clearly reaffirmed the importance of social reforms as a means of avoiding revolution, when he contrasted England with France in 1871 and 1848.[6] He favorably invoked the legacy of the earlier reformer, Robert Peel, who had declared in the 1830s that "the principal of my reform is to prevent the necessity of revolution .... I am reforming to preserve, not to overthrow." This was about pragmatism; upper- and middle-class concessions to labor were meant to be, and were, co-optations. National imperialist expansion would be the crowning glory that would instill pride and nationalist partisanship in those that had no direct interest in it. In 1875, as a means of ensuring greater revenues and glory, Disraeli saw to the purchase by the British government of a large portion of the shares of the Suez Canal Company, putting Britain firmly on track to control over that vital economic and strategic link from the Mediterranean to the Red Sea and the Indian Empire. In the wake of that transaction he led the way to make Queen Victoria the empress of India.

Jules Ferry, mayor of Paris during the Commune and two-time prime minister of France in the early to mid-1880s, is most often cited for his declarations of French racial superiority that aimed to justify imperialist expansion. Such ideological messaging at the time mobilized domestic support for imperialism and helped instill purpose and meaning in and for those responsible for imposing the colonial regimes. However, Ferry's most immediate and practical pro-imperialist argument warned of the exacerbation of the "social problem" within France should the country's markets abroad be lost to North American or other competitive producers. There was "a crying need" for France's industrial population to gain colonial markets for their industrial outputs: "Nothing is more serious," he asserted; "*there can be no graver social problem*; and these matters are linked intimately to colonial policy."[7] This was the spring of 1884. The merciless repression of the Paris Commune as well as the Berber and French *pied noir* uprising in Algeria had their intended chastening effects on the domestic and colonial enemies, but inevitably aroused fears among French elites of more of the same at home and abroad within the growing empire. Domestically, Ferry was a liberal reformer, known especially for his efforts to strengthen the institutions of French public and secular education. He shared this stance against the Catholic Church with the left, though they differed on the all-important specifics of the curriculum, which for Ferry centered on inculcations of nationalism and political doctrines that would purportedly help make the workers as reasonable and satisfied with their lot as the bourgeoisie was with theirs.[8] The two proposed bridges to the working classes, Disraeli's from the aristocracy and Ferry's from the liberal bourgeoisie, were from higher to lower terrains of social class, but they involved some mutual recognition. They served to soften the stances of the socialist movements, as they helped establish hybrid public and statist "socialistic" policies. In that way, they affirmed the principle and the culture of the "social," as opposed to the liberal and well-propertied individual. Yet, given the transformations of industrialization, the increasing importance of mass politics, and the realities of imperialist antagonism worldwide, they also helped to lay the basis for, and then fuel the growth of, xenophobic nationalism.

Bismarck was relatively cautious and skeptical about empire building, but he made his exceptions. He succumbed to the strategic pressure to join in on the "scramble for Africa," while also attempting to control and manage it; he convened and presided over the Berlin Conference that began in November 1884 and was essentially intended to ensure a stable and thoroughly self-interested imperialist carve-up of Africa. Germany now appeared to be playing a difficult, if not impossible, game of "catching up" as an imperial power on par with the British and French. Given Germany's position, to aggressively compete with British and French imperialism, for Bismarck, would have taken a recklessness on the international stage beyond what suited his strategic temperament—as it later suited Kaiser Wilhelm II's, not to mention Hitler's. The Kaiser grew impatient with Bismarck's caution, ousted him, and took control of German foreign and colonial policy, with disastrous consequences. However, before his ouster, when it came to outflanking the burgeoning German socialist movement and party, Bismarck's determination was clear and consistent in a way that set a precedent within Germany and beyond. While robust revenue flows from captive colonial markets could not be realistically expected, as they could be for the British and the French states, the German chancellor launched a systematic campaign to create what came to be known as a welfare state. Germany's rapid industrialization created both the need and the revenue for a more focused and systematic domestic solution to the "social problem." The British and the French, who prioritized imperial expansion to the point where their holdings had generated deep and complex political-institutional demands upon their states, created comparatively more makeshift welfare systems.[9]

Bismarck's second main front against the German socialists and their sympathizers was to attack their civil rights. His hostility was clear and direct, yet not particularly effective. In 1878, he used a second failed assassination attempt on Kaiser Wilhelm I as a pretext to propose and successfully advance "Anti-Socialist Laws" through parliament. These outlawed the gatherings, literature, and fundraising of the Socialist Workers' Party of Germany (SPD) and any organizations or individuals that were propagating socialist views to the public. Many socialists ended up in prison or exile, though the legislation did not block the actual election of socialists to parliament. In fact, their parliamentary numbers continued to grow while the laws were in effect, only at a slower pace than before and after. With the socialists held in check to that degree, Bismarck backed the most influential and fully institutionalized social reforms of the time, including state-funded retirement pensions and unemployment compensation. However, the chancellor's tactical support for workers began to crumble in the context of the likewise tactical and increasingly vocal support for them by Kaiser Wilhelm II, who assumed the throne in June 1888. In his maneuvers against Bismarck, Wilhelm went so far as to attack the Anti-Socialist Laws. In 1890, he forced the chancellor to resign, abolished the Laws, presented himself as a friend of the workers, and supported further social welfare programs, all with the intent to undermine the influence of the SPD and its ideology. Meanwhile, and most notoriously, he got reckless abroad, antagonizing just about all great power states, including Britain, France, Russia, and Japan. Despite their highly consequential differences on foreign policy, as well as the personal and domestic political differences between Bismarck and the Kaiser, they both used statist means to outflank the socialists, breaking ground for Germany's version of rightwing populism, if not the national socialism of the 1917–45 period.[10] Remarkably, these tactics did not stop the SPD from becoming the largest party in the *Reichstag* by 1914, but the new statist supports, combined with the turn toward extreme and insidious nationalist politics, blunted the socialists' anti-imperialist and internationalist resolve, so that when the critical moment came in mid-1914, their parliamentary representatives voted for war.

Though it showed some broad structural similarities with its European rivals as an advanced capitalist industrial state, the United States was also distinctive in a number of ways. Its industrial, urban, and demographic expansion from 1871 to 1914 made it the world's largest industrial power, producing approximately one-third of the world's manufacturing output and 43 percent of its steel.[11] Between 1880 and 1910, the US population increased from fifty million to ninety-two million. Around twenty million of the new Americans were immigrants, mainly from Southern and Eastern Europe, who affected the country's ethnic complexion irreversibly. The country's urban population increased from over 25 percent of the total in 1870 to over 45 percent in 1910, including the rapid growth of cities of over a hundred thousand inhabitants, all of which now had large neighborhoods of recently arrived poor immigrant laborers and their families, mostly in their own ethnic enclaves. They pushed for better wages and working conditions, which meant serious and expensive concessions from their mostly white—and now "nativist"—male employers. In the eyes of preestablished middle- and upper-middle-class white Americans, the new laboring populations were necessary for their own economic advancement, yet displayed an extra-pronounced and threatening "ethnic" and "foreign" character. They were conspicuous in dress, skin tone, accent, and language, and therefore were easy targets for attacks from white nativists.[12] Some of the legacies of the complex societal, state, and cultural differences on the European historical scene were recombining into a complex and conflicted set of socioeconomic and political inequalities—racist, classist, and sexist—as they moved onto the modern American stage. Meanwhile, the indigenous peoples of the country, and most of those of African origin that had been enslaved, shipped to the American colonies and sold as chattel, fared far worse than any of the rest.

In terms of imperialist expansion, the United States had definite long-term geostrategic advantages over other advanced capitalist states at the time, even though it lagged behind the formal colonial annexations by the British and French of far-flung lands and peoples. The western territories offered vast outlets and resources, which to some extent relieved the social and political pressures of industrialization. That helped to relieve the political pressure on the American elites to establish any systematic state-sponsored welfare system until the ground-up labor pressures upon the Roosevelt administration led to the New Deal during the Great Depression of the 1930s. The other major factor in this postponement was the absence of any "old regime"–type feudal and aristocratic elements that remained powerful influences within the major European societies and states. A politically unencumbered business class, with an obvious and unapologetically brutal predominance over labor, was the vanguard of American westward expansion in the late 1800s. It is no wonder why the United States was the last of the industrially advanced states to devise a welfare system designed to minimize the vagaries of capitalist development. While the French and the British cases contrasted significantly with that of Germany, all three contrasted most sharply with the United States, due to the vast, resource-rich lands to the west inhabited by a wide array of peoples that were as conquerable and subject to genocide by the American settler and state forces as the Herero and Namaqua peoples of Southwest Africa were for the German colonizers. According to a United Nations inquiry in 1985, the German "General von Trotha issued an extermination order; water-holes were poisoned and the African peace emissaries were shot. In all, three quarters of the Herero Africans were killed by the Germans then colonizing present-day Namibia, and the Hereros were reduced from 80,000 to some 15,000 starving refugees."[13] The European imperialists had to contend with relatively defenseless indigenous peoples in areas of the world far from home, as in Africa, India, and Indochina. But they also had to contend with other European rivals while, for the time being, the Euro-Americans had only the indigenous peoples to subjugate, which, given the extreme imbalances of power involved, favored the settler colonialists overwhelmingly.

America's ideals and practices of liberty and justice were rooted in Enlightenment liberalism as much as were those of France and Britain, but also more specifically in popular sovereignty, radical republicanism, and the experience of the war for independence from monarchical Britain. While these ideas and practices tended to be exclusive to, and jealously guarded by, citizens of mainly Northern European origins, it remained important and promising that the largely agrarian society of the United States up to the 1840s–50s showed a remarkable openness to radical democratic politics. The "free labor" arguments that were drawn from those politics became a highly effective political-ideological force for the abolitionists in their drive against the slave labor system of the South. With the Union victory over the South in the civil war of 1861–5, those arguments had the potential to develop in numerous directions, including one that would strengthen the bonds among laborers, and generate widespread sympathy for them, against the march of unfettered industrial capitalism. For the American business classes to realize their visions of "manifest destiny," those potentials had to be quashed. On the other hand, many believed that to abolish slavery, only to move on with other forms of systematic exploitation of men, women, and children, such as sharecropping, or the intensification and expansion of wage-based factory labor—or of "wage-slavery" as the reformist Knights of Labor put it in the early 1880s—would violate the spirit of the Thirteenth Amendment that constitutionally assured emancipation. In fact, the 13th Amendment remained wide open to abuse because of its statement that "neither slavery nor involuntary servitude, *except as a punishment for crime whereof the party shall have been duly convicted*, shall exist within the United States, or any place subject to their jurisdiction."[14] The response of the predominant parts of the white leadership and police forces across the South was to see to it that "emancipated" Blacks were arrested for petty and trumped up crimes, slapped with automatic convictions from complicit judges, and thrown back into involuntary servitude and permanent disenfranchisement. In a system of penal labor, or "convict leasing," large prison labor camps were established and mostly filled with Black men. Also on a general level, for the first time on such a scale, Black men were culturally vilified and attacked as threats to decent white society and to white women in particular. Prior to the civil war, the predominant image of Black men in white society had been naturally obedient and subservient.[15]

Still, some of the prominent radical Republicans who had helped lead the fight for free labor against the slave labor of the American South had not given up hope for further, more expansive and inclusive emancipations. The news of the radicalism of the Parisian Communards of 1871 inspired and emboldened many labor activists, radical reformers, and others who voiced serious doubts about the moral qualities of capitalist industrial society. These included middle-class radicals who aspired to be labor leaders or advocates for radical democracy in the United States, such as the abolitionist Wendell Phillips; the radical Republican senator, William Sumner; and the editor of the *New York Tribune*, Horace Greeley, who all sang the praises of the Communards. They were roundly attacked for doing so, but Greeley's *Tribune*, which had Marx (and indirectly Engels) on the payroll from 1852 to 1862, remained perhaps the largest and most influential newspaper in the country in 1871. Nor was Sumner's voice drowned out on the sidelines of politics or print media. On the other hand, the news of the radicalism of the Commune sent shudders through the new and rapidly growing urban conglomerations of white middle- and upper-class Protestants, which seemed to be falling into the grips of an unwitting crypto-Marxist expectation that a social revolution of the new urban laboring masses was on its way.[16] A *New York Times* editorial, "The Lessons of Paris," put it in a nutshell: "This rabble, this crowd of revolutionary socialistic laborers, having arms in their hands, and adventurers from all countries to lead them, seized control of the city, and held down the vast multitude of the well-to-do and orderly, as easily as Napoleon had trampled on them."[17] A "common ruin" would follow from the well-to-do classes abandoning responsibility to lead and to rule, as the French middle and upper classes had done when they resigned themselves to the *coup d'état* of 1851 and the Second Empire under Napoleon III that lasted to the crises of the Franco-Prussian War. The editorial chastised the French ruling classes but warned of what happens when the *canaille*, the rabble, the "pack of dogs," have a shot at power. As shown by historian M. J. Heale, the alarm in New York City and beyond was that the "reds" were out to "organize hell in France," and the threat seemed imminent to many in the United States.[18] For most American elites, the Commune was foremost about the supposed threats to private property, even though the Commune confiscated only Church property; elite indignation was also focused on the execution of the archbishop of Paris on May 24, 1871. By that point, thousands of Communards had *already* been shot on site by army troops, but there was no sympathy for them. It was also quickly forgotten that French elite and state forces in the first place betrayed their own people to the Prussians, which prompted the radical politics of self-protection in the first place.

One of the most important aspects of the Commune and the Franco-Prussian War that triggered it was that for the first of several crucial times in modern history, international war had set off a social revolution, in this case a fully spontaneous one. While the politics of the Commune provoked significant opposition and alarm in the United States and beyond, the next such historical moment came with Russia's Bolshevik Revolution of 1917, which sowed divisions within the surge of leftist politics out of the First World War, and, through fascism and rightwing authoritarianism, a tidal wave of anti-socialist politics worldwide. For now, the dominant classes of the United States saw French radical democrats as representative of a new collective menace, close on the horizon, coming for their property and privilege. It was fuel for paranoia. As with the liberal middle classes in the advanced countries of Europe, with their revolutionary ideological origins in the Enlightenment, the liberal middle classes of the United States largely abandoned their radical heritage and principles. They advanced only as far as their narrow interests took them. They believed they saw the socialists on the rise and it was time to protect their gains. This meant containing and, where necessary, attacking the new working classes and their cause of liberty and justice for all. The reaction of the majority of the predominating social forces in American society to the Paris Commune was among the more dramatic developments that anticipated the later surge of anti-"bolshevism" in the United States and worldwide.

Meanwhile, a series of labor strikes began that were suppressed with deadly force by varying combinations of federal, state, and private security forces. The depression years of 1873–9 brought deflationary pressures, frequent wage cuts, and mass layoffs that led to spontaneous, but increasingly organized, protests. Three consecutive wage cuts were imposed on railroad workers in 1876–7, prompting the Great Railway Strike of 1877, in which, countrywide, approximately one hundred laborers were shot and killed by police, federal troops, and Pinkerton security forces. May 1886 saw the nationwide general strike for the eight-hour day. On May 1 and 2 in Chicago, the protests were peaceful, but on May 3, two strikers were killed outside a harvesting machine factory, and a meeting was called for the following day at Haymarket Square. At the meeting, someone—it was never determined who did it—lobbed a bomb at the police, setting off a staccato of death and injury between strikers and protesters on the one side, and strikebreakers and police on the other. Eight policemen and four workers died from their wounds, and scores were injured on all sides. May 5 saw the Bay View Tragedy in Milwaukee, where the governor of the state, Jeremiah Rusk, called in National Guard forces to stop ironworkers and their sympathizers from striking and marching in favor of the eight-hour workday.[19] Seven strikers and their supporters were shot dead, including one child. The list of further strikes and deadly responses against them is long. From 1877 to 1917, at least six hundred striking laborers or labor organizers were killed. For the time being, little could match the violence meted out to the Parisian Communards, but in terms of deadly state and corporate violence against laborers who were simply seeking higher wages and better working conditions, the United States was second to none.

Demonstrations and protests occurred countrywide, amounting nearly to a general strike that revived and intensified the anti-labor anxiety and antagonism that had been simmering since the news from Paris of 1871. In full solidarity with the cause of the Railway Strike, but also with the Parisian Communards and the thousands of them that had been massacred, a localized general strike was called and a worker's Commune proclaimed in Saint Louis, Missouri—a premier railway hub linking rail lines from all directions. The repression of that Commune resulted in eighteen deaths and hundreds wounded at the hands of federal troops. Across the country, upwards of one hundred strikers were killed by federal troops as well as vigilantes and Pinkertons hired by the railroad corporations. As the violence took its toll, the harsh social character of industrialization went unchanged as a prime motivator for leftwing organization and protest.

The ideological and legal weapons used to justify the anti-labor violence and severely restrict the organizing rights of white laborers in the south and all laborers elsewhere in the United States were in the arsenals of the classical liberals, Social Darwinists, and Supreme Court majorities. Culturally and legally, they "reconciled" the extreme socioeconomic inequalities of the unfettered industrial capitalism of the Gilded Age with what were passed off as traditional American notions of liberty, reduced purely to the realm of individual choice and action, regardless of social setting. Strong individual white men were front and center, showing unfettered "nature" in full bloom. Labor unions, union organizing, and any state interventions that regulated economic activity in favor of labor were deemed to be threats to pure individual liberty. The poor and disadvantaged were simply and naturally worthy of their fates; any inherently antagonistic dynamics between owners and laborers were as natural as the differentiations of Darwin's tortoises of the Galapagos Islands. For the Supreme Court under Melville Fuller from 1888 to 1910, the epitome of freedom was found in contractual relations between individuals. It was *laissez-faire* maximalism that unconditionally supported the new model of large corporations that was taking shape at the time. The actual social class character of industrial society was denied by means of ideological, political, and juridical individualism. Labor was legally prohibited from unionizing; culturally, workers were encouraged to identify with their ethnic and racial groups. Each class and group was in its rightful and natural place; it was *nature's* divide and rule. Any interference in the arrangement would produce dire consequences for civilization. The highest expressions of freedom were found where individuals entered into contracts with one another, as in the individual laborer's wage contract with his employer.[20]

The Example of Colonial India and the South Asian Diaspora

The assaults on leftists in the advanced capitalist countries, where labor was exploited at points of production—in the factories—had certain parallels in the colonized worlds, where potential elite and middle-class manufacturers and merchants were blocked from advancement by colonial regimes. India, for example, had little in the way of an industrial working class but plenty of aspiring entrepreneurs who were denied both market opportunities and political power. They trended more and more against colonialism and got attacked for it. Though clearly far-flung from one another and with differing social class characters, these "core" and "peripheral" country conflicts took place within the same structurally conjoined systems of industrial capitalist production and the aggressive trade policies of the British. An important point that arose from this set of differences was that the politics of "right" versus "left" took shape and played out differently in each part of the world. They had different social bases and political targets, yet they both took place within the parameters of those vitally interconnected domestic and international systems of production and trade; in a myriad of ways, they both called for either the reform or the overthrow of their prevailing economic and political orders. Capital versus labor was the strongest dynamic shaping politics in the advanced capitalist countries. While that undergirded the power of its empire, it was mainly Britain's trade policies that blocked the subcontinent's potential productive power and fueled the anti-colonialist nationalism. British colonialist policies created very fertile ground for radical political reformism, if not outright rejection of colonial rule. The main vehicle to those ends was the *swadeshi* movement for economic self-sufficiency, which, since its inception, contained the potentials for becoming a movement for political independence.

With the Sepoy Rebellion of 1857, India already demonstrated the potentials for anti-colonialist politics. Meanwhile, the political-economic dynamics of the situation drew the attention of Marx, some of whose articles appeared in the *New York Daily Tribune* of the 1850s. He explained that the efficiencies of British textile production, which relied on the rare system of capitalist manufacturing, but also on low wages and low cotton prices, whatever their sources—American, Egyptian, or Indian—allowed British producers and merchants to undercut the viability of traditional Indian textile production. As Marx put it, "[it] was the British intruder who broke up the Indian hand-loom and destroyed the spinning-wheel. England began with driving the Indian cottons from the European market; it then introduced 'twist' into Hindostan [*sic*], and in the end inundated the very mother country of cotton with cottons."[21] The British intrusion into the Indian economy continued largely unabated at the turn of the century but with a larger array of manufactured commodities added to the cottons. That intrusion fed anti-colonialist economic and political nationalism that brought on and then combined *swadeshi* with *swaraj*, or the politics of self-rule.

The epicenter of India's anti-colonial politics in the late nineteenth and early twentieth centuries was the region of Bengal, whose population was approximately eighty million. Around 75 percent of the total were Hindu and predominated in the west of the region. The remaining were mainly Muslim and predominated in the east. Bengal's capital, Kolkata, was Britain's seat of power in India and its premier port city. Bengali merchants, manufacturers, and others from both religious backgrounds, though mainly Hindu, clearly saw the imbalances in productive and market power, as well as the opportunities for economic gain that would accrue to them, but only if they gained greater political power. Even Bengali *zamindari* landlords that had historically enjoyed strong British tactical support tended toward anti-colonialist nationalism. On one level, this was all about the making of the Indian national and anti-colonial bourgeoisie, but most immediately worrisome for the British was the movement's intercommunal character. Hindus and Muslims in the region had significant common political ground as *Bengalis*—enough to trigger the virtual reflex of divide-and-rule politics on the part of the British authorities. Lord Curzon, the Viceroy of India, and Herbert Risley, the Home Secretary, were both masters of such tactics. Risley was at the cutting edge of the Social Darwinist–oriented racialist ethnography of the time, variations on which, as we have seen, characterized elite conservative thought and permeated state policies throughout most of the advanced capitalist world and its colonial territories. Curzon and Risley officially divided Bengal between a mainly Hindu west, which incorporated neighboring parts of Bihar and Odisha, and a Muslim east, which now would include Assam. As Risley put it, "Bengal united is a power; Bengal divided will pull in several different ways …. One of our main objects is to split up and thereby weaken a solid body of opponents to our rule." However, once the "Curzon Line" of partition was implemented in 1905, it mostly produced a double backfire of increased anti-colonialism and bloodshed, none of which ceased even after the British succumbed to the pressures and lifted the partition in 1911.[22]

The Indian National Congress (INC) had been established in Mumbai in 1885. Eventually it was central to the movement for independence, but its earliest leaders—all socially elite and highly educated—aimed to reform Britain's Indian Empire, not overthrow it. One of the Congress's avowed principles was to be open to people of all faiths, yet it was predominantly Hindu. By the early 1900s it had also factionalized into "moderates" and "extremists"; the former challenged the British to reform education and administration, and to extend freedoms of speech, the press, and religion to some of its imperial subjects; the latter also advocated for those rights and reforms but argued that violence was justified as a means of attaining them and that the final goal was complete independence. In immediate response to the British partition of Bengal, but also to the *de facto* exclusiveness of the INC, the Muslim League was created in Bengal in 1906. It mirrored the INC as an organization mainly composed of educated middle-class professionals aiming to advance their civil rights and political interests. For the British, this splitting of their opposition was taken as a success, but on a more important level, for everyone involved, it created far more problems than it solved. The emergent anti-colonialists were emboldened by the obviously divisive and provocative character of British policy, even though they were also divided by it. But the policy instilled within the movement a more incendiary dynamic than would have likely otherwise developed. It all intensified anti-British politics, but it also fueled the intercommunal Muslim–Hindu mutual antagonism and eventual slaughter on the road to independence in the 1940s. Furthermore, the partition of Bengal strengthened the drive for independence by boosting the *swadeshi* movement for economic self-sufficiency, whose tactic was to boycott all British imports—textiles, but also sugar, salt, and luxury goods—and to favor Indian-made products. In Bengal and across much of British India, there were protest marches, public bonfires of British-made clothing, and spontaneous and organized outbursts of protest songs, the most famous of which was "Vande Mataram," whose opening line roughly translated as "Mother, I bow to thee." Bengal's Lieutenant Governor Fuller outlawed the song for "Mother India" in November 1905 on the dubious grounds that it was an affront to Christians as well as Muslims.[23] There were public humiliations of anyone—adults or children—shouting the slogan "Vande Mataram." Any homes scrawled with the slogan were destroyed. In other words, the dividers and rulers outlawed the song and the slogan because they claimed they were divisive.

The violent crackdown on the protests created a surge in student militancy that became another major target for repression. In October 1905 the government of Bengal issued the Carlyle Circular, which threatened to withdraw all government funding for individuals and institutions that took a nationalist turn. It backfired, spurring the establishment of independent national schools that drew in significant financial support from wealthy anti-colonialists. April 1906 then saw one of the more infamous attacks on anti-colonialist protesters with the use of the *lathi* charge: police attacking with long sticks of bamboo or cane, sometimes bristling with metal studs. The British ordered a *lathi*-wielding force of ethnic Gurkha troops recruited mostly from Nepal to break up a politically charged provincial conference of Muslim and Hindu activists in the East Bengal city of Barisal. There, a resolution was being drafted on the fast escalating politics of self-rule. Bal Ganghadar Tilak, a member of the "extremist" wing of the INC, likened the British authorities' treatment of the anti-colonialists to that of the Russian czarist police against their domestic opponents.[24]

Most of the leading figures in the growing movement for Indian autonomy or independence before 1917 were cosmopolitan, middle class, and well educated in British institutions either within colonial India or in Britain. Some were British, even drawn from the ranks of the imperial administration. Allen Octavian Hume had Scottish origins and was the lead figure in the creation of the INC. He was a botanist, an ornithologist, and an administrator in the Etawah district of the north-central United Provinces, close to where the anti-British Sepoy Rebellion broke out in 1857. Hume witnessed the Rebellion as the commander of a locally recruited brigade that was formed to repress it. But after the war, he called out the British authorities for their cruelty and ineptitude that led to it. From then on, Hume was a committed liberal critic of British policy. He focused on the problems of poverty and mismanagement in India and the need for radical reforms, especially in education. He met strong opposition from prominent Indians and Britons. In 1879, his criticisms got him dismissed from his administrative position by the Viceroy and Governor General of India, Lord Lytton. Hume then adopted a firm nationalist stance on behalf of India in the early 1880s, declaring himself to be an Indian native, while drawing support from several other very dynamic and reform-minded individuals.

Among the leading anti-colonialists there were significant tactical disagreements. Dadabhai Naoroji espoused a mix of liberal and socialist views, with his socialism looming larger over time. Tilak, on the other hand, was a conservative Hindu on religious, cultural, and social questions, though he was open to essentially Bakuninist anarchist tactics in order to throw off British rule. He was also a highly revered figure among the emergent working-class populations that had formed in the railway, construction, coal mining, and jute manufacturing sectors. Naoroji became one of Hume's top supporters and collaborators; he was from a Parsi cotton trading family in Mumbai, who began arguing in the 1870s that Britain was draining India of its wealth through colonial dominance and exploitation. His later book, *Poverty and Un-British Rule in India* (1901), elaborated that argument in the face of British claims that they were civilizing, dignifying, and economically benefitting their colonial subjects. His analysis powerfully influenced those that embraced independence but who otherwise followed mutually opposing tactics, such as Tilak on one side, and later the nonviolent Mahatma Gandhi on the other. In the INC, Naoroji was originally affiliated with the moderates but gradually steered leftwards.[25] Increasingly, he was drawn to the socialist thought and politics of the time. He had a prolonged friendship and correspondence with the British socialist Henry Hyndman, as well as periodic contact with the prominent Marxist Karl Kautsky. Naoroji joined the Second International in 1904 and attended its 6th Congress in August, where he advocated for Indian self-rule (*swaraj*), albeit under "British Paramountcy."[26] Clearly, he represented the potentials for more radical anti-colonialist politics within India and the rest of the colonized worlds that would challenge and invoke the wrath of the imperialist states.[27]

Tilak was a religious and cultural Hindu nationalist and social conservative with top-notch caste origins. His famous expression "*Swaraj* [self-rule] is my birthright and I shall have it" implied a call to arms. He agitated against British rule through popular Hindu religious festivals and legends of warriors, landing himself in prison at the hands of the British in 1897 and again in 1908.[28] His quasi-official reputation within the budding independence movement was as the lead "extremist." One of Tilak's disciples, V. O. Chidambaram Pillai, was a radical nationalist entrepreneur who in 1906 founded the Swadeshi Steam Navigation Company (SSNC) between India and Ceylon that competed with the British India Steam Navigation Company (BISNC) in the same seas. In 1908 he encouraged labor strikes against British-owned and managed textile mills at Madura (later Madurai), Coral, and Tinevelli, which produced for local and regional markets. The strikes brought significant success at the Coral Mills where, after a work stoppage lasting several days, workers received higher wages and Sunday holidays. Pillai combined anti-colonialism, leftwing labor tactics, and competitive entrepreneurialism, which speaks to the dynamic intersections of such "core" and "peripheral" social forces and politics on the world stage. It was a radical amalgam with potentially revolutionary consequences formed against British colonial practice in India, with the leftwing labor part of it found within Britain, the United States, and other advanced capitalist states. It proved effective and threatening, prompting British authorities to imprison him for four years, which ruined his company. Again, right versus left in the colonized worlds was not what it was within the imperialist home countries, but there were crucial areas of interplay and overlap.

It may be objected that British maneuvers against the budding anti-colonialist movement in India do not properly fit into the category of anti-"socialist" or anti-leftist politics. The argument would be to the effect that, at least for the most part, those in India opposing British rule included some large landowners (*zamindaris*) who had turned to liberal nationalism, educated national bourgeois elites, leading religious nationalists, and some increasingly socialist-oriented figures such as Naoroji. The Indian working class was still relatively small, composed mainly of railway workers, coal miners, and jute and textile mill workers, and they were mostly not organized. There was very little industrialization and, as of yet, little mass basis for socialist politics of the European sort; landless peasants who worked the large *zamindari* estates revolted sporadically but were also not organized on anything approaching a national level. Only a few of the more militant among the anti-colonialist nationalists explicitly espoused leftist or socialist politics of the sort that were operative in Europe and the Americas. British opposition against all these social forces, therefore, was anti-*nationalist*. However, this was the point: to be an anti-colonialist nationalist was to be on the political left. This was the distinctive historical territory of anti-colonialism and anti-imperialism in the worlds colonized by the great power capitalist states. Some nationalist players on the scene in British India showed clear signs of a positive interest in various sorts of socialism, including labor militants whose numbers were growing and organizing in the period running into the First World War. Labor politics merged with the *swadeshi* movement in 1906 and 1908. Tilak, who some argue was a rightwing religious nationalist precursor to modern India's rightwing *Hindutva* nationalists, was a heroic figure for many ordinary laborers that showed up *en masse* outside the courthouse in Bombay in 1908 when he was charged by a British judge with sedition. Unlike many of their conceivable counterparts in Europe in the years approaching 1914, most of whom abandoned their socialist and internationalist commitments, those in India pursued a sustained and increasingly stronger line of anti-imperialism in the years prior to the Great War, for the duration of the war, through to the next one, and all the way independence in 1947. In the early 1900s it was a disparate movement, yet it threatened Britain's manufacturing and trade positions and policies, as well as its strategic stature on the world scene, as much as, or more than, any leftist political tendency did within Britain at the time. The combined *swadeshi* and *swaraj* movements were activating the full forces of imperialist coercion and censorship when the socialist Second International was ceasing to be a problem for the great power states.

Another side of this power relationship is that leftwing politics in the colonized world were playing the role that paralleled the revolutionary role that liberalism had once played in the Atlantic world. As we have seen, this had run its course in its countries of origin; liberalism had become conservative, if not reactionary. In places such as India, left politics functioned in important ways for the national bourgeoisie just as liberalism did for the subjects of British colonies in North America, but also for those within the northwest European states that experienced radical transformations in liberalism's revolutionary heyday. In India, socialism then increasingly worked as a political and ideological vehicle that facilitated the rise of the Indian business and intellectual elite. It served them very well, while it also soon helped spawn a mass movement for independence. Liberalism as it had been known in the West was not an option; it had been the ideology of their oppressors, but they used the natural and civil rights aspects of it, combining those with elements of socialism and leftwing nationalism. Though it started off with certain limits, namely, that it was mainly for elite men just as the revolutionary liberalism had been in the Atlantic world, it was on the way to becoming a far more mass-based phenomenon on the way to national liberation from colonial rule.

The international émigré front within and outside of Britain's empire was an area of overlap and linkage between the working-class radicalism of the more advanced industrial countries, on the one hand, and the more nationalist anti-colonialist radicalism growing in India, on the other. Partly through exposure to and involvement with some of the working-class political organizations in the western United States and Canada, namely, the International Workers of the World (IWW) and the Socialist Party of Canada, though also independently of them, agitation within South Asian immigrant communities in the western United States and Canada against the Raj took on a more definite form.

Canadian white nativist workers in the western province of British Columbia of the early 1900s showed a pronounced and often violent resentment against South and East Asian immigrant labor in general. Expansion of railways, light industry, mining, agriculture, and forestry in western Canada presented a need for employers that was not sufficiently met by white labor; "oriental" immigrant labor was also cheaper, and there was no problem for most employers in fomenting ethnic antagonisms within the ranks of their workers. The pattern was similar in Northern California and much of the Pacific Northwest of the United States, as well as, for that matter, much of the rest of the industrializing world. An economic and financial squeeze triggered by a number of failing Canadian banks in 1906 only raised the stakes and intensified the antagonism between the workers of differing complexions, physical features, and clothing. For the angry white workers, Sikhs stood out because of their brightly colored turbans that made them more obvious targets for discrimination and violence. But a deeper reason why Sikhs got targeted was because of their roles in maintaining British rule in India. Theirs was a double-edged sword: their military reputation was outstanding, yet there was no guarantee they would remain loyal to the Crown. They could be as effective against colonialism as they had been in support of it. Even though the government of Canada needed little prodding on the anti-immigration front at the time, British authorities encouraged Canada, a member of the Commonwealth, to crack down specifically on Sikh immigration. This was done under cover of broader restrictions on immigration as laid out in the Acts of 1906 and 1910, together granting executive- and arbitrary-type authority to block the entry into Canada of anyone deemed unfit for Canadian "requirements" or its "climate." A 1908 regulation also stipulated that all immigrants had to have sailed a "continuous journey" from a port in their native country, and upon arrival each individual had to have at least 200 dollars cash in hand. Logistically and financially, both would shut the doors to a great majority of potential Asian immigrants. But, again, the Sikhs were the top target.

Looking through the experience of the Sikhs into the larger demographic of South Asian immigrants in the US Pacific Northwest and Canada's British Columbia and beyond, the *Free Hindustan* newspaper came out in Vancouver and Seattle in 1908, presenting itself as "An Organ of Freedom, and of Political, Social and Religious Reform." Relative to the structures of imperial power over India, which it targeted, it was a militant reformist program that argued for a radical liberal democratic model along the lines of the German revolutionaries of 1849.[29] It soon was joined with another radical nationalist publication, *Bande Mataram*, which was issued by Indians in Paris. Both publications circulated throughout the South Asian diaspora. The swells of anti-colonialism grew further still in 1912–13, as a small, but organized, group, mostly of Sikhs, but also of other South Asians of all backgrounds, formed the *Ghadar* movement in San Francisco—*Ghadar* meaning "revolt" or "revolution" in Urdu. They were more clearly militant in their rhetoric and practice; they created educational and consciousness-raising groups in their own Indian immigrant communities; they launched sabotage operations within and ran weapons into India. In their immigrant milieu, regardless of the varying class and particular national and/ or religious backgrounds and identities of the Sikhs, Hindus, and Muslims, all of them faced serious and sometimes violent discrimination from their "host" peoples and acted on the need for a broader Indian national solidarity. Their top geographical coordinate was the Punjab, where much of the sabotage was carried out, but their real and potential influence looped through just about all South Asian communities elsewhere in the world and back across much of British India.[30] The first printing of the party's publication—*Ghadar*—declared that it "conveys a message of rebellion to the nation once a week. It is brave, outspoken, unbridled, soft-footed and given to strong language. It is lightning, a storm and a flame of fire …. We are the harbinger of freedom." With gusto, it declared itself "The Enemy of the British Race."[31]

Some of the founding members of the *Ghadar* movement had close connections with the IWW, otherwise known as the "Wobblies," in San Francisco. Pandurang Khankhoje was an internationalist, socialist, anti-imperialist fugitive and activist whose biography was not unlike that of the Vietnamese anti-imperialist nationalist Ho Chi Minh. Khankhoje traveled the world and worked odd jobs, his mind always set on the liberation of his country from imperialist subjugation. In far-flung Astoria, Oregon, while facing discrimination from employers at a lumber company, he got a welcome introduction to socialist labor politics by an IWW organizer. One of his colleagues and a cofounder of the *Ghadar* Party, Lal Har Dayal, was also an internationalist anti-imperialist, first drawn to Kropotkin's anarchism while at Oxford on a scholarship, then to Bakunin's more militant strain when he moved to the United States and joined the IWW in San Francisco. He also had a pronounced philosophical bent, seen in his statement of 1912 that "above the East and the West, far from the present misery of both, shines the light of truth, freedom and social cooperation, that beckons us."[32]

The rise of the Ghadarites began to confirm the worst fears of the British, namely, that anti-capitalist labor politics in the core countries would combine with militant anti-colonialism in the periphery, doubling the threat of each one alone. As Peter Campbell has shown, the Secretary of State for India, Lord George Hamilton, wrote to Curzon in September 1897 that the "real danger to our rule in India" would be "the adoption and extension of Western ideas of agitation and organization." He saw the same problem among Indian students in London. In 1909, Lord John Morley, Secretary of State for India since 1905, argued against Indian emigration to Canada, in part because of the "socialist propaganda in Vancouver, and the consequent danger of the East Indians being imbued with socialist doctrines."[33] This problem was not a figment of their imaginations. They proceeded to convince their Indian, Canadian, and American colleagues in intelligence, immigration, and police forces to coordinate a more focused system of surveillance and repression. They also sent a young inspector from the Calcutta police department, William C. Hopkinson, to have a close look at the persons, activities, and plans of the *Ghadarites* in the United States and Canada. He provided useful information on the movement and its members to his superiors but got fatally enmeshed in the factionalism between pro- and anti-British Sikhs from San Francisco up to Vancouver. He was shot and killed by a radical left Sikh figure in Vancouver in October 1914.

Meanwhile, a highly political odyssey with a tragic ending unfolded from the eastern to the western hemisphere and back, involving a Japanese ship, the *Komagata Maru*, and its mostly South Asian passengers. Gurdit Singh, a well-off fisherman of Punjabi Sikh origins who lived in Singapore, saw the injustice of the racially based Canadian immigration restrictions and decided to at least test them, if not outmaneuver them. He chartered a Japanese ship in Hong Kong and found several hundred South Asians to sail on it to Vancouver. Most of the passengers were Sikh, the rest Hindu and Muslim. Singh himself had expressed support for the *Ghadar* movement already in January 1914, and a significant number of the Sikhs aboard the ship—now renamed the

Guru Nanak Jahaj—were nationalists willing to pose at least soft challenges to British rule.[34] The ship left Hong Kong in April, arrived in Vancouver in May, whereupon the Canadian government refused it permission to dock. Between then and mid-July, tensions mounted to the point where the Canadians sent a tugboat to pull the boat out to sea; in retaliation, the passengers hurled lumps of coal at the tug. Various Canadian military regiments were mobilized before negotiations took place, through which the passengers of the ship agreed to sail to Calcutta. They had little choice. A few of the passengers were allowed entry into Canada, but not the vast majority of them. In October, the ship arrived in Calcutta—still the seat of British power in India—where the British authorities insisted the majority of the passengers immediately board trains for the Punjab. Most refused to do so and, as they walked from the port toward the city, colonial police opened fire, killing at least twenty of them.

At that tragic final stage of the *Komagata Maru* Incident, the First World War was raging. Fighting on the western front in Europe had already turned to stalemated trench warfare. Four years of carnage and deep uncertainty were in store. The British had a lot to worry about, while more and more people under its rule and under that of others saw that for them, the destabilizations inflicted by the great power states upon each other held the promise of national liberation from colonial rule. Many, if not most, colonial peoples under British rule remained loyal to the Crown, but some resorted to working with its great power enemies, particularly the Germans, just as the latter were eager to work with any enemies of the British, including Indian, Irish, and Russian revolutionaries.

There was no mistaking the influence of the political atmosphere partly created by the IWW within the San Francisco Bay area and its seaport. Several of the group's leading members were also students at the University of California at Berkeley. Many among them became Communists after 1917. The British took notice early on, sounding the alarms through their own and their colleagues' intelligence services across the diaspora in the Americas, Europe, North Africa, Southeast Asia, the Middle East, and Japan.[35] The Colonial Office in British Guiana circulated among its officers the translation of an article that referred to the strong North American branch of the *Ghadar* movement, "Indian News of Mutiny, San Francisco, U.S.A." Its call was to "brave Hindumen, take your arms instantly … 56 years have elapsed since the mutiny of 1857 – another is urgently needed." The article explained that the English were draining "Hindustan" of its wealth, "ravishing" Indian women with impunity. It was a Hindu nationalist screed. Conservative Indians accused the *Ghadarites* of being a "black snake from America" whose bite would be fatal, but the author of the article used that as a point of power and pride, arguing that it was out to attack the "white snake" of English oppression. The black snake was righteous, the white one evil. A Colonial Office comment on the folder simply read "this enclosure is rabidly seditious." The stakes and fears of the British were compounded as the Great War began in August and anti-colonial militancy increased, not just in the Indian diaspora. While many in India remained loyal to British rule, various dissident groups from the prewar years amplified their oppositions. British intelligence reports from Southeast Asia—Thailand in particular—described the "malevolent" Muslim shopkeepers from South India that had moved across to Bangkok to agitate against the British from the outside. In late 1914, as the war was shaking the foundations of the great power states, the Muslim subjects were allegedly conspiring with a "pseudo Turkish Colonel," who was in close touch with the German legation in Bangkok, against the British and in favor of Germany and the Central powers.[36] It was recommended that their relatives still within South India be monitored as well as informed of that fact. The report also showed concerns about the disaffected Muslims of the small French colonies in Pondichéry and Karikal, in southeastern India, as well as the extent to which the French in Indochina were going to face increasing unrest.

The above problems are specifically illustrated by the so-called Hindu-German Conspiracy. By the spring of 1914, US immigration authorities had zeroed in on the radical nationalist Lal Har Dayal for deportation to India. However, instead of submitting to their control, Har Dayal went clandestine, made his way to Switzerland, then to Berlin, where he joined with students that had formed the Indian Revolutionary Committee. The *Ghadarite* organization and movement was now expanding, planning and coordinating worldwide. February 1915 saw an attempted uprising—the *Ghadar* Mutiny—meant to take place within India and across the diaspora against British rule. It was stopped at the last minute by the British, partly because of the information on the *Ghadarites* and their activities in the United States and elsewhere provided by the then-deceased Hopkinson.[37] The Defense of India Act followed quickly, allowing arbitrary arrests of any dissenters within the Raj; hundreds of suspected mutineers in the Punjab and beyond were rounded up and put on trial in Lahore. Over one hundred got life imprisonment and forty-two were executed. The uprising was squelched, but the movement and its conspiracies were not; they continued through the volitions of the *Ghadarites* and also through German support. Within a month of the thwarted uprising, the German Foreign Office stepped in and recruited Har Dayal and many other like-minded Indians to the Berlin India Committee (BIC), which planned a series of anti-British operations ranging from propaganda campaigns, to arms smuggling, assassinations, as well as sabotage of the Suez Canal and a number of naval bases in India and East Asia. The plans took shape from 1915 to 1917 and became known as the Hindu-German Conspiracy (a misnomer since it also included Muslims and Sikhs); Indian anti-colonial nationalists on the US and Canadian west coasts remained involved. When the United States declared war against Germany in April 1917, the British were able to successfully pressure the US government to launch criminal investigations against the *Ghadarites* in the United States, who were working with the German Foreign Office to foment anti-British unrest. A number of *Ghadar* suspects were subsequently arrested and tried by a district court, then by a federal grand jury in San Francisco. All of this became a riveting news event on the popular American level. In April 1918, eight of those on trial were indicted for military conspiracy against the UK, which requested their extradition to India. However, widespread American sympathy with the movement's anti-colonialism turned in its favor. Instead of extradition to India and either execution or life imprisonment there, the *Ghadarites* were imprisoned in the United States with varying sentences of less than two years.[38]

The Indian immigrant anti-colonialists got a significant break, but this was hardly the trend. The larger picture of this latter part of the war showed two things: first, the greater military advantage of the Allied states over the Central Powers because of the US entry into the war on the western front in Europe; second, sharper opposition of the

Allied states and/or empires against any calls for national liberation from colonial rule, social revolution, or even for peace. Germany shared this type of fundamental hostility with its great power enemies, except when it came to the strategic opportunities leftist politics offered to sabotage their enemies' war efforts. Calls for peace, social revolution, liberation, or any combination of the three were getting louder from various factions of the socialist and anti-colonialist movements worldwide. Especially since 1917 in Europe and Russia, there was a major swell of both pacifist and revolutionary opposition to the murderous insanity of the war. Despite the tensions and factionalism among them, anti-colonial, pacifist, and revolutionary leftists got increasingly interwoven with one another worldwide, as shown in the overlapping networks of *Ghadarites*, Irish Republicans, and Egyptian nationalists—all of whom sought to drive imperial Britain out of their respective countries of origin. The United States, Canada, France, Ireland, India, Russia, and, with its "enemy of enemies" angle, imperial Germany in its utterly desperate and pragmatic support of Lenin, were rife with radical leftist politics.

Figure 2 Child laborer in South Carolina, United States, 1908. In the words of the photographer and witness Sara R. Hine.

A little spinner in the Mollohan Mills, Newberry, S.C. She was tending her "sides" like a veteran, but after I took the photo, the overseer came up and said in an apologetic tone that was pathetic, "She just happened in." Then a moment later he repeated the information. The mills appear to be full of youngsters that "just happened in," or "are helping sister." Dec. 3, 1908. Witness Sara R. Hine. Location: Newberry, South Carolina.

Source: Public domain; commons.wikimedia.org.

These particular forces were mostly not yet shaking the foundations of empires; Czarist Russian state power had collapsed and imperial Germany was teetering, but only due to the blows of the war, not the anti-war protesters. But for all the imperialist states, the radical political activity spurred harsh countermeasures. Two months after the Indian radicals were sentenced, American Socialist Party leader Eugene Debs was arrested for speaking in favor of peace and against the Espionage and Sedition Acts that had recently been passed by the US Congress. He was found guilty of sedition and sentenced to ten years in prison in September 1918. For the leading belligerent states to win their nationalist and imperialist wars, it was imperative that they aggressively oppose and undermine leftist opposition against them. No doubt, the German Foreign Office's wartime support for Indian, Irish, Egyptian, and Russian revolutionary and national liberation politics was a highly tactical and pragmatic matter, as it was for those whom they supported.[39] The fact was that the German imperial state also, meanwhile, had to contend with mass leftist demonstrations in Berlin and other cities.[40] Much of that activism was coordinated and directed by the German SPD, to the point where, wrongly, conservatives and Nazis quickly and opportunistically blamed them for Germany's defeat in the war. The accusations—summed up in the infamous "stab in the back theory"—never lost steam on the way to the next world war. Clearly, the "imperial solution" to the social problem that gave rise to radical leftist politics turned into a vast human tragedy that set the stage for even worse things to come.

Notes

1. Richard B. Day and Daniel Gaido, eds., *Discovering Imperialism: Social Democracy to World War I* (Chicago: Haymarket Books, 2012). This is a highly useful review of the contemporary debates on imperialism. Rhode's "solution" was recorded by his famous journalist friend and confidant, William Thomas Stead. See also Patrick Brantlinger, *Rule of Darkness: British Literature and Imperialism, 1830–1914* (Ithaca, NY: Cornell University Press, 1990).
2. See Eric Hobsbawm, *The Age of Empire: 1875–1914* (New York: Vintage, 1987), pp. 10, 9–12, and *passim*. His "strange death" quote comes from the title of a book by George Dangerfield, *The Strange Death of Liberal England*, published in 1935, republished by Stanford University Press in 1997.
3. Adam Hochschild, *King Leopold's Ghost* (New York: First Mariner Books, 1999).
4. See the article and discussion from 1970 by Eric Hobsbawm, at https://monthlyreview. org/2012/12/01/lenin-and-the-aristocracy-of-labor/.
5. See Vladimir Lenin, "Imperialism and the Split in Socialism," *Sbornik Sotsial-Demokrata*, no. 2 (1916). Available online: https://www.marxists.org/archive/lenin/ works/1916/oct/x01.htm.
6. See "Mr. Disraeli at the Free Trade Hall" (otherwise known as the "One Nation Speech"), *Manchester Guardian*, April 4, 1872.
7. Jules Ferry, On French Colonial Expansion. Internet Modern History Sourcebook. Available online: https://sourcebooks.fordham.edu/mod/1884ferry.asp. Italics mine.
8. John Merriman, *A History of Modern Europe: From the Renaissance to the Present* (New York: Norton, 1996), pp. 874–5.

9. Robin Blackburn, *Banking on Death - Or, Investing in Life: The History and Future of Pensions* (London: Verso, 2000), pp. 45–50.

10. See John C. G. Röhl, *Wilhelm II* (Cambridge: Cambridge University Press, 2014), pp. 188–94.

11. This was up from 26 percent in 1870. See Evan Luard, *The Management of the World Economy* (New York: Macmillan, 1983), pp. 4–5.

12. On population, urbanization, immigration to the United States, and emigration from Europe, see Hobsbawm, *Age of Empire*, tables 1–4, pp. 342–4. For general and specific data on growth in US manufacturing from 1871 to 1914, see *Historical Statistics of the United States, 1789-1945* (Washington DC: U.S. Government Printing Office, 1949), p. 179. On the emergent politics of anti-communism, see M. J. Heale, *American Anticommunism: Combating the Enemy Within, 1830-1970* (Baltimore, MD: Johns Hopkins University Press, 1990), pp. 21–41.

13. B. Whitaker, "The Whittaker Report" (United Nations Economic and Social Council Commission on Human Rights, 1985). "Revised and Updated Report on the Question of the Prevention and Punishment of the Crime of Genocide," p. 8, fn 12. See Report's reference to P. Fraenk, *The Namibians* (London: Minority Rights Group, 1985); http://www.preventgenocide.org/prevent/UNdocs/whitaker/section2.htm. See also Benjamin Madley, *An American Genocide: The United States and the California Indian Catastrophe, 1846-1873*, The Lamar Series in Western History (New Haven, CT: Yale University Press, 2017), Appendix Seven, pp. 534–7.

14. https://www.archives.gov/historical-docs/13th-amendment. Italics mine. Credit to Ava DuVernay's film documentary, "13th" (Kandoo Films, 2016).

15. Gene Grabiner, "Who Polices the Police?," *Social Justice*, vol. 43, no. 2 (2016), pp. 58–79. See also Duvernay's film documentary "13th."

16. Heale, *American Anticommunism*, pp. 21–41.

17. Editorial, "The Lesson of Paris," *New York Times* (1857–1922), May 30, 1871 (ProQuest Historical Newspapers: *New York Times*, p. 4).

18. Ibid., pp. 23–9.

19. Timothy Melgard, "Theodore Rudzinski and the People's Party: Defying Governor Rusk and Establishing Milwaukee's Labor-Based Political Tradition Following the Bay View Massacre," unpublished article, University of Wisconsin, 2013.

20. See Patricia Cayo Sexton, *The War on Labor and the Left: Understanding America's Unique Conservatism* (Boulder, CO: Westview Press, 1992), pp. 53–76.

21. Karl Marx, "The British Rule in India," *New York Daily Tribune*, June 10, 1853. Available online: https://www.marxists.org/archive/marx/works/1853/06/25.htm (accessed June 21, 2017). "Twist" was an advanced type of cotton yarn. Some of the ideas in this article are attributable to Marx's colleague, Frederick Engels.

22. As British Foreign Secretary during the First World War, Curzon drew his more famous proposed line of demarcation between Poland and Russia in 1919.

23. Aurobindo Mazumdar, *Vande Mataram and Islam* (New Delhi: Mittal Publications, 2007), p. 16.

24. Ibid., p. 19. See also, Richard J. Popplewell, *Intelligence and Imperial Defence: British Intelligence and the Defence of the Indian Empire, 1904-1924* (Philadelphia: Routledge, 1995), p. 75.

25. Naoroji was a remarkable figure. At a young age he was ordained a Zoroastrian priest. He was the first Indian to be appointed professor at Elphinstone College in Mumbai in 1855 and the first to establish an Indian company in Britain in 1855—a trading company in Liverpool called Cama and Company, which he quit three years later

because some of his colleagues steered it into the alcohol and opium trade. He set up his own cotton trading company in 1859. He established the London Indian Society in 1865, which was dedicated to discussing and disseminating Indian culture in Britain. Two years later he founded the East India Association in London, which had the more political purpose of presenting Indian critiques of British racialist views on empire. He followed that with the Indian National Association, which merged with the Indian National Congress in 1885. During the 1870s–80s, Naoroji got involved in politics in Mumbai and Gujarat. From 1892 to 1895 he served as the first Indian parliamentary MP in England, representing the Liberal Party in the Finsbury area of north London. During the election campaign for that position, Lord Salisbury commented derogatorily that the English voting public would not support him because he was a "black man." On that matter, see Antoinette Burton, "Tongues Untied: Lord Salisbury's 'Black Man' and the Boundaries of Imperial Democracy," *Comparative Studies in Society and History*, vol. 42, no. 3 (July 2000), pp. 632–61.

26. For a brief account of the proceedings of that meeting, including commentary on Naoroji's hesitation to come out for Indian independence, see the following: https://www.worldsocialism.org/spgb/socialist-standard/1900s/1904/no-1-september-1904/international-socialist-congress-1904 (accessed September 15, 2017).

27. Gregory Claeys describes Naoroji's call for an "imperialism of civilization," of "equal rights, equal duties and equal freedoms," instead of "barbarism" and "enslavement." *Imperial Skeptics: British Critics of Empire, 1850–1920* (Cambridge: Cambridge University Press, 2010), p. 139.

28. John Keay, *India: A History* (New York: Grove Press, 2000), p. 461.

29. For a PDF of the original version of the *Free Hindustan*, see the South Asian American Digital Archive (SAADA), or the following link: https://www.saada.org/item/20110901-312.

30. Maia Ramnath, *Haj to Utopia: How the Ghadar Movement Charted Global Radicalism and Attempted to Overthrow the British Empire* (Los Angeles: University of California Press, 2011), Chapter One, pp. 1–15; Sumit Sarkar, *Modern India: 1885–1947* (Delhi: Macmillan, 1983); Tariq Khan, "Living Social Dynamite: Early Twentieth-Century IWW–South Asia Connections," in *Wobblies of the World: A Global History of the IWW*, ed, Peter Cole, David Struthers, and Kenyon Zimmer (London: Pluto Press, 2017), pp. 59–73.

31. Ramnath, *Haj to Utopia*, Chapter Two, p. 4.

32. Har Dayal, "Woman in the West," *The Modern Review*, vol. XI (January 1912), p. 49. Cited in Emily Clara Brown, "Har Dayal: A Portrait of an Indian Intellectual." University of Arizona, PhD diss., University Microfilms, Inc., Ann Arbor, Michigan, 1967.

33. See Peter Campbell, "East Meets Left: South Asian Militants and the Socialist Party of Canada in British Columbia, 1904–1914," *International Journal of Canadian Studies*, vol. 20 (Fall 1999), p. 36.

34. Guru Nanak (1469–1539) was the founder of the Sikh religion.

35. This in British Guiana; see CO 26707 folder entitled "Seditious Newspapers," July 21, 1914. The author of the article further insisted that "a true-born Rajput" will "prepare for a mutiny against the English enemies and oppressors."

36. FO 628/31/343 4N 1315 titled "To India (communism)"; Bangkok, December 15, 1914.

37. Popplewell, *Intelligence and Imperial Defence*, pp. 236–58.

38. Ramnath, *Haj to Utopia*, pp. 88–94, and Chapter Three, "Enemies of Enemies…".

39. Ibid., pp. 46–7. See also Seema Sohi, *Echoes of Mutiny: Race, Surveillance, and Indian Anticolonialism in North America* (New York: Oxford University Press, 2014), Chapter Four.

40. John Horne, "Socialism, Peace, and Revolution, 1917–1918," in *The Oxford Illustrated History of the First World War*, ed. Hew Strachan (New York: Oxford University Press, 2000), pp. 227–38.

2

The Fascist Solution: From Anti-Socialism and Anti-Bolshevism to another World War, 1917–39

Anti-"communism" against the major varieties of the political left worldwide was at once the most common, unifying, and overriding political-ideological driving force in the history of fascism, Nazism, militarism, dictatorship, civil war, and world war from 1917 to 1939. Internationally, it was the chief political-ideological component of the foreign policies and colonialist strategies of Britain and France, and soon those of the aggressor states—Italy, Japan, and Germany—all fundamentally against the Soviet Union and its imagined, alleged, and real foreign policies and influences. At least within Italy and Germany in the later years of the First World War and afterward, the target was the broader left that included socialists. Within all of the societies and states of Europe, anti-leftist politics showed certain variable but fundamental continuities with the extreme nationalism of the pre–First World War era, as well as with the politics and violence against various forms of socialism dating back at least to the Revolutions of 1848 and the Paris Commune of 1871. Meiji Japan in the early 1900s and after the First World War showed clear continuities with later nineteenth-century oligarchical and imperial suppression of demands for expanded liberal democratic political rights beginning in the 1870s, which was followed by the outlawing and police repressions of various leftwing party activists and organizations that featured both reformist and revolutionary tendencies.

But it was after the Bolshevik Revolution of 1917 that anti-communism, interchangeable with "anti-bolshevism," emerged as a specific and critical addition to what had been treated as the already threatening forms of socialism that had existed up to the early 1900s. The new forms of anti-leftist politics combined with the old and together became central to the formation and tragically broad appeal of Italian fascism and German Nazism, while they also fused with the militarism of the Japanese imperial state, both at home and abroad. While there was a familiar aggressiveness in these politics that recalled various precedents from the long nineteenth century discussed in the prior parts of this book, the new anti-communism had a definite and unprecedented geostrategic dimension, as it targeted the territorially vast state of Russia now proclaimed by its leaders to be a revolutionary worker's state, as well as the locomotive force for socialism and communism worldwide. This was not only a political bonanza for fascism and Nazism; it also set the sights of the British foreign policy establishment on the Soviet Union as the primary enemy, which went far in blinding them to the dangers of those new forms of extreme and aggressive nationalist politics. In that manner, anti-communism became a crucial element in shaping the notorious policy of appeasement, which amounted to a *tacit* alliance between Britain and Nazi Germany against the Soviet Union from 1935 to 1939. This was true despite Hitler's intention to eventually bring Britain and the West European powers to their knees, an intention about which the British were largely incredulous, in large measure because of their fundamental anti-communism. In Spain, the rightwing military conspirators eventually led by General Franco declared anti-"communism" to be their main reason to attack and destroy the democratically elected and manifestly noncommunist and nonrevolutionary Popular Front government of the Second Republic in July of 1936, setting set off both a ferocious civil war as well as an *actual* social revolution for which the attack was declared to be the antidote. Without anti-communism, not only the Anti-Comintern Pact that brought together Nazi Germany, Japan, and Italy in November 1936, but the September 1938 Munich Agreement itself was unthinkable. By 1938 and right into August 1939, that is, up to the making of the Hitler–Stalin Non-Aggression Pact, the problem was highly enmeshed with the strategic and diplomatic problems that by then had finally made a second world war, one supposedly to be avoided at all costs, unavoidable. Now, in fact, it was just days away.

The new level and kind of oppositional drive began to coalesce among the Allied powers of the First World War once they intervened militarily in Russia after the Bolshevik Revolution of October 1917. Unlike what was seen across much of the rest of Europe, let alone Japan, from approximately 1918 into the late 1930s, there remains no doubt about the historical and revolutionary cataclysm that brought down the antiquated and brittle Russian imperial state and opened the way for the Bolsheviks to seize power. In all its territorial and national-cultural vastness and complexity, Russia experienced a historically rare series of developments: extreme structural devastations and material deprivations of the war, with defeats on the fronts, millions of casualties, hunger, mutinies, sabotage, and mass desertions. Only a loose coalition of liberals and socialists was needed to bring down the teetering Tsarist state in February, which was followed by a groundswell of popular and active opposition against the new government under Kerensky after it bowed to Allied pressure to keep Russia in the war. The further grim and destabilizing impact of the war then provided a strategic opportunity for the revolutionary Bolsheviks, with their ever-greater popular support and well-positioned soviet organizations in Petrograd, Moscow, and elsewhere, to successfully agitate and maneuver to seize state power in October.

Allied intervention in Russia followed quickly in early 1918, motivated most immediately by strategic concerns about German gains on the Eastern front as well as by potential Allied losses of war material left on war fronts, in ports, and on supply lines, including the Trans-Siberian railway. However, as the Great War then approached its end, the shared strategic and political-ideological interest among all the many intervening powers (the Japanese, the British, the United States, France, Canada, Greece, Rumania, Italy, Poland, the Czech Legions, and others) to defeat the Bolshevik takeover of the Russian state became the common driving force. The interventions involved a geographically and politically far-flung array of loose alliances between various international Allied forces and domestic Russian "Whites," united—if that—by their anti-Bolshevism. One of the most ardent advocates of a vigorous anti-Bolshevism was Winston Churchill, Minister of Munitions in 1917 and Secretary for War and Air beginning in January 1919, for whom Bolshevism was an unqualified threat to Britain, its empire, and western civilization in general. The Bolsheviks "destroy wherever they exist," he claimed, "like the vampire that sucks the blood from his victims." Strictly speaking, he fell short of calling for a full-scale anti-Bolshevik British military assault but argued with urgency for an aggressive intervention that would include strong material support for various Russian "Whites" as well as the deployment of British volunteer military forces.[1]

Prime Minister Lloyd George restrained Churchill, arguing that a British anti-Bolshevik intervention of the sort proposed virtually guaranteed a logistical and financial nightmare that would lay out the "surest road to Bolshevism in Britain."[2] The two leading figures' common anti-Bolshevism diverged on tactics. Lloyd George's approach, however, was not at all to ignore the Russian situation; for the time being, it combined internal destabilization with international containment, supporting nationalist movements in the Caucasus, and provisional-type governments established under several anti-Bolshevik military figures in the south, east, north, and northwest. The policy was "to arrest the flow of the lava – that is, to prevent the forcible eruption of Bolshevism into Allied lands." Indicating a degree of uncertainty about the actual threat beyond Russia to the west, yet informally endorsing Clemenceau's proposal of an anti-Bolshevik *cordon sanitaire*, the prime minister declared, "The Bolshevists may menace or they may not. Whether they do so or not, we should be ready for any attempt to overrun Europe by force." US President Wilson was significantly more committed in principle and practice to nonintervention in general. For him, national self-determination, free trade, and the League of Nations were the answers to any other sort of internationalism, Bolshevik or not. Wilson rejected Churchill's proposals out of hand.[3] Churchill sustained his more aggressive stance through the fall of 1920 and beyond, by which time British support for the White armies had officially ceased. With one crucial exception that concerned Poland in 1920, Lloyd George softened his policy under public pressure at home and from the United States. The fortunes of the Whites proceeded to sink in late 1919 and early 1920; Allied support for them began to wind down that spring, thereby critically contributing to their demise.

The Polish-Russian War that started in 1919 and culminated in the Battle of Warsaw in August 1920 stands out as one of the most important conflicts of the Russian Civil War and the foreign anti-Bolshevik interventions in it. It was also a particularly clear illustration of the civil war as a far-flung array of struggles for political power and territory. What was to be internal or external to Russia and its neighboring states, that is, borders, were a matter of ferocious conflict. Beginning in February 1919, the Polish army under General Pilsudski sought to secure what they believed to be their home territories to the east from Bolshevik encroachment. But they found the Bolsheviks, who were at war with the Whites and others elsewhere across Russia, to be militarily vulnerable, so they reached farther into war-torn territory with the hope of establishing a greater Poland, if not a Polish empire, that included Lithuania, the Ukraine, and Byelorussia. This put Pilsudski on Lenin's short list of White Generals—along with Yudenich, Kolchak, Denikin, and Wrangel—getting support from the Allies against the new Russia. This was only partially true, as the Polish forces were getting some French military supplies through the port of Danzig, but for Pilsudski they were not enough, and in any case, they were not decisive. A further problem for the Poles was that the anti-Bolshevik forces across Russia were falling to defeat, allowing the Bolsheviks to regroup in the spring and summer of 1920. This was not for a mere counterattack to save what they saw as rightful Russian territory, but for an advance on Warsaw, the power center of the newly independent, post–First World War Poland. To attack Warsaw was Lenin's determination; it was against the advice of Stalin and Trotsky, who both warned of the ferocity of Polish nationalism and of overextending Russian supply lines.

The political and the great power diplomatic and strategic circumstances surrounding this situation in August 1920 are very telling, for they revealed a certain determination on the part of Lloyd George and conservative elements within Britain to go to war against Bolshevik Russia just two years after the last part of the Great War. To explain this, it is helpful to look at the discussions and tensions between Churchill and Lloyd George over the issues at hand. Many at the time in and outside of Britain saw Churchill as a reckless warmonger, mostly because of the tragic failure of the Gallipoli campaign that was his brainchild, while Churchill viewed his prime minister not just as tactically mistaken but as essentially weak in the face of the alleged Bolshevik threat. Churchill insisted that Lloyd George was leading his Cabinet toward Bolshevism by not intervening more aggressively in Russia and then by not supporting the Polish cause. For his part, Lloyd George countered that the surest way to Bolshevism in Britain was to follow Churchill's advice, which would lead to certain financial catastrophe and political revolution. Either way, "bolshevism" seemed to be the ultimate issue. But Lloyd George showed another side of himself to Churchill and to the world as the armies of "world revolution" appeared to be converging on Warsaw. On August 4 he presented an ultimatum to Lenin's two foreign policy representatives in London, Lev Kamenev and Leonid Krasin, that he would send the British fleet into the Baltic in three days if the Russians did not stop their advance. As it happened, the Bolsheviks ignored the ultimatum, advanced toward Warsaw, the British did not send in their fleet, and the Battle of Warsaw ended with the dramatic and unexpected defeat of Bolshevik forces by Pilsudski's nationalist armies by August 20. The Bolsheviks were chastened. The war and the border question were settled in March 1921, with the Poles gaining more territory east of the "Curzon line" that the Allies had determined to be Poland's eastern border in 1918.

One cannot conclude from this episode either that the British were utterly bent upon going to war against Bolshevik Russia or that they were highly inclined to issue flimsy ultimatums. Not enough time passed to test the British, and the Poles defeated the Bolsheviks. However, as Lloyd George saw it, if the Russian revolutionary armies threatened Warsaw, they threatened Europe, and they had to be stopped. He had already been fairly explicit about such a development, so he was being consistent, which puts the question, if not the lie, to the notion that he and Britain's establishment were about avoiding war at all costs. The actual Allied interventions in Russia against the revolutionaries constituted warfare; they started before the end of the First World War but continued into the postwar period; the bellicose ultimatum from Lloyd

George carried the clear threat of war. There was war and serious inclinations toward more of it. It was also during those days just before the Bolsheviks were unexpectedly routed outside of Warsaw that the *Times of London* issued numerous editorial calls to its readers that Poland had to be defended by Britain "by all means at their disposal." A July 30 editorial suggests that Churchill, Lloyd George, and the *Times* editorialists are on the verge of advocating for war over Poland. However, looking toward the late 1930s, the editorial also says flat out that Poland was created as a buffer against the Bolsheviks, while the Germans also were wondering if they would be able to scrap the Versailles Treaty because they will be expected to force the Bolsheviks out of Poland. Clearly there is no shortage of uncertainty and complexity to the situation, yet there is a definite inclination on the part of Britain to go to war against the Bolsheviks over Poland and/or ally with the Germans to do so.[4] It may be unfair to consider the expressed desire to "avoid war at all costs" very strictly. It was obviously not a full commitment, because there is strong evidence that Britain would have gone to war to keep the Bolsheviks out of Warsaw and out of Europe. Had the Bolsheviks defeated Pilsudski's armies and taken Warsaw, the drumbeats for war would have been very loud in London and Paris, as well as Berlin. In that context, it is striking that the British never showed inclinations toward war with Nazi Germany during the critical 1933–8 period, until it was too late and they had no choice.

Far to the east, the original impulse on the part of the Japanese government under General Terauchi after the Bolshevik victory in 1917 was to somehow topple it, or at minimum, establish some kind of anti-communist buffer state in eastern Russia. The western Allied forces no doubt helped turn that into something apparently practicable in March 1918, when they invited Japan to participate in the broad counterrevolutionary effort. The Japanese stepped up resolutely, eventually sending in 70,000 troops instead of the 7,500 suggested by President Wilson; they also stayed in Russia nearly two years longer than any of the other intervening powers. However, the results were meager. In sporadic battles with the Bolsheviks and because of diseases, the Japanese lost nearly five thousand troops and failed to create the buffer state. They did gain Bolshevik assurances, for whatever they were worth, that they did not have strategic designs on Japan. In the end, the Japanese were pressured to withdraw, above all by the United States and Britain, who suspected Japan's undeniable imperialist motives that rivaled their own, regardless of their anti-communist dimension.[5] In other words, the anti-communism common to the current and emergent great power states of the time outside the USSR also already contained its real and potential geostrategic fissures that were only to eventually develop with an uncontrolled vengeance.

While the way to the Russian Revolution itself was opened by the severe internal dislocations caused by the Great War, the anti-Bolshevik counterrevolution was conditioned by the war's myriad exhaustions within the country and internationally. It was not well supported in the upper echelons of the Allied world, it was disorganized on its own, and it was poorly coordinated with the politically disparate and often ruthless White factions. To the extent that it had a clear goal, it failed, at least nominally. However, it succeeded in helping to create three precedents for the new Russia: the secret police, which was eventually turned viciously against all real or imagined opposition; the Red Army, which saved the Revolution and in the Second

World War saved the west from the scourge of Nazism; and extreme structural challenges of vast physical and institutional devastation. The Bolsheviks proceeded to consolidate power in the new Soviet Union, whose subsequent impact on the rest of the twentieth century—for or against, real or contrived—was clearly profound. Most strikingly, the original paradigm of the Bolshevik Revolution was then inverted during crucial periods and moments across Central and Southern Europe, as well as Japan and East Asia, during the twenty years following the end of the Russian Civil War. Actual leftwing revolutionary politics were weak both in absolute and relative terms, while concerted and often belligerent anti-"bolshevism," real or alleged, gained deadly momentum, most obviously in the ultimate aggressor states of fascist Italy, Nazi Germany, and imperial Japan, but also in the liberal capitalist states, with Britain in their lead. In Germany of 1919, revolution was handily defeated by the new communists' erstwhile Social Democratic comrades, who resorted to a tactical alliance with *friekorps* nationalist paramilitaries to eliminate their rivals and maintain a modicum of support from the conservative Prussian establishment. The short-lived "Hungarian Soviet Republic" of 1919 under Bela Kun was also defeated, from inside and out, and the country fell under the reactionary regency of Admiral Horthy, which launched violent attacks against the left and was eventually to turn to an alliance with Nazi Germany. Such events, including their defeat at the hands of the intensely nationalistic Polish forces, defied Bolshevik expectations and cast severe doubt upon their revolutionary internationalism, which came in for a full interrogation before it was abandoned in the new Soviet Union of 1924–5 and Stalin's "socialism in one state." Meanwhile, anti-bolshevism became the domestic and international war cry for rightists and conservatives of all stripes, moderate to authoritarian to fascist, as well as for many liberals, mostly in the face of either a phantom or a contrivance. Societies and states across Southern Europe were also in the throes of change, rife with instabilities and left versus right polarizations, including some minority sociopolitical elements on the left with declared commitments to social revolution that they were either unwilling or unable to carry out. The threat of "bolshevism," that is, of an approximate repeat of the Russian experience, was negligible. But other threats existed in the form of popular and democratic reformist pressures and demands that were exerted mostly through electoral majorities against established elites. The latter, in turn, were desperate to protect their positions.

Italy presents one of many distinctive examples of this problem, but a particularly crucial one given that the country was the cradle of the classic model of fascism, where it first emerged as a mass movement, a regime, and an example to the rest of the world. The makings of the Italian inversion of the experience in Russia were already in evidence by the fall of 1917. No doubt, the Italian "liberal state," as it was known, was seriously shaken by the circumstances of the war, and the constitutional monarchy and parliamentary system altogether did not constitute a paragon of good governance and stability. But it was not an unresponsive, autocratic state on the brink of collapse. Even after the humiliating defeat of the Italian armies at the hands of Austria-Hungary at Caporetto in October 1917—the nadir of the country's experience in the war—the trend under the new prime minister Orlando was toward recovery. On the left, there was a fairly robust reformism organized mainly in the Socialist Party (PSI), but very little in the way of revolutionary ferment parallel to that of Russia from the 1880s to 1917, let alone a Bolshevik-type political party. As for Benito Mussolini, as editor of *Il Popolo d'Italia* (*The People of Italy*) since October 1914, his trajectory was away from his early socialism and anti-militarism toward more and more ardent and bellicose nationalism. In 1915, he joined the war effort, gained battle scars, and turned them into political capital on the home front. His extreme nationalism and militarism was only then solidified by the national trauma of Caporetto. His newspaper set an aggressive pro-war tone and attacked the labor strikers at the northern Italian arms and equipment factories. This drew the favorable attention of British intelligence operative Samuel Hoare, recently transferred from Russia to Italy after the February Revolution, and later of appeasement fame due to his close and agreeable associations with Lord Halifax and Neville Chamberlain. By late 1917, Hoare was helping to finance Mussolini's journalism and political thuggery to the robust sum of £100 per week (estimated at £4600 in 2013 values).[6] The thugs that the future *Duce* dispatched to beat up the strikers at the munitions factories in Milan and Turin were a bonus. For the British, the impetus was supremely practical: do everything to keep Italy in the war against the Central Powers after revolutionary Russia pulled out of it. However, such practicality from its inception was even more laden with political-ideological consequence than the intervention in Russia. The difference was in its resounding success in Italy, however myopic, where the rhetoric of fear, generated so prolifically by the international anti-Bolshevik forces, found increasingly fertile ground, despite the lack of such an actual threat.

Even the shift to more radical politics and maximalist revolutionary rhetoric during the *biennio rosso* ("red biennium") of 1919–20 did not amount to the "bolshevism" as claimed by Mussolini. The Italian left, mainly through the PSI was electorally popular (gaining 32 percent of the national vote in 1919), while there were also elements among them and others, later including the small but vocal Communist Party after January 1921, that rhetorically espoused unmistakable revolutionary politics.[7] The radical period saw land seizures by landless peasants and factory occupations by workers that demanded higher wages and better working conditions. Discounting the radicals' revolutionary rhetoric, the Italian government initially conceded to many of the left's demands—for better labor contracts, more equitable land distribution, more progressive taxation, an eight-hour workday, a reduction in the number of workdays per year, wage increases for day laborers, and the right to unionize.[8] The Liberal-dominated parliament of 1920 then made concessions to urban and rural labor, including a more progressive tax structure and some legalizations of land seized by landless peasants, which showed a functional and reasonable responsiveness of the parliamentary system regarding some of the more blatant injustices of the time. However, while in the crisis-charged atmosphere of the times in which law tended to apply only tenuously, landowners and factory owners also had a choice that was distinctive to the Italian scene: accept the government's concessions to rural and urban labor, or use and encourage fanatically violent fascist paramilitaries to protect their particular interests against labor. The extra-constitutional choice had a "patriotic" ring to it, as the paramilitaries proclaimed themselves to be true Italians, that is, militant nationalists, in a "war against Bolshevism" and internationalism.[9] Beyond resonating for angry war veterans, such politics, ideas, and the perceived benefits that could continue to accrue from them struck a chord in the parts of the Italian body politic ranging from landowners and factory owners to broader swathes of the middle and upper classes, as well Liberal politicians and the King, all of whom saw a chance to stop the momentum of socialist reformism that only sporadically and rhetorically smacked of actual social revolution. They could more securely protect their immediate and perceived practical interests, now in the name of saving Italy from the convenient rhetorical threat of "bolshevism." For purposes of propaganda and political mobilization, that threat was extremely effective, even though this was clearly not Russia of 1917–21, nor even Germany of 1918–19. It was a combination of lower- and upper-echelon activism and manipulation, particularly by the tactically adroit Mussolini, that helped to shift momentum strongly in favor of the new major political form of fascism. The establishment of the National Fascist Party (PNF) in November 1921 institutionalized the movement and furthered its momentum. On October 28, 1922, King Victor Emmanuel III offered the position of Prime Minister of Italy to Mussolini, who proceeded to make his dictatorial and ultimately disastrous mark on Italy, as well as on its neighboring and more distant states and peoples.

Unlike the Russian Tsarist autocracy, with its constitutional-representative window dressing, Italy was a genuine constitutional monarchy. It was far more open; it had popular depth as it had incorporated new political parties and millions of new voters since 1912–13 and the establishment of universal adult male suffrage; it was capable of advancing much-needed reforms and of absorbing radicalism, while remaining steadfast and ultimately resilient in the face of defeat. The problem was the emergence, the nurturing, and the development of the fascist option. Once that alternative to legality presented itself so clearly and viably, landowners and industrial and financial elites chose it for the simple reason that by doing so, they would not have to concede any of their power and wealth to the laboring classes. That option and its narrowly self-interested appeal created and swung momentum in favor of those elites, soon sweeping along a majority of the remaining premier bourgeois elements of the Liberal State, along with the King. Mussolini became the man of the hour and of the next twenty years. He drew admiration from many prominent and disparate figures, including Churchill and Hitler, who were both favorably impressed by his anti-socialism and anti-communism, while Hitler became determined to lead the way to a German version of what Mussolini introduced to Italy.

While Spain was neutral in the First World War, the country found itself severely shaken in the late teens and early twenties. The summer of 1917 saw an urban-based general strike that was not particularly effective but which had some revolutionary overtones. The country had found markets for its agriculture and manufactured products in all of the main belligerent countries, but the latter part of the war brought high inflation, and the war's end brought a loss of the markets, a dramatic economic downturn, and the labor unrest of 1918–20 subsequently described by some journalists as the "bolshevik triennium." This mainly involved spasmodic attacks on large estates and some spontaneous land seizures by landless anarchist laborers in the latifundist regions of the south and southwest. Suggestive and sensationalist parallels were drawn in some press and political circles between Spain and Russia—just as Russian-Italian parallels were in Italy—generating fears and hopes in the extreme. But again, the utter collapse of the ruling political and institutional edifice of Russia, not to mention the particular political character of the Bolshevik party and its strategic position, were not being repeated in Spain any more than they were in Italy. "Bolshevist" claims were far exaggerated, but increasingly recognized by their present and potential propagators as useful political weapons. Casting an important contrasting eye on Italy, the Spanish agrarian left was also not crushed by extra-constitutional paramilitary *squadristi*-types financed by big landowners. Instead, for the most part, the boldest leftwing militancies of the entire stretch of 1917–21 were viciously and effectively crushed by established urban and rural police forces. However, the city of Barcelona from 1917 to 1923 was somewhat distinctive in this regard; periodic gun battles there between the *pistoleros* of the anarcho-syndicalists on one side and the proxies of the industrialists on the other did involve local rightwing party activists as well as paid assassins, both on the proxy side.[10]

Something that further distinguished Spain from Italy during the 1917–23 period was the comparative lack of overriding anti-leftist fervor that increasingly characterized and drove the growth of fascism in Italy. There were brutal crackdowns in Spain on the sporadic and mostly spontaneous leftwing militancies, but for the time being, there was no over-the-top, unifying anti-leftist religiosity. Nor was there any sufficiently broad extreme nationalist tendency necessary for mobilizing a mass fascist movement. Perhaps first and foremost, the country had a national heterogeneity of long-term historic proportions—Castilian, Basque, and Catalan—which put Italy in a light of striking national homogeneity, however highly regionalized it was on the level of national and cultural identity. Italy at least appeared to have a unified nationalist horizon, even though that was notoriously elusive, always tending to recede. But for Mussolini and the PNF, it was obviously useful enough as a political promise. Despite the later and prolonged authoritarian regime under Franco, Spain was not fertile ground for a mass fascist nationalist movement as was Italy, though of course that did not stop Mussolini's Italy from supporting Spanish right all along in terms of morale, war material, and troops.

Italy's extreme nationalist horizon, not to mention its imperialist horizon, proved to be delusory but appeared to many to be comparatively bright at the time. Indeed, they presented political opportunities whose violently aggressive sides were immediately felt by the Italian left and soon by the Ethiopians as well as Italy's neighbors to the east, south and west. The widespread bitterness and disgruntlement over the Great War amounted to a recruiting base for any nationalist social and political faction interested in extralegal coercion. Spain had little, if any, of the above: popular extreme nationalism was not an option; Spanish imperialism was dealt its final major blows in 1898, and the country had remained neutral during the Great War. The larger reason for the establishment of the rightist dictatorship under General Miguel Primo de Rivera that lasted from 1923 to 1930 was systemic: the traditional, elite-dominated *turno* system of controlling votes between two dominant parties was being fatally shaken by the emergence of mass-based politics, particularly on the left. The political insecurities nourished by such unpredictable forces for change then intensified the politics surrounding the defeat of the Spanish Army by Berber resistance fighters at

Annual in Morocco in July 1921. In 1923, the government succumbed to popular pressures to investigate King Alfonso XIII and the military for their failures and corruptions displayed in what was perceived to be the scandalous defeat. Backed by the King, Primo de Rivera and a group of supporting officers carried out a successful *coup* and established the dictatorship. The regime was harshest on the anarchists, at the time the most radical element of the Spanish left; they were criminalized, imprisoned, and tortured. The regime was soft on the socialists of the Socialist Workers' Party of Spain (PSOE), who largely inclined toward reformism. This was divide and rule, and the traditional anarchist versus socialist rivalry was therefore reinforced. Beyond that, the General's run as dictator lasted until January 1930, by which time he had alienated all of his political and agrarian elite supporters and was forced to resign. With popular fanfare, this opened the way for the establishment of Spain's Second Republic of 1931–6, which started out with a strong republican-socialist coalition but degenerated into severe tension and left- versus rightwing polarization. Extreme anti-leftist aggression from the right that surpassed anything seen in Italy was unleashed ferociously against the participants in the miners' strike of October 1934 known as the Asturias Rebellion, against which none other than General Franco led the charge of the colonial Army of Africa. Nearly two thousand miners were killed and thousands more were imprisoned and marked for life as political criminals. Shortly thereafter, as will be reviewed below, anti-leftist violence was launched by the Spanish right, including the fascist falangists, with extreme vengeance during the civil war of 1936–9.

Japan from 1914 into the 1920s, in certain clear ways, followed its pre–First World War economic trajectory: further capitalist industrial development during the war, particularly fueled by supplying Allied countries with war materials and provisions, and by moving in on markets that other belligerent countries had to abandon given the demands of the war. However, as was the case in the countries of Eastern and Southern Europe, regardless of whether they were belligerents, what followed was a postwar inflationary surge that set off widespread unrest. The so-called rice riots began in late July 1918, coinciding roughly with the Siberian Intervention on the international front, and were a response to across-the-board deprivations due to significantly increased prices on all sorts of everyday commodities. Though not initially ideological, the unrest played into the hands of, and helped fuel, the growth of a variety of leftist political organizations. These included preestablished anarchist, socialist, and other organizations that brought in students, workers, and women, as well as the new Japanese Communist party (JCP) that had been established in 1922. The Movement for Universal Manhood suffrage had been established in 1920; as intended, it was a serious and effective vehicle for greater political democracy. It was central to the fact of the dramatic expansion of male suffrage in 1925, when the electorate expanded from 3 million to 12.5 million voters. However, also continuing the pre–First World War political trajectory, virtually all leftwing groups were repressed, harassed, and then officially outlawed, in both Japan and Korea under the Public Security Preservation Law of 1925. On March 15, 1928, 1,600 known and suspected members of the Japanese Communist party were arrested and imprisoned; shortly thereafter, the 1925 law was changed to include the death penalty for anyone suspected of supporting changes in the prevailing system of private property. This was the period of so-called Taisho democracy and its immediate aftermath, the 1912–26 period of "political liberalization" that was worthy of that term only by the standards of rule of the late-19th Meiji oligarchy. It featured nothing close to a liberal democratic constitution and state. Unelected cabinet governments, the House of Peers, the Privy Council, and the elder statesmen or "*genro*"—all with origins in the Meiji oligarchy—retained broad constitutional powers that enabled them to block the growth of democratic electoral politics. In practice, this especially meant blocking and crushing the Japanese left.[11] Europe had already set the bar very high for such politics. Fascism and its attendant paramilitary thuggery against the left were already operative in Mussolini's Italy at this time, while in Spain, for example, anarchists were imprisoned by the thousands under the dictatorship of Primo de Rivera. Japan, in other words, was certainly keeping up with, if not staying ahead of, the anti-leftist curve on the coercive and legislative fronts. It was ahead of Germany during most of its Weimar phase, at least after the distinctive and vicious attacks by the SPD and *friekorps* against the radical left in 1918–19. Germany, of course, was full of potentials for such further assaults on the left, but they were not inevitable. In 1925–6, Adolf Hitler published his infamous *Mein Kampf*, in which he railed against liberals, leftists, and Jews for their supposedly endless treachery and laid out his plan for the global dominance of Germany through the thousand-year Third Reich. But there was still very little yet evident in 1920s Germany of the nightmares that were to come. The country had carried out imperialist aggression and internal repression in the pre-1919 period, and it had obvious potentials for more of the same, but Germany of 1919–32 was not an aggressive imperialist state practicing systematic internal political repression. It obviously had the potential for all that and far worse, yet none of that was inevitable. Japan, on the other hand, was already clearly on that track. What nearly clinched the rise of Nazism in Germany and dramatically accelerated Japan's repressive and expansionist militarism—and spelled doom for the left and others within those states and in many places beyond—was the variable impact of the Great Depression.

By some ordinary measures, Japan was hit by the Depression significantly less severely than was Germany, and even less so, for example, than the United States. Estimates for rural unemployment in Japan in 1930–1 are around 15 percent, while the cities saw rates of at least 20 percent. Figures on Germany overall are close to 40 percent, which more or less match the country's drop in industrial production. Amid the crisis, and with very significant success, Hitler took the political path to gain dramatically in the eyes of as much of the German electorate as possible. He promised jobs and he promised national glory; he promised to realize "true socialism," that is, an essentially nationalistic program whose use of the term "socialism," as in National Socialist German Worker's Party (NSDAP) only served as a measure of Hitler's awareness of two things: the popularity of the SPD since the late nineteenth century and his efforts to draw SPD members over to his NSDAP. He approved of Nazi-allied paramilitary forces attacking leftists in the streets in 1932, which also ended up benefitting his party and movement. He further advanced his prospects in late 1932 to early 1933 through his mastery at fooling and manipulating the traditional Prussian establishment figures, such as von Papen and Hindenburg, into thinking he was easily controllable and expendable. Once Hindenburg decreed him to be the new German Chancellor in January, Hitler moved extremely effectively on a number of fronts to gain dictatorial power and instill fear in all who opposed him, with leftists of all stripes the first to be arrested and thrown into concentration camps.

While Hitler and the Nazi movement were certainly the lead forces in their own rise to power, they also were able to take advantage of, and, in fact, depend upon, a wide array of political-institutional weaknesses, constitutional flaws, and national-cultural insecurities that characterized Germany at least from 1918 to the early 1930s. In some contrast, the actual lead forces in the consolidation of the Japanese militarist-imperialist and internally repressive state were rogue military elements that attained such a degree of military success in seizing portions of Manchuria in the name of Japan that the Japanese government, already deeply vested in expansionism one way or another, found itself incapable of opposing them. Major elements of the Japanese Imperial Army in Manchuria, known as the Kwantung army, had been playing the role of protecting Japanese rail lines and port areas that the country had leased from the Chinese. For them, the repercussions of the Depression created a turning point. They became disillusioned with any degree of democracy, with industrialists and bankers who were perceived to be pushing soldiers into poverty, and with governments that were reluctant to launch an unapologetic drive for empire. Furthermore, as they saw it, China of the warlords, the nationalist Kwomintang (KMT), and the budding Communist movement was vulnerable to predatory outside interests; that is, it was Japan's opportunity. They staged an attack on their own rail lines in Mukden, blamed it on the Chinese, and seized control of Manchuria. In 1932 they established Manchuria as a puppet state, referred to as Manchuko, under the Manchu emperor Puyi. In a way that offers some parallel with Hitler and the NSDAP's electoral successes of 1930–3, large portions of the Japanese populace, however ignorant they may have been about the Mukden Incident, also now saw the aggressive, imperialist expansionism in Manchuria and against the Chinese—the nationalist KMT in particular—as a rightful and resounding demonstration of national prowess. If Japan was to have any chance of being a respected and viable great power imperialist state and therefore no longer have to suffer humiliations at the hands of other, long-established imperialist states, there should be no turning back. Despite their differing lead forces and developments, Nazis in Germany and the militarists in Japan showed similar success in captivating domestic audiences with the promise of invigorated national glory, or the immediate and violent demonstration of it abroad. A characteristic part of this was an intensified assault on the left, or what remained of it in Japan, after the persecutions of recent years.

However, despite the domestic and international ideological and political drive against the left and/or Soviet Communism, the prowess of the Japanese Kwantung army in Manchuria may not have appeared as impressive as it was to many on the home front had it not been for the Chinese Communists (CCP) and the nationalist KMT's policy toward them. During the crucial years of 1931 to the end of 1936, the clear priority of the KMT under Chiang Kai-shek was to defeat the CCP in the struggle for domestic power, not to stop the invading Japanese. The Communists, in effect, drew fire away from the Japanese forces and thereby facilitated their expansionist successes in northern China. Japanese confidence and momentum grew. On the other side of the matter, KMT policy also played into the hands of the CCP, allowing them to don the mantle of patriotism as they also claimed to lead the way to justice for workers and peasants. Both in the short and long runs, KMT policy backfired. But for Imperial Japan, which had already annexed Korea since 1910, this was a major step in its expansionist thrust into other parts of Asia, including more of China, as well as Indochina, Southeast Asia, and the Pacific islands. The Japanese attempt to gain that rare status of a great power imperialist state was sufficiently marked by an aggressive anti-Communism to eventually guide it toward an alliance with Nazi Germany and fascist Italy. Of course, the mutual strategic calculus between the liberal capitalist states of Britain and the United States, on the one hand, and Japan, on the other, also had its impact on the formation of Japanese policy. Out of all this, it is no great leap of imagination to the December 1941 attack on the United States at Pearl Harbor and the entire Pacific War of 1942–5.

The British and French had rejected a request by the Japanese at Versailles in 1919 to sign a "racial equality" treaty. Japanese sensitivity on this matter, and its antipathy toward the other major Allied powers, did not go away. Two years later, members of the newly assertive English-speaking dominions of Britain (Australia and Canada, in particular) blocked any renewal or strengthening of the Anglo-Japanese alliance that had been first agreed in 1902 and carried through the First World War. As explained above, Allied collaboration over anti-Bolshevik operations then revealed particular fissures in 1921–2 over Japan's prolonged Siberian Intervention. In effect, Japan was cut off, freer to pursue its expansionist aims. Meanwhile, the prevailing militarist element in the Japanese government was still linked with samurai warrior-elite tradition that had assumed a modern political form in the Meiji era. Assessing the strategic character of the great powers of the west, the militarists identified strongly with the Prussian tradition, its persistence in modern Germany, and the Nazi rendition of it taking shape under Hitler by the mid-1930s. Germany looked strong on the international stage, and Britain did not. Furthermore, Hitler was reconsidering German financial and infrastructural support for Chiang Kai Shek's KMT. In what he saw as the imminent world historical battle against bolshevism, Hitler increasingly saw the Japanese as the premier military and like-minded force in the east. Accordingly, the Chinese nationalists would be militarily unreliable allies against Bolshevik Russia; they inspired no confidence in the *führer* that they could even defeat the Communists domestically. That task could also be more reliably left to Japan. On November 25, 1936, the Japanese government signed the Anti-Comintern Pact with Nazi Germany and fascist Italy, as the news from Spain was that German bombers were pounding Madrid, and pro-Republican Popular Front *madrileños*, supported by the International Brigades, were putting up stiff resistance. This was Nazi Germany's step away from China and toward Japan. The fall and the "Rape of Nanking" at the hands of the Japanese were on the horizon. The Japanese looked strong to the Germans, and vice versa. Each was on its way into the other's vortex to a significant extent, but Japan in particular was getting pulled into the vortex of the coming war in Europe that had "world war" dimensions due to the extensive colonial empires that the belligerent powers either already held or aspired to establish in East and Southeast Asia. The Nazi-Japanese alliance stretched from 1937 to 1945, that is, for the entirety of the Second Sino-Japanese War and the Second World War that officially began in 1939.

Returning to the situation in interwar Europe, perhaps the most outstanding case of a contrived "communism" being used as a propaganda tool to establish a rightwing authoritarian regime is to be seen in Portugal. A small-scale imperialist player with colonial holdings in Angola and Mozambique, but with next to no influence on the global strategic equation, the country presents a distinct and mostly domestic illustration of the problem highlighted both in this chapter and elsewhere, where it will be seen to seriously backfire on the Portuguese dictator. The rhetoric of António de Oliveira Salazar as the head of the rightwing authoritarian semi-fascist *Estado Nuovo* beginning in 1933 railed against a "communism" that, at the very most, played a minimal role in Portuguese politics and society. Even the anarchism that had predominated on the left through the late 1910s, as it had in Spain, was relatively very weak by the time of the establishment of the new corporatist state.[12] For Salazar—his advanced studies in finance notwithstanding—the real threat to Portugal was modern liberal middle-class industrial society and all its potentials for class conflict and instability.[13] Any advancement of such forces and development would have undermined the positions of the country's traditional ruling oligarchical families on the land and in the cities. The strategy appeared to be to stop modern economic development and liberal politics in their tracks, to freeze Portuguese history and society on the cusp of modernity. The best rhetorical means of justifying such a move was not to reveal his problem with the liberal middle-class forces of modernization but instead to contrive an imminent threat from the left. Neither anarchists nor communists played any serious role in the crisis that brought on the dictatorship of 1933–74. However, there was plenty of criticism of Salazar as the anti-communist dictator that, however unintentionally, by way of repression of anything suggestive of radical left politics at home and in the colonies, nurtured the communism that eventually did play a considerable role in the downfall of the regime he first created.[14] Salazar saw instability around him, called it "bolshevism," established a corporatist authoritarian Catholic dictatorship, and got British, Italian, and German approval and praise for doing so. The *Estado Nuovo* would go on to become the world's longest-standing non- and anti-communist authoritarian regime.

Neighboring Spain presents a similar example on the domestic front, though it is less clear-cut as a "contrived" threat from the left, since leftist politics were very lively during the period in question. Including this, but beyond it as well, there may be no better example of how a complex dynamic of anti-leftist politics and strategy led to the Second World War than the domestic and international history of the Spanish Civil War of 1936–9. On the domestic front, these politics included violent and systematic anti-"bolshevism" that was, in reality, against a democratically elected and nonrevolutionary government; internationally, they included crucial material support for that aggression by Nazi Germany and fascist Italy. British foreign policy makers, meanwhile, deep in their mode of appeasement of Nazism and fascism, and deeper still in their opposition against Communism, knowingly and deliberately refused to recognize the particularity and the general symbolism of the assault on political democracy of the rightist military attack on the popularly elected Spanish government.

As will be explained further below, Britain led the way toward looking the other way, while resorting to the charade of Non-Intervention in the Spanish Civil War.

The Spanish oligarchy—the monarchy, the army, the Church, and the big landowners—defended their various traditional, well-established institutional powers and *de facto* privileges with consistent intransigence. They were strongly inclined to see any calls for significant reforms in landholding, military, educational, political, and other structures as revolutionary threats. The domestic context of the 1917–39 period, therefore, gave them endless pretexts to maneuver to save "their country" from certain disaster. But the international context of the time, from the Allies against the Bolsheviks in Russia, to Mussolini's Italy, to Salazar in neighboring Portugal, to Hitler in power in Germany, and more, gave them various supportive models, as well as political and material backing and greater confidence, to actually make a military move against the supposed revolutionary threat with a serious chance of success.

By just about any standard of modernization and for the sake of societal stability, Spain needed reforms. This was particularly true in Andalusia and Extremadura in the south and southwest, where landless, impoverished, largely illiterate seasonal laborers, locals, as well as migrants from all regions of the country, altogether numbering close to two million, worked exceedingly large agrarian estates, the *latifundia*. It was a virtual invitation to social revolution yet, despite the severe economic strains and attendant unrest of 1918–20—the so-called bolshevik triennium—such a development was not taking shape.[15] The government of the time was fully able to dispatch its Assault Guard units to stop and roll back whatever spontaneous land grabbing took place. Nevertheless, a confluence of factors was combining to create larger real and perceived threats to elite political control of the country. First was the broad new reality of mass democratic political participation—since 1890 all males 25 and over had the right to vote; second was the rural and urban proletarian unrest of the post–First World War years; third, and more immediately, were the moves by the government of the time to reform and modernize the Spanish army, particularly its bloated officer corps, whose weaknesses and corruptions were revealed in their humiliating defeat at the hands of Rif tribesmen at Annual in Morocco in July 1921. Representing the upper echelons of the military, General Primo de Rivera established a dictatorship in 1923, backed by King Alfonso XIII and the rest of the traditional oligarchy, but also by the new financial and industrial elites, who feared the growing labor movement in Spain might gain excessive influence over the processes of modernization and reform. The dictatorship had a complex and serious impact on Spanish political life and society; among other things, it followed an effective "divide and rule" policy against the left, sowing further seeds of bitterness between socialists and anarchists. It was also not successful in addressing, let alone solving, any of Spain's pressing problems; probably most importantly, it backfired on the popular level, alienating more people than ever from the monarchy and military rule. The General displayed an astounding ability to alienate his own supporters. The final blow was the onset of the Great Depression. The regime collapsed in 1930. Municipal elections in April 1931 supported a majority of pro-republican candidates. King Alfonso XIII fled the country, and the Second Republic was declared. Its first two years, coinciding with the Great Depression, saw a dramatic increase in the number of strikes and the numbers of laborers involved.

They got strong political support from the republican-socialist coalition government. The Minister of Labor in that government was Francisco Largo Caballero, head of the Socialist party's (PSOE's) trade union movement, the General Workers' Union (UGT) described by some friends and enemies as the "Spanish Lenin." For most of his supporters, he was the spearhead of the reforms necessary to usher Spanish society into a social democratic modernity. For conservatives of all sorts, he was a premier part of the so-called red threat, which made partial sense in his case, as he periodically espoused revolutionary rhetoric and politics, though just as often opposed them. Elections in 1933 saw a swing to the right, represented by a coalition of oligarchical and conservative parties. All of the reform measures of 1931–3 were repealed. Part of the response from the left against those rollbacks was a general strike called for in October 1934. The strike failed on the grand logistical and political levels, but miners in the northern region of Asturias rose up very concertedly, showing a local revolutionism, which, in the moment, was supported by Largo Caballero. This served to confirm and strengthen the right's view of him. The uprising was readily crushed under the lead of General Franco, on orders from the government, with a ruthlessness and bloodletting not seen in Europe since the Paris Commune of 1871. Franco declared this to be a war against socialism and communism, that is, against "red" Spain. But for him and for conservatives generally, the "red" category included just about all political leaders, factions, and followers of the Spanish center-left political world. Those elements joined together in a new "Popular Front" coalition that came to power through the democratic elections of February 1936.[16] The situation only polarized further. Beginning on the following July 17, the entire swathe of Spain that voted for the Popular Front coalition was attacked militarily led by a cabal of rightwing generals and their supporters that aimed to seize power and declare a state of emergency throughout the country. But they only succeeded in throwing the entire society into a state of horrible civil war and unmistakable, widespread social revolution. First intended to crush a fictional revolution, now it triggered an actual one.

Demonstrating clearly that the order of the day was to avoid real or contrived social revolution at all costs, a stunning array of great power international political and military forces displayed a sameness of purpose as they lined up against either the Republic, the revolutionary elements within it, or both. That purpose produced an underlying unity between the soon-to-be deadly enemies: Nazi Germany, fascist Italy, the Soviet Union, Britain, France, and the United States. The Spanish Republic even turned on itself, with its nonrevolutionary forces in tension, then eventually at war, with its revolutionaries. Strictly speaking, on the international front, things did not start out this way. The Popular Front government of France under the socialist prime minister Leon Blum, came to the defense of its Spanish counterpart, politically and materially. Within days of the breakout of the conflict, and in response to the Spanish government's requests, Blum's government sent armaments, including aircraft, marked for the defense of the Republic. However, effective pressure on the French to end all such support came quickly. Anti-Republican Spanish foreign policy bureaucrats operating within France conducted logistical sabotage against the armament supply lines. France's conservative political establishment launched a systematic public relations and press campaign against any support for the beleaguered Republic. Perhaps most tellingly, the general secretary of the French foreign ministry, Alexis Léger, received reports that British officials were considering an alliance with the Germans if the French Popular Front government moved any further to the left. The positive test for that: any continued material support for the Spanish Republic. To the profound chagrin of Blum himself, the French government abandoned its sister Republic.[17]

As the French were aborting efforts to support the Spanish Republic, Hitler moved decisively to support those out to destroy it. Two German businessmen based in Morocco, both card-carrying Nazis, agreed to a request from General Franco to appeal to Hitler face-to-face to send military hardware to the Spanish rightist rebel forces. Rudolf Hess agreed to arrange the meeting, which took place on the night of July 25 in Bayreuth, Germany, during the height of the Wagner Festival. Fresh and fiery from a performance of *Siegfried*, his vision was to save Spain from the scourge of bolshevism emanating from Moscow. He was very giving. To the representatives of the Spanish rightist rebels, he guaranteed the war material they asked for, and more.[18] This included the Junkers-52 troop transport planes that, during the crucial days of late July and early August, ferried the Army of Africa from Morocco to mainland Spain, therefore probably saving the attempted *coup* from utter collapse and ensuring a bitter civil war. Using the original but now abandoned French moves as a pretext, Mussolini committed war material; ground troops that eventually numbered eighty thousand strong, and a fleet of bombers to the rightwing rebel cause.

A last-ditch effort on the part of the French came in a proposal from Blum to Samuel Hoare, First Lord of the Admiralty since June 1936 in the government of Neville Chamberlain. Blum approached him and others on August 5 with the argument that it would be to Britain's strategic detriment if the authoritarian rightists would gain state power in Spain. It will be recalled that Hoare had a long history of anti-communist politics, one of whose milestones was secret financial support he funneled to Mussolini in the crucial formative days of Italian fascism. Hoare saw no strategic problem with the Spanish rebels, particularly with Franco, the one emerging as the leader of the military assault, whom he saw simply as a good nationalist. Hoare dismissed Blum's strategic warning, and the French government, believing itself unable to go it alone without the more powerful British lead, changed its ways.

With strong suspicion of the German involvement in and knowledge of Italian support for the attack on the Republic, the French proposed to the British and the Italians that a "noninterference" policy be adopted toward Spain by all the great powers. In sharp contrast to their response to any and all previous French moves and propositions supporting the democratically elected Republic, the British were exceedingly receptive to such a notion. They moved forward with it effectively and cynically, turning it into the infamous policy of "Non-Intervention" in the Spanish Civil War. With very good knowledge of the large-scale German and Italian interventions in the conflict, the British and the rest of the representatives on the Non-Intervention Committee approved of those states officially signing on to the charade. Portugal, Italy, and Germany all signed on to the agreement by the end of August, when they were all known to be funneling military hardware to the *franquistas*.

The Soviet Union, having survived the vicissitudes of the Russian Civil War, subsequently faced a succession crisis when Lenin died in 1923. The power struggle that ensued saw Stalin prevail brutally over any and all domestic rivals, real and imagined, by the late 1920s. Forced agrarian collectivization, the liquidation of the kulaks, and famine followed fast; their combined death tolls up to 1937 reached close to fifteen million. By the time civil war and revolution broke out in Spain, Stalin had gone very far in creating a monstrous state in his own image. The murderous purges and show trials were underway in 1936-7. All perceived enemies were being liquidated; all of them were deemed "trotskyites" and traitors. These developments were not yet well known outside the relatively insular and highly repressed USSR, but conservatives, rightwing militarists, fascists, and the liberal capitalist establishment had already clarified and demonstrated their violent opposition against any and all things "bolshevik." On the other hand, Stalin still had an audience and a reputation to maintain internationally as the head of the supposed "worker's state" of the USSR. Through the Comintern in June 1935, he declared official support for the Popular Front policy, which insisted that revolution was off the table, while all liberal and leftwing political forces across the globe needed to cooperate against the grave threat of fascism. He was appealing to workers and to liberal bourgeoisies worldwide, which was to say he was indeed terrified of an attack by Nazi Germany and its allies against the Soviet Union. His still-worse nightmare was such an attack supported by the British, the leading foreign policy state of the liberal capitalist world. Stalin clearly recognized a more immediate threat posed by Nazi Germany against the Soviet Union, but he also recognized that Hitler presented an expansionist threat against the states and colonial territories of the liberal capitalist world. Soon after Hitler's accession to power in Germany in 1933, therefore, Stalin proposed to the British a "collective security" policy in the face of the Nazi threat, that is, against what Stalin saw as their common enemy. Among those in the commanding heights of power at the time outside of Germany, he may have been the most clear-sighted on these matters. The Popular Front policy that the Comintern followed beginning in 1935 was, in fact, the popular political corollary to collective security, which was offered by the Soviets to the British as consistently as it was roundly rejected by them, right into August 1939. At the beginning of the civil war in Spain, in late July 1936, Prime Minister Stanley Baldwin set Britain's tone clearly for the present and future regarding the USSR. "On no account, French or other," Baldwin insisted, "must he [Foreign Secretary Anthony Eden] bring us into the fight (in Spain) on the side of the Russians."[19]

In the meantime, Stalin followed a policy toward Spain that was derived from this hard and precarious international calculus. Without yet sending any material support to Spain, the USSR signed onto the Non-Intervention agreement on August 22. The diplomatic-strategic pressure from the fascist and liberal capitalist west on the Soviets not to meddle in the Spanish conflict was intense, but so was the popular liberal-left and leftwing pressure on them to come to the defense of the Popular Front government and its supporters as they faced the fierce military onslaught of the *franquistas*, Nazis, and fascists. The way forward for Stalin was to intervene on behalf of the Republic, but do so strictly according to the terms of the Popular Front: no revolution, and respect only for private property and all other liberal democratic institutions. This offered great hope for many in the Spanish world and beyond who were desperate for some kind of serious response against the march of fascism. But the undeniable reality within the

Republican zone of the civil war was that significant portions of its supporters had taken a revolutionary turn. Given his assessment of the world situation at the time, Stalin's decision to support the Republic materially came with a most fundamental and ominous anti-revolutionary imperative. With no shortage of irony, some would have to call it Stalin's anti-bolshevik imperative. In the end, the French fizzled vis-à-vis Spain's Popular Front government, the Nazis and fascists rose quickly to the murderous occasion, and the British looked the other way, glad to know the Republic's prospects were grim. The Soviet Union intervened to save face, but with the core intention of destroying the social revolution, not saving the Republic. If the British and the liberal capitalist states would have removed their anti-communist/anti-Soviet blinders and woken up to the actual dangers of Nazism and fascism, presumably at some point they would have maneuvered accordingly, in some pragmatic cooperation with the Soviet Union, and perhaps against the *franquistas*. But this did not happen.

The Munich Conference of September 1938 and the agreement that resulted from it is well known as the apex of Britain's appeasement of Nazi Germany. It was an affair to which the Soviet Union was not invited. This was a tragically consistent result of the particular dynamics of the three-way power struggle between the Nazi/fascist powers, the Soviet Union, and the liberal capitalist states that had started with clarity in June of 1935, with the Anglo-German Naval Agreement on the one hand, and the Comintern's announcement of the anti-fascist Popular Front policy on the other. In that first phase of the international power struggle between the three premier power systems of the twentieth century, the British engaged in what was a *tacit* anti-communist alliance with the Nazi and Fascist powers. Perhaps an even worse indication of the problem was that, once it was clear to the British in the spring of 1939, when Hitler took all of Czechoslovakia, that war with Nazi Germany was extremely likely, if not completely unavoidable, the British continued to refuse to work with the USSR. Soviet Communism, in their eyes, remained their fundamental enemy, not Nazi Germany. The last possible chance for the British establishment to "avoid war at all costs" was denied in the spirit—really the common pathology—of avoiding socialism and communism at all costs. In its execution, Nazi Germany's version of this pathology, of course, was very different from Britain's, but it was that pathology, nevertheless, that moved the world toward another world war. Neither the Hitler–Stalin Non-Aggression Pact, signed on August 23, 1939—nine days before the start of the Second World War in Europe—nor all that led up to it can be sufficiently explained and understood outside of this setting of the overlapping hostilities against the political left shared between the liberal capitalist and Nazi, fascist, and dictatorial societies and states of the era.

In much of the post–Second World War west, Bolshevism and Soviet Communism, Nazism and fascism, have been lumped together in the category of "totalitarianism." In a sense, they have been equalized; some say relativized. This was by no means the case in the interwar years among the great power states outside of the Soviet Union. The Allied powers intervened militarily, aligning with the Whites against the Reds in Russia during the civil war. Britain and a dozen other states, including Canada, France, Japan, and others, aimed to destroy the Bolsheviks. A distinct part of that effort and drive was Britain's threat to go to war against them over Warsaw in August 1920. The damage done to Russia by the Great War, by the revolution, and by the

Figure 3 Rosa Luxemburg, of Polish-Jewish-German origin and an ardent socialist internationalist. Believing the workers' movements of the advanced capitalist states would lead a world revolution, she became a German citizen and founding member of the Spartacus League in 1915; she joined the German Communist Party in 1919. Soon, she and Karl Liebknecht were assassinated by rightwing paramilitary *Freikorps* members, with the approval of the leadership of the Social Democrats, and no doubt to the satisfaction of the rest of the German establishment.

Source: Public domain; commons.wikimedia.org.

civil war, including all the foreign interventions in that war, were devastating. The interventions and the counterrevolution did not succeed in destroying Bolshevik power, but they certainly helped destroy its grounds for legitimacy and practicability. When Mussolini and fascism emerged in Italy, many in the liberal capitalist west were impressed. The British found a friend in Mussolini and his paramilitaries against the surge of Italian anti-war labor militancy. Drawn somewhat from that disposition and perception, when Hitler rose to power in Germany in 1933, many

Figure 4 Russia, 1921. Original text appearing after the image: "A soldier of the Red Army captured by the Whites. He confesses he is a Communist and is bound to a stake to be shot." Photographer: Williams, Albert Rhys, 1883–1962.

Source: Public domain; commons.wikimedia.org.

in the liberal capitalist west were miffed; there was a "wait and see" attitude. The situation was very different from the prevailing view of the liberal capitalist great power states toward the Bolshevik Revolution of 1917–22; there was not a hint of interest in doing anything to undermine the power of the new German regime. For many in the British establishment, there was a sense that the Germans were victims of the Versailles Treaty. Their sympathetic line was that the Germans had a right to reassert their power in some measured way on the international stage and, last but not least, the new German state could serve as a buffer against Soviet Russia.[20] Nazi Germany and fascist Italy respected private property and capitalism; especially under Stalin, the USSR clearly did not. Japanese militarism was, at least, anti-Soviet. A certain perceptual and political problem emerged from these fundamentals, blinding the liberal capitalist world especially to the dangers of Nazism and fascism, until another world war could not be avoided. The vortex had a horrific global force. The Second World War was the result of a deeply complex combination of political, strategic, socioeconomic, cultural, and ideological developments. However, the tragedy of World War Two's *Bloodlands*, as Timothy Snyder *describes* them in great detail in his book, simply cannot be explained and understood without focus on the widely shared, underlying, overlying, anti-leftist, and anti-communist drive on the parts of the liberal capitalist, fascist, and dictatorial states outside of the Soviet Union, up to 1939.[21]

Figure 5 Ku Klux Klan (KKK) parade, Washington, DC, September 13, 1926. From 1920 to 1926, the KKK gathered over two million members. The organization targeted non-whites and non-Protestants, which inevitably trained their eyes on leftists of all sorts.

Source: Public domain; commons.wikimedia.org.

Notes

1. See speech to the House of Commons, March 26, 1919, quoted in Martin Gilbert, *Winston S. Churchill, Volume IV, 1916–1922* (London: Heinemann, 1975), pp. 270, 288; see also references to the arguments of Major-General Radcliffe, concurring with Churchill, in support of a Finnish offensive against Petrograd.
2. *Documents on British Foreign Policy, 1919–1939, Vol. III*, p. 310.
3. See quote from President Wilson, in Gilbert, *Winston S. Churchill*, p. 244.
4. *Times of London* reported a July 15, 1920, statement by Bonar Law, at the time the leader of the House of Commons, that "if the Red Army invades Poland proper the Allies will come to her aid." The article is entitled "Poland's Frontiers," issue 42463, p. 14. See also "The Question of Poland." The Friday, July 23, 1920, issue 42470, p. 15, reads, "Trotsky assured his hearers that Poland would soon cease to be a defensive buffer against Russia. Far from being a buffer, she would become a 'Red bridge of Social Revolution for the whole of Western Europe.' " The *Times of London* editorial of July 30, 1920, is in issue 42478, p. 12.
5. Andrew Gordon, *A Modern History of Japan: From Tokugawa Times to the Present* (New York: Oxford University Press, 2003), p. 175.
6. Estimated at 5197.83 pounds sterling and 7158.06 US dollars, both in 2021. See https://wise.com/us/currency-converter/usd-to-gbp-rate and https://www.uwyo.edu/numimage/Currency.htm.
7. R J. B. Bosworth, *Mussolini's Italy: Life under the Fascist Dictatorship, 1915–45* (New York: Penguin, 2005), pp. 101–106.
8. William Brustein, "The 'Red Menace' and the Rise of Italian Fascism," *American Sociological Review*, vol. 56, no. 5 (October 1991), p. 654.
9. Bosworth, *Mussolini's Italy*, pp. 108–10, 124–6, 185.
10. Stanley G. Payne, *The Spanish Civil War, the Soviet Union, and Communism* (New Haven, CT: Yale University Press. 2004), pp. 9–10.
11. Germaine Hoston, *The State, Identity and the National Question in China and Japan* (Princeton, NJ: Princeton University Press, 1994), pp. 133–5.
12. Kathleen Schwartzman, *The Social Origins of Democratic Collapse: The First Portuguese Republic in the Global Economy* (Lawrence, MO: University Press of Kansas, 1989), pp. 180–4.
13. António Costa-Pinto, *Salazar's Dictatorship and European Fascism: Problems of Interpretation* (Boulder, CO: Social Science Monographs, 1995), pp. 181–7.
14. This was precisely the point of one of his most ardent critics from the republican military in the 1960s, Captain Henrique Galvao, himself a fierce anti-communist, who wrote an open letter to Salazar, arguing, "In this country, which is essentially anti-communist, and where communism could not even gather a thousand sincere supporters, Your Excellency set about manufacturing artificial communists in order to be able to (declare) constantly to the world that in Portugal there was only one political alternative: either Salazar or communism" (see D. L. Raby, *Fascism and Resistance in Portugal: Communists, Liberals and Military Dissidents in the Opposition to Salazar, 1941–1974* (Manchester: Manchester University Press, 1988), p. 158).
15. Jeffrey Paige, *Agrarian Revolution: Social Movements and Export Agriculture in the Underdeveloped World* (New York: Free Press, 1975), pp. 58–66. On the numbers of landless laborers and their backgrounds, see Stanley G. Payne, *The Collapse of the Spanish Republic, 1933–1936: Origins of the Civil War* (New Haven, CT: Yale

University Press, 2006), p. 8; and Jordi Domenech, "Rural Labour Markets and Rural Conflict in Spain Before the Civil War (1931–1936)," *Working Papers in Economic History*, WP-12-01 (January 2012), pp. 5–8. Available online: http://www.academia.edu/2371317.

16. Robert Whealy, *Hitler and Spain: the Nazi Role in the Spanish Civil War, 1936–39* (Lexington: University Press of Kentucky, 2004), p. 41.
17. Gerald Howson, *Arms for Spain: The Untold Story of the Spanish Civil War* (New York: St Martin's Press, 1999), pp. 33–5.
18. Michael Alpert, *A New International History of the Spanish Civil War* (New York: St. Martin's, 1994), p. 24.
19. A. R. Peters, *Anthony Eden at the Foreign Office, 1931–1938* (New York: St. Martin's Press, 1986), p. 229.
20. Ian Kershaw sheds light on these attitudes, their social underpinnings, and political consequences in Britain, in his book *Making Friends with Hitler: Lord Londonderry, the Nazis and the Road to World War Two* (New York: Penguin, 2004), pp. 1–64. See also the point made toward the beginning of this chapter on how the British clearly saw Poland as an anti-Soviet buffer state in the immediate post–First World War period.
21. Timothy Snyder, *Bloodlands: Europe between Hitler and Stalin* (New York: Basic Books, 2010).

3

The Second World War, 1939–45: From Anti-Communism to Anti-Communism

By mid-1939 the strong likelihood of war relegated Germany's international anti-communist politics into the background for about one year. Domestically, of course, such politics remained in full force through the system of concentration camps that held tens of thousands of leftist political prisoners, along with other "undesirables." At its minimum, the Nazi anti-socialist drive was sustained in those camps, but it was also evident in the fusion of anti-Semitism with anti-bolshevism that drove the policy of the ghettoization of the Jews in Poland following the invasion of early September 1939. Meanwhile, Hitler maintained his top particular strategic goal of destroying the Soviet Union, even as he directed the Nazi assaults on Northwestern Europe, Britain, and Southeastern Europe. The drive toward that goal then reached its maximum force in "Operation Barbarossa," the attack on the Soviet Union that began in June 1941. For its part, Japan's anti-communism was frighteningly evident in China against the Communists (CCP) under Mao Zedong in 1939–40. A Japanese military loss to the forces of the CCP in December 1940 led to its retaliatory policy of the "Three Alls"— kill all, burn all, and loot all—that was pursued for the duration of the war. Inevitably, at times it was also tied in with its war against the Kwomintang (KMT) nationalists under Chiang Kai Shek, who themselves had a pronounced inclination to prioritize the war against domestic Communism instead of the Japanese aggression. As part of its drive to conquer as much of East Asia as possible, Imperial Japan also battled Communist and Communist-nationalist forces in various parts of Korea, Indochina, Southeast Asia, and the Pacific Islands. Britain's anti-Communism was rendered relatively inoperative for some years, though it remained operative in the distrust of the Soviet Union for the duration of the Nazi-Soviet Non-Aggression Pact of August 1939–June 1941, as well as into late 1941 and beyond. But also during the 1939–41 period, British policy makers held out the hope of somehow drawing the USSR away from, and ultimately against, Nazi Germany. This was a version of the type of approach the Soviets had wanted from the British for some years prior to the war, when all they got was appeasement.

The Non-Aggression Pact represented an unexpected global strategic shift, the first of two that occurred during the war that led to unprecedented cooperation between prior enemies. It followed years of mutual hostility and it confounded many, not least Communist party leaders and members worldwide. The second strategic shift was the breaking of that pact, as the Nazis invaded the Soviet Union on June 22, 1941.

Barbarossa was designed and presented as a means to destroy "Jewish Bolshevism" and expand German *lebensraum*. Instead, the fateful attack lurched the Soviet Union and liberal capitalist powers into the formidable Grand Alliance, soon to include the United States, against the Axis forces, soon to include Japan. As Barbarossa tied down Soviet forces far to the west, the Japanese went for broke in the east: on July 2 the Japanese Imperial Conference resolved to expand further into Southeast Asia to realize the vision of their so-called Greater East Asian Co-Prosperity Sphere, despite the risks of war with Britain and/or the United States. For the anti-Axis alliance of the liberal capitalist powers and the Soviet Union, this was its most cooperative phase, lasting for approximately two years at most, until mid-1943. That thoroughly unlikely alliance—the only time in the short twentieth century that anti-Communism was not a prominent feature of the major liberal capitalist states—became the crux of the war, if not of the century.[1] The irony deepened, as it was the Soviet Union that delivered the decisive military blows against the best of *Wehrmacht* to save itself and, in effect, the liberal capitalist world and its imperial order, from the further scourge of Nazism. The last phase of the war, mid-1943 to August 1945, saw the Axis drive fall to defeat roughly simultaneously with a concerted and steadily rising resumption of the original anti-communist thrust on the part of the liberal capitalist states, now including West Germany and Japan, but with the United States now emerging in the lead role. In other words, the war was *not* settling the problem of "communism" but in fact dramatically reconstituting and expanding it. The common interests and perspectives of the great power imperialist states outside the Soviet Union that went so far in bringing on the war—through their myriad strategic and ideological drives that prominently included anti-"Bolshevism," anti-socialism, anti-communism, and so forth—were now embroiled in war and creating a vast array of new leftwing targets. Not only did the Soviet Union remain fully intact, but Communist regimes also were established in Eastern Europe, poised for victory in China, and threatening elsewhere, now more than ever. In addition to the defeat of the fascist model of capitalism and imperialism, what the war settled was that the United States would lead the charge against Communism and, eventually, against the extremely wide variety of noncommunist "leftist" politics worldwide. While this current chapter will track the main lines of anti-Communism that continued during the war, it will also show how, in times and areas where such politics were not prominent, the stage was being reset for the next round of conflict, the so-called Cold War.

On August 11, 1939, Hitler insisted that "everything I undertake is directed against Russia. If the West is too blind or too stupid to recognize this, then I shall be forced to come to an understanding with the Russians, strike at the West, and, after its defeat, turn with all my concerted force against the Soviet Union." On August 29, less than a week after the signing of the Nazi-Soviet Non-Aggression Pact, Hitler explained to the baffled Japanese ambassador to Germany, Hiroshi Ōshima, that "in no ways was he altering his fundamental anti-bolshevist policies; one had to use Beelzebub to drive away the devil; all means were justified in dealing with the Soviets, even a pact such as this."[2] Hitler's intent to destroy "Jewish Bolshevism" now necessitated the attack on the obstinate British and French, which he, Rippentrop, and others had admonished for not seeing the need for a full anti-Soviet alliance. Though Chamberlain hoped to the last minute and beyond that Hitler's "reasonable side" could and would prevail, the strategic and human price for the rejection of a full alliance was harsh: Poland fell to the Nazi *blitzkrieg* in September, while its eastern portion was soon devoured by the Soviet Union.[3] April–June 1940 saw the fall of Denmark, Norway, Luxembourg, Belgium, Holland, and France. Amid the varying socioeconomic, political, and infrastructural dislocations of the invasions, the Nazis found willing collaborators, most infamously Quisling in Norway and Pétain in France. Britain came under assault from the *Luftwaffe* and was back on its heels by the end of August–early September. The Japanese government and military had, at first, been shocked by the Nazi-Soviet pact, because they were keen to maintain a strong relationship with Germany and Italy but not unduly antagonize Britain and the United States. But now, with the colonies and strategic resources of the now-beleaguered Dutch, French, and British in East and Southeast Asia up for grabs, Japan rode a new wave of expansionist enthusiasm beginning in mid-1940. The Imperial Japanese Army (IJA) launched its initial incursions into French Indochina in early September, aiming to block the flow of war material to the Chinese communists (CCP) and nationalists (KMT) along the Kunming-Haiphong railway. Those aggressions combined with German pressure to quickly force the French collaborationist Vichy regime to concede the key ports Haiphong and Saigon to the Japanese. On September 27, Imperial Japan, Nazi Germany, and fascist Italy signed the Tripartite Pact that established the wartime Axis alliance, while Hitler made sure to scuttle whatever remote chance existed for the USSR to join the Axis. In fact, already in June–July 1940, Hitler was clamoring to prepare for "the great and true task: the conflict with Bolshevism."[4] The official command to the *Wehrmacht* to prepare for Barbarossa was issued on December 18, 1940; its launch date was slated for the following May 15.

Preparations for the German invasion of the Soviet Union proceeded at an uneven pace, in part due to the sheer logistics of the massive operation. But, contrary to Hitler's expectations and claims, Britain under Churchill's leadership as of May 1940 was neither falling to defeat nor making a "deal" with Nazi Germany. Britain stood strong and became stronger in terms of war manufactures, particularly warplanes, as well as morale. They also had full material backing—"all aid short of war"—from the United States and, by March 1941, the formalization and expansion of that through the Lend-Lease Act. While Hitler had believed the United States would inevitably join the war on Britain's side in the near future, rather than instilling caution in him, it only further convinced him that the time was now to make his greater mark on the world. His determination persisted even after the series of postponed Nazi land invasions of Britain in the fall, and after the scrapping of the plan altogether by the end of 1940. Meanwhile, developments in southeastern Europe created further problems for the *Wehrmacht*. Having militarily subjugated Albania already since April 1939, Mussolini's armies launched an invasion of Greece in October 1940. But the Italian aim for nationalist glory and conquered territories alongside those of Germany was blocked by a tenacious Greek defense and counteroffensive that pushed Mussolini's forces back into Albania. Italian military weakness and vulnerability were in full display, revealing an unacceptable strategic soft spot for the German military and its grandiose aims against Bolshevik Russia. To further focus Hitler's anger, a successful pro-British and popular *coup d'état* took place in Yugoslavia in late March 1941, betraying the previous government's commitment to the Axis. The German invasion of the Soviet Union, planned for the spring so as to maximize the time before the onset of the Russian winter, had to be postponed to secure the Balkans militarily. German ground and air invasions of Yugoslavia and Greece came in April and May, with the city of Belgrade coming under particularly fierce and destructive aerial bombing named nothing other than "Operation Punishment." During the following few years, under Axis occupations and following them, Yugoslavia and Greece were to become sites of some of the most complex and violent Communist versus anti-Communist politics experienced anywhere in the war-torn west.

A situation with compelling parallels and distinctions took shape in northern Indochina, to where Ho Chi Minh returned in May to organize a national liberation movement against both the Japanese and the French.[5] Compared to the fast and hard Japanese aggressions of the time, Indochina as a whole had been subjected to a slower French colonial subjugation beginning in the 1860s. Its liberation would also be relatively slow—taking until the 1970s—yet punctuated by horrific conflict and deprivation. Ho Chi Minh's return to Indochina followed numerous personal and increasingly political adventures on the high seas and in assorted jobs in New York, London, Paris, and elsewhere. Explicitly in the spirit of the American Declaration of Independence, he and his nationalist colleagues' appealed to US President Wilson at the Versailles conference in 1919 to support the liberation of Vietnam from French rule. This went nowhere, except to open the future Vietnamese leader to the revolutionary anti-imperialist politics of Vladimir Lenin. In 1920, Ho became a founding member of the French Communist Party. He spent 1923–1940 between Moscow, China, and Hong Kong, where he cofounded the Indochinese Communist Party in 1930, and where he was arrested by British police and jailed from 1931 to 1933. As an indication of Ho's relatively independent position vis-à-vis the Comintern's party line, his return to northern Indochina in May 1941 was prior to the Nazi invasion of the USSR and Moscow's subsequent call for armed anti-fascist resistance. The Viet Minh Communist-nationalist movement was bound for a long, tragic, but ultimately victorious struggle for independence that had a profound global significance.

With the invasion of the Soviet Union begun on June 22, 1941, Nazi anti-Communism and anti-Semitism shifted to the forefront with a vengeance. The USSR now faced the largest land invasion in human history: four million highly armored and mechanized *Wehrmacht* troops moving across the 1,800-mile border in three main army groups—North, Center, and South—aiming for Leningrad, Moscow, and Stalingrad, respectively, and all their regional strategic assets, including infrastructure, minerals, industries, and land and water routes. While Hitler demanded a "war of annihilation," Stalin issued the call to Communist parties in all Axis-occupied countries, east and west, to organize Popular Front–style, anti-Nazi/fascist resistance centered tactically on mass mobilization and guerilla warfare. The former tactic was similar to the 1935–9 Popular Front political line of nonrevolutionary anti-fascism, but with a unique urgency that also motivated the new call for guerilla warfare. The potentials for the emergence of mass-based, armed movements with unmistakable leftwing political complexions were clear.

The Nazi-Soviet war is known for its bloodletting on all sides, but this morbid sensationalism should not deflect attention from its specific historical character and context. The invasion was motivated by perceived national geostrategic interests, which set off a long paroxysm of violence. From the Axis side, it was also tied in with an inexpungible modern political, ideological, and nationalist drive that Hitler forced into the overriding mission of destroying "Jewish Bolshevism." In his rhetoric, Hitler declared the ultimate need to eliminate Jews in the west; one of his brazenly and absurdly false, yet characteristic, claims was that Jews started both the First World War and the present one. In other words, there was nothing exclusive about his identification of the Jews with Bolshevism; capitalist Jews in the west, including the United States, controlled everything from behind the scenes and were also an eventual socio-biological threat to the fictional Aryan race. But there was no doubt that, for Hitler and many of his underlings, the premier political evil of their times was Bolshevism, fused as it was with Jewishness. The urgent task was to eliminate it, while the need to deal with the broader Jewish threat only loomed vaguely in the future. On the day of the invasion of the USSR, the Reich Press Chief issued an extended comment with the essential message that "the Jews pulling the strings behind the Soviet scene have remained the same .... Plutocracy and Bolshevism have an identical starting point: the Jewish striving for world domination." Two weeks later came a follow-up: "The Jew pushed the peoples of the Soviet Union into this indescribable misery by way of his devilish Bolshevik system." A poster in Axis-friendly Romania asked, "Who are the masters of Bolshevism?" It showed a "Jew in a red gown, with side curls, skullcap, and beard, holding a hammer in one hand and a sickle in the other. Concealed beneath his coat [were] three Soviet soldiers."[6]

The initial order from Hitler to execute "anyone who doesn't give us a straight look" on the eastern front was modified by mid-July to include a series of explicit directives to kill all Jews. Stalin had called for anti-Axis partisan resistance war within the USSR as of July 3. Somewhat under the cover of anti-partisan operations, top Reich Security Chief Reinhard Heydrich, gave the order to encourage local "avengers" to carry out pogroms, execute all Jewish political and administrative functionaries, and to eliminate all Jewish prisoners of war. Soon, *einsatzgruppen* and various other SS units, as well as Order Police Battalions, local collaborationist units, and Wehrmacht troops were killing Jewish men, women, and children indiscriminately. After all, it was claimed, each one must have been ultimately supportive of anti-Nazi partisan activity. In the second half of 1941 alone, the Nazis murdered at least six hundred thousand, and as many as one million Jews.[7]

Especially since 1937, Japanese imperialist aggression and expansionism in China and Korea entailed systematic, large-scale murderousness and abuse, most notoriously the Nanking Massacre of 1937–8 and the institution of sex slavery throughout the conquered territories. For the sake of its economic might as an advanced capitalist industrial economy and its competitiveness as an imperialist state—now highly inclined to redraw the lines of imperial power in the Pacific—Japan primarily needed oil but also rubber and a great variety of minerals and metals. The Dutch East Indies had oil and rubber; British Malaya rubber and tin; Indochina had rice, rubber, coal, tin, and zinc. Hostility with the United States and Britain was increasing, yet up to 1938

Japan remained highly dependent on the United States for at least 80 percent of its oil, 74 percent of its scrap iron for making steel, 60 percent of its machine tools, and the bulk of its main metal alloys. Total dependence on US imports ran close to 33 percent. By 1939 they depended crucially on American copper. Already in 1938, potentially explosive tensions were evident from the Japanese side as Army vice-minister, Tojo Hideki, publicly presented the British and the United States as Japan's top threat. He further explained that western powers exploited Southeast Asian colonial resources only for their own purposes, but even more importantly and directly, they—specifically Britain and the United States—supported Chiang Kai Shek and the KMT in China against Japan. Starving the KMT could be accomplished by severing its supply lines from Southeast Asia.[8] In July 1940, the Japanese persuaded the beleaguered British to close the Burma Road into China; Japanese confidence and ambition grew. With France and Holland under Nazi occupation and Britain back on its heels, Prime Minister Fumimaro stated in August the advantages that expansion beyond China, Korea, and northern Indochina would hold for the Japanese and all Asian peoples under their sway. All would conjoin in the "Greater East Asia Co-Prosperity Sphere," as described with flourish by the Foreign Minister Mastuoka.

It was already clear to American policy makers that it was of vital interest that Britain retain control of its Southeast Asian colonies in order to maintain the flow of strategic minerals to the US economy and military. Roosevelt viewed Japanese actions and pronouncements with imperial contempt and suspicion, reinforced by the groundswell of popular American anti-Japanese sentiment roused by what they knew of the recent murder and abuse in China. The two powers were on a likely collision course. Neither necessarily wanted war, but both foresaw its possibility, with the Japanese at a clear disadvantage in case it should happen. In that context, the commitment of the United States, first to Britain, but eventually to China and other allies as well, became formalized by the Lend-Lease Act of March 1941, which facilitated the transferal of American war material, food and billions of dollars in loans to its embattled allies. The thin veneer of US neutrality was gone.

It was imperative for Japan to stem any potential threat from the Soviet Union against its position in China, including Manchuko. The Soviet Union, facing potentially tremendous trouble from the west, wanted no entanglements at any points east. In particular, it needed to prevent any Japanese incursion into the People's Republic of Mongolia, the *de facto* Soviet Republic located on China's northern border that shared a border with Japan's puppet state of Manchuko. The treaties signed in April addressed all of these matters; despite the numerous strains of the unfolding war, they settled them for the duration. The Soviet-Japanese neutrality pact made the two states into bedfellows no more or less than the "Communazi Pact" did for Nazi Germany and the USSR. Just as the Germans got a free hand against the west, the Japanese were now freer to advance on the rest of Southeast Asia. The Japanese imperial establishment resolved to do exactly that, though in a step-by-step manner it vaguely intended to avoid war with the United States. The situation in the west was mixed: the Nazis were potentially on the verge of defeating the USSR, yet Britain stood undefeated and was backed strongly by the United States. When the Japanese gambled in July to take the rest of Indochina from the French, Roosevelt promptly ordered a freeze on all Japanese assets in the United States, and he soon imposed a full embargo on US oil and steel exports to Japan. Secretary of State Cordell Hull was out front on this matter. He rejected all Japanese attempts at compromise over China and Indochina, insisting that Japan abandon both completely and commit to free trade throughout the Pacific.[9]

Japanese diplomatic efforts continued amid increasingly loud and resonant factional voices for war. It was also at this time that Japanese strategists began devising plans to militarily debilitate the United States long enough to seize numerous European and American colonial territories throughout Southeast Asia. Emperor Hirohito intervened to mend the factionalism in October, tipping the scales further in favor of war. He appointed a new prime minister, General Tojo, the anti-Communist hero of Japan's Kwantung Army in China, in other words, a battle-hardened ideologue and veteran of imperialist expansionism. Tojo opened extensive internal discussions about possible terms of settlement with the United States, resulting in two compromise positions that would allow Japan to keep its territorial gains in China, while expanding no further. These were presented to the Roosevelt administration in November and summarily dismissed. The fallback for Japan was the high-risk strategy of a hard hit against the US Pacific fleet, from which the assumed recovery would take long enough for the conquest of Southeast Asia. The United States would then not go to war; it would be a *fait accompli*. In the moment and according to plan, Japan attacked Pearl Harbor and conquered across Southeast Asia.[10] However, the damage done to the United States was not only far from fatal but it also lurched the country into a merciless war against Japan and its western allies that would also do two broader things: expand the geographical and historical breadth and depth of the conflict to make it an unmistakable world war, further fuel a variety of leftwing anti-fascist and anti-colonialist political-military movements, and facilitate the American postwar rise as the preeminent power and anti-Communist state on the world stage.

During the following six months, Imperial Japan knocked the European powers out of their colonial strongholds in Southeast Asia and re-subjugated its territories and peoples. Much of this, but not all, was done by sustained military force. The European colonial armies of the region were generally trained and equipped to suppress internal revolts, not external invasions, while the loyalties of their lower-echelon troops, drawn from the colonized peoples, tended to be insecure. In Malaya, the Japanese faced British, Indian, and Australian forces allied with large numbers of indigenous and ethnic Chinese troops. Hundreds of these were led by the Malayan Communist Party (MCP) that had been outlawed for ten years until one week into the invasion, when the British released all leftist political prisoners and began cooperating with the MCP. The liberal capitalist-imperialist alliance with the Soviet Union in the west was now clearly extending to the east and its equally grim strategic situation. Allied forces in Malaya were defeated within two months, though the Communist-led element among them remained and continued to build upon a core cadre in the inland jungle regions. From that base, they launched a full-scale insurgency after 1945. The Philippines, under US dominance since the Philippine-American War of 1899–1902, was under the military sway of Field Marshall Douglas MacArthur, who had been granted rather vast sums of money and air power in anticipation of a Japanese attack. The actual attack destroyed the American fleet of 100 B-17 "flying fortresses" while it also apparently shook the determination of the General, who led his forces into various stages of retreat that finally brought him to Australia in February 1942, where, he declared, "I shall return," and he did. In 1945, as Supreme Commander of the Southwest Pacific Area, MacArthur returned to lead the reassertion of American power over the Philippines and more.[11] In the meantime, Japan completely overpowered the Philippines by May 1942. With Holland under the firm grip of the Nazis, the Dutch East Indies were similarly overwhelmed by March, though initially, on the popular level, there was significant enthusiasm for the new imperialists, self-proclaimed as the "light of Asia," who would treat their same-race subjects with understanding and decency. Indonesian nationalists of the 1930s, including Sukarno and Mohammad Hatta, had already believed that a Japanese military move against the Dutch and other European powers throughout the region would mean an opportunity for Indonesians to realize their independence. At least with that end in mind, they also appeared favorably inclined toward the Imperial Japan's racialist rhetoric. Meanwhile, the Indonesian leftist of the 1930s, Amir Sjarifuddin, though not clearly affiliated with the Indonesian Communist Party (PKI), followed the Popular Front line against the Axis in the late 1930s, and was one of the few to organize resistance against the Japanese. The nationalist Sutan Sjahrir also did so, in secret cooperation with Sukarno, the most popular of Indonesian politicians of the time, who had made a deal with the Japanese: support them in return for being allowed to cultivate Indonesian nationalism. Sjarrifuddin and Sukarno were to fall prey to Indonesian and American anti-leftism during the Cold War.[12] The new Japanese conquerors quickly reneged on their own racialist promises by establishing sex and labor slavery, and commandeering all possible raw materials and manufactured items for their war machine.

Thailand and Burma allied with Japan, also with some outright enthusiasm for the latter's racialist rhetoric. But the hard reasons had to do with Thai designs on parts of French Indochina, over which the Japanese now had top leverage, and the Burmese quest to be rid of British colonial rule. With that same goal in mind, the Indian nationalist Subhas Chandra Bose organized the Indian National Army (INA) in 1942–3 as a collaborationist force with the Japanese against the British in India and Burma and wherever they could be of use. Bose had met face to face with Hitler's representatives in Berlin in the spring of 1941, and with the *führer* himself in May 1942, when they reaffirmed the British as their common enemy. Aside from vague material promises the Nazis made to Bose that were never kept, the perceived strategic and tactical options, if not priorities, of the Indian nationalist, and many others throughout South and Southeast Asia on the popular and leading levels, were sufficiently clear: if necessary, use the upstart imperialist powers against the established ones to advance toward national liberation. The use of one or more allied or rival imperialist power against any other was what was to be expected, and what happened, in all cases. Among the softest, but most dramatic and successful, cases was that of colonial India, where Mahatma Gandhi and Jawaharlal Nehru faced various jail terms for their refusal to come out against the Japanese unless the British first promised to "quit" India. For his part, Bose in 1942–3 eluded British reach while building the INA. His recruits were from India itself, from Indian colonial troops captured by the Germans in North Africa and from various colonial Indians of the diaspora in Southeast Asia, especially including troops captured by the Japanese during the Battle of Singapore.

The British were clearly not in the position of strength they had largely enjoyed for many decades; the empire was being shaken at its foundations. At least by May 1940, it was the *Luftwaffe* that overshadowed any leftist or anti-colonialist threat. However, having withstood the German assault, it was clear that the June 1941 Nazi attack on the Soviet Union meant a potential for a British-Soviet anti-Axis alliance that could help Britain's position worldwide. Only a spectacular German defeat of the Soviet state, which Hitler and some British and American analysts had predicted, would quash such a possibility. The British-Soviet alliance took shape, but slowly. In a broadcast speech on the day of the invasion, Churchill evoked the historical profundity of the moment, established his anti-Communist credibility forged over the past twenty-five years, but explained that British support for the USSR was now, by necessity, in the works. The support was for the ordinary people—peasants, workers, and soldiers, in the Russia "where there are still primordial human joys, where maidens laugh and children play"—but it was also and ultimately about protecting Britain, he stated, because a German victory over the USSR would put it in position for another direct blow against Britain.[13]

Stalin first appealed to Churchill on July 18 to open a second front in northern France, and/or in the Arctic, in order to release pressure on the USSR. Churchill doggedly resisted such a move for at least one and a half years, arguing a lack of military preparedness. Suspicion in Soviet circles, of course, was that the British priority was not the defeat of Nazi Germany but to encourage a mutual German-Soviet pulverization that would allow Britain the freest and most effective reign across Eurasia. The Soviet ambassador to Great Britain, Ivan Maisky, reflected in his memoirs that "three years of stubborn struggle by the Soviet Union were required before the second front in France at last opened, and then only because the Western Powers were afraid that the Red Army might come to Berlin before they did."[14] The evidence for or against deliberate stalling on this is not sufficient, though it is entirely plausible that Churchill did it, always with enough reason to claim he didn't, given his political position and the hard calculus of any imperialist state, in wartime, in relationship to its rivals.[15]

Somewhat aside from Churchill's particular disposition, and let alone the question of a second front, urgency did not characterize British and American policy makers during the summer of 1941 with regard to material support for the Soviet Union. The logistics were difficult, but there was plenty of room for criticism and recrimination. Responding to the criticism from Stalin, Molotov, and Maisky, Churchill and Anthony Eden lost no opportunity to note that when the British could have used some help from the Soviets during the period of the Nazi-Soviet Non-Aggression Pact, they did not get it. The USSR had supplied Nazi Germany as it lashed out against Western and Southeastern Europe. Now the tables were turned, but of course some were more determined than others to offer support. Though his War Department had predicted the USSR would be crushed in six weeks, Roosevelt became more optimistic and favorably inclined toward supporting it, especially after his close adviser and top New Deal architect Harry Hopkins returned from a Moscow trip in late July, confident that the Soviet Union would survive the Nazi onslaught. The US Congress, on the other hand, driven by its core-value anti-Communism, refused to vote in favor of granting Lend-Lease privileges to the USSR, while US Secretary of State and free market militant Cordell Hull suggested to the Soviet Ambassador to Washington, Konstantin Umansky, that perhaps a deal could be reached if Stalin would unequivocally declare freedom of religion in the Soviet state.[16]

On August 14, the principles of the Atlantic Charter were first broadcast. It was a statement of common Anglo-American and western Allied purpose. It was a way of stating who they were and who they were not; how they were not like their enemy, or enemies. The Americans were the lead authors of the agreement reached between Churchill, Roosevelt, and their advisors that included commitments to the right of peoples to choose their own government; admonition against territorial self-aggrandizement and territorial changes opposed by the peoples concerned; free trade; improved labor conditions, economic development, and social security; and international stability, open access to the seas, and disarmament.[17] Among other things, the agreement had the strong mark of American strategic and business interests and tended to undermine their British equivalents. This was further confirmed by early 1942, when language in the Charter that protected Britain's system of Imperial tariff preferences, which privileged trade relations within the various entities of the empire, was eliminated. American negotiators believed any such preferences were inimical to American interests and a maximally robust system of world trade.[18] The notion of having to conform to the principles of the Charter repeatedly irritated many figures in the upper echelons of global power at the time and, to some extent, since, yet it remained the basis for the postwar Charter of the United Nations. The commitment to free trade within the Charter had eighteenth-century classical liberal origins, while it anticipated both postwar American free trade policies as well as the US-led hyper-free trade trend of the era of neoliberal economic globalization since the 1970s. It was the free trade maximalists such as Cordell Hull that anticipated the neoliberalism of everyone from Ronald Reagan and Margaret Thatcher to Bill Clinton and Barack Obama. As will be explained in the chapters on the post–Second World War period, some of the politically conservative among them prefer to describe as "socialist" anything but free trade and free markets. Politically speaking, the principles of the Charter that clearly favored democracy and self-determination were used and abused in numerous ways by all the great powers concerned, including the Soviet Union. It became a standard of sorts for measuring hypocrisy or the lack of it.

In light of those questions as well as related matters of timing, Britain's strategic priorities focused on North Africa, the Suez Canal, and the Middle East, which meant that there was common ground with the Soviet Union in Iran. Especially for the British, this was about seizing the oil fields of southeastern and eastern Iran, and doing whatever possible to keep the oil of the Caucasus from falling under German control. For the Soviets, it was about securing supply lines from the Persian Gulf up to the Caspian Sea along the Trans-Iranian Railway. "Persia's value as an oil producer and as a potential route for supplies to the Soviet Union was obvious."[19] British imperial forces came from the south and the Soviets from the north in a coordinated surprise attack on August 25, 1941—that is, two weeks after the initial pronouncement of the Atlantic Charter. The pretext was that the Iranian government of the time, though it had declared neutrality, was pro-German. This was highly debatable, but in the event, the Iranian armed forces were overwhelmed, King Reza Shah was replaced by his son, Mohammad Reza Pahlavi, and a new government was installed under Prime Minister Mohammad Ali Foroughi. Resistance against the invasion and occupation was only scattered and sporadic, yet in a way portending developments in the postwar decades, Iranian nationalist identity, sentiment, and resentment were strengthened. Furthermore, the Soviets encouraged the establishment of the pro-Moscow Tudeh party, which remained a small, though vocal, party that was to draw fire in the early 1950s from the Shah and his American and British allies. They staged a successful coup against the popularly elected Mossadeq in 1953 and imposed the Shah, who remained in power until the tumult of the Islamic Revolution in 1979. During the Second World War and after, political expediency tended to prevail, of course, over the principles of the Atlantic Charter, whenever deemed necessary by those with the interests and capacity to make their strategic marks.

Realizing the potential problem of the imagery and the substance of neglecting to assist the Soviet Union for too long, on August 15, 1941, Roosevelt and Churchill had informed Stalin of their cooperative efforts to supply the USSR with as much aid as possible; the qualification was that such decisions would be affected by demands on other war fronts, present and future. Appeals by Roosevelt to Congress and the American public resulted in Lend-Lease privileges being extended to the Soviet Union in September. The same month saw a joint Anglo-American mission to Moscow that led to Roosevelt's announcement on November 6 of a one-billion-dollar aid package for Russia under Lend-Lease. From July to November, Churchill's foreign secretary, Eden, reiterated to Soviet authorities the lack of military and material preparation for a second front. In early December, he could and did promise to send British fighter planes to Russia, to be released only when success was achieved against Rommel's armies in North Africa.[20] These were all important beginning steps, but again, they were not proportionate with the scale of the crisis for the Soviet Union. Maisky countered to the promise of the fighter planes that this was a paltry promise given the many hundreds of thousands of Soviet troops and civilians losing their lives or barely surviving in those first months of the invasion. In some contrast to the other major British figures on the scene, it was with noticeable sympathy that the British ambassador in Moscow, Stafford Cripps, attempted to confirm the desperation of top-level figures and ordinary people in the Soviet Union as they faced the Nazi onslaught. But Cripps, the Labor politician, was sidelined in the main discussions between the Tory politicians of the British War Cabinet.[21] In addition to the vast numbers of Soviet troops that were killed and/or taken prisoner during these months up to December, upwards of one million Jews were massacred in the same period by the notorious Nazi mobile killing units— the *einsatsgruppen*—and their local collaborators.

A notable shift in British action on the Soviet crisis occurred as Nazi forces became stalled in their attempt to take Leningrad, while outside of Moscow in November the snow and the cold forced them into a standstill. On November 14 it was determined that Eden would make a personal visit to Moscow to discuss matters of supply and coordination between Britain, the USSR, and ultimately the United States. Eden arrived on December 7, two days after the start of a Soviet counteroffensive, in the virtual moment of the Japanese attack on Pearl Harbor, and four days before the German declaration of war on the United States. The British could not contain their relief about the news from Pearl Harbor, followed by the German declaration, as these items now guaranteed full US entry into the war against the Axis. From there on, always subject to tensions and differences, the relatively mild, yet significant, Anglo-Soviet tensions of 1939–41 gave way to the recognition of common strategic interests reinforced by the full involvement of the United States in what was now the most global and grave strategic crisis humanity had ever experienced. Now and for the following one-to-two years the overarching interests of the British and the United States compelled them to push their anti-communist politics aside for purposes of fighting with the Soviet Communist state against the Axis alliance.

British maneuvering on these matters was then the first to show signs of a return to normalcy. Long accustomed to imperialist intervention, Britain also had immediate interests in the outcomes of the conflicts on the European continent. The shift began after the western Allied victory at Second Battle of El Alamein in October–November 1942, when Churchill was tempted to ring the bells of victory over the Axis. The moment roughly coincided with the rising power of Communist anti-Axis resistance organizations and movements, most importantly in Greece, Yugoslavia, and France. As the war now looked very winnable, it was time to maneuver for postwar power. On the local levels throughout Axis-occupied Europe, the British as well as the United States had potential *de jure* and *de facto* allies in a variety of hard-driven anti-Communists—some that had collaborated with the Axis and some that had not. As will be seen, these included everyone from figures such as Charles de Gaulle in France, George Papandreou in Greece, and Marshall Badoglio in Italy, as well as more ground-level prospects that included local French collaborationist *gendarmes*, Greek anti-Communist police and paramilitary forces, as well as royalist military officers and troops in the Greek forces in the Middle East. Such institutions and currents became vital for the successful resurgence of British and US anti-Communism but were also reminders that the main problem those states had with extremist anti-Communist politics was when they were also turned against the liberal capitalist states. The Nazi-led forces that had done this were now going down to defeat, so that whatever ground-level anti-leftist forces that had collaborated with the Axis were now potentially useful for what was to become the British-led drive in its perceived spheres of influence to undermine leftist power. The British maneuvering took on interesting parallels with what had been a fairly constant line of anti-leftist politics and strategy on the part of the Axis occupation powers against anti-Axis resistance throughout occupied Europe. This was, by definition, anti-leftist in its political character, and especially anti-Communist, since it was the Communist parties that proved to be the most effective at organizing mass-based anti-fascist political and military resistance movements.

An example of the return of British anti-Communist politics was clear in Greece by the summer of 1942. The prior September had seen the establishment of the Greek Communist Party's (KKE's) National Liberation Front (EAM), aiming to be a mass-based anti-Axis political resistance movement. In October, the republican anti-communist officer Napoleon Zervas established the National Republican Greek League (EDES) as an alternative to the EAM. The KKE then created the Greek National

Liberation Army (ELAS) in April 1942, which caught the attention of the British Special Operations Executive (SOE). Elements within the SOE were keen to support EDES as a counterforce to the EAM-ELAS. That summer, the SOE funneled twenty-four thousand gold sovereigns into the hands of Napoleon Zervas, the main leader of EDES. The agreement was that Zervas would head into the mountains of central Greece to organize armed resistance. But by the end of the summer he remained inactive in Athens, which led the SOE to threaten to betray him to the Gestapo. With that prod, he proceeded to set up guerilla-style operations in the mountains, taking in recruits from any and all non- and anti-Communist backgrounds, including plenty of committed royalists that had been supporters of the 1936–40 Metaxas dictatorship. In other words, there were vital ground-level currents of undiminished anti-Communism that fed into British grand strategies and tactics of the time. The SOE's intent to build up that political-military faction against the EAM-ELAS was, at that point, precautionary, yet it showed unmistakable and unsurprising continuities with the British imperial strategy in the past and, within one year, would grow to into the overarching strategy of British policy toward anti-Axis resistance in Greece, namely, to support EDES and undermine the EAM-ELAS, with an eye on reestablishing uncontested British hegemony over Greece in the postwar period.[22]

Seeing to the reestablishment of a state to their liking in France after the war proved a far easier task for the British than it was for them in Greece. For reasons partly structural and partly geostrategic, French resistance came without civil war. The French economy and society had a more modern and developed character whose industrial structure and infrastructure allowed for two things: first, they could both be commandeered more easily than their Greek equivalents for war production purposes by the occupation powers, which meant a less harsh and provocative plunder regime and therefore less of a cause for resistance; second, those structures indicated the relative successes of the upper social and economic echelons of France in creating a firmly established bourgeois society. These things facilitated both the interests of the occupation regime, meaning both the Nazis and their Vichy collaborators, and subsequently the reestablishment of those ruling strata, both socioeconomic and political, after the war. Another distinguishing feature was the year-long period after the Fall of France in June 1940, when a smattering of anti-Vichy conservatives, including de Gaulle and the many he famously rallied from his position as leader of the Free French movement in London, resisted the occupation, when the Communists of the PCF did not, instead adopting an anti-war stance due to the dictates following from the Nazi-Soviet Non-Aggression Pact. As Robert Paxton, put it, "conservatives dominated the resistance until June 1941."[23] The price many PCF members paid was in prison time, since the government proscribed the party after the war began in 1939; on the other hand, the many that went underground were able to accustom themselves to clandestine operations that soon served them very well. Meanwhile, the conservatives and Gaullists—typically staunch anti-Communists and anti-socialists profoundly antagonistic toward the prewar Third Republic and the prominent role of the left within it—did not resist the occupation with anything approaching armed and aggressive, mass-based tactics, but they had a strong initial lead on those that did. Despite his own fears and those of the Americans, which became clear by 1943, de Gaulle and his followers never really lost their lead, even when the June 1941 Nazi invasion of the Soviet Union spurred the PCF into action. While he had to work with the PCF and the left, de Gaulle's shrewdness, his British backing, his anti-Communist determination, the anti-revolutionary anti-fascist politics of the Popular Front, the structural and institutional constitution of the French economy and society described above, as well as the actual Anglo-American second front opened at Normandy in mid-1944, all favored the return of the main elements of the prewar French establishment. This is all in spite of the claims by de Gaulle that the PCF tried to seize power in Paris and then in the countryside in 1944, the evidence for which is scant, at best. In his memoirs, de Gaulle manages to present himself as the spearhead of a French republican nationalist anti-communist crusade.[24]

The French Vichy collaborationist anti-Communists were, of course, also deeply hostile toward the Third Republic, fulfilled by its destruction and inspired by the Nazi determination to destroy Bolshevism, wherever it may have existed. In November 1940, the Vichy authorities ordered leftists to be ousted from local governments; the following July 1941 saw the establishment of the Legion of French Volunteers against Bolshevism as well as the Anti-Bolshevik Action Committee, a group equal parts anti-Semitic and anti-Bolshevik, directed by the notorious collaborator Paul Chack. Though they characteristically misrepresented the political character of their targets, the timing of the creation of these organizations had its logic, as the PCF anti-Nazi/Vichy Popular Front–style nonrevolutionary resistance operations were dramatically escalating by August. Two top German officers were assassinated in October, which was met by vastly and disproportionate hostage taking and reprisal executions, directed especially against Communists and labor organizers. At that time, Jean Moulin was in London getting directives from de Gaulle to unite the disparate factions of the resistance within France, where he returned in January, and where, had it been of any interest to him, he could have visited the exhibition at the dazzling Salle Wagram in Paris, "Bolshevism against Europe," organized by Chack. Bolshevism was exhibited as the great threat, and the Nazi mission was to destroy it. But not everyone was convinced. Concerted resistance increased significantly over the following year, in November helping to lead to the German decision to occupy the entire country instead of assigning a large swathe of the south to Marshall Petain and his Vichy government. In January 1943, the demoted, but still functional Vichy authorities and the Germans also established the political and paramilitary group *Milice française*.[25] The range of its social and political composition included veterans of the prewar fascist *Accion Française*, to those that wanted to avoid being sent to Germany for labor service, to those that had suffered at the hands of the resistance and later the Allied bombings. Its mission was to fight "Communists" and help round up Jews for deportation. Its harsh and torturous tactics instilled particular fears in resistance circles due to its members' often close familiarity with local social networks and physical terrain. Its estimated membership grew to 25,000–35,000 by the spring of 1944.

De Gaulle's exhortations to the French to resist the Axis were of an imperialist-nationalist sort from start to finish; his rhetoric expressly precluded emancipation for those under the French empire in Southeast Asia and Africa, where the top strategic priorities, respectively, were Indochina and Algeria. For de Gaulle, French "greatness" was predicated on the maintenance of the empire after the war, a message that found qualified sympathy from the British.[26] No doubt this was, on the other hand, an invitation to all manners of anti-colonial activism, including left-oriented Communist and nationalist political and military movements.[27] The United States, with its long-term free market agenda, was skeptical of de Gaulle's postwar vision, not because of its subjugations of peoples, but because it promised imperial tariff preferences for its colonies similar to those of the British. But for the present, the United States recognized the Vichy regime, since it would keep France "less Nazi"; they later believed de Gaulle was too close to the Communists and too willing to speak with the Russians. Cordell Hull was particularly vehement and alarmist regarding de Gaulle and the Communists, stating that the general "has permitted to come under his umbrella all the most radical elements in France."[28] Given his own interests, de Gaulle was probably doing the right thing; after all, it was *his* umbrella and recognized as such by the potentially dissident leftist elements within what became the Committee of National Liberation by January 1943. Meanwhile, at that point in the war, British disdain and anger toward the Vichy regime strongly drove their French policy, making them appear somewhat soft on Communism, certainly compared to their antagonists, but also to their American allies. This was all remarkably close to the common anti-Communism that got the world into this second war in the first place. It became increasingly easy for the victors and vanquished outside of the Soviet Union to come together under the new US anti-Communist lead after the war. Despite the gradations of the anti-Communist politics of the warring states outside of the USSR, the commonalities were emerging as the paramount force.

The interests of the French establishment, more or less backed by the British and the United States, had de Gaulle as a potential lead figure in the reestablishment of postwar power. It is again instructive to consider the contrasting situation in Greece, which had a large anti-communist constituency, yet was short on outstanding and unscathed conservative or liberal anti-Communist figures that could have been close equivalents to de Gaulle. However, when their desperate and perceived need arose, the British found a most useful figure in Papandreou, the liberal republican anti-Communist whom they installed as prime minister of the Greek government-in-exile between April 1944 and January 1945. During this critical time, for the interests of the British and the conservative and anti-Communist elements of the Greek establishment, Papandreou drove a political wedge between the Communists within EAM-ELAS on the one hand, and the organization's more numerous supporters who were more republican and non-Communist (as opposed to anti-Communist). Also, very much *unlike* the French example, it was a last-minute scramble rather than one that emerged in the opening moments of the catastrophe of the invasion and occupation. It reflected the tenuous but—with some strong prodding from the outside—potentially still viable institutional establishment of Greece's conservative propertied classes. This was to be anti-Axis resistance with simultaneous and subsequent civil war as well as an anti-Communist, anti-leftist victory. The most critical turn toward civil war occurred from February to the end of 1944, when the British successfully built up and led a tacit alliance of anti-EAM-ELAS interests within Greece and in the Greek armed forces in the Middle East, and while the EAM and the KKE that organized and led it, for the most part, attempted to reconcile with the republican elements of that alliance. Tremendous tension between these forces broke into armed hostilities in Athens in December. Shortly following the end of the Axis occupation, and six months before the formal end of the war in Europe, leftist elements within Greece were now at war with the British and their domestic Greek military forces that had been purged of all leftwing republican members. British snipers were perched on the Acropolis as their warplanes strafed the city's working class neighborhoods. At this point, the country was deeply predisposed toward more civil war that was to break out again, but more extensively, in 1946–9.

Italy's experience during the Second World War was loaded with nearly all the war had to offer on all sides. It was a domestic fascist regime and an international fascist aggressor state; it was the site of Nazi-fascist occupation and anti-fascist resistance; it was a fierce battleground between the western Allied military forces on the one side and the *Wehrmacht* and their Italian collaborators on the other. For some historians, it was the scene of a "civil war" of the resistance elements against the Italian collaborators with the Nazi occupation of 1943–5, including Mussolini and those that supported his Social Republic of Salò.[29] The fact that the Italian experience ran the gamut as it did entailed certain continuity as well as a rupture for the left. Originally from below and above, Italy reached its distinctive fascist incorporation in the immediate years after the First World War, which meant the Italian left was outmaneuvered and repressed by fascism until the fall of Mussolini in July 1943. From then until the German withdrawal of April 1945, the left organized the mass-based resistance coalition whose overarching structure was the Committee of National Liberation (CLN), which even, as of December 1943, included the center-right Christian Democratic Party (DC). But, as in most of the rest of occupied Europe, the Communist Party (PCI) played the more dominant and active role in the anti-Axis war. The guerilla units of the CLN faced the fire of the die-hard *squadristi* of Mussolini, the puppet governor of Salò, just as they faced off against the Nazis. Meanwhile, the British and the Americans became increasingly alarmed at the growing strength of the CLN and especially that of the PCI. They did everything possible to dissuade the CLN from exerting its political and military strengths.

This period of rupture and resistance rejuvenated the various factions of the left that had long been stifled; they inflicted significant damage on their Nazi-fascist enemies, and along the way managed to regain confidence. They committed themselves to the establishment of a constitutional liberal and representative democracy, which is what they got. However, they were in for a shock. As Italy fell squarely into the western allied sphere of influence, the new Italian Republic proved to be very manipulable from the outside, in particular by the American CIA, whose secret funds flowed abundantly into the coffers of the Christian Democrats (DC), enough to secure an unexpected victory for that party in the elections of the immediate postwar period. From the moment of the fall of Mussolini, the DC became a magnet for hundreds of thousands of his supporters, making it the premier vehicle for Italy's "soft exit" from fascism. In the meantime, the PCI and the rest of the left held considerable local political influence and maintained pride in the achievements of the wartime resistance until such memory was destabilized by figures such as De Felice during the neoconservative years of Reagan and Thatcher, followed by Italian prime minister Silvio Berlusconi in the 1990s. For Italian elite and middle-class interests, the war was a disaster, but its fascist synthesis, and Mussolini's top-down ouster by the Grand Council, as western Allied bombs rained down on Rome, and their armies moved up from the south, all served the establishment very well. Change came abruptly in 1943 but in a domestic and international setting still enabling them to keep the left quite neutralized.

Abrupt change also came to Yugoslavia, but through an invasion and occupation that was designed to, and actually did, destroy the highly fragile prewar multinational political structure of the country. Within a few months of the April 1941 four-way Axis invasion, recovery for the country's prewar political establishment was a lost cause, though that did not stop various factions from fighting for it.[30] The most important developments of the Yugoslav civil war and revolution took place from June 1941 to November–December 1943, the period characterized internationally by the strongest cooperation between the liberal capitalist powers and the Soviet Union. The circumstances domestically and internationally worked rapidly in favor of the Yugoslav Communist Party (KPJ) under Josip Broz Tito after the Nazi invasion of the USSR, so any anti-Communist interests, even those within Yugoslavia, were either caught off guard or simply helpless. The Croatian fascist *Ustasha* movement was assigned by the Nazis to control the so-called Independent State of Croatia (NDH) that included the large multinational region of Bosnia-Herzegovina. The NDH, as it was conspicuously designated, quickly launched a genocidal campaign against the Bosnian Serbs. They did it in a largely preindustrial manner that even shocked the Nazis because it was perpetrated by a poor, Slavic state instead of the "advanced" and industrialized Aryan Germany. The monstrous campaign drove tens of thousands of the Bosnian Serbs into the arms of the KPJ. Especially beginning in June, the party that had amounted to only a few hundred members on the eve of the invasion organized a pan-Yugoslav anti-fascist resistance movement with which no other sub-Yugoslav nationalist faction—neither the *Ustasha* nor the Serbian collaborationists or royalists—could effectively compete. It was an exceedingly complex, bloody, and ferocious affair, but the Yugoslav Partisans under the command of the KPJ leader Tito found themselves in a uniquely powerful and advantageous domestic and international situation that drove them on to a revolutionary outcome. With their growing independence and strength, they "persuaded" the British, who really had no choice in the matter, and they defied Stalin, who could also simply not control them. In 1920, the government of Kingdom of the Serbs, Croats, and Slovenes had voted to outlaw the KPJ after its impressive pan-Yugoslav electoral victories. Twenty-three years later, in the abyss of the war, that particular and self-interested decision was vindicated for those with attachments to Serbian-dominated pre–Second World War Yugoslavia. It was hardly a consolation, because what was left of the old regime was stripped of its power at least by late 1943. On the European scene, the Yugoslav case was unique: a small Communist party unexpectedly rose to the pinnacles of power and held on, due to an overwhelmingly favorable constellation of domestic and international forces.

The rest of Eastern Europe was a greater "loss" for the anti-communist west, but the reasons for this mainly involved the movement of the Red Army westward, through Eastern Europe, against the last dregs of the German armies, not because of any great independent anti-fascist resistance movements. All of the states of the region had Communist parties that were necessary and exceedingly useful for the Soviet Union's extension of its hegemony, but none had anything approaching the popular base, power, and independence of the Yugoslav party. All the prewar regimes of Eastern Europe outside of Yugoslavia—nationalist, dictatorial, pseudo-fascist, and anti-Communist— were dislodged and/or destroyed by the war. The USSR saved itself from the scourge of Nazism, and expanded as it did so, simultaneously saving the west from an even more protracted and unpredictable struggle against it. The plan of Churchill, Roosevelt, and Stalin, agreed at Yalta in February 1945—nearly a ground-level fact at the time of the conference—was to close in on Nazi Germany from all sides, then divide it. The Soviets were in a prime position to dominate the entire region "from Stettin in the Baltic to Trieste in the Adriatic," as Churchill put it in famous speech in Missouri in March 1946, and they did so for decades. Ordinary Allied troops were soon to liberate the concentration and death camps of the Third Reich. They bore witness to the horror of the Holocaust of the Jews, the Roma people, homosexuals, and transsexuals; the people that actively resisted Fascism and Nazism and got criminalized and killed for it. It had been a campaign of mass annihilation of innocents whose most murderous and technologically systematic phase raged since early 1942. High-level figures in the British and US governments had been aware of that genocidal effort at least since mid-1942. Word had spread from those who escaped from Poland, reached London, and informed the Polish government-in-exile, who passed the information on to their British hosts, who passed it on to the Americans, who, for "strategic reasons" did next to nothing, when they most probably could have saved at least hundreds of thousands of lives.[31]

While Axis-occupied Europe and East and Southeast Asia shared the profound and overlapping ground of the politics of national liberation from imperialist aggression, the tactical orientations for or against the older imperialist states versus the newer Axis states presented contrasts. The colonized world, one without even relatively sovereign states established in some measure to serve local interests, featured nationalist and anti-imperialist politics that included a significant willingness to collaborate with the Axis powers toward national liberation that was ultimately, hopefully, free from all foreign domination. Of course, this was more easily envisioned than achieved. The most obvious and general differentiating factor across all states and territories involved was the particular relationship each one had with the imperial and colonial powers. At base, this involved the presence or absence of state power, which by definition and in reality meant strong imperialist states and weak colonized territories, or, in the case of China, a nominally independent, but vast and fledgling, state overrun by competing domestic factions as well as by the Japanese.

From 1927 to 1937, Chiang Kai Shek very consistently maintained that the Chinese Communists (CCP) under Mao Zedong were the main enemy of his nationalist movement and organization, the KMT. This held true despite the Japanese invasion of Manchuria in 1932 and the establishment of the puppet state of Manchuko that resulted from it. Chiang, the KMT, and its National Revolutionary Army (NRA) were then beneficiaries of considerable Nazi economic and military support in the mid-1930s. Yet, as evidence of the particular pathology of Chiang's anti-communism, it persisted into the early part of the Second Sino-Japanese war of 1937–45, when the man who was comfortably dubbed the *Generalissimo* had to be virtually forced by his own officers to lead his forces against the Japanese invaders, whom the Communists were already fighting, or face mass military desertions. In the eyes of many ordinary Chinese, Chiang lost credibility. He and the Japanese, despite their obvious grounds for mutual antagonism, shared a common anti-Communism, which threatened to backfire on his entire effort to prevail as the head of a centralized modern Chinese state. As he put it at the time, "the Japanese are a disease of the skin. The Communists are a disease of the heart."[32] This was his strategic judgment and choice, no doubt loaded with the emotions of his conservative blend of Chinese Confucian as well as Christian cultural identities and attachments. However, just as the British and the American leaders did in their ways, Chiang deprioritized his anti-communism for much of the war. Out of immediate strategic necessity, he finally cooperated with the CCP against the Japanese, though his fundamental antipathies were never far beneath the surface. Somewhat aside from these strategic choices, he was notoriously corrupt on the financial front, particularly with wartime loans received from the United States. His armies squeezed the peasants for taxes and coercively conscripted men for service; inflation raged out of control in areas under the sway of the NRA. Instead of mobilizing the peasantry for the war effort and for a greater future political goal, he was destroying the fabric of their lives—in vain. The spring 1944 Japanese Ichi-Go offensive against the NRA, which was meant to destroy American bases on the Chinese mainland and open a safe route to Indochina, was a disaster for the NRA and Chiang, and a substantial gain for the Communists. Even to the chagrin of the Americans on the scene, Chiang was again seen as prioritizing his anti-Communism, which, in effect, shed the better light on the CCP; they were fighting the Japanese concertedly and continuing their pro-peasant policies as a means of further building their mass political base.[33] The circumstances Chiang faced were extremely challenging, but if he had any great strategic intelligence, it was not evident, as the main effects of his maneuvers tended to be gains for his Communist archenemies.

The Japanese had been falling to defeat at the hands of the United States since the crippling of the Japanese Navy at the Battle of Midway in May 1942. But it was a protracted defeat for the IJA, which for the duration of the war kept virtually the entirety of Southeast Asia in its grips. The brutally exploitative treatment meted out by the IJA to peoples under its force throughout the area, provoked resistance: some nationalist, some communist, some mixed. In August 1945, as the inhabitants of Hiroshima and Nagasaki were being incinerated by the atomic bombs, the revolutionary nationalist Viet Minh of Indochina were poised to fight "Free France," if necessary, for independence. Shortly after the Japanese surrender in September, the people of Korea found themselves divided. A vague agreement between the "big three" reached at Yalta in February 1945 was imposed upon them, dividing the Korean peninsula between a Soviet-controlled north and a US-controlled south. The doubtful commitment was to unity and independence at some later date. The real result was that Korea was in for an extremely rough experience of civil and international war that would cost 2–3 million lives by 1953. Meanwhile, British Malaya was set up for an anti-colonial war that got further internationalized by the support of the United States on the British side, and the Soviet Union and China supporting the Malaysian Communists. In the Philippines, the Communist-led People's Anti-Japanese Army, which had grown strong on the main island of Luzon, also resisted the US-backed postwar Philippine government. Instead of an all-out anti-colonial revolutionary civil war, which was to occur in Indochina, the United States had conservative nationalist allies in the country strong enough to entrench its influence. This led to the US support for the likes of the brutal and corrupt "nationalist" dictatorial figure, Ferdinand Marcos, beginning in the 1960s.

Anti-colonialism in Indonesia in nationalist, Communist, and combined forms that got their starts against the Dutch in the prewar period were only intensified, expanded, and reconstituted by the Japanese occupation of 1942–5 and by the postwar attempt by the Dutch, backed by the British, to reimpose the pre–Second World War colonial order. Suharto was a product of both the Dutch Colonial Army and the Japanese occupation forces, which allowed him to organize a Defense of the Fatherland group as long as it deferred to Japanese authority, yet his trajectory was ultimately nationalist and ferociously anti-Communist. He overlapped in his wartime experience with Sukarno, the political figure who became the first president of Indonesia but who leaned to the nationalist left and had significant sympathies for the Indonesian Communists (PKI). As Indonesia was forced more and more into the Cold War mold on the side of the United States, Suharto's prospects soared, while Sukarno's and the PKI's dropped precipitously. Suharto was later to become an extremely useful figure for the United States during the some of the hottest and bloodiest spells of the Cold War.

British colonial rule in India and Burma, already facing powerful anti-colonialist challenges, was clearly shaken further by the war. For the British, whose priority had been India, Burma proved to be the more difficult place to stem the tide of radical leftist politics. Part of the difference was the fact that Burma had fallen under Japanese occupation and suffered all attendant dislocations that India was spared. The Burmese Communist Party had played a central role in resisting the Japanese; the party established the Anti-Fascist Organization (ASO) in August 1944 that was a local replication of such organizations throughout Axis-occupied parts of the world.[34] After the war, the same organization was reestablished as the Anti-Fascist People's Freedom League (AFPFL) that retained a strong left-leaning character and retooled to resist the reimposition of British colonial rule. The AFPFL had some success as a political coalition, but as a governing bloc, it faced an insurgency from within, pressed by remnants of the KMT forces that continued getting support from the United States precisely because of the risk that Burma would swing squarely into the Soviet camp. Meanwhile, in 1947, several of the ASO's leaders were assassinated. The country remained fraught with such tensions, which shifted in favor of a US-backed rightwing dictatorship in the 1960s and a purge of the left. In India, Britain had been successful in denying the radical left any role in the movement for independence; the nationalism of Nehru and Gandhi suited the British well. Their orientations and the precedents they set also went far in defining modern India. It would be several decades later, only after the defeat of the more obvious and immediate threat of Soviet socialism, that India's "socialism," showing a strong dose of economic statism and protectionism, would fall into the sights of militant neoliberalism.

The common anti-Communism of the great power states outside of the Soviet Union got ripped apart by internal imperialist rivalry, leading to another world war, which reaped a grim harvest of 45–60 million lives. During the war, the fires of anti-Communism were kept alive most brightly by Nazi Germany and the Axis alliance. This was most obvious in the largest military operation the world had ever seen, the Nazi invasion of the Soviet Union, which was intertwined politically and ideologically with anti-Semitism. The Holocaust in its entirety cannot be separated from Hitler's and the Nazi anti-socialism and anti-bolshevism, nor, of course, from the war itself. Against resistance in occupied Europe, the Axis forces mounted constant anti-"bolshevik" military, political, and even cultural campaigns. In the east, the Japanese declared that Communism had to be eliminated from all areas within its so-called Co-Prosperity Sphere. The antipathy against Communism that the Japanese shared with Chiang Kai Shek played quite directly into the hands of the Chinese communists, leading to what became one of the biggest communist targets for the American-led post–Second World War alliance. Especially the latter two years of the war in the west and east saw the British and the United States return to their normal anti-leftist

Figure 6 "Paul Robeson, world famous Negro baritone, leading Moore Shipyard [Oakland, CA] workers in singing the Star Spangled Banner, here at their lunch hour recently, after he told them: 'This is a serious job—winning this war against fascists. We have to be together.' Robeson himself was a shipyard worker in World War I."

Source: The National Archives and Records Administration, NARA 535874.tif; unknown author or not provided; public domain; commons.wikimedia.org.

dispositions. The capitalist democracies' and Soviet Communists' common enemy of Nazism and fascism were falling to defeat. It was, therefore, time to revert to more standard practice for postwar power purposes. Before the war, the anti-leftist drive was clearly subject to volatile internal strategic rivalry. The most important outcome of the Second World War in the history of anti-leftist politics was the unification of those common lines of anti-Communism on the part of otherwise antagonistic states into one, unified American-led drive.

Notes

1. Eric Hobsbawm, *The Age of Extremes: A History of the World, 1914–1991* (New York: Vintage, 1996), p. 7.
2. The quotes are drawn from Lorna Waddington, *Hitler's Crusade: Bolshevism and the Myth of the International Jewish Conspiracy* (New York: Tauris, 2007), pp. 156–7. The first is from a conversation with the high commissioner to the League of Nations.
3. A letter from Chamberlain on September 10 referred back to August discussions between "Goering & Hitler & Halifax & me" that "gave the impression ... that it was possible to persuade Hitler to accept a peaceful and reasonable solution of the Polish question .... But, what happened to destroy this chance?" Chamberlain suggests that Hitler was not "merely talking through his hat," but "at the last moment some brainstorm took possession of him – maybe Rippentrop stirred it up – and once he had set his machine in motion he couldn't stop it." The British prime minister at one point described Hitler as a "paranoiac," yet the overall picture is of a largely reasonable man. Robert Self, ed., *The Neville Chamberlain Diary Letters, Volume 4, The Downing Street Years, 1934–1940* (Burlington, VT: Ashgate, 2005), pp. 443–6.
4. R. A. C. Parker, *The Second World War: A Short History* (New York: Oxford University Press, 2001), p. 60.
5. Ho's birth name was Nguyen Sinh Con; he started using Ho Chi Minh around the time of his return to Indochina.
6. Robert Gellately, *Lenin, Stalin, and Hitler: The Age of Social Catastrophe* (New York: Alfred A. Knopf, 2007), p. 417.
7. Saul Friedlander, *The Years of Extermination, Nazi Germany and the Jews, 1939–1945* (New York: Harper Perennial, 2007), pp. 198–208.
8. James L. McClain, *Japan: A Modern History* (New York: Norton, 2002), pp. 470–3.
9. Perry Anderson takes a very hard and insightful look at Cordell Hull's role as a free trade maximalist in shaping US policy on the international stage during his long tenure as FDR's Secretary of State, 1933–44. See Anderson's article "Imperium," *New Left Review*, 83 (September/October 2013), pp. 4–111.
10. McClain, *Japan*, pp. 476–82.
11. MacArthur happened to have established his anti-Communist *bona fides* in the crackdown on American veterans of the First World War and their families, the "Bonus Army," that had marched on and camped out in Washington, DC, in 1932. As Army Chief of Staff during the Hoover administration, MacArthur had insisted that the Bonus Army had been fatally infiltrated by Communists and pacifists and needed to be broken. He notched up a victory commanding the actual infantry and cavalry charge against the demonstrators.

12. Sukarno became Indonesia's first president in 1945. Sjahrir and Sjarrifuddin became the first and second prime ministers of Indonesia, from 1945 to 1947 and from 1947 to 1948, respectively. Sjahrir shifted politically to the right, fell out of favor with Sukarno, and was first jailed, then marginalized in the postwar era. Sukarno himself would fall in 1965 to an anti-"communist" coup led by General Suharto. Sjarrifuddin was executed in 1948 for involvement in a Communist rebellion. See Adrian Vickers, *A History of Modern Indonesia* (New York: Cambridge University Press, 2005), p. 86.

13. "Minister Winston Churchill's Broadcast on the Soviet German War," British Library of Information, London, June 22, 1941. Available online: http://www.ibiblio.org/pha/policy/1941/410622d.html (accessed March 16, 2015).

14. Ivan Maisky, *Memoirs of a Soviet Ambassador: The War, 1939–43* (New York: Charles Scribner's, 1968), p. 163. See also John Keegan, *The Second World War* (New York: Penguin, 2005), p. 311, for the contention that "in 1941 there was no chance of a Second Front." For Stalin's first appeal, see "Personal Message from Stalin to Mr. Churchill," July 18, 1941, pp. 20–1, in *Correspondence between the Chairman of the Council of Ministers of the USSR and the Presidents of the USA and the Prime Ministers of Britain during the Great Patriotic War, 1941–1945, Volume One.* Available online: http://www.marx2mao.com/Stalin/WWIICv1wm.pdf.

15. For an extended discussion of the matter of a second front, see Gabriel Kolko, *The Politics of War: The World War and United States Foreign Policy, 1943–1945* (New York: Random House, 1968), pp. 14–20.

16. Cordell Hull, *The Memoirs of Cordell Hull*, vol. 2 (New York: Macmillan, 1948), pp. 976–7.

17. Ibid., p. 15.

18. See the reflections of Cordell Hull on the making of the Atlantic Charter, in ibid., pp. 974–6. For an excellent and penetrating discussion of American "grand strategy" at this time as well as prior and since, see Perry Anderson, "American Foreign Policy and its Thinkers," New Left Review, 83 (September–October 2013), pp. 5–167.

19. Graham Ross, ed., *The Foreign Office and the Kremlin: British Documents on Anglo-Soviet Relations, 1941–45* (New York: Cambridge University Press, 1984), p. 15.

20. Anthony Eden, *The Memoirs of Anthony Eden, Earl of Avon, Volume Two: The Reckoning* (New York: Times, 1964), pp. 328–9.

21. On Cripps, as well as on other War Cabinet and Foreign Office communications, see Ross, *The Foreign Office and the Kremlin*, pp. 69–79. John Keegan dismisses the issue of a second front in 1941 as a practical impossibility in *The Second World War*, pp. 311–16. See also Maisky, *Memoirs*, pp. 155–83; Eden, *The Memoirs of Anthony Eden*, pp. 317–18, 317–29.

22. Procopis Papasratis, *British Policy towards Greece during the Second World War, 1941–1944* (New York: Cambridge University Press, 1984); see also Philip Minehan, *Civil War and World War in Europe: Spain, Yugoslavia and Greece, 1936–1949* (New York: Palgrave Macmillan, 2006), pp. 148–51.

23. Robert Paxton, "The Bottom of the Abyss," in *Collaboration and Resistance: French Literary Life under the Nazi Occupation*, ed. Oliver Corpet and Claire Paulhan (New York: Five Ties, 2009), p. 15.

24. Charles de Gaulle, *War Memoirs, Volume III, Salvation: 1944–1946* (New York: Simon and Schuster, 1960), p. 10; pp. 10–15, 273–6.

25. Robert O. Paxton, *The Anatomy of Fascism* (New York: Vintage, 2004), p. 218.

26. John E. Dreifort, *Myopic Grandeur: The Ambivalence of French Foreign Policy toward the Far East, 1919–1945* (Kent, OH: Kent State University Press, 1991), pp. 218–22.

27. On the matter of the two great French betrayals of the universality of liberal and liberal nationalist principles, one the attempt to suppress the Haitian Revolution in 1801 and the other to launch colonialist aggression against Indochina, Algeria, and the West Indies following the liberation of France from the Nazis in 1945, see Vijay Prashad, *The Darker Nations: A People's History of the Third World* (New York: New Press, 2007), pp. 3–15.

28. Kolko, *The Politics of War*, pp. 68–70.

29. The "civil war" thesis was originally and most forcefully advanced by the conservative, nationalist, anti-communist historian Renzo de Felice. Part of his intent was to deflate the long-standing and popular claims of the left that the resistance went far to salvage Italy's politics, reputation, and memory from the scourge of fascism. The thesis gained traction in the 1980s and 1990s as part of a larger Italian conservative quest for a shame-free nationalist politics; it turned fascism and anti-fascism into moral equivalents. The fact that to this day there remains no common reference to the Italian Civil War suggests that there is plenty of reason to doubt it, while there is no such disagreement as to whether or not fascism prevailed in Italy for over twenty years and was indeed an inspiration for and then a critical ally of Adolf Hitler and the Nazi regime. See Renzo De Felice, *Breve Storia del Fascismo* (Milan: Mondadori, 2001). (The author died in 1996.) Note that even De Felice puts the term in quotation marks in the title of his chapter "Salò e la 'Guerra Civile'," p. 113. The author's great accomplishment is his four-volume biography of Mussolini (Turin: Eindaudi, 1965–97). As a highly acclaimed response to De Felice's argument, see the recent translation into English of Claudio Pavone, *A Civil War: A History of the Italian Resistance* (New York: Verso, 2014), whose original Italian edition was published in 1991 as *Una Guerra Civile: Saggio Storico sulla Moralità nella Resistenza* (Turin: Bollati Boringhieri).

30. The four powers that invaded and occupied Yugoslavia were Germany, Italy, Bulgaria, and Hungary.

31. David Wyman, "The Abandonment of the Jews," in Donald L. Niewyk, *The Holocaust*, 2nd ed. (New York: Houghton Mifflin, 1997), pp. 256–68.

32. Kolko, *The Politics of War*, pp. 205, 211–12.

33. Ibid., pp. 200–5, provides a particularly vivid assessment and account of the dynamics that "lay the conditions for the triumph of communism." The quote is from p. 203. On the inflation, see Keegan, *The Second World War*, p. 281.

34. Keegan, *The Second World War*, pp. 547–51.

Part Two

The US-led Global
Anti-Communist Solution

Introduction

After the relentless and deadly international power struggles between the great power imperialist states that reached their peaks from the late nineteenth century to the end of the Second World War, the United States came out on top. This was just the latest consequence of the specific long-term eruptions of the "contradictions of liberal bourgeois society" of the pre–First World War era that continued to heave forth their consequences into the twentieth century.[1] But there was much more to come. The arc of European imperialism that had risen so dramatically in the late nineteenth century was falling about as fast as the American empire was rising, with both trends involving and promising a tremendous amount of conflict and warfare against a broad array of left-oriented anti-colonialist and anti-imperialist forces. In 1945, after allying victoriously with one another and other states against the Axis powers, the United States and the Soviet Union moved as far as possible from their wartime partnership and became pitted against one another in contention for global hegemony in the Cold War, while anti-colonialist rebellions gained strength across the colonized worlds and popular leftist anti-imperialist politics swelled in much of Latin America. Intertwined as the Cold War was with the anti-colonialist wars for national liberation—so many either Communist- or socialist-led—their combined worldwide death toll reached 20–25 million.

The strategic dynamics of the Second World War had submerged the common anti-Communism of all the warring states outside the Soviet Union, but in the postwar liberal capitalist west and Japan, anti-Communism reemerged under the American lead more strongly and concertedly than ever. This was in rough proportion to the world's abundance of old and new targets, whether real or fabricated. Furthering the upheavals of the First World War, the Second World War's invasions, occupations, dislocations, and demands created conditions for the rise of highly organized and often powerful resistance and anti-colonialist movements—all of them national liberation movements—in French Indochina, British India, Dutch Indonesia, and colonial Africa, and across Eastern, Southeastern, and Southern Europe. Virtually all of them claimed some significant allegiance to one version of "socialism" or another and opposition against fascism and/or colonialism. Some were Communist-led and leftwing nationalist, as in Indochina; some were noncommunist leftwing, as in Chile; others combined social democratic and Third World liberal nationalism, as in India. Some had conservative nationalist religious overtones, also as in India, which were leftwing at least in their stand against imperialism, and remained dependent upon the successes of the more clearly left-leaning anti-colonialist groups.

All such developments were varyingly antithetical to the interests of the manufacturing, business, and political classes of the imperialist states. But, for those states, Communism—especially Soviet Communism—was the priority enemy, which suggests that there may have been room for varieties of socialism, social democracy, and welfare state politics to develop under the cover of the Cold War. One of the main contentions and organizing themes of the following Chapters 4–6 is that, with some important exceptions and changes over time, there was indeed that room. In the broad framework of modern anti-leftist politics, the 1945–91 period involved a two-stage campaign with an approximate ten-year overlap. First came the multipronged US-led crusade across most of the world against Communism, which persisted with escalations and de-escalations up to the fall of the Soviet Union in 1991, but—crucially—got expanded in around 1980 to include all leftist politics. The shift and expansion of this political assault was interwoven with, and mainly driven by, economic change and its complex consequences, namely, the systemic downturn in the rate of profit on capital investment that first appeared in US corporate reports in the late 1960s, gaining force and increasing political consequence into the 1970s and 80s.[2]

There was one main part of the world, however, where the Cold War provided little, if any, cover for any sorts of leftwing politics—Latin America. There, in collaboration with landed and business elites, as well as police, military, and paramilitary forces, the United States did its utmost against any and all leftwing politics throughout the whole period. They tended to brand them all as "Communist," a term that was used, of course, to imply a kind of metaphysical evil that justified all manner of political repression. Though it was not always successful, it is arguable that the model for the post-1980 US-led campaign against *all* leftist politics worldwide was originally forged in Latin America, over which the United States had maintained a *de facto* interventionist regime since the declaration of the Monroe Doctrine of 1823. However, somewhat aside from that for now, the period worldwide involved counterinsurgency wars and/or *coups d'état*—successful or not—such as those in Greece, China, Iran, Korea, Guatemala, Vietnam, and Chile. Wherever they could, the United States, Britain, and France launched anti-Communist propaganda as well as periodic political-military campaigns that were designed to prevent, undermine, or destroy any real, potential, or fictitious Communism. Some of the targets were large and numerous in terms of population and territory. After all, by the 1960s, around one-third of humanity lived in states that were nominally Communist—approximately one billion people living in the USSR, Eastern Europe, the People's Republic of China (PRC), North Korea, and Cuba. Outside those states, the potential areas for Communist gains were seen to be virtually everywhere. For anti-Communists and often anti-leftists more broadly, the world constituted a complex combination of real, imagined, or contrived threats, as well as political and strategic opportunities, both domestic and international. Once the campaign became clearly wholesale against anything deemed leftist in the 1980s, financial leverage held by US-dominated institutions such as the World Bank and International Monetary Fund (IMF) became the weapon of choice in the effort to free up as many investment opportunities as possible across the world. Economic globalization and neoliberalism were coming into full force, gradually in some times and places, but like crude shock therapy elsewhere, as in Jamaica in the late 1970s and early 1980s. The social safety nets were being clipped down to nothing in the Third World under the sway of the United States where, meanwhile, the rug was also getting pulled from beneath organized labor and relatively democratic politics. In strong contrast with the years of the modern liberal consensus of approximately 1945 to the early 1970s, the political center had shifted right. Privatization, deregulation, and free markets became the mantras. Oligarchy, plutocracy, and neofascism were the likely and actual outcomes, but so was the resurgence of leftwing politics.

Notes

1. The reader is reminded here that Eric Hobsbawm did not explicitly carry the argument he made in *The Age of Empire* about the contradictions of liberal bourgeois society into *The Age of Extremes*, his monumental work on the twentieth century. The analysis presented here tries to explicitly draw out the implications of that original focus, or at least of a version of it, through the twentieth century up to the present.
2. See Robert Brenner, "The Economics of Global Turbulence," *New Left Review* (Special Issue), 1, no. 229 (May/June 1998).

4

Soft on Social Democracy, Hard on "Communism": Britain, the United States, Greece, China, Korea, and Indochina

Britain and the United States

The ambition to undermine the entire universe of leftwing politics was far from anything most major conservative politicians could imagine, let alone implement, in the capitalist-imperialist and allied states during the first stage of the Cold War. Especially seen in retrospect, the British Conservative Party's 1945 platform was a virtual paean to social democracy, presented by the party leader, Churchill, who had selected Ernest Bevin from Britain's Labor Party to preside over the program's implementation. Churchill and Bevin were both firm anti-Communists and, while not by any means identically inclined on the domestic political front, were both yet very accepting of softer forms of leftist politics—Bevin, of course, more than Churchill. The Conservative platform called for an "all-out housing policy" for the sake of family life but also to ensure steady employment and robust national health. It was to be a mixed economy at the very least, in which "local authorities and private enterprise must both be given the fullest encouragement to get on with the job." It is explicitly open to price controls, rent controls, and committed to "the best use of land in the public interest." It called out compassionately for "a nation-wide and compulsory scheme of National Insurance," as well as "old-age or retirement pensions" and a "comprehensive health service ... available to all citizens."[1] It was an example of the normalcy of the clear distinction between Communism and social democracy; reject the former and accept the latter. As it happened, the commitment to social democracy was unequivocally confirmed by the landslide victory of the Labor Party under Clement Atlee in the 1945 elections. The Labor government nationalized the Bank of England, as well as the coal, iron, electricity, and telecommunications industries; it committed to full employment, health, and social security for all. They established a national insurance scheme to protect against job losses, accidents, and ill health. Clearly, Labor outdid the Conservatives on the social democracy front, both in their program and their political victory. But just as clearly, the political center in Britain had shifted dramatically to the left. This was true on much of the world stage outside of the Communist states.

The state social welfare system devised in the United States at the time was not nearly as generous as the British one; most importantly, it did not follow a program of nationalization. Touted as the great bastion of the systems of capitalism and free enterprise, and largely dominated by such interests, the United States only reluctantly lurched onto the modern liberal welfare trend, including dramatically increased state-sponsored jobs programs in infrastructure and the arts, during the Great Depression. Despite its comparative limits, the New Deal was popular, politically successful and showed decades-long staying power. For better or worse, it may have staved off social revolution; at least it probably helped avoid severe social unrest. But it is instructive to see that the New Deal was attacked at its inception in a way that echoed past anti-leftist politics and anticipated more in the future. Coming from likely sources, such as *laissez-faire* fans of Herbert Hoover, the attacks also came from across party lines, that it was "socialist" and "communist." Of course, this was another way of claiming it was a betrayal of a particular notion of capitalism—a system conceived to be maximally free-market and *essentially* American. Sharp criticism of the New Deal as a leftist regime came especially from southern Democrats—"Dixiecrats"—who feared stronger labor and civil rights for Black people, while conservative anti-Semites attacked it as the "Jew Deal." During the latter part of the Second World War, conservatives and business leaders attacked it for these same reasons, but more successfully. Never far from center stage, they maneuvered their way back to it, though without entirely displacing labor. The main advantage of the business class at the time was the resurgence of the US economy, ironically enough because of the high rate of wartime military spending by the government—military Keynesianism—that was getting the country out of the Depression. But once the war ended, price controls and rationing were lifted, inflation increased, and overtime production diminished, with the combined result that real wages dropped precipitously.

What followed was the biggest strike wave in US history. In 1945–6, over four million workers struck countrywide, in diverse sectors, including film, automobiles, electricity, coal, steel, and railroads. In response to the railroad workers that struck nationwide in the spring of 1946, Truman threatened to call out the US Army to run the railroads and draft all strikers into the armed forces. In a speech addressing the situation in May, Truman requested "permanent legislation leading to the formulation of a long-range labor policy designed to prevent the recurrence of such crises and generally to reduce the stoppages of work in all industries for the future."[2] Particularly with the Cold War anti-Communist rhetoric heating up in the media, many middle-class Americans got nervous about the labor unrest, grew hostile against labor and the left, and voted accordingly, helping the Republicans gain control of both houses of Congress in the mid-term elections of November 1946.[3] Truman's call for restrictions on labor was closely akin to the legislation that took shape by mid-1947 as the Taft-Hartley Act, which banned closed shop unions (those that obliged employers to only hire union members), curtailed rights to strike, allowed employers to sue unions for damages caused by strikes, allowed for a sixty-day "cooling off period" before any major strike, prohibited union contributions to political campaigns, and legally obliged union leaders to take anti-Communist oaths. Knowing his effort would fail, Truman attempted to veto the legislation, but Congress prevailed. When campaigning in 1948,

Truman promised to repeal Taft Hartley but instead left the legislation intact, as it largely remains seventy years later. Overlapping with, but also expanding, the assault on left-leaning labor to include Communist party members and any "subversives," the McCarran Internal Security Act (also known as the Concentration Camp Law) passed both houses of Congress in 1950, even overriding a veto from Truman—no stranger to anti-Communism. The directions pointed further and further rightward.

Truman had acceded to the presidency upon Roosevelt's death in April 1945. Despite the hostility against labor on display against the railroad strikers, he presented himself as a New Deal Democrat on the domestic front, though he updated the 1930s policy package as he touted his Fair Deal, promising national health insurance and a broad commitment to civil rights. Internationally, of course, he was a hard anti-Communist. But he was in the shadow of the extensive high-level experience of his predecessor and was also highly susceptible to the advice of the upcoming hard-core cold warriors within and close to his administration, such as his secretary of state James Byrnes, and James Forrestal, his secretary of the Navy and later secretary of defense. With Byrnes, he strode confidently into the Potsdam Conference to greet Churchill and Stalin on July 17, beaming with the declaration that, one day earlier, the United States had detonated an atomic bomb in the New Mexican desert. He had deliberately delayed the convening of the conference until the successful explosion. He and his top conferees—Truman, Stalin, and the new British prime minister Atlee, who replaced Churchill—together acknowledged and officially recognized certain ground-level strategic realities, especially Soviet dominance in Eastern Europe, including eastern Germany. Berlin was divided between the two Allied sides: the USSR would occupy the east of the city; France, Britain, and the United States the west. The agreement guaranteed logistical and political complications and gave way to some of the tensest standoffs of the Cold War, including the Berlin Airlift of 1948 and the 1961 Berlin Crisis. German society and economy was to be de-Nazified, which meant outlawing the Nazi party and breaking up the industrial cartels.[4] Japan was called upon to surrender or face utter destruction, though it did not do so fast enough for the leading Americans. Three weeks later, with Byrnes's encouragement, Truman ordered the atomic bombings of Hiroshima and Nagasaki as a means of accelerating the achievement of three intertwined goals: forcing Japanese surrender, doing so quickly enough to keep the Soviets out of postwar Japan, and presenting a "tough" aura to Stalin and the world.

The United States came out of the war not just relatively unscathed but also far and away as the world's paramount industrial and military power. The country suffered 292,000 military deaths, as opposed to Russia's astounding 25 million civilian and military deaths (14 percent of the total population). The terrain, towns, and cities of the USSR saw some of the most ferocious and physically destructive fighting of the war, while the United States saw nothing of the sort. The American economy surged during the war, up 15 percent per year from 1940 to 1944, so that by 1945 it produced at least half of the world's industrial output, and its economy was three times the size of the USSR's. As pointed out by Paul Kennedy, "the United States was the only country that became richer – in fact, much richer – rather than poorer because of the war." Topping it off, the country held nearly two-thirds of the world's gold reserves.[5] Militarily, the

United States was vastly superior to any other state; it was the lone power with atomic weaponry until 1949 and had demonstrated its willingness to use it. If any state power in the world was in a position to influence or threaten others, or not be threatened by them, it was the United States. However, while this strategic situation could conceivably have put the United States at ease in the face of the existence of Communism—again, whether real, fictional, or some combination of the two—instead, as a matter of ideological conditioning and expediency, leading Americans at the time decided to "scare the hell out of the American people" regarding the Communist threat.[6]

The story of Henry Wallace helps illustrate the crucial shift in the terms of US foreign and domestic policy that was taking place in the mid-1940s. Wallace was Roosevelt's vice president up to January 1945, but his days had been numbered since the prior November. That was when he advocated friendly relations with the Soviet Union, along with a non-Communist leftwing program for the United States, and got pilloried and purged for it. The Depression, the collapse of capitalism, sympathy for labor, and the New Deal of the 1930s, plus the war, the victorious alliance with the Soviet Union against fascism, and the preeminently practical demands of the war—all still lingered. But evidently, these positions had to be abandoned in favor of a systematic campaign to make the world safe for American capitalism and its allies. Stealthily, conservative members of the Democratic National Committee forced Wallace out of the vice presidency in 1944, replacing him with the far more conservative and pliable Truman. Roosevelt mustered no opposition to the maneuver. Anyone outside of the "containment versus rollback" loop was just not a part of the conversation. When Roosevelt died, Truman kept Wallace on as secretary of commerce, a role that he had played throughout the war, but then fired him in September 1946 for giving another Soviet-friendly speech. Wallace went on to establish the Progressive Party and in 1948 ran on a leftist platform—desegregation, civil rights, gender equality, national health care, and a friendly approach to the Soviet Union. He was now squarely in the crosshairs of what had become the anti-Communist establishment; he came under heavy fire as a Communist sympathizer, got trounced in the elections, and largely receded from politics. By 1952, he recanted his earlier views on the USSR, declaring in a weekly news magazine that "more and more I am convinced that Russian Communism in its total disregard of truth, in its fanaticism, its intolerance and its resolute denial of God and religion is something utterly evil."[7]

A number of major factors were quickly combining into early Cold War American anti-Communism both as a strategic matter and popular propaganda tool. In February 1946, the US State Department sent a query to their embassy in Moscow as to why the Russians were refusing to join the two newly established and American-dominated financial institutions of the post–Second World War era, the IMF and the International Bank for Reconstruction and Development, later to become the World Bank. George Kennan, the deputy chief diplomat at the embassy, took the opportunity to write up an extended account of how the Soviet leadership viewed the outside world. His "Long Telegram" was highly influential, purporting to explain how Stalin and the top figures in the USSR viewed the position of their country vis-à-vis the outside world. Kennan argued, first, that it was a matter of Soviet paranoia and propaganda that the USSR faced "capitalist encirclement," which allowed for "no permanent peaceful coexistence" with the capitalist states; second, capitalist and socialist countries constituted two mutually antagonistic centers engaged in a zero-sum game for global dominance. Third, the capitalist world was fraught with "internal conflicts"—the main one between the United States and Britain—that could not ultimately be solved by peaceful means. Fourth, wars between the capitalist states could present revolutionary opportunities for the USSR, providing it remained militarily powerful and ideologically committed. Fifth, "smart capitalists, vainly seeking escape from the internal conflicts of capitalism, incline toward wars against socialist states," so there was always the chance that capitalist states would try to overthrow the USSR. Finally, certain political party players in the capitalist world were favorably inclined toward the USSR. They are described as "communistic" and "democratic progressive elements" that must be encouraged and used. In contrast, moderate socialists and social democrats were "false friends of the people" and "serve the interests of reactionary capital." Unsurprisingly, Kennan concluded that Soviet foreign policy was designed to do everything possible to advance the USSR and reduce the power of its adversaries. This included setting capitalist states against one another, supporting "democratic-progressive" forces, and waging a "relentless battle ... against socialist and social democratic leaders."[8]

But Kennan proceeded to explain that the Soviets had it all wrong: "Experience has shown that peaceful and mutually profitable coexistence of capitalist and socialist states is entirely possible." As a way of attempting to dismiss Marxist theory in general and Stalin's particular doctrinaire take on it, Kennan argued that internal conflicts in advanced countries were not about capitalism but arose "from advanced urbanism and industrialism as such, which Russia has thus far been spared not by socialism but only by her own backwardness." He insisted on the truism that "internal rivalries of capitalism do not always generate wars; and not all wars are attributable to this cause" and "to speak of possibility of intervention against USSR today, after elimination of Germany and Japan and after example of recent war, is sheerest nonsense." The capitalist world was "quite capable of living at peace with itself and with Russia." Kennan's premise and claims were that the United States was civilized, reasonable, and fair, that the United States and the USSR could, in principle, get along well, if it were not for the fact that Stalin and the Soviet elite were diabolical and paranoid. Despite the practical dangers of brinkmanship implied in the "containment" approach, on the face of it, Kennan's rhetorical stance stayed just short of aggressive. This left him vulnerable. He was soon accused of being "soft on communism" from the likes of Joe McCarthy, in whom Kennan saw a "hysterical" form of "anti-Sovietism." Kennan helped plant the seeds of such hysteria, then declared his opposition to it.

Regarding the matter of Soviet Communism versus social democracy and its variants, Kennan reaffirmed the common distinction of the time in the liberal capitalist states, asserting that "no sane person has reason to doubt [the] sincerity of moderate socialist leaders in Western countries. Nor is it fair to deny success of their efforts to improve conditions for working population whenever, as in Scandinavia, they have been given chance to show what they could do." According to Kennan, and quite accurately, Stalin painted the social democrats in the liberal capitalist west as enemies—"false friends of the people." Aside from his rhetorical and professional strategic constructs, Kennan was a highly elitist figure intrigued with Social Darwinist racialism and had little confidence in democracy. On that level, Perry Anderson presents him very convincingly as an erratic anti-Semite and white supremacist.[9] With his remarks on social democracy, Kennan was responding to Soviet rhetoric that critiqued the social and economic injustices in the United States and the rest of the liberal capitalist west. For the most part, social democracy and welfare state politics in the capitalist states were, for Kennan and for many others in the American establishment, very useful propaganda props in the polemics of the Cold War.

Sowing the seeds of fear and suspicion, and providing a potential blueprint for anti-Communist inquisitions, Kennan listed a number of civil society organizations within and among the capitalist states that were vulnerable to Soviet penetration and should indeed expect it, including "labor unions, youth leagues, women's organizations, racial societies, religious societies, social organizations, cultural groups, liberal magazines, publishing houses." The Soviets will attempt "to disrupt national self confidence," "hamstring measures of national defense," and "increase social and industrial unrest," all "to stimulate all forms of disunity." He foresaw that "poor will be set against rich, black against white, young against old, newcomers against established residents, etc." In other words, Kennan predicted a systematic program of Soviet intervention and subversion in the capitalist states and among the "colonial backward or dependent peoples," one aiming to ruin those states and bring victory for the Soviet system worldwide. Although he portrayed the USSR as weak compared to the United States and not on track toward any "adventuristic" Nazi-style expansionism, Kennan conveyed a dark and endlessly insidious prospect. The real hope was in maintaining "the health and vigor of our own society." Communism, he said, "is like a malignant parasite which feeds only on diseased tissue." Once he read the telegram, Secretary of the Navy James Forrestal, a man already advocating a more confrontational policy than Kennan's, was instrumental in bringing Kennan back from Moscow and placing him in a prime scholarly and advisory position in Washington, DC, at the National War College.

The Long Telegram was the basis for Kennan's so-called "X" article that was published in *Foreign Affairs* magazine in July 1947. It was there that the term and the idea of the "containment" of Communism appeared as a policy recommendation. The United States should embark "with reasonable confidence upon a policy of firm containment, designed to confront the Russians with unalterable counter-force at every point where they show signs of encroaching upon the interests of a peaceful and stable world."[10] The telegram and the article were immediately and in the long run crucial in setting the terms of the debate within the US foreign policy and political establishment at the time. In the context of what was happening in the upper echelons of foreign policy making in the United States, Kennan's analysis and prescriptions regarding Soviet power were clearly meant to appear steady and confident, not alarmist and aggressive. He did not explicitly suggest any need for a militarily offensive stance against the USSR, which, again, later made him vulnerable to those that towed a harder line than his. But in reality, "containment" could and in some cases did easily become a step towards a more aggressive "rollback" policy—successful or not—of attempting to force the Soviets or their allies out of positions they occupied. Containment was brinkmanship, always prone to boiling over. This was a fine line that was always a matter of situational politics, not that of abstract policy. But on an ultra-abstract, transcendentalist, yet crudely nationalist plane, Kennan topped off his famous "X" article with a fitting dose of American exceptionalism: the "thoughtful observer," he wrote, "would experience a certain gratitude to a Providence which, by providing the American people with this implacable challenge, has made their entire security as a nation dependent on pulling themselves together and accepting the responsibilities of moral and political leadership that history plainly intended for them to bear."[11]

Anti-Communism in Greece

Evidence of Kennan's influence and of the more general new phase of US power was abundant on the world stage, famously so with regard to Greece and Turkey. To examine this shift in the US disposition from late 1944 to late 1946 as it played out in Athens, it is instructive to go back to certain remarks made by Reginald Leeper, the British ambassador to Greece from 1943 to late 1946. He had been a lead figure in organizing and directing a political and military effort against the Communist-led leftwing wartime resistance movement, the National Liberation Front (EAM) and its military wing, the Greek National Liberation Army (ELAS). In the post-occupation setting, he strove to keep Communists and their sympathizers out of the Greek government. Severe tensions over that issue led to the deadly December Events of 1944, in which British and anti-EAM-ELAS Greek military forces fought elements of the ELAS forces. Though Roosevelt mounted no attempt to block the British attack in Athens, he had to distance himself from it because American popular opinion saw it as arbitrary and heavy handed. He explained to Churchill in mid-December, "As anxious as I am to be of the greatest help to you in this trying situation, there are limitations imposed … by the mounting adverse reaction of public opinion in this country."[12] In mid-January 1945, when the fighting had ceased for the time being, with the ELAS on the losing end, Leeper wrote the following to a colleague in the Foreign Office: "Inside Athens, of course, we British are all heroes, without discrimination. And I am glad to say the Americans are dirt. Our neutral Allies cut the most ignominious figure during the five weeks that the battle lasted." He wrote that they were frightened, "wanted appeasement," and descended into "an orgy of stars and stripes."[13] The ambassador continued his invective at length before settling down to order several more cases of whiskey for the Athens embassy. Clearly, British foreign policy players were playing the anti-communist/anti-leftist role in Greece up to that time and into 1947. But by late 1946, the American ambassador to Greece, Lincoln MacVeagh, was apologizing to his new British counterpart in Athens, Clifford Norton, because the US government "had woken up so late in the day to what was at stake in Greece." He "indicated that the US Government were prepared to consider supplying material and arms to us to hand on to the Greeks." MacVeagh sent a telegram to the State Department, "the gist of which was that the US must be prepared without delay to provide Greece with up to $80 million in cash or kind for 1947."[14] In mid-February 1947, the British embassy in Washington, DC, informed the American undersecretary of state, Dean Acheson, that in thirty days, Britain would cease its financial and material support for the Greek and Turkish governments. Britain had just given up its control over Palestine and had agreed to independence for India. Its treasury was bankrupt; all it could do now was follow the lead of the United States but persuade the Americans along the way that they needed to step in and play the right anti-leftist roles in order to secure the global dominance of their common liberal capitalism.[15]

On the following March 12, the American president delivered his anti-Communist "Truman Doctrine" speech to Congress, declaring that the "very existence of the Greek state is today threatened by the terrorist activities of several thousand armed men, led by Communists, who defy the government's authority at a number of points, particularly along the northern boundaries." He said Greece's government was "unable to cope with the situation" and "needs supplies and equipment if it is to restore the authority of the government throughout Greek territory." The British Government, "which has been helping Greece, can give no further financial or economic aid after March 31." The United States was its only hope: "There is no other country to which democratic Greece can turn." Channeling Kennan and Churchill, among others, Truman put the world in stark terms:

> One way of life is based upon the will of the majority, and is distinguished by free institutions, representative government, free elections, guarantees of individual liberty, freedom of speech and religion, and freedom from political oppression. The second way of life is based upon the will of a minority forcibly imposed upon the majority. It relies upon terror and oppression, a controlled press and radio; fixed elections, and the suppression of personal freedoms.

Greece in the spring of 1947 was not democratic. It had not been anything remotely so since the establishment of the anti-Communist Metaxas military dictatorship in 1936, which was backed by the King of Greece, George II. The country remained in the grips of a civil war that had raged periodically since the fall of 1943 under the Axis occupation. Since early 1945, highly strained by the consequences of dictatorship, occupation, and civil war, the country saw a spate of anti-EAM "white terror" attacks by groups of fanatical anti-Communists—mainly wartime collaborators and hard-core monarchists. There was no favorable ground yet established for democratic electoral politics. Justifiably, the Greek Communist Party and many of its sympathizers abstained from the elections of March 1946, arguing that the violent political climate was inimical to free and fair elections. However, driven to desperation and strategic ineptitude on the eve of the elections, some members of the party and its remaining wartime military forces carried out a guerilla-style attack on a police station in northern Greece. It caused fatalities and triggered the 1946–9 civil war. Truman's "democratic Greece" was a fiction. It was a ruthlessly anti-Communist, anti-leftist state; for the great powers, it was a strategic state neighboring the oil-rich Middle East, the Suez Canal in Egypt to the south, and the Dardanelles waterway from the Black Sea through western Turkey to the Aegean and Mediterranean seas. US State Department officials wrote up the first drafts of Truman's speech, highlighting the investment possibilities and access to oil across the Middle East for American corporations if the United States could gain overriding influence in both Greece and Turkey. The Soviets, meanwhile, were pressuring the Turks off and on for shipping rights through the Dardanelles. But according to Truman, Acheson, and Vandenburg, the draft speeches sounded too much like annual corporate investment reports and might appear cynical to the American voting public. Vandenburg had a better idea, to supposedly trump the cynicism, but in actuality doubling down on it; he told Truman to simply "scare the hell out of the American people."[16] Truman agreed and delivered to the US Congress and to the American people conditioned to be susceptible to such fear mongering. Congress was wowed, and so were a lot of ordinary people. Greece got $300 million and Turkey $100 million. It was only three months later that the $13 billion Marshall Plan (officially named the European Recovery Program) was announced. If the US business and investment interests were to satisfy themselves, and the country to fulfill its imagined "destiny," American manufacturing needed access to natural resources and markets, while American finance needed the US dollar as the world's dominant currency. All of this required bulwarks against command-economy style Communism. But when it came to selling it to the American voters, it was about "good versus evil," "democracy versus totalitarianism," not about the preeminently practical and strategic interests of business and finance.

The United States was extremely well positioned for that rare opportunity: to create a dominant global empire, with all its attendant problems and challenges. Anti-Communist hysteria was proving most effective in advancing that venture on the popular level of American politics. It was easy, all encompassing, and fit sufficiently well with the Anglo-Saxon white supremacist culture of "manifest destiny." For many, despite the astounding ignorance on which it was predicated—which does not excuse it—anti-Communism was heartfelt. For the more cynical it was a tool to sustain that heartfelt support for what they defined as American interests. This was a combination of massive power, interests, arrogance, ignorance, and cynicism—an outstanding and distinctive case of ideological hegemony, crucial for its impact worldwide. In its language and imagery, the anti-leftist part of it fit the pattern of the hysterical rhetoric of the early nineteenth century against figures such as Robert Owen and Henri de Saint-Simon; in its implementation, it often displayed the fully violent character that was consistent with the turn that it originally took at Peterloo in 1819 and Paris of 1848 and 1871. There was little perceived need or place for a reasoned critique, or for serious restraint from force or the threat of it; it was always much closer to a war cry. The hysteria was licensed by the alleged beastliness and moral derangement of its target, but of course also by the threat that it posed to class and state power.

Anti-Communism in China, Korea, and Indochina

China

In the late 1940s, anti-Communism was as central to British, American, French, and Dutch policy in East and Southeast Asia as it was to the British and Americans in Southeastern Europe and Western Asia. In both areas, those states faced Communist-led, anti-imperialist rebellions fueled by decades, if not centuries, of exploitation, racism, and abuse at the hands of the great power states and those that collaborated with them locally. It was also a matter of Communist confidence and strategy inspired and modeled after the original Bolshevik victory in Russia, by the Soviets retaining their grip on state power up to the Second World War, and then dealing the decisive military blows against the Nazi military machine during the war. Finally, it was about the dislocations of the war, which resulted in a spate of Communist-led anti-colonial movements across East and Southeast Asia in the wake of the Japanese surrender in September 1945. The immediate question for the remaining imperialist powers was how to regain control over their colonies, if that could be done at all. But paramount was the question of China, a mostly agrarian society and state that had been in the throes of radical instability at least since the Taiping Rebellion of the mid-nineteenth century. Since 1927, civil war ensued between the military forces of the Chinese Nationalists (KMT) led by Chiang Kai-Shek and the Communists (CCP) led by Mao Zedong. Out of those conflicting currents, the relative power position of the CCP grew to be much stronger than its Greek counterpart. Its greatest strategic opportunities were given to them by the Japanese, first with the occupation of Manchuria that began in 1931, but more importantly, by the Japanese invasion of China that began in 1937. Amid such challenges, Chiang and the KMT tried to face off against the foreign onslaught but prioritized their anti-Communism. This both weakened the KMT and gave the CCP a golden opportunity to prove its nationalist credentials—their commitment to China's territorial integrity and national well-being. Meanwhile, the CCP also pursued much needed and highly popular land reforms, which were an anathema to Chiang. The CCP fought effectively against the Japanese, even though they did not rush to the defense of the KMT when the latter were under attack by the Japanese or their collaborators.[17] All these differences aside, the American diplomatic disposition regarding China underwent a shift similar to that in Greece; in both cases, nuanced analysis inclined toward anti-Communism showed some signs of life, only to be replaced by blunt anti-Communism.

Just as Roosevelt backed Churchill's anti-Communism in Greece, despite some distaste about its cynicism, he quietly sided with Britain's general hard-line against the Communists regarding postwar power in China. In August 1944, he sent a special emissary to China, General Patrick J. Hurley, a Republican who, with some doggedness and "a lot of hootin' and hollerin," did all within his capacity to enforce a hard US anti-Communist diplomatic line. The effort was undertaken in the guise of creating a coalition between the KMT and the CCP, and it took time—to recognize it as a vain effort. But the general policy drive that emanated from the top would combine with domestic US politics, as well as the facts on the ground in China, to help crystallize a hard anti-Communism toward China and anywhere else there was even a hint of such a political form. In the meantime, for a number of "China hands" in the State Department at the time, Hurley was a problem. According to Philip D. Sprouse, who worked as a US Foreign Service officer on China from the mid-1930s up to 1950, and was the director of the Office of Chinese Affairs in 1949–50, Hurley was "a 'bull in the china shop' and ... an absolute disaster." He was really the decisive force in our policy toward China in those days, and he accused all the China specialists of those days who had served on his staff or served on Stilwell's staff, of being pro-Communist and espousing the Communist cause rather than the Nationalist Government. The State Department itself had no power, no authority, and apparently President Roosevelt had given Hurley pretty much of a free hand, because he ignored the State Department.

Sprouse continued that "Hurley … was ignorant, he was arrogant, he was bombastic, he was a fool in some ways, and you wonder why FDR ever appointed him to China to begin with."[18]

Sprouse was an understandably frustrated officer that displayed a relatively pragmatic—and therefore suspicious—anti-Communism and paid a personal and professional price for it. A similar fate struck John Paton Davies Jr., a member of Stilwell's staff and friend and colleague of George Kennan's. Davies led the so-called Dixie Mission to establish direct US relations with the Chinese Communists in the mountainous east-central Yan'an area in 1944. His overall strategic assessment was that the Nationalist KMT had no viable future in China, so he clashed bitterly with Hurley, who kept angling for a coalition between the CCP and the KMT, and falsely accused Davies of sabotaging the negotiations.[19] At Hurley's request, Davies was pulled from China in January 1945 and reassigned to Moscow, where he developed close ties with Kennan. But Hurley kept running up against resistance from the "China hands" that believed that the United States could and should try to work with the Communists because they had a strong independent base and could be kept away from the Soviet Union.

In addition to the veteran American analysts of China, Hurley also had to contend with prominent Democrats who had dim views of Chiang Kai Shek and his KMT, relatively favorable impressions of the CCP, and entertained hopes of keeping it away from the Soviet Union. The possible alternate strategies and relative American pragmatism were evident in Democratic Senator Mansfield's report to Roosevelt from his visit to China in early 1945. According to Mansfield, "the biggest single problem in the country today" was not a Communist threat but "this disunity within China itself." He stated that US "military and diplomatic representatives are doing all that they can do to close this breach (between Chiang and the Communists) and bring about greater cooperation among the Chinese." Further, the

> Communist Party is the chief opposition group in China. They are not Communists in the sense that Russians are as their interests seem to focus on primarily agrarian reforms. Whereas they used to execute landlords and expropriate their estates to divide up among the peasants, today they try to cooperate with landlords or anyone else who will help them in their fight against Japan. There are more reformers than revolutionaries and they have attacked the problems most deep-seated in agricultural China, namely, high rents, taxes, interest rates, and they have developed cooperatives and a system of local democracy.

Regarding the KMT, whom the British still strongly supported at the time, Mansfield wrote that it

> is hated more every day and this is due to fear of the army and the attitude of tax collectors; and is proved by the revolts of the peasantry, the party criticism by provincial leaders, student revolts against conscription and the fact that many Chinese will stoop to anything to get to America and, once there, to stay there. It is corrupt. It speaks democratically but acts dictatorially.

The aim of "American influence ... has been to try to get the divergent elements in China together ... to prevent a possible civil war; to bring about as great a degree of unification as possible to carry on the war; and to help the Chinese to help themselves in settling their own internal problems." Hitting a cautious final note, he suggested there was "a bare possibility that the present crisis which confronts China may be a means of bringing these two groups together." Certainly this was a damning portrait of the KMT; its leadership was narrowly egoistic, inefficient, opportunistic, corrupt, and without courage. The Communists were presented in a nearly opposite manner; agrarian reformist more than revolutionary, not getting resources from Moscow; committed and courageous against the Japanese, and popular with the peasants, who increasingly hated Chiang, the dubious "nationalist."[20] Along with the rest of the western powers, the United States was still fighting more or less alongside the CCP against the common enemy of Japan, so it was easier to look upon them more favorably, just as many in the United States did toward "Uncle Joe" (as Roosevelt referred to Stalin) and the USSR during the war. But it was still a serious and comprehensive analysis with sustainable policy implications that were just left to collapse. It was also a window for the American government and people, soon to be shut, onto practical reality in China. From the top down, and in combination with domestic pressures from various archconservative lobby groups, the trend was toward an adamant pro-KMT stance, just as its fortunes were dropping, and an anti-CCP stance, just as its power was rising. Many like Mansfield and the China hands were sympathetic with the principles and programs of Roosevelt's New Deal and had close-up familiarity with the situation in China. They were relatively open-minded about the needs and possibilities for reform in societies across the world, sometimes even radical versions of it, as with China.

Hurley lost his patience by November, when he submitted his resignation, returned to the United States, and testified before a Senate panel that most of the US Foreign Service analysts in China were Communist sympathizers out to sabotage US cooperation with the KMT. Partly informed by Davies, Kennan agreed that the United States could work with the CCP and communicated that to General George Marshall, Hurley's successor in China, whose post lasted from December 1945 to February 1947. Though the stately Marshall cut a sharp contrast with Hurley in terms of style, demeanor, and his appointment as Ambassador to China, his stated mission was the same as his predecessor's, to bring the CCP and the KMT into a governing coalition. Marshall was now caught dead center in the confused and contradictory US policy toward China and the attempts to apply it. On the face of it, he did not reject the apparently pragmatic view that was purported to be US policy, yet behind that he authorized major and exclusive material and financial support for the KMT in March of 1946. Mao's and the CCP's suspicions were only further aroused that the United States fully intended to only support the KMT. Dealing within China, Hurley's problem was his personality; Marshall was statesmanlike, but his mission and actions led to the same predictable failure. According to Lanxin Xiang, the "inherent contradiction" in US policy toward China was an aim for unity, undermined by actions that only sowed further disunity. Furthermore,

> General Marshall was not simply the victim of this inherent contradiction in the US China policy; in part he was its author. It was his decision in March to start an aid project to China – one exclusively for the Nationalists. The project involved such matters as training military personnel and providing equipment for the KMT army, air force, and navy, as well as Lend-Lease supplies, surplus material sales, and sea and airlifts to the KMT troops to Manchuria and North China.

He had Truman's full support for all these measures.[21]

Many diplomats and analysts within the foreign policy establishments of the liberal capitalist states saw in Mao and the CCP a chance to help create an "Asian Tito."[22] This would be a leading Communist who, like Josip Tito of Yugoslavia, had a powerful and independent social base, tremendous popular respect, and strong, if not explicit, opposition against Stalin, and possibly against the Soviet model generally. Aside from the fact that the great power states did not choose Tito to rule Yugoslavia the first place, pragmatic support for such a figure in China might have resulted in less explosive tension and deadly conflict. But that chance was precluded by the opportunistic and phobic fixations of doctrinaire anti-Communism. Regarding China, top-level American anti-Communist continuity was clear, though it was somewhat hidden and slowed at first amid the discussions and debates of the China hands that had been students of and advisers on the country since the 1930s and through the war. "New Deal" Roosevelt and "Fair Deal" Truman were hard anti-Communists but still tolerated some discussion and dissent within their State Departments. Yet even that tolerance was soon to get minimized, if not forced out completely. The trend was already unmistakable by 1946–7 and gained strength during the following several years. The period of Marshall's ostensible and failed efforts to unify the rival camps in China was precisely the time when those camps girded themselves for and relaunched their civil war. To be sure, this does not put the blame on Marshall, but only reveals how ineffectual US policy had become toward China. Doctrinaire anti-Communism was leaving no room for constructive policy-making.

After a series of failed negotiations to arrive at a ceasefire, outright and sustained conflict between the CCP and KMT began in April 1946. Marshall certainly failed in his attempt to appear neutral in the conflict, as he only ceased providing war material to the Nationalists at the end of July 1946.[23] For several months, the KMT's superiority in troop strength, training, and weaponry served them effectively, but they began to fall in 1947 to the Communists' superior leadership, organization, popularity with the vast peasantry, and guerilla war tactics. The United States resumed financial support to Chiang in May 1947, but it was far too late. When the CCP seized control of what had been Soviet-occupied and strategically crucial Manchuria in 1948—outmaneuvering the KMT in doing so—defections of Nationalist troops to the Communists numbered in the hundreds of thousands. The Communists took the major cities in 1949, and on October 1 declared the establishment of the People's Republic of China (PRC), while the Nationalists fled to the island of Taiwan and established the rival Republic of China (ROC). Secretary of State Dean Acheson tried to wash his and the Truman administration's hands of the matter, writing in July 1949,

> The unfortunate but inescapable fact is that the ominous result of the civil war in China was beyond the control of the government of the United States. Nothing that this country did or could have done within the reasonable limits of its capabilities could have changed that result; nothing that was left undone by this country has contributed to it. It was the product of internal Chinese forces, forces which this country tried to influence but could not.[24]

Yet the red baiting surged. Acheson and Truman came under fire for what was construed by the "China lobby" to be nothing but weakness in the face of the Communist menace. The precedent this set in American politics for at least the next twenty years was utterly tragic. Jumping a few years ahead, historian Ellen Schreker writes, "It was in part to avoid a replay of the loss of China scenario that … Kennedy and Johnson, dragged the United States so deeply into the quagmire of Vietnam."[25]

In the spring of 1947, Marshall had already returned to the United States to formulate his plan for West European reconstruction. At that point, American Cold War anti-Communism was crystallizing rapidly in both foreign and domestic policy—the Truman Doctrine in March, the Marshall Plan and Taft-Hartley in June, and Red China emerging. The House Un-American Activities Committee (HUAC), originally established in 1938 without major consequence, was reconvened in 1945, then amplified with a vengeance in October 1947, when it went after the Hollywood Ten group of film screenwriters, directors, and producers with its infamous lead question: "Are you now or have you ever been a member of the Communist Party?" There were plenty of precedents for this round of anti-leftist politics in the United States, in the assaults on labor from the 1870s up to and into the First World War, and in the "Red Scare" that followed it. But the early Cold War in the United States produced an escalation, expansion, and virtual consecration of an ideology that proved a dangerous accompaniment to the global expansion of American power. It notoriously and easily fed the likes of Joe McCarthy, whose deceitful accusations from February 1950 to the fall of 1954 about hundreds of supposed Communists and their sympathizers within the State Department resonated strongly as "facts" within much of the frightened American body politic.[26] Soon after the PRC became an actual fact, Mao signed a Treaty of Friendship with the USSR and got recognition from the pragmatic and trade-hungry British. At home, the United States embraced red baiting, which spanned everything from "who lost China," to attacks on left-leaning Hollywood screenwriters, to the high-profile trial of Alger Hiss, accused of being a spy for the Soviets, to advertisements for cleaning agents warning of "Bolsheviks in the bathroom." It was a dark and difficult enough time within US politics and culture, but the global implications of it were proving to be extremely serious for millions of people.

Following the Soviet detonation of an atomic bomb in August 1949, and the Communist victory in China the following October, Truman requested an updated global strategic analysis from the Departments of State and Defense. The request was to "undertake a reexamination of our objectives in peace and war and of the effect of these objectives on our strategic plans, in the light of the probable fission bomb capability and possible thermonuclear bomb capability of the Soviet Union." The request tended to prefigure the response, particularly in the hands of its lead author, Paul Nitze, successor to George Kennan as the Director of Policy Planning for the State Department, and otherwise a man mostly in and out of investment banking, law, and politics. Nitze sidelined Kennan and others whom he considered soft on Communism. Submitted in April 1950, the document, known as NSC 68, represented and advocated a more explicitly offensive type of anti-Communism than that found in Kennan's prescriptions. The avowed strategic imperative of "containment" escalated to "rollback," with the insistence that "a vigorous political and military program" was necessary "to check and to roll back the Kremlin's drive for world domination."[27] China was now also targeted, of course, but the main focus remained on the Soviet Union. The new policy approach was not to be applied consistently at all, and when it was, it usually failed. It was tried against North Korea, where it failed, unless success was measured in the infliction of ultra-devastating human and physical consequences that promised extremely difficult beginnings for the regime that survived. It was tried again in the Bay of Pigs fiasco against Cuba in 1961.[28] It was not applied to Soviet dominated Eastern Europe, nor to East Germany in 1953, Hungary in 1956, or Czechoslovakia in 1968. The risks of all-out war were deemed too great. Taking it at face value, its only success was in 1983 against the Cuban-backed regime on the small Caribbean island of Grenada.

Korea

Korea at the end of the Second World War was a beleaguered and factionalized quasi-state that had endured decades of abuse at the hands of imperialist Japan. The country was subordinated to Japan as a protectorate in 1905, annexed and occupied outright since 1910, and faced incipient civil war over the question of postwar state power in 1945. Korea at that point was deeply affected by early Cold War geopolitical dynamics, as the Allied states agreed that the USSR would occupy the north and the United States the south of the country, divided roughly in half by the border at the 38th parallel. The Allied division was very much a pragmatic "facts on the ground" great power state agreement, just as was the looming division between Eastern and Western Europe. The agreement regarding Korea was made by Roosevelt, Churchill, and Chiang Kai Shek at the Cairo conference in November of 1943, namely, that the "aforesaid three great powers, mindful of the enslavement of the people of Korea, are determined that in due course Korea shall be free and independent."[29] Yet both the Korean and European situations were also extremely likely to get racked by Cold War strategic and ideological tensions that were potentially devastating.

At the moment of Japanese surrender in September 1945, Korea was alive with the legacies of radical leftwing resistance against the occupation. Some of it was Communist, some of it non-Communist left, both radical and moderate; some of it was nationalist anti-communist and aligned as much as practicably possible with China's KMT. For each faction, the aim was the same: to unify Korea. The new occupations of the two halves of the country did not quell the domestic rivals' ambitions; instead, by presenting to them new sets of political parameters and opportunities, they most likely undermined the prospects for unification. On the left there was a striking shift toward unity on the parts of most of the factions, north and south, from moderates to radicals to Communists. On the other hand, the nationalist anti-Communist right mostly rallied around the United States and its likely ally, Syngman Rhee.

Following their pattern in postwar Eastern Europe, the Soviets backed the Korean Communist Party (KCP), though they had to help rebuild it politically and organizationally. The remains of the party that had been splintered since the 1920s was spread far and wide; as many as twenty thousand came back from exile and service in the Red Army in Soviet Union, including Kim Il Sung, the first Premier of North Korea, who was a captain; others returned from China, where many had joined the CCP.[30] Those that had stayed in Korea and fought a guerilla-style war against the occupiers also now joined the revived party. At the outset of the post–Second World War period, the KCP became the go-to organization for Communist and non-Communist leftists, whose numbers were significant in the People's Committees that had been formed toward the very end of the Japanese occupation. The KCP continued that function until it was the only political party option in the country. However, Communist and non-Communist leftists had been more numerous and active in the south than in the north. Both anti-leftist nationalists in the north, and leftists of all sorts in the south, if they did not flee their respective areas, were essentially trapped in what for them was quickly becoming enemy territory.

General MacArthur was the commander in chief of US Army Forces in the Pacific and therefore the man most responsible for overseeing the US occupation of Japan and the south of Korea. After its punishing defeat at the hands of the United States, Japan was undivided and rebuilding its industrial capacity with American funds and expertise, while Korea was just coming out from beneath decades of occupation by Japan, wrought by left versus rightwing political tensions and divided north from south between the archenemies of the Cold War. If MacArthur had the Machiavellian aim to instill fear rather than love and hope in a wide swathe of the population for which he now had responsibility, he got off to a flying start. He decreed that that the technical, administrative, and police forces established by the Japanese occupiers, still including some Japanese officers, including General Abe, as well as considerable numbers of their ethnic Korean collaborators, such as the collaborationist landed gentry of the south, would essentially remain established. Given the brutalities of the occupation as well as the strong left-leaning demographic of the region, this was deeply offensive for most of the people of the area; for many it just continued the trauma of the occupation and war. This was an iteration of the basic pattern also seen in Greece, where members of the "security battalions" had been formed by, and collaborated with, the Axis occupation forces were welcomed into postwar anti-leftist police forces under the approving eyes of the British and later the Americans. In the US occupation zone of Korea south of the 38th parallel, MacArthur addressed his decree to the "Korean People," indicating he and the United States did not recognize the newly established government under the KPC in the north. To administer the south, he assigned responsibility to Lieutenant General John R. Hodge, who, based mainly on reports from Japanese authorities that remained in the US-directed "Military Government," quickly sounded the alarm "that the communists will seize by direct means the government in our area" and recommended that the United States work closely with Rhee to stop the threat.[31]

While Hodge further reported that the Japanese remaining in the south were both viciously anti-leftist and set upon extracting from the country anything they could before they were forced out, his top focus stayed on the perceived leftist threat, reporting in early November 1945, "Communistic activities are reaching point where they may gain control unless positive action is taken. Am sure most radical elements are Russian instigated but cannot get positive proof." He had a prescription and anticipated some of its fallout, writing, "When it becomes necessary to take drastic action, it may be expected it will be followed by a flood of wails both by Korean and Russian Communists and by American press against discrimination, suppression of 'civil liberties' etc."[32] Similar to what happened in the western theater of the Second World War, where the United States took up the postwar anti-Communist cause that had been central to the defeated western Axis states, the fierce anti-leftist thrust of those states' eastern ally, Imperial Japan, was clearly continuing, now under American direction.

In early 1946, the situation in much of Korea seemed to crystallize in favor of the broad spectrum of the left but inevitably in favor of the KPC. On February 8, the Provisional Peoples Committee for North Korea was established as the North Korean central government; one week later, the Korean Democratic People's Front was established in Seoul, the major city of the south; it consisted of upwards of forty leftwing organizations, including the KPC. Meanwhile, rightists were purged from all administrative posts in the north. Such developments bolstered the US determination to consolidate its control over the south of Korea. The rhetorical and strategic justification, if not the firm belief, was that the Soviet Union intended to do everything possible to unify the entire country under its power and create a "people's democracy" of the sort it was creating in Eastern Europe. The Central Intelligence Agency (CIA) articulated this view four days after the November 14, 1947, United Nations vote that called for foreign troop withdrawals and free elections throughout the country by the end of March 1948. The CIA stated, "Soviet tactics in Korea since V-J Day have consistently and clearly indicated a firm intention to accept no settlement which would not insure the acquisition of Korea as a loyal Soviet satellite in the Far East."[33] This view was consistent with the combined determinations of the cold warriors—Kennan, Truman, the Dulles brothers, MacArthur, and so forth—as well as General Hodge, whose "rough justice" collaborationist and nationalist anti-communist allies in the police forces in the south were now under the direction of Rhee. But with the Soviets boycotting the United Nations on the expressed belief that no free elections could be guaranteed amidst the widespread factionalism and instability, the United States successfully pushed for free elections exclusively in the south. To no one's surprise, this offended a great many Koreans who feared such elections as a step toward a potentially permanent partition of the country. Anyone outwardly opposing the step was labeled a "Communist," normally as a prelude to violent persecution. For the time being, the people of the island of Jeju, off the south coast of Korea, got the worst of it. In April 1948, the "people's committee" of the island organized a popular celebration of their survival against all odds during the years of war and occupation. The festivities were inevitably combined with lively expressions of opposition to the partition of the country between the two rival great power states. For that, Rhee's police opened fire on the left-leaning islanders participating in the event, which triggered an uprising against the police and the new regime generally. The police escalated to the extreme, massacring thirty thousand to sixty thousand of the islanders—horrific in itself, yet only to be repeated during the coming Korean War.[34] National Assembly elections took place in May, in which the left was suppressed and got no representation. Rhee was elected president in July. He ordered the creation of a list of suspected Communists that soon added up to approximately three hundred thousand people, 10 percent of whom were immediately jailed. By 1949, the whole lot was branded as the "Bodo League" and in imminent danger of paying the ultimate price. The Democratic People's Republic of Korea was declared in the north in September 1948. In December the United Nations recognized the Republic of Korea in the south as the only legitimate government on the peninsula. At that point, the mutual nonrecognition of the two start-up regimes and their equally opposed foreign allies were set upon violently contentious terrain.

North Korea launched its military attack in June 1950 against South Korea, where Rhee's police and paramilitaries were attempting to crush leftist forces that were potential allies of the north. The invasion was not exactly Soviet directed, but the USSR had been supplying military hardware to the north and did not try to stop it. Trying to counter the US priority in East Asia of rebuilding Japan, which was the USSR's main rival in the region, Stalin had been supporting and supplying North Korea since 1945 and may have encouraged the attack to show bravado as well as distract US attention from Europe. He also created cover for himself. When the United States soon proposed in the United Nations Security Council that a UN force be created to push back the North Korean incursion, the Soviet representative on the Council was conspicuously absent. Stalin was concerned that blocking the vote would unacceptably heighten the risks of all-out war with the United States, though he also later privately explained to the head of the Czechoslovak Communist Party that the empty Soviet seat in the Security Council was a gesture of solidarity with Mao's China, which Stalin considered to be entitled to a seat on the Council, whereas the United States had seen to it that Taiwan (the ROC) had the China seat. Higher still on the strategic level, Stalin calculated that, with the United States bogged down in Korea, it would be less able to prepare for an all-out anti-Soviet war.

Under the command of General MacArthur, the UN forces were initially back on their heels in the face of the North Korean invasion but managed to hold on and stabilize themselves in the far southern area of Pusan. From there they prepared a naval counterattack in the far northwest of the south, at the port of Incheon, near the capital, Seoul. The plan succeeded as dramatically, as had the north's initial invasion. North Korean forces were forced all the way up to the border with Communist China at the

Yalu River. In effect, at least, "American leaders had decided to go beyond containment .... They had decided to experiment with the possibilities of a rollback strategy."[35] But this backfired. Fearing a US-dominated regime on its doorstep, Mao's China responded with a massive troop commitment backing North Korea. In one month, the combined Korean-Chinese forces pushed the US-led UN forces back into the south, taking the city of Seoul in January 1951. The war continued for two and a half years around the 38th parallel, the prewar dividing line between north and south. While the US/UN forces regained the northern territories of the South, including Seoul, they did not make further headway on the ground against the large, disciplined, and fervent armies of the North Koreans and Chinese. That was the ground war.

The air war, in contrast, was in the largely uncontested hands of the US/UN forces. With the US Air Force in the lead, the bombing of North Korea in the wake of the retreat of the US/UN forces from the north was a classic "scorched earth" campaign—indiscriminate and murderous. MacArthur nearly outdid himself, flirting with genocide in calling for an atomic attack. In July 1950, he requested ten to twenty "A-bombs" to destroy all tunnels and bridges in the border regions of North Korea's neighboring states so as to create a "cul-de-sac" advantage for the US/UN forces.[36] "Sweeten up my B-29 force," he pleaded. However, for tactical, practical, and public relations reasons, his request was denied. For the time being, the American Joint Chiefs of Staff determined that conventional forces would win the war, though consideration of the atomic option continued. What was "conventional" included hard counterinsurgency operations and the use of napalm and flamethrowers at points across South Korea against actual and suspected leftist and Communist guerillas. But the situation in North Korea was worse. In September 1950, British journalist Reginald Thompson wrote that "handfuls of peasants defied the immense weight of modern arms with a few rifles and carbines and a hopeless courage ... and ..."—referring to napalm—"brought down upon themselves and all the inhabitants the appalling horror of jellied petrol bombs." In the end, "every village and township in the path of war was blotted out."[37]

At least in effect, here was a message to the people of North and South Korea and the world: if it wished to do so, the anti-Communist superpower would conduct a strategically unnecessary and genocidal bombing campaign against a weak state that was backed to some extent by the considerable forces of the Chinese and Soviet Communists. But this was only the first phase of the campaign, to be followed by two that were worse. According to Cumings, the "Chinese entry into the war caused an immediate escalation of the air campaign. From early November 1950 onward, MacArthur ordered that a wasteland be created between the fighting front and the Chinese border, destroying from the air every 'installation, factory, city, and village' over thousands of square miles of North Korean territory." On November 8, 70 B-29s dropped 550 tons of incendiary bombs on the Sino-North Korean border city of Sinuiju, incinerating it and a large portion of its inhabitants. The following week, Hoeryong was torched with napalm. By the end of November, a large portion of the expanding area between the Chinese border and southward to the war fronts was burning. The capital city of Pyongyang was targeted with aerial bombing in December; the United States dropped seven hundred bombs weighing 500 pounds each, in addition to dropping napalm and many tons of unpredictable delayed-fuse bombs that promised particular dangers for first responders and civilians. The following January, General Ridgway ordered two further strikes on the capital, "with the goal of burning the city to the ground with incendiary bombs." "Tarzon" bombs—12,000 pounds each and never before used in war—were dropped where the Kim II Sung leadership was bunkered in the town of Kanggye, but also to destroy bridges and dams. Other cities large and small were destroyed and "torched" as the US/UN forces retreated and their enemies approached. With no more targets remaining, American bombers unloaded their surplus ordnance into the sea. By 1952 just about all major buildings and vital food and water infrastructure in northern and central North Korea were completely destroyed. The remaining population survived in underground facilities and caves, where complexes of dwellings, schools, hospitals, and factories were built. American political-military authorities used aerial bombing as a type of psychological warfare to break any resistance, which only served to strengthen it. In South Korea, many clearly still sympathized with the North Koreans, prompting the call-up of the decorated American General, James Van Fleet, who had recently overseen anti-leftist campaigns in Greece. Van Fleet headed up "Operation Rat Killer," which began in December 1951 and resulted in the deaths of nearly twenty thousand suspected South Korean leftists.

Two to three million civilians were killed in the Korean War. South Korea endured approximately 415,000 military and civilian deaths, and more than 1.3 million casualties; North Korean fatalities reached an estimated 1.5 million, including 1 million civilians and over 520,000 soldiers. Bombing and napalm killed civilians by the hundreds of thousands, but many were also killed by ground troops, war-related illness, and starvation.[38] The proportions of fatalities to overall populations in Korea as a whole outdid any country in the Second World War, with the possible exception of Yugoslavia, as well as the later war in Vietnam. Minimum estimates are around 10 percent, the highest at 20 percent.[39] Around nine hundred thousand Chinese soldiers died in the conflict, and over forty-four thousand Americans, including more than eight thousand missing. Nearly four thousand UN troops from a variety of US-allied states—Australia and New Zealand, Britain, Greece, and so forth—were also killed.[40] With civilian and military fatalities in the hundreds of thousands and growing steadily, this can be seen as a bitter response to the defeat of the American "rollback" policy. But the evidence also suggests a larger and longer-term strategy that recalls the Allied anti-Bolshevik intervention of 1918–21, which failed, both on the face of it as well as substantively. However, there were severe consequences from fact that the Whites and the Allies pummeled Bolshevik Russia from within and without from 1918 to 1922. The devastations that combined with those of the war up to 1917 severely challenged the Bolsheviks' prospects creating a viable and legitimate regime, as the primary institutional options quickly became the secret police and the Red Army. Regarding North Korea, as the US Secretary of Defense Robert Lovett advised in 1952, "if we keep on tearing the place apart, we can make it a most unpopular affair for the North Koreans. We ought to go right ahead." The bombing did not turn the North Korean population against its government, but the scorched earth beginnings of the regime held little promise for the political character of whatever society and state it would build in a world of sustained and sometimes obviously extreme anti-Communism.

Indochina

While the United States was maneuvering and then warring against the Korean left, it was also supporting the French empire's shaky efforts to reassert control over Indochina, the "pearl" of their empire. France and its empire had been highly destabilized by the Nazi invasion, occupation, and establishment of the collaborationist Vichy regime. That combined with the December 1941 Japanese attacks across Southeast Asia to present a potentially fatal set of challenges to the colonial grip on Indochina. Though the French colonial administration remained largely intact during the war, afterward France was weak vis-à-vis the surging and increasingly concerted and aggressive anti-Communist United States. The converse of all of this was the rise of the Vietnamese Communist-nationalist left. The world war was the moment for Ho Chi Minh and the Viet Minh to establish themselves as the lead anti-colonialist force throughout the area, though their power position was seriously uneven. They built a strong base in the northern territories of Tonkin and Annam (later to become mostly North Vietnam), and a lesser force in Cochinchina (later mostly South Vietnam), Laos, and Cambodia. Given the strategic ascendancy of the United States, its policy positions on French matters—domestic and international—were crucial. Leading elements in the French colonial establishment may have been willing to fight any anti-colonial movement, but the increasing American political and material support on which France came to depend was conditional. The United States wished to see an anti-Communist nationalist movement to which the French would grant autonomy and, ultimately, independence. In other words, the United States supported French colonialism, but only in the service of anti-Communism. If a viable organization and movement of the sort they wanted actually existed, the Americans would have pushed for it as a vehicle for independence, and the French would most probably have succumbed to the pressure. Indeed, where the American vision was closer to realization was only where the Viet Minh had a clandestine presence, in Cochinchina, where the French colonial economic and administrative power and influence was strongest. There, in June 1949, in cooperation with anti-Communist nationalists, the French set up the "State of Vietnam"—otherwise known as the "Bao Dai solution." He was France's puppet emperor, nominally at the head of the government also in Tonkin and Annam. It was an important step toward the preferred American solution. However, if Bao Dai's power had any viability, it was only in the south. Throughout Indochina, the individual political figure that most impressed and concerned the French and the Americans was Ho Chi Minh.[41]

Ho's biography reveals a history of appeals to the western great powers, first and foremost to the Americans, for support in his quest for liberation from French colonial rule and Vietnamese independence. The Americans would appreciate this, or so went Ho's assumption, as it was their country that was the first to achieve its independence from colonial rule in 1776. However, certain representative and leading great power, postrevolutionary, American men—Woodrow Wilson at the Versailles Conference in 1919 and Harry Truman in 1945—arrogantly and fatally dismissed the Vietnamese leader's pleas. No doubt there was a racist and great power chauvinist dimension to the dismissals, but that quickly combined with the fact that Ho gave up on the United

States and the liberal capitalist-imperialist west. In 1919 he sought support for his cause among renegade French socialists who broke away in 1920 to establish the French Communist Party, of which Ho became a founding member. He led the Viet Minh national liberation movement that formed in 1941 against the Japanese, and, as an integral part of the Allied war effort, he worked with the American Office of Strategic Services (OSS) in the war against Japan in 1944–5.[42]

At the Potsdam Conference of August 1945 it was agreed that Indochina would be temporarily divided at the 16th parallel. The agreement allowed temporary occupation of the north by Chinese troops committed to Chiang Kai Shek, who did not oppose the Viet Minh, allowing them to solidify their base in the north, strengthen elsewhere, and declare the Vietnamese Democratic Republic in September. Meanwhile, the British, who were assigned temporary control of the south, facilitated France's aim of reasserting its authority in the area. Clearly, France would soon have to confront the problem of Ho and the Viet Minh, who were not keen on accommodating any imperialist intentions. A few weeks following negotiations of dubious sincerity on both the French and the Viet Minh sides in early March 1946, as French naval forces were heading toward Haiphong harbor in the north as a show of force and sign of possible attack, the Viet Minh launched guerilla operations against the French and their collaborators' positions in the south. The fighting continued to the end of October, when Ho agreed to a *modus vivendi* with the French colonial minister, Marius Moutet, a socialist who was sympathetic with the Viet Minh's cause. The agreement was for peace and civil liberties, including freedom of speech and press, which unleashed a wave of popular expression favoring unification with the north under the Viet Minh. However, French military authorities in Saigon would not have it. Facing a possible total loss, they schemed to provoke war in the north. Defying the *modus vivendi*, and overriding opposition in their own top ranks, quasi-rogue French forces found an incident—gasoline smuggling—and made it a pretext to bomb the harbor of Haiphong in November, killing thousands of civilians and occupying the city. However, unfortunately for the French military hawks in Saigon, the results were disappointing. The Viet Minh cadres in Haiphong evacuated the city and regrouped in remote rural and jungle areas. For the time being, no one was putting up a fight; there was no sufficient justification for further French military action. But in fact, the Viet Minh, under the highly capable General Giap, were solidifying their remote positions and aggressively eliminating any active anti-communist nationalist forces.[43]

A parliamentary impasse in Paris led to the resignation of Prime Minister Bidault and the temporary administration of Léon Blum, the veteran socialist who, as prime minister, got outmaneuvered by French hardline conservatives during the early stages of the Spanish Civil War in 1936. In accord with Ho Chi Minh's appeals, Blum wanted peace with the Viet Minh and telegrammed accordingly to Saigon, where the message was to be immediately relayed to the Viet Minh leader. However, the French hardliners sat on the orders, instead seeking to provoke a military crisis with the north. The obstruction and provocation worked in the short run. Amid an uneasy standoff, the French managed to lure some sections of the Viet Minh forces in and around Hanoi to launch attacks on the French positions. Open warfare ensued, in which French forces gained the upper hand. When Blum learned of the developments, he was furious, yet was quickly overwhelmed with accounts of doubtful veracity from Saigon, as well as from the French press, that put the blame squarely on the Viet Minh. Domestically and internationally, Blum was again outmaneuvered and isolated. Particularly for the French, it became "the dirty war" for its grey areas separating enemies from allies— inherent in the uncertainties of fighting guerilla forces instead of regular armies, and a sadly familiar theme in the American experience that followed in the 1960s–70s. What allowed the Viet Minh to survive in the first few years of the war were its tight organization, popular and independent base, effective use of guerilla tactics out of remote jungle hideouts, and the skilled leadership of Ho Chi Minh and General Giap. Until 1950, they got little to no outside support for their operations; their only option was guerilla warfare, which wore on the French but did not defeat them. But in their fall 1949 victory, the Chinese Communists recognized North Vietnam as an independent state, and the USSR followed suit. Both states offered ample material support that allowed Giap to shift to very effective regular military operations. At least as of May 1950, the United States was eager to financially and militarily support what it saw as the French war against Communist aggression, but it was to no avail.

From 1945 to the victory of the Chinese Communists in 1949, US policy is typically seen as showing ambivalence, though this was not as to whether or not anti-Communism was their central tenet. It was mainly in contrast to the extremism of their anti-Communism from 1950 onward, the template text for which was NSC 68. A 1948 policy statement shows the somewhat softer approach:

> Our long-term objectives are: (1) to eliminate so far as possible Communist influence in Indochina and to see installed a self-governing nationalist state which will be friendly to the US and which, commensurate with the capacity of the peoples involved, will be patterned upon our conception of a democratic state as opposed to the totalitarian state which would evolve inevitably from Communist domination.

They acknowledged correctly the problem of Ho Chi Minh and what he represented: "Our greatest difficulty in talking with the French" is that "we are all too well aware of the unpleasant fact that Communist Ho Chi Minh is the strongest and perhaps the ablest figure in Indochina and that any suggested solution which excludes him is an expedient of uncertain outcome." But the same document shows a phony type of restraint on military support:

> We have ... declined to permit the export to the French in Indochina of arms and munitions for the prosecution of the war against the Vietnamese. This policy has been limited in its effect as we have allowed the free export of arms to France, such exports thereby being available for re-shipment to Indochina or for releasing stocks from reserves to be forwarded to Indochina.[44]

The British offered a fairly clear and pessimistic eye on French dilemmas that did not bode well for either French or American interests.[45] A report from their embassy in Hanoi of May 1949 was striking in its suggestions, that for the people in Tonkin, which was the area comprising most of what later became North Vietnam, "France and not communism is enemy No. 1. The Viet Minh have taken pains to improve in every possible way the lot of the peasant, at the expense of the rich middle classes and mandarins. They have not always succeeded ... but where they have failed, clever propaganda has placed the blame on the French." Furthermore, "it must not be forgotten that HO CHI MINH is a national hero to a large portion of the population." Propaganda against Communism, therefore, "is rendered particularly difficult."[46] The all but explicit warning out of this assessment was that a military effort to dislodge him and his movement from power would also, no doubt, be "particularly difficult."

The shift to American anti-Communist NSC68-style extremism was clear at least by mid-1950. On May 8, Secretary of State Dean Acheson announced,

> Foreign Minister (Schuman) and I have just had an exchange of views on the situation in Indochina and are in general agreement both as to the urgency of the situation in that area and as to the necessity for remedial action. The United States recognizes that the solution of the Indochina problem depends both upon the restoration of security and upon the development of genuine nationalism and that United States assistance can and should contribute to these major objectives.[47]

The secretary further stated that

> the United States Government, convinced that neither national independence nor democratic evolution exist in any area dominated by Soviet imperialism, considers the situation to be such as to warrant its according economic aid and military equipment to the associated states of Indochina and to France in order to assist them in restoring stability and permitting these states to pursue their peaceful and democratic development.

The following week it was announced that a "small military aid group" was to be established in Indochina "to supervise the extension of military assistance to that country." The first American grant to the French war effort was $10 million in 1950, and it grew to $1.1 billion in 1954, overall "paying for 78 per cent of the French war burden."[48]

Along with Korea, Indochina was drastically affected by at least three major things: the successful Soviet atomic bomb detonation, the Communist victory in China, and the toxicity of domestic McCarthyist anti-Communism. The intensification of American hostility crystallized in National Security update NSC 68, issued in April 1950 as the textual license for the extremism. The document also reflected a shift in American strategic priorities, from ensuring that France and all of Western Europe constituted a bulwark against Communism, to preventing any more of Asia from falling into Communist hands. Up to then, it was "the fear of French rather than Vietnamese communism that made the United States refrain from intervening to stop the war" in Indochina.[49] From this point onward, despite their dim prospects so clear in retrospect, US material and financial support for the French war in Indochina was virtually guaranteed. So was the tragedy. Even voices from within the system issued warnings about it for anyone capable of listening. The US Ambassador to France at the time showed a deep appreciation of the complications and their potentials. Very aware of the strength of the Viet Minh, he wrote that the

> US ... finds itself supporting joint effort of France and non-Communist nationalists of three associated states. Yet these two forces, brought together only by common danger of Communist imperialism are inherently antagonistic and gains of one will be to some extent at expense of other. Therefore, implementation of US policy, more particularly by US Government officials in Indochina, is highly difficult and delicate.[50]

By early 1952, the inexorability of tragedy was apparent, as seen in US policy statements on the problem of Communism in Southeast Asia, that first came to light in *The Pentagon Papers* in 1972. It was all about the "domino theory," that one country's fall to Communism would lead to the same in neighboring countries, extending from East Asia (including Japan) to India, throughout most of Middle East, and ultimately destabilizing Western Europe. Without US "action" it would be a veritable apocalypse.[51] Guided by such thinking, the United States supported French forces as they attempted, but failed, to defeat the Communist-nationalists in the north. Their war was not politically popular in France, nor could any of the forces—the majority non-French colonial troops—fight with anything resembling the purpose and morale possessed by the Viet Minh.

The Viet Minh defeated the forces of the French empire at the battle of Dien Bien Phu in the spring of 1954. For the two imperialist states, two fears were operative and intertwining: first, that of Communism and how it would block the paths to American expansion—or, as it was often put, block the development of "democracy"; second, the French fear of the loss of their empire. According to Premier and Foreign Minister, George Bidault, in late November 1946, any loss or humiliation in the northern part of Indochina would ultimately mean the loss of the rest of Indochina, as well as of French North Africa—Tunisia, Algeria, and parts of Morocco. The French fear was well founded; their empire was in free fall. The American fear was not as well founded, though the systematic anti-Communist aggressions it led to, or which were carried out in the guise of anti-Communism, functioned to expand and distinguish its empire.

What happened in China, Korea, and Indochina from 1946 to 1954, including the Communist-nationalist victory over the French empire at Dien Bien Phu—not to refer to the post–Second World War establishment of Soviet hegemony over Eastern Europe—amounted to a greater swelling of the leftist political seas that began with the Bolshevik Revolution in 1917. In the complex of antagonisms between what was now the US-led system of capitalism and liberalized markets on the one side, and the complex phenomena of leftwing politics on the other, the post–Second World War circumstances produced new Communist states. As a whole, they mounted a major challenge to the American quest for hegemony, east and west. On the face of it, it was not irrational to see the world in "binary," or "bipolar," terms. However, the relative independence of the Yugoslav Communists from Moscow put doubt to such thinking, as did the ponderings of the American and British foreign policy analysts about Mao

Figure 7 Mao Zedong and Chiang Kai-Shek toasting to the victory over Japan, 1945. From 1925 to the end of the Chinese Civil War in 1949, Mao the Communist and Chiang the Nationalist were fierce rivals, though sometimes reluctant allies. The Communists were victorious in the Civil War, and the Nationalists fled to Taiwan.

Source: Public domain; commons.wikimedia.org.

Zedong or Ho Chi Minh as the possible Titos of Asia. Close on the horizon was also the Sino-Soviet split, while so much of the rest of the world was shaping up as the anti-colonialist Third World, which, more thoroughly than anything, challenged the notions and realities of bipolarity.

Notes

1. "1945 Conservative Party General Election Manifesto, Winston Churchill's Declaration of Policy to the Electors," Conservative Manifesto. http://www.conservativemanifesto. com/1945/1945-conservative-manifesto.shtml (accessed February 3, 2019).
2. Truman speech quoted from http://historymatters.gmu.edu/d/5137/.
3. Eric Foner, *Give Me Liberty!: An American History, Volume Two, from 1865* (New York: Norton, 2017), pp. 922–33.
4. Efforts to break up the cartels persisted only until the Korean War (1950–3), when anti-Communism within the US-led western alliance reached full throttle. See Henry B. Wend, *Recovery and Restoration: U.S. Foreign Policy and the Politics of Reconstruction of West Germany's Shipbuilding Industry, 1945–1955* (Westport: Praeger, 2001), pp. 109–82.
5. Paul Kennedy, *The Rise and Fall of the Great Powers: Economic Change and Military Conflict from 1500 to 2000* (New York: Vintage, 1987), pp. 357–8. For an excellent

critical assessment of the American foreign policy establishment, see Perry Anderson, "Imperium," *New Left Review*, 83 (September/October 2013), p. 22. Eric Hobsbawm, *Age of Extremes: A History of the World, 1914–1991* (New York: Vintage, 1996), p. 258.

6. Thomas J. McCormick, *America's Half Century: United States Foreign Policy in the Cold War and After* (Baltimore, MD: Johns Hopkins University Press, 1995), p. 78.

7. Henry A. Wallace, "Where I Was Wrong," *The Week*, September 7, 1952. Quoted from Steven Stoft, *Ripped Apart: How Democrats Can Fight Polarization to Win* (Berkeley, CA: PolyScience Press), p. 80.

8. "George Kennan's 'Long Telegram,'" February 22, 1946, History and Public Policy Program Digital Archive, National Archives and Records Administration, Department of State Records (Record Group 59), Central Decimal File, 1945–9, 861.00/2-2246; reprinted in US Department of State, ed., *Foreign Relations of the United States, 1946, Volume VI, Eastern Europe; The Soviet Union* (Washington, DC: United States Government Printing Office, 1969), 696–709. Available online: http://digitalarchive.wilsoncenter.org/document/116178.

9. See Perry Anderson, *American Foreign Policy and Its Thinkers* (London: Verso, 2015).

10. George F. Kennan, *American Diplomacy, 1900–1950* (New York: Mentor, 1952), p. 119.

11. Ibid., p. 121.

12. WO/106/5433 Roosevelt to Churchill, T. 2354/4, No. 673, December 13, 1944.

13. FO 800/276 Gr/45/1 Leeper to (recipient name handwritten and illegible), January 12, 1945.

14. FO371/67032 R6109 No. 2642, C. Norton to Foreign Office, December 13, 1946.

15. McCormick, *America's Half Century*, p. 72. See also FO371/67033 R2817, Lord Inverchapel (aka Archibald Clark Kerr) to Foreign Office, February 15, 1947, where he reports he has Acheson's assurance that the United States will step in to supply the Greek government with military and financial aid.

16. On the background discussions about the type of messaging the US president should use in the speech, in other words, the speech's cynical and manipulative subtext, see Anderson, "Imperium," pp. 33–4.

17. John Keegan, *The Second World War* (New York: Penguin, 1989), p. 547.

18. James R. Fuchs, "Oral History Interview with Ambassador Philip D. Sprouse," February 11, 1974, accessed online at Harry S. Truman Presidential Library & Museum, pp. 53–4 in the written transcripts of the spoken words, and *passim*. See also Warren Cohen and Philip D. Sprouse, "Ambassador Philip D. Sprouse on the Question of Recognition of the People's Republic of China in 1949 and 1950," *Diplomatic History*, vol. 2, no. 2 (Spring 1978), pp. 213–17. General Stilwell commanded US and Chinese forces in the Second World War Burma Campaign, and was appointed by Chiang Kai Shek as his chief of staff of operations in China. But Stilwell had a falling out with Chiang, whom he criticized as corrupt and more concerned with fighting the Communists than the Japanese occupiers. He was consequently removed from his post. See Barbara Tuchman, *Stilwell and the American Experience in China, 1911–45* (New York: Macmillan, 1971).

19. Wilson D. Miscamble, *George F. Kennan and the Making of American Foreign Policy, 1947–1950* (Princeton, NJ: Princeton University Press, 1993), pp. 215–16. Also, according to Lanxin Xiang, "Hurley was sent to China with a two-fold purpose: to bring about unification of China under Chiang Kai shek, and to 'keep an eye on European imperialism.'" See his *Recasting the Imperial Far East: Britain and America in China, 1945–1950* (New York: Routledge, 1995), p. 4.

20. January 3, 1945, Mansfield to Roosevelt, *Foreign Relations of the United States* (FRUS): Diplomatic Paper, 1945, The Far East, China, Volume II. 893.00/1–1645, Document 2, pp. 8–12.
21. Xiang, *Recasting the Imperial Far East*, pp. 73–4. The exclusive US material support for Chiang came in the same month of Churchill's "Iron Curtain" speech in Fulton, Missouri. Both surely bolstered Chiang's confidence in US support for his cause.
22. Ibid., pp. 230–4.
23. Having failed in his mission in China, Marshall returned to the United States in January 1947 to take up his post as Truman's secretary of state.
24. Dean Acheson, "Letter of Transmittal" of the "China White Paper" to President Truman, August 1949. Originally published as "United States Relations with China, With Special Reference to the Period 1944–1949," Department of State Publication 857–3, Far Eastern Series 30. Reissued with the Original Letter of Transmittal to President Truman from Secretary of State Dean Acheson and with a New Introduction by Lyman P. Van Slyke (Stanford, CA: Stanford University Press, 1967), p. 16. Available online: https://archive.org/stream/VanSlykeLymanTheChinaWhitePa per1949/Van+Slyke%2C+Lyman+-+The+China+White+Paper+1949_djvu.txt.
25. Ellen Schrecker, *The Age of McCarthyism: A Brief History with Documents*, Second Edition, (New York, Bedford/St Martin's), p. 106.
26. Ibid., pp. 71–9.
27. "A Report to the National Security Council by the Executive Secretary on United States Objectives and Programs for National Security" (NSC 68), Washington, DC, April 14, 1950, pp. 39, 35 (pp. 50 and 55 in the photocopy of the original document).
28. On Korea, see McCormick, *America's Half Century*, pp. 100–6.
29. *FRUS*: "Diplomatic Papers, The Conferences at Cairo and Teheran," pp. 448–9.
30. The twenty thousand figure comes from a report from Kennan to Dean Acheson. See *FRUS*, 1945, The British Commonwealth, the Far East, Volume VI, 895.01/4– 1745: Telegram, Kennan to the Secretary of State; Moscow, April 17, 1945.
31. *FRUS*, 740.00119 Control (Korea)/11–1345; The Assistant Secretary of War (McCloy) to the Under Secretary of State (Acheson), Washington, DC, November 13, 1945. Regarding the Japanese remaining in the Military Government of the south, see two items: first, *FRUS* 740.00119 Control (Korea)/1–2246: Telegram, Benninghoff to the Secretary of State, Seoul, January 22, 1946; second, a study favorable to the US role in South Korea, but also informative: Hakjoon Kim, "The American Military Government in South Korea, 1945–48: Its Formation, Policies and Legacies," *Asian Perspective*, vol. 12, no. 1 (Spring–Summer 1988), pp. 61–64.
32. *FRUS*, 740.00119, Control (Korea)/11–245: Telegram, Lieutenant General John R. Hodge (in Seoul) to General of the Army Douglas MacArthur, at Tokyo, November 2, 1945.
33. See CIA document "Implementation of Soviet Objectives in Korea," dated November 18, 1947. Available online: cia.gov/readingroom/docs/DOC_0000256631.pdf (accessed September 21, 2019).
34. Chalmers Johnson, *Blowback: The Costs and Consequences of American Empire* (New York: Henry Holt, 2000), pp. 98–100.
35. McCormick, *America's Half Century*, p. 103.
36. Bruce Cumings, "On the Strategy and Morality of American Nuclear Policy in Korea, 1950 to the Present," *Social Science Japan Journal*, vol. 1, no. 1 (April 1998), p. 58 and pp. 57–70, *passim*.

37. The quote is found on p. 61 in the above article by Cumings and is drawn from journalist Reginald Thompson's book, *Cry Korea: The Korean War, A Reporter's Notebook* (London: Macdonald, 1951).

38. Mark Clapson, *The Blitz Companion: Aerial Warfare, Civilians and the City since 1911* (London: University of Westminster Press, 2019), p. 152.

39. For the arrays of estimates, see "Death Tolls for the Major Wars and Atrocities of the Twentieth Century" at http://necrometrics.com/20c1m.htm#Ko (accessed November 6, 2019). The 20 percent estimate is from Hugh Dean, *The Korean War: 1945–1953* (San Francisco, CA: China Books and Periodicals, 1999), p. 149.

40. See Dong-Choon Kim, "Forgotten War, Forgotten Massacres: The Korean War (1950–1953) as Licensed Mass Killings," *Journal of Genocide Research*, 6, no. 4 (2004), pp. 523–44.

41. On the complex political dynamics of the First Indochina War, see Stein Tønnesson, "The Longest Wars: Indochina 1945–75," *Journal of Peace Research*, vol. 22, no. 1 (March 1985), pp. 12–18. On the contrasting political economies of the northern versus southern parts of Indochina, see Jeffrey Paige, *Agrarian Revolution: Social Movements and Export Agriculture in the Underdeveloped World* (New York: Free Press, 1975), pp. 278–333.

42. The OSS was the precursor to the American CIA, which was founded in September 1947.

43. The main material for the above account is drawn from Tønnesson, "The Longest Wars: Indochina 1945–75," pp. 12–18.

44. *FRUS*, 1948, The Far East and Australasia, Vol. VI. Executive Secretariat Files, Lot 57 D–649; "Department of State Policy Statement on Indochina," September 27, 1948.

45. On the concerted character of British anti-Communism, see FO 959/41, "Anti-Communist Policy."

46. May 31, 1949. Capitalizations of " 'Ho Chi Minh" are in the original.

47. This statement from Secretary of State Acheson, May 8, 1948, is quoted in "Editorial Note" in document 515 (see https://history.state.gov/historicaldocuments/frus1950v06/d515).

48. Ibid; also document 519, "Acting Secretary of State (James E. Webb) to the Secretary of Defense (Johnson)," May 16, 1950. See also Neil Sheehan, Hedrick Smith, E. W. Kenworthy, and Fox Butterfield, *The Pentagon Papers: The Secret History of the Vietnam War* (New York: Bantam Books, 1971), pp. 9–10; and document 2, "1952 Policy Statement by U.S. on Goals in Southeast Asia," pp. 27–32, and *passim*.

49. Tonnissen, "The Longest Wars," p. 18.

50. *FRUS*, East Asia, document 522, "The Ambassador in France (David K. E. Bruce) to the Secretary of State," Paris, May 31, 1950.

51. *FRUS*, 1952–1954, East Asia and the Pacific, Volume XII, Part 1. Report to the National Security Council by the Executive Secretary (Lay), "United States Objectives and Courses of Action With Respect to Communist Aggression in Southeast Asia," Washington, DC, February 13, 1952.

Cold War Bipolarities versus Complex Realities: Examples from Africa and the Middle East

It is important and instructive to not fixate on the fixations of anti-Communism. In China, North Korea, and Indochina the various currents of leftist politics got subsumed under some combination of Soviet or Chinese Communist influence and in that respect constituted a set of relatively clear and specific leftist targets. But at that time as well as now, politically and analytically, the angle of a "bipolar" world does little to no justice to the varieties of socioeconomic, political, and cultural life throughout most of the world at the time, which, in effect and by intent, presented resistance against unbridled capitalism, colonialism, imperialist propaganda, and other forms of exploitation. The Non-Aligned Movement (NAM), which was organized by several Third World leaders (Tito, Sukarno, Nasser, Nkrumah, Nehru, and others) as a hopeful means of navigating a third way between the two superpowers, is only the most obvious reference to the complexities of the world at the time that spontaneously or deliberately defied the bipolarity. However, given what happens in the late twentieth and early twenty-first centuries, it is also important to keep in mind that, in foreign and domestic policy circles across the liberal capitalist states, the preoccupation with anti-Communism was often, though not always, strikingly accompanied by praise for various forms of social democracy in Western Europe, for the "liberal consensus" in the United States, and for cooperatives and traditional communal forms of property and social relations wherever they existed—just as long as they were non- or anti-Communist. In the late 1940s and early 1950s, the American CIA had a favorite acronym for some of that vast swathe of the world's sociopolitical spectrum, the "NCL"—the Noncommunist Left. US and British intelligence services attempted to maintain and further drive whatever wedges they could between the Communist and noncommunist left areas of the political spectrum, both at home and abroad. It was challenging enough for them to do so domestically in the more economically advanced states, and it is clear that there were serious "terminological" differences, say, between the US "China hands," on the one hand, and the doctrinaire anti-Communists, on the other, as to how to exactly describe the political character of the Chinese Communists.

However, as British and American analysts admitted, it was often downright vexing for them to formulate and disseminate propaganda across much of the Third World, which composed most of the world's peoples, so many of them colonized by the advanced capitalist imperialist states. The colonized worlds featured wide varieties of non-modern social, political, and cultural structures that were difficult enough to understand for western academics and professional political analysts. But for imperialist Cold War propaganda purposes, what appeared to function sufficiently in the great power states often did not do so in the colonized worlds. The further from the centers of imperial power—not just literal geographical distances, but also the distances stemming from social differences within states or colonial territories—the greater were the tendencies toward cognitive and political gaps, ambiguities, and radical instabilities. The Cold War terminology of strategic bipolarity—Communism versus anti-Communism—had grown out of the rivalries between, and was current within, the great power states, including both superpowers, but to the extent the terms were used in the colonies, they certainly did not translate as the intelligence services wished. In China, in the views of the foreign policy establishments of Britain and especially the United States, the meanings and significances of the terms were nearly turned on their heads. Elsewhere, in most of the Third World, translating the terminology and propagating it effectively in multiple languages and political-cultural milieus often became as much of a stretch as the overall efforts to maintain colonial power, which, never stable in the first place, was now crumbling.

In his *Scenes from the Anti-Nazi War*, the prominent historian of Africa, Basil Davidson, tells of how Field Marshall Jan Smuts, prime minister of proto-apartheid South Africa during the Second World War, warned his close friend Winston Churchill about developments in Axis-occupied Italy and Southeastern Europe in August of 1943. Smuts warned that "with politics let loose upon those peoples, we may have a wave of disorder and whole-sale Communism set going all over those parts of Europe." On the still larger level, Smuts warned, "The Bolshevization of a broken and ruined Europe remains a definite possibility, to be guarded against by supply of food and work and interim Allied control." Churchill considered the comment "prescient."[1] Davidson remarked that Smuts should know what he was talking about, since he presided over one of the most racially oppressive states in the world. The two racist state leaders, one an internal colonialist, the other a global imperialist, certainly knew what was going on in terms of their own power positions and threats to them. Along with various colleagues in the recent past and near future, they would largely succeed in suppressing and containing the radical left in Western Europe, including Greece. At least for the time being, they could do little about the strategic facts of Soviet power over Russia and Eastern Europe, or the strength of Communism in China. But now the war against the radical left was, in a sense, pushed deeper into the third world, which was full of its own sorts of specific conditions for radicalization that had been growing since the nineteenth century. Though Britain and United States basically agreed on maximal use of the non-Communist left against the main enemy, significant tensions also existed between the two powers, as one was a crumbling colonial empire and the other an emergent economic, financial, and military superstate. Both sides were evident in distinctive ways in British and US affairs in Africa, as they had been in East Asia.

British and US Anti-Communism in Parts of Sub-Saharan Africa

Extensive discussions took place at middle and upper foreign policy levels in the late 1940s–early 1950s about how, for "publicity" or propaganda purposes worldwide, to define and present the "enemy" of Communism to peoples who, for diverse reasons, may have found it an appealing idea. Peoples across the world were targeted, including various peoples of Africa under colonial rule. A November 1949 British report entitled "Communism in Nigeria" concluded that

> one has only to read the contributions of Nigerians to the local press and study the phraseology of the memoranda and petitions they submit to Government to realize the extent to which this insidious propaganda is beginning to take hold of their minds, and it is now accepted that the stage where Government must take active measures to combat this evil before the interests of the country are materially damaged by those who are being duped into the belief that the easiest way to reach their political goal is to ride there on the back of the communist tiger.

While an American CIA report from the same period stated that, in Nigeria, "Communism is almost non-existent," the British report conveyed palpable anxiety that it was gaining momentum. They may have seen something that was not there, or kept a better watch on the situation because it was one of "their" territories. In either case, the author of the British report was John S. Macpherson, colonial governor general of Nigeria; he continued to explain how negative messages about Russian Communism were generally difficult to sell in an Africa where most peoples were still under the yokes of the European imperialist states. He candidly presented what he saw as the obstacles to a successful propaganda campaign:

> First … the conviction that alone of the European or Western Powers, the Soviet Union has sincerely and successfully waged war against the colour-bar and has in fact eliminated all forms of racial discrimination within its territories. This shining virtue tends to offset, in African eyes, the great bulk of the crimes that are charged against the Soviet Union by its enemies. The second conviction is that whatever form of tyranny may exist within the Soviet Union and its satellite states, it cannot be nearly as bad as the tyranny believed to be practiced by the White communities in South Africa – a tyranny very close to home which the African resents much more than he does the distant tyranny of the Kremlin,

and

> to denounce the activities of the Soviet Government and its puppets while remaining silent about South Africa inevitably smacks, to the African, of hypocrisy.

A final conviction from the colonial Governor was that "in her struggle for freedom Nigeria is entitled to accept help from any quarter, no matter how mixed the motives that prompt the offer." He then suggested, without much confidence, "It will require the greatest skill to develop an anti-Communist propaganda that will remove or by-pass these obstacles but I am convinced that the attempt must be made" and "the target of all information and propaganda must be the literate African population."[2] Yet there was concern about that population, too, especially the members of the elites who found a chance to study in the United States and the UK. While the colonial governor of Sierra Leone, G. Beresford-Stooke, saw little cause for concern in his territory, he warned that

> perhaps the most effective point of infiltration for informed communist doctrine would seem to be through the contamination of African students studying in the United Kingdom and the United States. Our experience indicates that it is in the United Kingdom in particular that the source of Communist inspiration is to be found, and it is in applying counter measures to the source that the most effective results can be expected.

Furthermore, "in any case it is not doctrinaire communism which is the present danger but the likelihood of growing discontent and disaffection stirred up by Cominform misrepresentation of our colonial aims and policy."[3] However, as shown with frustration by the governor of British Somaliland, Gerald Reece, it was feared that doctrinaire communism also had its potentially broad appeal. First, Reese vented that "in a country like this it is exceedingly hard to know how best to deal with Communist propaganda." To his colleagues in the Colonial and Foreign Offices, he questioned whether or not "we should substitute the word Bolshevism for Communism, because some Somalis are already commenting on the fact that Communism, using the word in its original sense, is obviously a good idea because it involves a leveling of the classes and a form of existence closely akin to that of their own in olden times."[4] The Foreign Office's response came through Ralph Murray, Director of the Information Research Department that was specifically set up for anti-Communist propaganda purposes. Murray wrote, "Using 'Bolshevism' would be "ill-advised," because it suggested "old-fashioned reaction of the '20s and an anarchist revolutionary creed. It is important that we should not be tarred with suspicion of old-fashioned reaction." Murray was a committed social democrat, presumably not a fan of the far more *laissez-faire* American economic model, but along with leading Americans, a staunch anti-Communist. Evoking the negativity of the anti-"Bolshevik" reactionary politics of the 1920s made sense from a Labor government appointee, as many of the top Foreign and Colonial Office figures were at the time.[5] They were also basically well attuned to the importance of the varieties of social and cultural forms across the Third World. The problem, of course, was that peoples over whom they were assigned to maintain colonial power were socially, politically, and culturally different from themselves but also defying their power with uneven, but increasing and undeniable, success. Yet Reese persisted with his suggestion of using "Bolshevism" instead of "Communism" in a way that illustrated both the difficulties of general political surveillance and of distinguishing anti-colonialist nationalism from anti-colonialist communism—let alone any other forms of anti-colonialism. Of course, these difficulties pervaded politics across the colonized worlds and in the seats of power in London and especially Washington, DC. The colonial governor resorted to dictionary definitions, which described Communism as the " 'vesting of property in the community', with 'each member working to his capacity and receiving according to his wants.' " He reiterated how very good this sounded to ordinary Somalis. On the other hand, a Bolshevik was defined as "an advocate of proletarian dictatorship by soviets, or a Russian communist." In the end, Reese called for vigilance, citing a memo from an officer of the East Africa High Commission that warned how "subtle and clever" the Communist agitators could be, as they start off very quietly, yet insidiously, and are suddenly leading an effective general strike, if not something even more threatening. He refers to a recent situation in Britain's Kenya Colony: "You may remember that although it was almost certain that Jomo Kenyatta had organized the big strike at Mombasa a few years ago, it was found quite impossible to prove anything against him in this connection because in his actions and talk he was so very subtle and clever."[6] Kenyatta was an anti-colonialist nationalist, not a Communist, despite assumptions and persecutions to the contrary; nor was he a lead organizer of the Mau Mau Rebellion of 1952–60. But he was definitely an enemy of British colonial authorities, who did not understand or ultimately control him.[7]

In July 1950, Governor Reece again requested "an alternative to the word 'Communism' for use in publicity in Africa," this time to S. H. Evans, Britain's Acting Director of Information Services. Evans's response was that the words "Communism" and "Communist" were "capable of a quite definite association with traditional forms of communal life such as exist in many parts of Africa, in the Pacific and elsewhere, or with a naïve conception of the perfect social order based on a literal adherence to the precepts of the New Testament." He suggested, "Semi-sophisticated Somali's cannot understand why communism is bad when it appears to provide for a manner of life to which many of them are accustomed or which appears to be right, and there are many other territories where a similar point of view might be expressed at any moment." There was also the problem of translating "Communism" into native languages, where, "almost invariably such a system would have to mean a system which places all people on the same level of personal wealth and status ... which would be descriptive of everyday life among 99% of people with a communal system." Evans was troubled that "we are really faced with ... the task of convincing the Colonial people that the word 'Communism' as used by the Communists, does not mean what they think it means." The best he could suggest was the term "Russian Communism," while stating that he and his colleagues "do not consider it by any means ideal."[8]

Expounding on the same themes and line of discussion, Juxon Barton of the Colonial Office offered a wide-ranging anthropology, along with lamentations about those that took the New Testament literally:

In the Colonies we have various stages of communal life which ranges from the pure type in the Pacific and amongst pastoral tribes in East Africa, e.g., the Somali and Masai, to the most individualistic systems in certain parts of West Africa and to some degree in Malaya. Moreover, it is to be remembered that with the extensive growth of missionary teaching there is very frequently a most literal adherence to the precepts of the New Testament, and I think we shall soon have the natives pointing out that the Disciples had all things in common. Putting it in another way, what we are about to do is set out on an extensive campaign against a debased political and administrative philosophy the present names for which will inevitably be associated in the minds of all but the really educated natives with what is thought good in their own methods of living.

Barton goes on to address another crucial and related question:

I have been trying to translate Communism into the native languages with which I am acquainted and invariably the translation would have to mean a system which places all people on the same level of personal status and wealth, and I find that in Swahili this is indeed the classical translation. Quite obviously we will get into most frightful difficulties if we use a word capable of that translation, for it would be descriptive of ordinary life amongst 99% of people with a communal system. Moreover, it is not only a question of our using a word not capable of favorable translation into a native language. Another unfortunate corollary is that when many African natives are attempting to describe some form of philosophy they often do so by saying, "The religion of...."

The exasperated Barton concludes, wishfully, "The best words would be either 'Stalin-Stalinist' or 'Russia-Russian' or 'Kremlin-Kremlinist', all of which are incapable of mistranslation or misinterpretation."[9]

For the authorities that ruled them, the colonial territories were prime territory for confusion, desperation, and paranoia over who were the enemies. It was horribly easy to resort to indiscriminate and violent repression to supposedly solve this problem, as the British did against the anti-colonialist Mau Mau movement, or the Kenya Land and Freedom Army (KFLA), as they called themselves. In that case, the British also fell back on an updated variant of Social Darwinist pseudoscientific ethnography—the "ethnopsychiatry" of Dr. John Colin Carothers—that argued that traditional African peoples in the first stages of literacy and some degree of modernization were extremely inclined toward primal savagery. It was a perfect feed into a rationale for a vicious crackdown, but they also made use of tactics they had honed against the Malayan anti-colonialist insurgents, many of whom were Communists.

On that front, as explained in a speech by Malcolm Macdonald, commissioner-general for the United Kingdom in South East Asia and later the last colonial governor of Kenya,

we can kill, as we are doing to quite good effect in Malaya now, Communist terrorists by bullets; but we cannot kill Communist ideas by any military weapons alone. We can only defeat them by counter-ideas, by better ideas of our own. We have got to prove to the peoples of South East Asia that Communist ideology and Communist practice will be just as tragic an experience for them as it is proving to be for many people in Eastern Europe, and that their salvation lies in the Democratic camp.

The pride Macdonald showed in killing the Malayan anti-colonialist "Communist terrorists" with bullets was reflective of a deeply rooted and deadly pathology, which was anti-leftist, but not exclusively so. Yet, in some other respects, the commissioner-general was right; they needed superior ideas to win these wars, but they would also have needed to implement them in in practice. If the practical versions of the ideas of the "Democratic camp," or the "democratic way of life," were to be found at all, it was far away in the "mother country," not in Malaya or the Kenya Colony. In both of those places, the British ultimately resorted to bullets and other vicious means of force, including torture.[10] It was as far a cry as possible from the ideas and fruits of the "democratic way of life."

In Malaya's British-declared Emergency of 1948–60, there were actual Communists targeted, many of them ethnic Chinese; in the Kenya Colony Emergency, there is little to no evidence that Communists had any significant involvement in or influence upon the Mau Mau uprising. However, suspicions and assumptions exactly to the contrary were rife within British colonial, settler colonial, and allied circles across Africa. According to A. S. Cleary, "South Africa, along with the majority of white settler communities scattered throughout Africa, portrayed the revolt as something between full-blown Communist insurgency and Asian and/or communist instigated anti-White terrorism." Oliver Lyttleton, secretary of state for the colonies from 1951 to 1954, considered rumors entirely credible that the Soviet Union supported the rebellion through their embassy in Ethiopia. He denied this in parliamentary proceedings but then reiterated the same point in his memoirs published in 1962. Meanwhile, a secret 1954 British intelligence report alleged the uprising to be "directed and financed by Indian Communists."' But, according to Cleary, such allegations "could only be damaging to the United Kingdom's primary aim of shoring up its monopoly over the international relations of the colony, and so they were quietly pushed to one side."[11] Anti-Communism was undoubtedly a highly operational tenet of British colonial policy at the time, one not easily separable from imperialist anti-nationalism. The worldview of most of the colonial officials saw the Mau Mau as Communist and nationalist. While those policies and dispositions against those political forms drove the crackdown against the Mau Mau, there was official denial that communism, nationalism, or any combination of the two, were actual factors in the uprising. Ironically enough, that denial jibes somewhat with postcolonial scholarship on the movement, at least since the 1990s, which tends to downplay the value of either of those historical categories for understanding it.[12] Instead, there are more particularistic cultural explanations for the rebellion that diverge clearly from the studies used by the British. The result is a complex irony, namely, that British colonial authorities assumed the existence of something that was not there, only to deny that assumption officially and resort to classic nineteenth-century nationalist-imperialist pseudoscience about savagery. Equipped accordingly with the work of Carothers, Louis B. Leaky, and others, they claimed the Mau Mau were nothing but impulsive primal savages, mainly fighting each other and eminently controllable. They were said not to be Communist, not nationalist, not inspired by Indian leftists of any sort; they had no connection with or similarity to any other anti-colonialist movements elsewhere. The colonialists' approach exuded the insecurity and desperation of a declining imperialist state, as did the violence they meted out to their enemies. As for the character of the Mau Mau rebellion, the official explanation for it was presented in a racialist vein in the Corfield Report, while the historical and anthropological explanation of it tends to stress the severe violation of the cultural dignity of those involved in it, and their militant efforts to recover it. Anti-Communism was on the minds of the colonial authorities and surely helped to fuel the aggressive crackdown on the Mau Mau. It was a type of fiction that helped to shape the hard realities of the Kenya Colony.

But something more fundamental was going on in Kenya that ties in with everything else in this study: the displacement of peoples from their traditional relationships and environments due to one form or another of modernization. This form was "colonial modernization." As it had been one way or another in most of the rest of the world, the general process was driven and sustained by capitalist economic dynamics but also selectively guided by classical liberal political-economic policies that, in this case, supported the white settlers and facilitated the exploitation of the non-white colonized. Facilitated politically by the colonial government and the newly built railway lines within the colony, white settlers expropriated some of the best potential agricultural lands in the Kenyan highlands and turned them into coffee plantations producing for export. The settlers got Black laborers to work the plantations as tenant farmers or wage laborers. For the sake of the settlers, but rationalized as a "civilizing" experience for the laborers, the latter were displaced from their traditional lands and communities and subordinated on and around the plantations. The lands they now worked were often those held in common by their ancestors in precolonial times. While people were ripped from their original social fabrics, they still did not forget or deny who or what they were in their own pasts and vis-à-vis their colonial masters. Those that joined the Mau Mau were mostly ethnically Kikuyu, but also Embu and Meru—all from the central highlands. The movement was very specific to the area and not a widespread popular national, nationalist, or nationalist-Communist movement. But its goals lined up with those of nationalists and Communists across the colonized worlds: to drive out the colonial powers and somehow regain their lost dignity and independence. The Mau Mau movement was a response to top-down, rapid, and highly racialized colonial-style modernization. Beginning in the late 1940s, some members of the subjugated group organized and rebelled, and the white settlers and colonial authorities were compelled to defeat and destroy them. Especially from 1952 to 1954, the fighting was ferocious all around, until the British colonial forces gained the upper hand and held it in the face of diminishing attacks that lasted until 1960. In 1955, the Colony and Protectorate of Kenya printed a study of the Mau Mau by Dr. J. C. Carothers, the "ethnopsychiatrist" and colleague of Marshall McCluhan. Carothers explained that Mau Mau "arose from the development of an anxious conflictual situation in people who, from contact with the alien culture, had lost the supportive and constraining influences of their own culture, yet had not lost their 'magic' modes of thinking. It arose from the exploitation of this situation by relatively sophisticated egotists." By taking certain oaths, Carothers argued, the men cut themselves off completely from their traditional culture and embraced and found solidarity in utter savagery. The study also stated that it "seems most likely that hypnosis plays a part in these assemblies" where the oaths are administered and argues that men with the same psychological makeup in Britain would be in asylums for the mentally ill.[13]

Captured Mau Mau fighters were detained in "rehabilitation" camps and often subjected to severe torture. In the notorious Hola incident of 1959, camp guards beat eleven of the rebels to death for resisting the forced regime of hard "redemptive" labor. Some argue this was the moment that the colonial "civilizing mission" in Kenya, and even generally, was finished. While this is plausible, it is widely believed to have been the final catalyst for the Kenyan independence movement and for the British to let go of the colony. In defeat, the Mau Mau rebels suffered 11,503 deaths; British and colonial forces lost 167 troops and 1,819 "loyalist" civilians, including Africans and Asians. Thirty-two European civilians were killed in the fighting.[14] In June 1963, Jomo Kenyatta—one of the "relatively sophisticated egotists" referred to by Carothers in 1955 and imprisoned by the colonial government on false charges—became prime minister of a new, independent and majority-ruled Kenya. An infamous postindependence official study of the Mau Mau movement, called the Corfield Report, drew heavily from Carothers's ethnopsychiatry, as well as from the famous paleoanthropologist Louis B. Leaky. One of the conclusions of the Report was the following: "Without the freedom afforded them by a liberal Government, Jomo Kenyatta and his associates would have been unable to preach their calculated hymn of hate and to exploit, through the medium of perverted witchcraft and intimidation, the almost inevitable grievances which must accompany the rapid evolution of a primitive society."[15]

In the imperialists' discussions regarding Kenya and much of Africa, as well as regions beyond, there was frequent reference to the "communal" character of their social and cultural structures and values. This was a problem when it came to formulating and implementing anti-Communist propaganda, even where there may have been no Communism at all. In effect, if not by intent, this often involved a preemptive assault against the potential for the rival ideology and system to gain any footholds in what they referred to as "their territories." However, two things about the Mau Mau Rebellion (1952–60) go to the heart of the matter: first, *the* most crucial assault in the Kenya Colony that created the conditions for the rebellion was precisely against those "communal" social forms found to be so culturally and politically problematic for the anti-Communist propagandists. The communal forms had to be destroyed to create the labor for the Kenya Colony to thrive, yet that assault created social forms and politics that the colonizers believed to be either actually or potentially communist. Second, the Mau Mau forces were brutally defeated militarily by the British and their local allies but politically crucial in leading Kenya to independence and majority rule. In other words, the colonizers created the conditions for the Mau Mau rebellion, which many colonial officials saw one way or another as Communist, repressed it ruthlessly, then decided— or realized—their colonial power there was no longer practically or morally viable. Like many situations across the colonized world, it was a chronologically condensed as well as distinctively violent version of what happened originally in the few cases of the transition to capitalism in what became the "advanced capitalist world." But, the conditions were crucially different, and their dynamics became too much for the colonizers to handle. From an "internal colonialism" angle, elites in the advanced capitalist states for the most part managed to hold onto their power and privilege, instead of getting overthrown or ousted by any subordinated groups and classes.[16]

Algeria

The 1954 victory of the Viet Minh over French colonial forces at Dien Bien Phu inspired anti-colonialism across the world. But outside of Indochina, the impact was perhaps nowhere as clear, important, and immediate as it was in Algeria. Ferhat Abbas was one of the leading figures within the National Liberation Front (FLN) that led the liberation struggle to Algeria's independence in 1962, when he reflected, "Dien Bien Phu was more than a military victory. It is a symbol for all time. It was the Battle Valmy of the colonial peoples, an affirmation of Asian and African man against the European and a confirmation of universal human rights. At Dien Bien Phu France lost its sole claim to a presence in Indochina – the right of the strongest."[17] Several years later, Jean Captain Pouget, formerly of the French Expeditionary Corps in Indochina reflected, "The fall of Dien Bien Phu marked the end of the colonial period and the beginning of the era of third-world independence. Today there is not a revolt, rebellion or uprising in Asia, Africa or America that fails to invoke General Giap's victory. Dien Bien Phu has become decolonization's 14th of July."[18] Each of these testimonies from mutually opposed figures on the global stage was cast generally; it was a major defeat for France as an imperialist state and victory for anti-colonialism worldwide. However, for the sake of highlighting the virtually fixed character of American anti-Communism worldwide at the time—blind to so much except the real, potential, or imagined "Communist threat"—it is also important to consider the more particular political character of the Indochinese victory within a comparative framework.

The Viet Minh was a Communist-led leftwing nationalist organization and movement, which evidently secured American support for the French war against it. The Algerian FLN had a far stronger nationalist, noncommunist anti-colonialist leadership and composition, which might have elicited sympathetic treatment from the United States, especially given its larger political-cultural context. In January 1951, the CIA reported that Communism "was hampered throughout North Africa by a hostile Mohammedanism" and by "the vigorous native nationalist movements." In Spain's Moroccan and Saharan colonial territories, "the Franco government has successfully suppressed all possibly Communistic activities." Even by May 1952, the American ambassador to Egypt—where Nasser was two months away from leading a successful coup against the British-backed Egyptian monarchy—reported that France had Algeria under control, and that there was little to no Communist influence on Algerian anti-colonialist opposition.[19] But by September, the CIA reported that Algerian nationalists and Communists were showing a willingness to ally with one another against the French. In fact, by this point the Algerian Communist Party (PCA) had come out in favor of independence and was therefore already tacitly allied with the nationalists.[20] Suspicions of nationalist-Communist cooperation persisted into the critical time of mid-1954, yet they tended to be inconsistent and often just nebulous. The French governor-general of Algeria, Roger Leonard, downplayed the suspicions. According to the American ambassador to Egypt, the Governor claimed that "he has the local nationalistic parties under control," though "there may be trouble stirred up by terrorists from abroad"—alluding to "recent exposure by his police of Spanish Communist activities." As for the French defeat at Dien Bien Phu, it would "undoubtedly have repercussions in Morocco and in Tunisia," and "it was inevitable that there would be some repercussions in Algeria," because it would be taken as an "indication of the weakening of French control, with the resulting increased possibility of success for nationalistic activity." However, Leonard was said to have no concern about domestic nationalist or Communist unrest; the latter "were not in a position to do anything," even though they might create trouble if they get a chance. He said that "if difficulty arose it would come from terrorists sent into Algeria from abroad" such as from the Arab League or from Communists. He told the US ambassador that "his people had unearthed in the last week a very definite resurgence of Spanish Communist activity in Algeria. He said that the movement had been a very closely coordinated one in which each cell contained only about three people. Nevertheless, his police had discovered it and, he believed, had suppressed further activity."[21] Two things stand out about Leonard's remarks: first, given that the Algerian revolution was less than six months away from boiling over, his sparse awareness of the potentials for unrest was astonishing; second, since at least the specters of Communism were raised by him and the Americans, however much they were sometimes downplayed, there was a convenient array of pretexts for the two great power states to do what they wanted. The default came into play: anti-Communist geopolitics for the United States, which meant strategically securing the southern Mediterranean and, in turn, defending France's colonialist war against the Algerian independence movement.[22]

Though John F. Kennedy was firmly lined up with domestic anti-Communism, joining the chorus with Joe McCarthy and others of criticism and suspicion of the State Department because it "lost China" and was probably infiltrated with "reds," he still showed some signs of being outside of that default zone of his country's foreign policy in the 1950s. In April 1954, midway through the distant battle for Dien Bien Phu, he warned against US "involvement" in Indochina. He spoke critically of French colonial rule and in favor of an Indochinese independence movement supported by "the people." He said that uncompromising French rule only presented an opportunity to Ho Chi Minh. As seen above, the United States was already deeply vested in the French colonial cause, though this was not widely known. Kennedy may or may not have known about it, but his criticism of the Eisenhower administration's support for the French war was a worthwhile voice of opposition. In July 1957, he delivered a similarly principled and critical stand against the same administration for its support of France's war on Algeria's independence movement. He made a plausible case for the *zeitgeist*, pleading with those that disagreed with him to realize "that man's desire to be free and independent is the most powerful force in the world today." He meant to present an enlightened anti-Communism, arguing that denying freedom to those aspiring to it would only play into Communist hands. The results in North Africa could be as disastrous as, or worse than, what happened up to that point in Indochina. Kennedy's views did not prevail; he seemed principled but also detached from realities in Indochina. Looking ahead, further skepticism is warranted based on his Bay of Pigs invasion of Cuba in 1961 and his responsibility for anti-Communist "mission creep" in Vietnam. Unsurprisingly, it was similar with regard to Algeria. According to Miloud Barkaoui, once Kennedy became president, he assumed a hardline US cold warrior stance toward the matter. He wanted the French war to end, but only on terms that fitted within the developing US dominated strategic framework. Kennedy "went to great lengths to press for a settlement but through direct negotiations between France and the Algerian nationalist leaders and away from the U.N. or any other international organization; a settlement that would perforce guarantee France and the West's strategic interests in the region and keep the new state out of the Soviet sphere of influence."[23] This is not to pin something on Kennedy that was primarily Charles de Gaulle's and France's responsibility, while US policy toward it was mostly the doing of the Eisenhower administration. Their concern was that French submission to the FLN would cause unrest within France and play into the hands of the Communists. Still, with the power of the presidency, Kennedy came late to the Algerian question and shed any signs of dissent from the party line.

The course of the Algerian war was vicious, notoriously rife with atrocities and torture on all sides. The potential was realized for the explosiveness of all the society's social divisions combined. The war was racialist, classist, religious, individually traumatic, and pathological; a powerful minority—approximately one million—overprivileged French and other European settler *colons* faced off against ten times as many socially diverse native Algerians. Four to five hundred thousand French troops fought tens of thousands of FLN guerilla fighters across the country. Estimates of the war's total death toll range from three hundred thousand to one million, the vast majority native Algerians.[24] The late-nineteenth-century thrust of French imperialism, often justified as a necessary means of supposedly solving the "social problem" of the new working classes domestically, ultimately produced a bloodbath in Algeria and nearly a collapse of capitalist democracy within France.

The Middle East: Fighting the Cold War, Planting Seeds for the "War on Terror"

Getting into another part of the world where the dynamics of the Cold War and anti-colonialism played out in great and often painful drama, a reminder is in order as to what was happening on the grander historical scales of propaganda and reality. US and British anti-Communist propaganda presented a bright picture of their own societies, cultures, and political systems, relentlessly denigrating their enemies' systems, while excusing their allies' travesties. This would be expected from any state power with formidable enemies, but in these cases and others, vis-à-vis Soviet Communism, the capitalist democracies could tout some impressive domestic accomplishments. While they were not justified in taking credit for capitalism itself, they did so anyway, at least implicitly. But that economic system obviously turned into a profound and sustaining precedent for modernity in all its vicissitudes, just as it generated greater relative material comforts for more and more ordinary people within the few countries where it emerged. Despite its booms and busts and inherent mal-distributions of public and private goods and opportunities, the system had a proven capacity to "deliver the goods." But liberal capitalism could also sing its own praises for the expansions of civil rights and electoral representative politics that dignified larger and larger portions of their populations. These were by no means automatic accompaniments to capitalist production. To the extent they had developed, they were the results of concerted and courageous social and political movements, hard-fought battles, and sacrifices. These things provided substance and viability to the propaganda points that were also relative to the repression and greater hardships experienced by the peoples of the Soviet Union, the East European states then under its domination, and the peasants and workers of China, Southeast Asia, and wherever else leftist politics appealed. Soviet problems, for example, included poor developmental legacies, damages sustained in the First World War, the civil war, foreign interventions, and threats of more of the same. This is not the place to attempt to do justice to the question of how those legacies helped lay the precedents for the terrors and crimes of Stalinism, but it is undeniable that the extremely challenging beginnings of the Soviet regime, combined with the flaws it displayed as a political system in the early-to-mid 1920s, gave rise to Stalinism. This whole line of discussion is important, but the argument running throughout this book is that there was and is also a very dark core dynamic to the system of capitalist production and liberalized markets. It has been operative within the few societies where those combined systems were strong, as well as elsewhere in the world where they were and are weak and subjugated by the strong states. American propaganda relentlessly masked and denied these problems, which are just too deadly and dangerous to ignore.

Naiveté about the problems is fully evident within the United States, from where it would be transplanted internationally through a number of channels running mainly from the State Department. "America is the answer to Communist propaganda abroad," declared the head of a State Department propaganda chief in December of 1948 at a gathering of the Institute on World Affairs in Riverside, California. "The existence of this country is the answer, in so far as this country is known." His purpose was to promote the newly established US Information and Educational Exchange Service that would back the broadcasting of US propaganda, mainly by radio—"Radio Free Europe" and many more like it—across most of the world. Given his position at the State Department, this was not just an opinion from a genuine believer and cheerleader, but a universal proposition, delivered to a community of interested residents of Southern California, of the sort that could justify anti-Communist interventionism across the world, as applicable in Southeast Asia as it was everywhere else, including the Middle East. Given the perceived potentials for Communism everywhere, the United States would have to answer it everywhere, by all possible means. Though the British were losing the global reach that the United States was gaining, they still reached far and wide, showing great compatibility with the United States on the propaganda front, namely,

> H.M.G. have decided that the developing communist threat to the whole fabric of Western civilization necessitates the adoption of a new publicity policy designed

primarily to give a lead and a stimulus to all truly democratic elements in Western Europe in withstanding the inroads of communism. The new policy will, with special variations, apply also in the Middle East and possibly in certain Far Eastern countries.

Sounding like a *bona fide* bourgeois Leninist, Mr. Bateman of the Foreign Office revealed, "The main target will be the broad masses of workers and peasants in Europe and the Middle East." He wrote, "Our principles offer the best and most efficient way of life," that "this ideology has its basis in the value of civil liberty and human rights," and that "we shall make a positive appeal to democratic and Christian principles."[25]

However, the problem in the foreign policies of the powerful capitalist states was the ease with which these principles and policies could be jettisoned in favor of cynical strategic moves for resources and transport corridors anywhere in the world, so often justified by real, potential, or fictional leftwing threats. Such moves were to be highly and distinctively consequential for peoples across the world, not least in the Middle East. In the longer run—at least into the 1990s–2010s—the consequences continued to reverberate within that region, but also hit the "homelands" of the imperialist states and some of their allies. The region was as complicated as any other but distinguished mainly by a number of high-stakes strategic and historical features that never ceased to be in play: vast untapped reserves of oil, the waterways to transport them (especially the Suez Canal and the Straits of Hormuz in and out of the Persian Gulf), and the border with the Soviet Union that stretched from Turkey in the west to Iran and Pakistan to the east. It was divided between Arabs, Turks, Persians, rival sects of Islam, and, as of 1948, the new state of Israel. Its Zionist core dated back to Britain's Balfour Declaration of 1917, which promised a homeland for the Jews in Palestine that would come at no expense to the Palestinians or any others in the area. All of these peoples and states, including the Israelis, had deep-seated reasons dating back to the Crusades, if not earlier, to distrust the great power Christian states of Europe and North America. It was historical terrain that made the imperialist and interventionist politics of the twentieth century and since—typically anti-leftist in their justifications, as well as undeniably racist—as extremely likely as they were risky. As we will see, in its own history of the *coup* against the Mossadeq government of Iran in 1953, the CIA described the problem as "blowback."[26]

A 1950 British Foreign Office report on "Communism in the Middle East" provided a survey of the politics of the region that is useful a retrospective guide to anti-Communist "actionable intelligence." The large picture suggested there was mostly little concern about the matter, as it stated that "in most Middle Eastern countries … the communist party has gained no great degree of influence over the populations. This is due partly to the natural antipathy between Islam and Communism and partly to the repressive action taken by the governments concerned – in no country, save Israel, is there a legal communist party." The Kurds were briefly mentioned as an exception, and political leaders of the region were said to sometimes pretend communist sympathies "as a form of blackmail designed to extract concessions from the Western powers." But there was no reason to see these as anything but bluffs. There were even signs that some Middle Eastern countries—Israel, Lebanon, and Iraq—were "tending to abandon neutralism in favor of closer relations with the democracies." However, the Israel–Palestine issue presented serious challenges. There were "indications that communist propaganda may be having some effect amongst the Arab minority, arising from … what they consider to be the Israeli practice of racial discrimination." Jordan had no Communist party, but it did have "the Arab League for National Liberation," which was "purely communist" and "whose propaganda has had some effect on the very large Palestinian refugee element in the country." The Syrian Communist Party was illegal, yet sustained by "ten thousand paying members and a further number of sympathizers." The report said it was well organized and in collaboration with its Lebanese counterpart, which had around twelve thousand members, and with which it shared a joint committee. Again, the Kurds stood out with serious communist sympathies, but the report suggested that this "is largely due to the inefficiency of the Syrian Government's measures to ensure security in the Jezireh, and it is intended to draw their attention to the unfortunate results of their policy."[27] The Iraqi Communist Party, also illegal, had two thousand members and minimal influence, though again communism had significant appeal in the Kurdish areas. The United States showed some alarm about the leftist politics of the Kurds of Syria, Iraq, and Iran, which they believed were fomented by the USSR, but the British persuaded them not to be overly concerned about them.

At about the same time, there were signs of some doubt on the part of American policy advisors as to the favorability of the perception of the US status in the Middle East. The report stated,

It must be recognized that at the present time the prestige and position of the US in the Near Eastern area is at a low ebb. Such friendship and esteem as the US held at the end of World War II were quickly dissipated through our Palestine policy which in Arab eyes represented the antithesis of everything which they believed the US represented. Our support of the UK in its relations with Iraq and Egypt and our support of the French in North Africa have done nothing to increase American prestige. The bitterness engendered by these policies is deeply rooted and the attitude of the Arab States towards the US, in fact the Western world, have increasingly reflected their belief that the US support of Israel and the UK in the Near East will govern US policies, even when these are to the detriment of what the Arabs believe to be their legitimate interests. While Communism and Mohammedanism are mutually incompatible and while there is among the Arab States a degree of fear and hatred of Communism, it is necessary to realize that the attitude of the Arab States toward Communism is not based on an understanding of the ideological conflict involved, but on considerations which are more or less those of expediency.[28]

Perhaps speaking precisely of expediency, the blaring exception to the tendency on the part of the Americans and the British to downplay the potentials for the development of Communism in the Middle East was how they treated the situation in

Iran. The CIA in July 1949 published an extensive and detailed report on the Iranian Tudeh Party, presenting it as both strong and menacing:

> The Tudeh Party continues to represent a significant threat to Iranian stability. By virtue of its broad popular appeal and vigorous organizational methods, it is the only contemporary political organization in Iran which has achieved any real degree of support among the people. Moreover, despite its pretense of being only a national reform movement, the Tudeh Party is, for all practical purposes, the Iranian Communist Party and is unmistakably under Soviet influence.[29]

The Tudeh Party had been established in Tehran in September 1941 shortly after the Allied occupation of Iran that was designed to keep the "Persian corridor" open for the common war effort and keep the region's oil out of the hands of the Axis powers. The party was strongly influenced by the Persian Communist Party (PCP), which had originated in the 1920s but by that point had been effectively repressed. However, the new party was by no means a disguised reiteration of the old one. Its program was influenced by Marxism and Leninism but also included an explicit Iranian nationalist and liberal parliamentary and civil rights line that was absent from the PCP's more ethnic Azerbaijani and official Soviet orientation. After the war it remained friendly with the Soviet Union but was not subservient to it. However, with major investments and control over resources at stake, most of the leading foreign policy figures in the liberal capitalist Cold War great power states characteristically lacked any appetite for nuance. For the CIA, the small but sophisticated Tudeh Party was a "vehicle" in Iran for Soviet Communism.

Discussions between US and British officials in July 1950 showed further suspicions of the Tudeh Party. The American determination was that the

> U.S. and U.K. should, insofar as possible, assist the Iranian Government to strengthen its position and should consider what steps should be taken in the event of an uprising in Azerbaijan or a *coup d'état* by the Tudeh Party. It was agreed that the U.S. and U.K. should study the question of whether the loss of Azerbaijan alone to the Soviets would be fatal, and at exactly what point in Iran the stopline should be laid down.

Completing the picture of the threat was the hypothetical "question of demolition of Iranian oil wells in case of Soviet attack." The matter was discussed and "the U.K. representatives stated that their government is examining ways and means of dealing with this matter."[30]

The fact was that the British as well as the Persian monarchy that they presently supported faced growing popular opposition, led by the elite French- and Swiss-educated Mohammad Mossadeq. He was a prominent member of the *majlis*, Iran's parliament, who generated a major discussion of the unacceptability of foreign violations of Iranian sovereignty. For several years, Mossadeq had been arguing in parliament and publicly for the nationalization of the Anglo Iranian Oil Company (AIOC) in its entirety, claiming that the oil wealth was naturally Iran's.[31] Nor was there any doubt that oil sales revenues in Iranian hands could help finance the socialistic reforms and developments he and his supporters envisioned. The *majlis* voted to nationalize the AIOC in March 1951. Mossadeq's popularity within and outside of the government compelled Mohammad Reza Pahlavi, the Shah (king), to appoint him prime minister in April. However, given Mossadeq's agenda and its popularity, the pretexts, suspicions, and warnings for the British and the United States just kept piling up—all intertwining with the perceived and alleged politics of the Tudeh Party and the supposed Communist threat that it directly represented. A June 1951 British report from Tehran stated, "I should warn you that the present degree of infiltration of Persian Government Departments by Communist sympathizers might entail some risk of leakage of information from other countries to the Soviet Union." Similarly from the British embassy in Baghdad several days later, it was written that in Persia "there has been a crop of cover societies for Tudeh activity, a method which might well be extended to other areas." And in the British efforts to coordinate anti-Communist strategies between the Middle Eastern states, "the Iraqi Security Services would not be prepared to cooperate with their Iranian counterparts because they believe them to be penetrated by the Tudeh Party."[32]

Most prominently of all, both Churchill and Clement Atlee not only warned the United States that the Tudeh Party was a means for the USSR to infiltrate Iran, but they also appealed to the Truman administration to collaborate with the British to overthrow the Mossadeq government and establish a monarchical dictatorship under Reza Pahlavi. Since they evidently did not wish to go it alone, they needed to persist in their efforts to get the United States to collaborate. They had grounds for optimism. Though Truman had refused to authorize any such final move, toward the end of his tenure in late 1952, his State Department's position on the matter fell just short of a call to intervene. Although a Communist takeover of power in Iran was not foreseen as probable in the coming year, the State Department's alarm was still very strong, as seen in a November 1952 National Security Report: "If present trends continue unchecked, Iran could be effectively lost to the free world in advance of a possible Communist takeover of the Iranian Government. Failure to arrest present trends in Iran involves a serious risk to the national security of the United States."[33] In fair detail, the report suggests it would be a colossal and disastrous surrender of the "free world" to the Soviet Union and Communism. The entire Middle East would likely be lost to US power and influence. Given what had been done in Greece and was happening in Korea, there was no doubt about the United States' inclinations toward anti-Communist and anti-leftist military interventionism. By late 1952 at least, earlier warnings about the Tudeh Party and the dangers of Soviet intervention in Iran were so magnified that the final task was virtually assigned to the incoming administration of Eisenhower and Secretary of State John Foster Dulles. They assumed power in early 1953 and in June approved the CIA's "Operation TPAjax,"[34] which they coordinated with MI6's "Operation Boot," with the common aim of overthrowing the legitimately elected and popular Mossadeq government and installing Shah Reza Palavi as the sole ruler of the country. The Shah initially supported nationalization and rejected proposals for a *coup*, but by early August 1953, he buckled on both points when warned that he, too, would get the boot if he did not cooperate.[35]

The execution of the *coup* was rough. In Tehran, Britain's MI6 had placed Colonel C. M. Woodhouse, who was fairly fresh from undermining the Communist-led resistance against the Axis occupation in Greece. According to journalist Robert Fisk,

> Woodhouse visited Washington after Eisenhower's presidential election victory and outlined his plan to the Americans: Operation Boot was to use an organisation of … disenchanted army and police officers, parliamentary deputies, mullahs, editors and mob leaders to seize control of Tehran while tribal leaders would take over big cities, no doubt with the weapons the colonel had dumped in northern Iran.[36]

Woodhouse's declared aim was to support "resistance" in Iran against Mossadeq, his National Front alliance, and the Tudeh Party. The hard-core of the colonel's constituency meant royalists, big landowners, and those with vested interests in the return of the AIOC to the British. Mossadeq's agenda favored none of them. Since the nationalization in 1951, oil production had dropped precipitously due to practical problems in the transition, but also due to various forms of logistical, infrastructural, and financial sabotage by the British. As they saw it, the nationalization of one of their biggest property investments in the world could not be allowed to succeed, either practically or symbolically, for the British or, conversely, for the Third World.

The initial attempt at the *coup* in February was bungled; it created further chaos that prompted the Shah to threaten to flee the country, which was used by the plotters to paint the Shah and the grand Persian monarchy as victims of combined Mossadeqist-Communist subversion. The second try came on August 16, which again failed militarily but created new levels of disorder and strain. In response, widespread Tudeh-led demonstrations called for the monarchy to be abolished; the party pressured Mossadeq to adopt the same line, but he didn't. According to Fahkreddin Azimi, "Mossadeq had not sought the party's backing and would not do so in 1953." Amid the crisis, the Shah fled to Iraq, which put fears into royalist social and military circles that their monarchy would be abolished. Support from the military for Mossadeq had been steady, but now it started crumbling.[37] The teetering prime minister chose not to mobilize popular support for his cause. He and his supporters were apparently shocked; they lacked resolve, making him and themselves vulnerable to military moves and maneuvers by the royalists, the United States, and Britain. On August 19, the Shah was installed as the sole leader of Iran. He quickly organized and directed the state security services (SAVAK) to effectively and often torturously silence any opposition. This went on for the next twenty-six years, until the Iranian Revolution overthrew him. In the actual developments of 1951–3, Britain and the United States targeted the Tudeh Party because it was a supposed "vehicle" through which the USSR was bound to threaten the national securities of the great power states and their interests across the Middle East. But in the end they used the existence of the party to justify the destruction of the popular and democratically elected Mossadeq and his government because it nationalized the AIOC. For that, they installed the Shah in power as a monarchical dictator. In the words of Azimi, "the Anglo-American efforts to restore the Shah to a focal role unmistakably indicated that to them the project of democracy was far too risky to be allowed to take root in Iran."[38]

While the US and the British governments collaborated to overthrow Mossadeq, they did not do so against Nasser, despite his provocations and the extremely high stakes in Egypt. One of the chief concerns of France and the United States regarding the Algerian insurgency had been that weaponry from the Soviet Union was being sent to Egypt through Libya and passed into FLN hands through the long and porous Libyan-Algerian border. This was the truth of it. As of 1952, Egypt was under the rule of Gamal Abdel Nasser, who came to power through a *coup d'état* of military officers against the British-backed monarchy of King Farouk. The monarchy was ousted and so were the British, who had occupied the country since 1882. But their ouster did not supersede Britain's majority and France's minority shareholdings in the company that owned and operated the Suez Canal, which was the main transport line for Middle Eastern oil to Western Europe. While Nasser advocated a socialist and neutralist line for Egypt, one very similar to that followed by Mossadeq in Iran, one might expect that the nationalization of such a major piece of property in Egypt would bring on a similar covert operation.

Nasser's vision was to create pan-Arab national solidarity, transform the economies of Egypt and other Arab republics along socialist lines, and check the influence of the great powers in the region. His "neutralist" line aimed to play the United States and the Soviet Union off of one another for the ultimate benefit of Egypt and the rest of the Middle East. In all their Cold War bipolarity, the United States was not comfortable with this, particularly when, in 1955, Nasser was procuring arms from Czechoslovakia in return for Egyptian cotton. As a means of drawing the Egyptian leader solidly toward the United States, Eisenhower and Dulles offered Egypt financing to build a great hydroelectric dam on the Nile at Aswan, in southern Egypt. Though the dam would be a boon for agriculture and electrification throughout the Nile Valley, it would inextricably strap Egypt into debt to the United States and the World Bank. Nasser recognized this and got defiant. He stalled, maintained his dealings with Czechoslovakia, officially recognized the People's Republic of China, and, with great publicity, arranged for a Third World summit meeting with Tito and Nehru in Cairo in July. In response, the Americans rescinded their offer to finance the dam, never imagining two consequences: first, that the Soviet Union would be able to step up and support the dam's construction, which they did beginning in 1960, and, second, that Nasser would have the guts to nationalize the Suez Canal, which he did almost immediately upon getting the dam's termination notice from the United States, on the eve of his much heralded Third World conference.[39]

Nasser's move on the Suez Canal sent shudders through the French and British foreign policy establishments, while earning him hero status across Egypt, the Middle East, and the rest of the Third World. This was such a blow to the strategic position, revenues, and imperial egoism of the French and the British that they hatched a plan to retake the canal, recruiting the Israelis to spearhead the military operation. Between Israel and Egypt there was major tension. With the warfare and displacement of Palestinians that came with the establishment of the state of Israel in 1948 in very recent memory, Nasser positioned himself as the leading anti-Zionist in the Arab world, antagonized

Israelis with exorbitant taxes on goods destined for their country that passed through Suez, and periodically sent paramilitaries into Israeli territory to harass civilians. While the Israelis had already responded with small-scale military incursions, they were inclined toward a major attack on Egypt. Meanwhile, the Egyptians were receiving Soviet arms, and the Israelis were developing a robust political military alliance with the French, who supplied them with nuclear technology as well as conventional arms. The Israelis showed little hesitation in agreeing to the secret tripartite campaign to retake the canal. They struck first in October against the Sinai Peninsula but fell into a deadlock with Egyptian forces around the Suez, at which point the British and French demanded that both belligerent forces withdraw from the Sinai and engage in peace talks. Nasser refused; this was sovereign Egyptian territory. Britain and France brought in their bombers against Egyptian positions around Suez. However, to the perpetrators' surprise, the United States intervened to stop the entire operation. They had not been consulted about it; if they had they likely would have rejected the proposal. They were not fond of any of the alternatives in Egypt; King Farouk, his circles, and their British connections that had been overthrown by Nasser would have been a step backwards; the Muslim Brotherhood would have meant a theocratic state that would have been more difficult to control than Nasser's Third World socialist and nationalist secularism. Nor was there any significant Communist presence in the country, despite Nasser's tactical dealings with the Soviets and East Europeans.

Soon Nasser would link his politics with those of the NAM of Third World states that tried to navigate a third way between the United States and the Soviet Union. Because he was a noncommunist rather than an anti-Communist, he was difficult for the Americans to assess as to any threat he posed to them. He was effective at playing the great powers off of one another, which he demonstrated in his relations with the United States and the USSR, both of which he had funneling financial and material aid to Egypt in the early 1960s, including Soviet support for the Aswan Dam. Britain and the United States had plenty of suspicions about Nasser, but once they decided he was not a Communist, they got pragmatic; they accepted his state socialist programs, including land reform and nationalization of industry. Such acceptance was roughly consistent with the acceptance of social democracy in Britain and New Deal policies in the United States. However much the contexts of those settings differed, this was part of the larger pattern of the tolerance of some leftist politics in the First and Third worlds, as long as their practitioners were either anti-Communist or reliably noncommunist. Another example of this was to be seen in India—independent since August 1947—under the leadership of the Fabian socialist Jawaharlal Nehru. He had also been arousing American animosity and suspicion for years for being soft on the Soviets and voicing anti-imperialist politics. However, to the delight of the State Department and Eisenhower in 1958, he came out explicitly against Communism.[40]

Judging from the situations across North Africa, the Middle East, and beyond, the United States, Britain, and France were finding it extremely difficult to handle both the Third World left as well as the tensions with the Chinese and Soviet Communists and their real or fictional allies. Nevertheless, for purposes of controlling the Middle East and its oil, the United States and Britain in 1953 secured Iran—with its long border with the USSR—as an anti-Communist state for at least the following twenty-five years. One could also perhaps see the latent rivalries between the United States, Britain, and France revealed by the Suez crisis as a problem, yet it resulted in the United States batting down the other two. The Americans even got firm with the Israelis over their refusal to promptly withdraw from the Sinai, though that did not set the pattern of US policy toward Israel. The United States also largely had its way in Western Europe, where its actions in 1956 against the French, in particular, decisively accelerated the establishment of the European Coal and Steel Community as a means of solidifying West European anti-Communist unity. The French got the US message that it was time to finally agree with the West Germans and others to the establishment of that core institution that later became the European Economic Community (EEC) and then the European Union (EU).[41]

But the United States was also taking hits. Soviet Premier Khrushchev, who succeeded Stalin after his death in 1953, threatened nuclear attacks on Britain, France, and Israel if they did not withdraw from Egypt, while the United States' allies were concerned that they did not see an effective response, whether or not the Soviet threats were credible. The French established a nuclear weapons program outside the framework of NATO, while also continuing to support Israeli nuclear weapons research and development.[42] While these were not blows to the American plan for a committed anti-Communist Western Europe, Khrushchev's threats of rocket attacks came as he was strategizing to crush the Hungarian uprising, which the United States did nothing to support. Meanwhile, despite their violent move against the Hungarian dissidents, the Soviets launched a major Leninist rhetorical campaign in favor of decolonization, which helped put them in a better light across the Third World. Following that, there was a rapid succession of new Third World states celebrating their freedom from formal and traditional colonialism. The arc of US power was still rising but encountering myriad oppositions across the world where the ideas and politics of liberation and anti-colonialism had powerful momentum. In contrast to that, the USSR was gaining strategic confidence and some apparent moral high ground vis-à-vis the Third World. Close on the horizon was the potentially incendiary Cuban Missile Crisis, as well as American "mission creep" into South Vietnam.

Overall, the problem was that the capitalist imperialist states were fighting wars against enemies very much of their own creation, though they also did so in necessary collaboration with reactionary allies in the same states or territories. The politics of Mossadeq and the Tudeh Party in Iran, Egypt's Nasser and the Algerian FLN—to name only a few of the countless examples—were fundamentally and highly attributable to the indignities and offenses of British and French imperialism. Saudi Arabia was a different, but equally outstanding, example. It was a conservative ally that was staunchly anti-Communist, brooked no internal opposition, and was hostile toward Nasser and Arab socialism in general. The royal House of Saud was at the top of a theocratic monarchical state that cultivated and sustained a robust tradition of Wahhabist Islam, which was partly predicated on deep hostility toward the western powers. For the United States, among the Wahhabists were enemies in gestation. For Britain and the United States, the Saudi state was nothing if not a double-edged sword.

Meanwhile, aside from the situational politics of the Suez Crisis, support for Israel that was central to US Cold War strategic interests in the Middle East, which, aside from the key Israelis, made for few friends and many sworn enemies in the region. None of this discounts the importance of the domestic vagaries of politics or the socioeconomic entrapments that tended to shape people's lives far from Cold War imperialist maneuvers. Local socioeconomic, political, and institutional structures and the people that represented them provided necessary domestic leverage for the imperialist states to advance their interests. Nor does it deny the agency and courage of the anti-colonialists, or excuse any of their political misjudgments, misdeeds, or crimes. But their politics were specific responses to repressive power configurations that the great power states had established or reinforced upon their worlds during the preceding many decades.

Britain and the United States ousted their challengers in Iran; the French engaged in ferocious warfare against the FLN before granting Algeria independence in 1962. At first uncertain about Nasser in Egypt, the Americans under Eisenhower and Kennedy accommodated him, believing he was actually the best means of fighting Communism in Egypt and the Arab world.[43] Yet for the Muslim Brotherhood in Egypt, Nasser's secularism and dealings with the United States and the USSR were constant reminders that they saw him as a traitor. They saw his comrade and successor, Anwar Sadat, in the same light. Sadat warmed up ever closer to the United States; in 1979 he agreed to a US-sponsored peace treaty with Israel over the Sinai. For that, members of the Muslim Brotherhood assassinated him in 1981 in Cairo. By that time, despite their profound sectarian differences, elements within both the Shia and Sunni Muslim worlds were highly emboldened and radicalized by the 1979 revolution in Iran that overthrew the US-backed Shah, his domestic allies, and security state. It was a moment of rare Muslim unity against perceived common enemies. Now a militant Islam was taking the battle to the United States as the "Great Satan," and, after the Soviet invasion and occupation of Afghanistan, to the USSR. The United States supported the Afghan anti-Soviet war with money and sophisticated weaponry. In the words of the American national security advisor Zbginiew Brzezinski, when he spoke face to face with the Afghan *Mossadeq* guerilla leaders in the Afghan-Pakistan border region in 1979, "your cause is right and God is on your side."[44] Once they ousted the Soviets from Afghanistan in May 1989, the Afghan militants and their Arab volunteer forces, many from Saudi Arabia—most famously Osama bin Laden—turned their sights on the United States.

While these were only some of hardly foreseeable specific contingencies of US policies in the Middle East, given the long- and short-term legacies of religious fanaticism, racism, imperialism, colonialism, and the two world wars, few of these tragedies were surprising once those legacies were reactivated by specific dynamics of the Cold War. The main patterns of conflict in the Middle East, and the precedents they set, cannot be understood sufficiently without priority consideration of the "blowback," or the unintended consequences, of US and British anti-Communist and anti-socialist policy throughout the region, but especially toward Iran in the early 1950s, and the US prosecution of its anti-Communist agenda in Afghanistan in the late 1970s–80s.[45]

Figure 8 Jomo Kenyatta with leaders of the Lembus people that had protected him from British colonial persecution in the 1950s. The Lembus gave refuge to Kenyatta in their forest while he was evading arrests in the 1950s. Kenyatta was viciously targeted and persecuted as a Communist by the British colonial authorities in their Kenya Colony during the 1950s, though he was a noncommunist nationalist and anti-colonialist. He became the first prime minister of independent Kenya beginning in 1963.

Notes

1. The quote and Churchill's response is to be found in Winston S. Churchill, *The Second World War, Volume Five: Closing the Ring* (Cambridge: Houghton Mifflin, 1951), General Smuts to Prime Minister, August 20, 1943, p. 537. For Basil Davidson's presentation of the matter, see *his Scenes from the Anti-Nazi War* (New York: Monthly Review Press, 1980), pp. 17–18. Apartheid in South Africa was established constitutionally and legally in 1948; before that it existed in fact.
2. See report on "Communism in Nigeria" in CO 537/6567.
3. George Beresford-Stooke to James Griffiths, Secretary of State for the Colonies, March 9, 1950. Folder CO/537/6567, document 96038/1/41. The Cominform was the Communist Information Bureau that was established by the Soviet Union in 1947 after the formal dissolution of the Comintern (Communist International) in 1943.

4. Gerald Reece to A. B. Cohen of the Colonial Office, Folder CO/537/6556 document 96038, March 18, 1950. For Murray's response, see document PR/18/29/G Murray to Blackburne, April 22, 1950, in the above CO folder.

5. Clement Atlee and his Labor government lost the general election of October 25, 1951, to the Conservatives, thus bringing Winston Churchill back as prime minister.

6. Reese to Lambert, May 23, 1950; unnumbered document in folder CO/537/6556.

7. See Jeffery M. Paige, *Agrarian Revolution: Social Movements and Export Agriculture in the Underdeveloped World* (New York: Free Press, 1975), for some special insights on the Mau Mau Rebellion (pp. 69, 97).

8. Colonial Office (CO) 537/6556 folder entitled "Anti-Communist Propaganda Terminology," document 96038/1/H/50, PR. 18/29/50, S. H. Evans to F. R. Murray, FO, July 6, 1950.

9. CO/537/6556 96038/1/H, handwritten note from Veronica Ware to Juxon Barton, second page in the folder, unnumbered document dated June 9, 1950.

10. Caroline Elkins, *Imperial Reckoning: The Untold Story of Britain's Gulag in Kenya* (New York: Henry Holt, 2005. For a review of the book, see Marc Parry, "Uncovering the Brutal Truth about the British Empire," *The Guardian*, August 18, 2016. Available online: https://www.theguardian.com/news/2016/aug/18/uncovering-truth-british-empire-caroline-elkins-mau-mau.

11. A. S. Cleary, "The Myth of Mau Mau in its International Context," *African Affairs*, vol. 89, no. 355 (April 1990), pp. 234–6, 243.

12. For a comprehensive critique of the work of Carothers, as well as others, see Jock McCulloch, *Colonial Psychiatry and the African Mind* (London: Cambridge University Press, 1995).

13. J. C. Carothers, *The Psychology of Mau Mau* (Nairobi: Colony and Protectorate of Kenya, Government Printer, 1955), pp. 15–19, and *passim*. Available online: https://ufdc.ufl.edu/UF00023305/00001/18j.

14. Basil Davidson, "The Motives of Mau Mau": Review of *Unhappy Valley* by Bruce Berman and John Lonsdale, *London Review of Books*, vol. 16, no. 4 (1994).

15. For a critique of Carothers and others, see Marouf Hasian Jr., "The Deployment of Ethnographic Sciences and Psychological Warfare During the Suppression of the Mau Mau Rebellion," *Journal of Medical Humanities*, no. 34 (2013), pp. 329–45, p. 339.

16. For a widely applicable theoretical framework on this approach, see Michael Hechter, *Internal Colonialism: The Celtic Fringe in British National Development* (New York: Routledge, 1998 (first published 1975)).

17. *Time Magazine*, October 13, 1958; Saliha Belmessous, *Assimilation and Empire: Uniformity in French and British Colonies, 1541–1954* (New York: Oxford University Press, 2013), p. 200. Also, Robert D. Kumamoto, *International Terrorism & American Foreign Relations, 1945–1976* (Boston: Northeastern University Press., 1999), pp. 92–109. The Battle of Valmy took place just outside of Paris in 1792. It was the first great victory of the French revolutionary forces against their reactionary monarchical state opponents, effectively saving the revolution. Abbas's reflections also recall Thucydides's "Melian Dialogue" regarding the problem of "might" versus "right."

18. Alain Ruscio, "Dien Bien Phu, Symbol for All Time: The Fall of the French Empire," *Le Monde Diplomatique*, July 2004.

19. Cairo, May 8, 1952, Doc. 50. *Central Intelligence Agency*, Memorandum No. 346, January 24, 1951, pp. 3–4. *FRUS*, 1952–4, Africa and South Asia, vol. XI, Part 1, Ambassador in Egypt (Caffery) to the Department of State.

20. The PCA defied its French counterpart, the PCF, which refused to support the FLN's cause. Instead it advocated for peace and unity. The PCA officially joined the FLN in 1955.

21. "The Consul General at Algiers (Lewis Clark) to the Department of State," No. 238 Algiers, May 19, 1954. Subject: Political Situation in Algeria. https://history.state.gov/historicaldocuments/frus1952-54v11p1/d164.

22. Miloud Barkaoui, "Managing the Colonial Status Quo: Eisenhower's Cold War and the Algerian War of Independence," *Journal of North African Studies*, vol. 17 (2012), pp. 125–41. Available online: https://doi.org/10.1080/13629387.2011.586402.

23. See also by Miloud Barkaoui, "Kennedy and the Cold War Imbroglio: the Case of Algeria's Independence," *Arab Studies Quarterly*, vol. 21, no. 2 (Spring 1999), pp. 31–45. Available online: https://www.jstor.org/stable/41858283.

24. On the death tolls, the overall character of the Algerian war, and extended commentary on Frantz Fanon, see Vijay Prashad, *The Darker Nations: A People's History of the Third World* (New York: New Press, 2007), pp. 119–33.

25. Both of these items are found in FO 1110/24, PR 41. The first is from a speech by Douglas Schneider, Acting Chief, Public Affairs Overseas Program Staff, Department of State, delivered at the Institute on World Affairs, Riverside California, December 6, 1948; the second is written by Charles H. Bateman of the Foreign Office, and is entitled "Communism – New Publicity Policy" and dated February 12, 1948.

26. The term was chosen by the late Chalmers Johnson as the title for his excellent, critical, and prescient book, *Blowback: The Costs and Consequences of American Empire* (New York: Henry Holt, 2000).

27. The Jezireh region is in northeastern Syria. The quotations are from FO 371/91177, item E1017/1, entitled "Communist Influence in the Middle East."

28. See https://history.state.gov/historicaldocuments/frus1950v05/d93.

29. "The Tudeh Party: Vehicle of Communism in Iran," ORE 23–49, July 18, 1949. Available online: https://www.cia.gov/library/readingroom/docs/DOC_0000258385.pdf.

30. https://history.state.gov/historicaldocuments/frus1950v05/d85. "Azerbaijan" as referred to in the memo was the ethnically Azerbaijani area of the northwest corner of Iran adjacent to Soviet Azerbaijan.

31. Up to 1935 the name of the majority British-owned company was the Anglo Persian Oil Company; since 1954 it has been British Petroleum (BP).

32. See FO 371/91177, items E1017/7, from June 11, 1951; E1017/9 (Memo to Herbert Morrison, British Foreign Secretary) from June 27, 1951; and E/1017/10, September 13, 1951.

33. "A Report to the National Security Council on United States Policy Regarding the Present Situation in Iran," NSC 136/1, November 20, 1952. https://history.state.gov/historicaldocuments/frus1952-54v10/d240.

34. The "TP" was for the Tudeh Party, while the criterion for the choice of Ajax is not clear. It may have been to evoke a mythological hero, a corporate household cleaning agent launched in 1947 that was "stronger than dirt," or both—with the dirt being "Communism."

35. Milani Abbas, *The Shah* (New York: Palgrave Macmillan, 2011), Chapter 10. Available online: https://www.offiziere.ch/wp-content/uploads-001/2019/08/The-Shah-Abbas-Milani.pdf.

36. Robert Fisk, "With Sten Guns and Sovereigns Britain and US Saved Iran's Throne for the Shah," *The Independent*, March 15, 1997.

37. Fakhreddin Azimi, "The Overthrow of the Government of Mosaddeq Reconsidered," *Iranian Studies*, vol. 45, no. 5 (September 2012), p. 702.

38. For a trenchant, detailed, and persuasive historical and historiographical analysis of the overthrow of Mossadeq, see Fakhreddin Azimi, "The Overthrow of the Government of Mosaddeq Reconsidered," *Iranian Studies*, vol. 45, no. 5 (September 2012), pp. 702, 711, 693–712, *passim*.

39. Thomas J. McCormick, *America's Half Century: United States Foreign Policy in the Cold War and After* (Baltimore, MD: Johns Hopkins University Press, 1995), pp. 122–3; Prashad, *The Darker Nations*, pp. 51–2.

40. See 1958 CIA document on Nehru, displaying downright giddiness at Nehru's explicit rejection of Communism. For the CIA, Nehru was now categorized with the dissident Yugoslav social democrat, Milovan Djilas. "Nehru on Communism: An Awakening," https://www.cia.gov/library/readingroom/docs/CIA-RDP78-02771R000400010002-2.

41. See Perry Anderson, "Under the Sign of the Interim," in *The Question of Europe*, ed. Peter Gowan and Perry Anderson (New York: Verso, 1997), pp. 51–71.

42. http://www.wisconsinproject.org/countries/israel/nuke.html.

43. Peter Mansfield, *A History of the Middle East*, 2nd ed. (New York: Penguin, 2003), p. 271.

44. CNN Documentary *Cold War* (released in 1998), Episode 20, "Soldiers of God: 1977–1988."

45. The situation of Afghanistan and related matters from the 1970s to recent times is addressed further in Chapter 7 of this book.

6

Anti-Leftist Politics in Western Europe, Latin America, and the United States to the 1970s

Western Europe: Anti-Communism and Social Democracy

From the standpoint of anti-leftist politics and their consequences worldwide, the first of the three most salient features of the West European situation from 1945 to the 1970s was that the entire region was in the anti-Communist camp. But second, while the northern states were politically and electorally social democratic and anti-Communist, Portugal and Spain were rightwing anti-"Communist" dictatorships, and Greece was engulfed in civil war, which made Italy after 1948 an exception to the pattern. Of course, its fascist legacy was still extremely fresh, which meant it was a fertile field for anti-leftist maneuvering for the remaining fascist demographic, and for the interventions of British and American intelligence operatives, at least up to and through the elections of 1948. Liberal capitalist machinations in favor of a dictatorship to succeed Mussolini's would have been nearly impossible domestically and internationally, but not out of the question. Portugal under Salazar and Spain under Franco persisted as straightforward anti-leftist dictatorships that had origins in the interwar era. At minimum, they were anti-Communist, anti-socialist, anti-anarchist, and anti-liberal. Salazar's regime collapsed in the "Carnation Revolution" of April 1974, Franco's a year later upon his death. After its civil war of 1943–9, Greece was a repressive anti-Communist security state with the trappings of electoral democracy, until those trappings actually transformed into a substantive threat to the security state, at which point a full-on military dictatorship was established from 1967 to 1974.

The third striking feature of the West European scene was the enthusiastic embrace of social democracy in the states and societies of northern Europe, including Britain. Such enthusiasm was accompanied by hard anti-Communist policies at home and abroad, that is, especially the French, British, and Dutch in their colonial territories, but beyond them as well. British foreign secretary Ernest Bevin stated clearly in January 1948 what he believed to be Britain's commitment to social democracy and against Communism:

The Russian and the Communist Allies are threatening the whole fabric of Western civilization, and I have drawn attention to the need to mobilize spiritual forces, as well as material and political, for its defence. It is for us, as Europeans and as a Social Democratic Government, and not the Americans, to give the lead in the spiritual, moral and political sphere to all the democratic elements in Western Europe which are anti-Communist and, at the same time, genuinely progressive and reformist, believing in freedom, planning and social justice – what one might call the "Third Force."

In an apparent attempt to show sympathy with the humanistic values of cooperation as opposed to the evils of Soviet Communism, the British minister of defense offered a concise country-by-country account of the vitalities of the cooperative movements long established throughout Western Europe, suggesting the government make use of them in their propaganda efforts.[1]

The endorsement of the idea of social democracy against Communism was clear, but so was the suggestion of a potential rift between the United States and Britain at the time over ideology and economic policy. The latter was not necessarily serious. William Edwards, head of the British Information Services in the United States, feared the Americans would object to British emphasis on the value of social democracy as a "controlled" form of capitalism, "in which the great majority of people in Britain believe, whereas the Americans would presumably be extolling their own principles of capitalistic free enterprise."[2] But his US counterpart, Bill Stone, had no problem with that. He acknowledged the differences and said that

so far as he and the members of his Department were concerned, he foresaw no difficulty because he appreciated that in an appeal to the broad masses of workers and peasants in Europe and the Middle East (which he also accepts as the main target) it would be futile to preach the doctrines of unrestricted capitalism which are still fashionable in some quarters of the United States. On the other hand, he admitted that it would be impossible for the State Department to preach social democracy in the way we understand it without incurring severe criticism from Congress.[3]

While the British Ministry of Defense also suggested the Communist presence and threat was low within various sectors of British society, they conducted plenty of surveillance. On the international front, a "Russia Committee" established by the Foreign Office had found that "the growth of Communism in Italy and France was … causing concern, and it was difficult to undertake counter-measures in these countries, other than by propaganda and covert assistance, where possible in the Social Democrat movements."[4] The Italian and French Communist parties indeed played important roles in their countries' politics; they rode waves of popularity based on their lead positions in anti-fascist wartime resistance. As the British issued warnings about them in early 1948, the US State Department and CIA were busy with systematic, covert "counter-measures" against them. Each situation was distinctive, but not particularly different. The French Communist Party (PCF) was more or less as highly revered as its Italian counterpart was for its heroic resistance activity during the war. But the shift into the full-blown Cold War put both in new and difficult positions. With his fingers on the financial spigots of the European Recovery Program—the ERP, popularly known as the Marshall Plan—US secretary of state George Marshall, fresh off of his failure to boost the fortunes of Chiang Kai Shek against the Chinese Communists, refused to indulge the prospect of any significant Communist power in France. The writing was on the wall. The major socialist party of the time, the French Section of the Workers' International (SFIO), did some of the dirty work when it ceased its support for the PCF in the three-way coalition with the Christian Democrats that ruled the country up to 1947. But pressure upon the PCF also came at the trade union level, where a CIA-funded American Federation of Labor (AFL)-Congress of Industrial Organizations (CIO) campaign encouraged the establishment of a new, anti-Communist, social democratic style union—Workers' Force (FO)—that drew significant numbers away from and reduced the political leverage of the PCF dominated union, the General Confederation of Labor (CGT).[5]

In Italy prior to the April national elections, the United States conducted a similar, but more systematic, covert financial and propaganda campaign. Its aim was to promote the Christian Democrats and demote the Communist Party (PCI), which was joined with the Italian Socialist Party (PSI) in a coalition called the Popular Democratic Front for Liberty, Peace and Labor (FDP). The PCI had played a central role in the resistance against the Nazi occupation of Italy from 1943 to 1945 and against the collaborationist Social Republic of Salò headed by Mussolini, who had become an obvious Nazi puppet. Under the lead of Togliatti, the party openly committed itself in 1944 to liberal democratic and constitutional government. Togliatti also served as minister of justice as well as deputy prime minister in the years 1944–6. He supported the referendum of 1946 that endorsed the Republic. With its great prestige among many Italians, the coalition with the PSI had reasonable expectations of a strong electoral showing. The rival Christian Democratic Party (DC) contained many non-fascist elements, but it was the main vehicle into which members of the National Fascist Party (PNF) had flooded as a means of covering up their support for Mussolini, fascism, and the Axis alliance. It had support from the vehemently anti-Communist Vatican, which had given its blessing to Mussolini, as well as from prominent and ordinary past members of the Liberal Party that had disintegrated in the early years of Fascism.

The CIA and State Department interventions were multipronged, including letter-writing campaigns from Americans to Italians that extolled the virtues of the American way, Hollywood stars celebrating the bonds between US and Italian culture, and Cardinal Spellman preaching the sacred bonds between the two countries and condemning the evils of Communism. There were sensational propaganda shows made out of the arrivals of US provisions to hungry and war-ravaged Italians at the country's various seaports and inland along rail lines; finally, the US military staged major demonstrations of its might off the Italian coastlines in the days prior to the elections. It was time for a show and possibly an intervention in case the show did not succeed. Secretary of State Marshall threatened to stop aid immediately if the PCI/PSI coalition won the elections. Many of the local and national Italian newspapers carried sensational headlines stating exactly that. The campaign succeeded. The election results favored the Christian Democrats (DC) enough to exclude the left from power at the national level for the following twenty years. Fitting the pattern of social democratic anti-Communism across much of Europe, Premier Alcide de Gasperi invited the small, social democratic and explicitly anti-Communist Social Unity party into his government. Beyond that, the United States and its newly acquired domestic Italian allies strictly disfavored the PSI and all leftists that were not anti-Communist.[6] Whether or not it wished to, the Soviet Union was in no position to counter the campaign.

While the efforts to pit Christian democracy and social democracy against Communism continued on the domestic fronts of Western Europe that were not anti-Communist dictatorships, there were movements on the transnational level toward Western European military and political unification. Three interrelated strategic factors aligned strongly in favor of those developments. First were the sheer devastations of the war, second was the strategic imperative of preventing another one, and third was US pressure to solidify Western Europe as an anti-Communist bloc. The military alliance came first, with the establishment of the North Atlantic Treaty Organization (NATO) in 1949. Following that were the negotiations that eventually led to what became the European Union. With an eye on neutralizing the "German problem," as it was known, the French took the main initiatives, but specifically spearheading the project was Jean Monnet, the cosmopolitan businessman and banker who was appointed by Charles de Gaulle in 1945 as the head of a planning commission whose mission was to regenerate the French economy. Living off and on in New York City, Monnet operated within elite east coast circles that included Truman, Eisenhower, Dean Acheson, John Foster Dulles, Averell Harriman, and others.[7] Their immediate and overriding interest was not in rates of profit but in protecting the potentials for them through not just anti-Communist political structures, but military ones as well, which they got through NATO. On a fairly standard and popular level, Monnet shared that anti-Communist predisposition, while he also showed social democratic–style sympathy with organized labor. Out of Monnet's unique combination of basic politics, his high status economic policy position in France, his supranational institutional vision, and his connections with leading Americans of the time came certain decisive influences and pressures that led to the original institutions of the European Union (EU). Beginning in 1949, Monnet took up the American challenge to the French to devise an anti-Soviet "United States of Europe," including a determination vis-à-vis West Germany that would prevent its rearmament. Monnet proposed a systematic pooling of strategic resources and production between France and Germany that would render another war between the two states extremely unlikely. This was the blueprint for the Schuman Plan, announced in May 1950, which was realized in 1952 in the establishment of the European Coal and Steel Community (ECSC), composed of France, West Germany, Italy, Belgium, Luxemburg, and the Netherlands. Its functions got expanded beyond coal and steel into a full-blown free-trade zone with the creation of the European Economic Community (EEC) in 1957.

While anti-Communism and Western Europe were getting reconstituted under the US lead at the supra-state level through NATO and the EEC in Northwestern Europe, the direct legacies of anti-Communism from the era of fascism and world war remained in force in Southwestern and Southeastern Europe. The dictatorships in Portugal and Spain, and the one soon to be established—or reestablished—in Greece, were ugly reminders of fascism and war that brought Europe to the point of do-or-die unification in the first place. Simply put, the two world wars were necessary conditions that convinced the French and the West Germans that they needed to pool their strategic and greater economic resources or risk annihilating themselves and others. However, even this was not quite enough. As explained above, the sufficient condition for the French and West Germans to agree to a common market came out of the Suez Crisis, in which the United States asserted its hegemony by neutralizing French and British imperialist impulses. In other words, getting at the specificities of the establishments of the ECSC and EEC means tracking the role of the United States, whose Cold War mission also, of course, had a bearing on the southern European dictatorships.

Although the liberal capitalist states were complicit in Franco's victory in the civil war that ended in 1939, they tried somewhat to shun Franco's Spain from the Second World War to the early 1950s because of its wartime collaborations with Nazi Germany and Fascist Italy. Franco's Blue Division fought for the Nazis on the Eastern Front against the Soviet armies. But the distance maintained from Spain by the United States closed quickly and unsurprisingly. The American bottom line in the late 1940s tended to favor Franco. By late 1950, now deep in the Korean War as well as so much in the grips of McCarthyism at home, Franco's Spain was seen by much of the US foreign policy elite as a reliable and useful anti-Communist state. Truman buckled under their pressure, exerted mainly through Secretary of State Acheson, and the United States offered Spain full diplomatic relations and generous financial consideration. Under Eisenhower in 1953, the United States signed the Pact of Madrid with Franco, which opened the way for more American financial and military aid to Spain and, in return, US rights to build military bases on Spanish territory. During these years, Franco's repression of what remained of the Spanish left continued with ferocity.[8]

Portugal under the Salazar dictatorship since 1932 was even less of a problem for the United States than Spain was in the 1940s–50s. The regime kept a relative diplomatic distance from fascism/Nazism in the interwar and war years. This was true despite the fact of its dictatorial and strictly anti-leftist political character that it had in common with fascism; of course, the same could be said, with variations, for Spain, Greece, and to a significant extent, post–Second World War Italy. Speaking geo-strategically, Britain had gained access to the airfields of the Azores islands in 1943, which paved the way for US-Portuguese agreement later that year that provided US rights to the same airstrips. During the early period of the following Cold War, the strategic importance of the Azores for the United States remained high, making for a great friendliness of the Eisenhower administration toward the Salazar dictatorship. Portugal was invited to be one of the founding members of NATO in 1949. US support was somewhat shaken by the Kennedy administration, which attempted to articulate an anti-colonialist line in general, but one particularly against the Portuguese presence in Angola, Mozambique, Capo Verde, Goa in India, and East Timor. This did not fly well in Lisbon. Marcelo Caetano, a Portuguese extreme rightist politician who succeeded Salazar as dictator in 1968, expressed the spirit of the Portuguese imperialists already in the 1930s: "Africa is more than a land to be exploited … Africa is for us a moral justification and a *raison d'etre* as a power. Without it we would be a small nation; with it, we are a great country." This sentiment persisted to the bitter end. Nor did the soft American criticisms of colonialism and rhetorical support for electoral democracy outweigh the strategic value of the Azores. Salazar conceded nothing, and John F. Kennedy relented. The end of the Portuguese dictatorship and its colonial empire would only come with a groundswell of anti-colonialist politics, especially in Angola in the 1960s–70s, but also in Mozambique, Guinea, East Timor, Goa, and within Portugal itself. The result was a surge of rebellious leftist politics within Portugal from the early 1970s to the "Carnation Revolution" of 1974, when Caetano was overthrown and eventually replaced by the Socialist government of Mário Soares.[9]

But the surge of mainly leftwing nationalist politics across the fast crumbling Portuguese empire also opened up a perceived opportunity for the viciously anti-leftist Indonesian dictatorship under General Suharto to invade and occupy East Timor. The violence meted out by the Indonesian military on the East Timorese was murderous, if not genocidal. Ten years earlier, in 1965–6, Suharto had come to power in a rightwing military coup, which was justified as a means of supposedly protecting Indonesia from the Third World leftwing nationalist Sukarno and the Indonesian Communists (PKI). But the violence was indiscriminate against all suspected leftists in a manner that anticipated the 1975 massacres of East Timorese independence-minded nationalists. The pretext for Suharto's power grab in the 1960s that overthrew the leftwing nationalist Sukarno regime was clearly anti-Communist, though it targeted all opposition, real and alleged. The invasion of East Timor was somewhat less obviously presented as an anti-Communist operation, but Suharto and his top officers and propagandists still declared that the major East Timorese resistance organization, Fretilin, was a Communist organization and needed to be destroyed. The two waves of political violence launched by Suharto killed at least a half a million Indonesians (1965–6) and one to three hundred thousand East Timorese. Both campaigns were very significantly marked by anti-leftist politics; politically and militarily, the Suharto regime was vigorously backed by both the United States and Great Britain.[10]

Outside of that world of collapsing Portuguese power, and at the opposite end of the Mediterranean, all the efforts of the Greek anti-Communist establishment to control domestic politics from the 1930s to the early 1960s were once again getting out of hand. While the political demographic of the leftwing resistance mostly remained alive, further structural changes also took place in the country since the early 1950s that further opened the way for popular center-left politics. Greece had shown that political tendency in the EAM-ELAS resistance movement of the Axis occupation period, but the Communist domination of it was too much for the bourgeois political parties, the British, and the United States to accept, so they went to great lengths to destroy it. The hard-core of the anti-Communist establishment of the entire era was in certain military factions, mainly including the Sacred Bond of Greek Officers (IDEA), which had support from the CIA, and the rightwing Greek Rally party and the National Radical Union (NRU). In the post–Second World War and civil war period, they saw Communist threats potentially anywhere, whether they existed or not. But a new and dramatic practical and perceptual challenge for them came in the early to mid-1960s when the Center Union Party arose under George Papandreou.[11] What the anti-Communist establishment saw in the 1964 national electoral victory of the Center Union Party was an open door for the dreaded and outlawed Greek Communist Party (KKE). This was not the case, but that did not matter. Though this would not guarantee anything, part of the subtext was that few knew that George Papandreou did the bidding of the British in the fall of 1944, when he saw to it that as few Communists as possible would have any power in the postwar Greek government. This was nothing if not a further provocation for civil war in the political atmosphere of the time.

However, in 1967, in the face of a new round of national elections, it appeared as though Papandreou's Center Union would not win a majority of parliamentary seats. They were therefore likely to resort to a coalition government with the leftist United Democratic Left (EDA), which all the rightists suspected of being a Communist front party. Seeing this on the horizon, rival factions of die-hard anti-leftist elements in the Greek military and politics made their plans for *coups d'état*. A group of colonels struck first, most famously led by Yiorgos Papadodopoulos and his colleagues with the IDEA group. They seized power on the night of April 21, 1967, declaring martial law and arresting and imprisoning hundreds of leftists, many of whom they quickly subjected to torture. Furthermore, the colonels convinced the CIA and the State Department of the necessity and legitimacy of their anti-Communist *coup*, which secured political-military and financial support from the United States until the regime collapsed in 1974.

It is difficult to convey the traumatic legacies of these politics, but it is helpful to jump ahead to October 2012 in Athens. At that time, neoliberal austerity reigned, and the neo-Nazi politics that it nurtured—though in conjunction with the refugee problems that resulted from the neoliberal US triumphalist wars in the Middle East—took shape in the Golden Dawn party. It was clear that the memories, traumas, and hatreds of the past remained very much present in certain recesses of the Greek political world. A group of anti–Golden Dawn and anti-austerity protestors were rounded up by the police in Athens and taken to the "Attica General Police Directorate (GADA) – the Athens equivalent of Scotland Yard," where they were subjected to torture similar to that inflicted by Americans on Iraqi prisoners at Abu Ghraib. The account in *The Guardian* newspaper read,

> One man with a bleeding head wound and a broken arm that he said had been sustained during his arrest alleged the police continued to beat him in GADA and refused him medical treatment until the next morning. Another said the police forced his legs apart and kicked him in the testicles during the arrest. "They spat on me and said we would die like our grandfathers in the civil war," he said.

A second group of detained protesters said they "all had to go past an officer who made us strip naked in the corridor, bend over and open our back passage in front of everyone else who was there … he did whatever he wanted with us – slapped us, hit us, told us not to look at him, not to sit cross-legged." The police denied any wrongdoing whatsoever, but the protesters' account was graphic and credible:

All we could do was look at each other out of the corners of our eyes to give each other courage. He had us there for more than two hours. He would take phone calls on his mobile and say, "I'm at work and I'm fucking them, I'm fucking them up well." In the end only four of us were charged with resisting arrest. It was a day out of the past, out of the colonels' junta.[12]

Latin America: The United States and Anti-Reformist Anti-"Communism"

Though Latin America largely avoided the physical devastations of the world wars, no doubt it was highly impacted, if sometimes indirectly, by the wars, global power struggles, and socioeconomic changes of the 1875–1945 era. The entire region had its distinctions: relatively weak capitalist development largely as legacies of Spain's or Portugal's relative economic weaknesses; large indigenous populations mostly excluded from the fruits of independence, liberty, and opportunity enjoyed by the minority of landed elites and small middle classes of each society; and a tendency toward state-level factionalization of those elites and their supporters. The combination of the above forces involved political volatilities and tendencies toward civil war that erupted most dramatically in the Mexican Revolution of 1910–20. But the earlier, grand-scale variant affecting the historical fate of Latin America vis-à-vis the United States goes back to 1823. When most of the states of South and Central America had been, or were soon to be, established through wars of national liberation against Spain and, in the case of Brazil in 1822–5, against Portugal, the United States claimed the entire western hemisphere as its sphere of influence. The original spirit of the Monroe Doctrine had a slight element of anti-colonialism and anti-interventionism in it, directed as it was against the European imperialist states of the time. But the more the US empire advanced through its settler colonial phase to its more global and overseas phases, the more the Monroe Doctrine was used as a declaration of US western-hemispheric hegemony and a license to intervene if, when, and where, it pleased. By the end of the Second World War, the United States was the most powerful capitalist imperialist state on the planet, while the trajectories of Latin America's societies mostly involved domestic instability and political-military weakness and vulnerability.

Of course, the United States had also experienced its severe instabilities, most especially its civil war of the 1860s, but this was not between oligarchs and their social bases; it was between slave and free states, that is, between competing models of capitalist development. Its resolution in favor of "free" versus slave labor only facilitated capitalist development that expanded dramatically from the 1870s onward. Stepping back a bit, this is also to say that, while a few parts of Northwestern Europe were in the early throes of industrialization in the nineteenth century, with all their attendant politics based mainly on the "social problem" of the new working classes, the new agrarian and landed oligarchical states of Latin America were both struggling socioeconomically in the transforming world system and on notice that their emergent and fully industrializing great power neighbor to the north, the United States, was watching them with great interest.

In the mythology of the times, particularly in the eyes of its predominant elites and religious figures such as Josiah Strong, the United States was fulfilling what it proclaimed to be its divinely approved mission. In the context of the Mexican-American War of 1846–8, that mission got weaponized. The Monroe Doctrine became inextricably tied in with American exceptionalism and the religious nationalism of "manifest destiny," that is, with the subjugation of the peoples and territories further and further westward, until it reached the western seaboard of the continent. The next horizons were to the south and around the Pacific. South America was also a settler colonialist world but economically weaker and with different demographic configurations. Within a few decades, early industrialization in some states of the region created a swell of leftist politics, including anarchist, feminist, and socialist, to be followed by more socialist politics, and, after 1917, some Communist politics in the cities and countryside. These became targets for domestic elites in Latin America and in the United States, who found common purpose in finding people, or training them—as they did at the institutions that eventually became the School of the Americas in 1963—to do the frontline dirty work of neutralizing and/or eliminating their perceived leftist enemies.

The imperialist camp was politically victorious in the United States, despite the significant opposition to it from formidable figures such as William Jennings Bryan. But it was specifically President Theodore Roosevelt's 1904 "Corollary" to the Monroe Doctrine that revealed the new US resolve. In response to anything in the hemisphere deemed to be "chronic wrongdoing," the United States would be justified in exercising "international police power" against it. From that point on, the frequency of US interventions in countries across South America was astounding, as if the entire region was a US appendage. Up to 1933, it was Cuba, Panama, Nicaragua, Honduras, Mexico, and the Dominican Republic. Under Franklin Roosevelt and during the Great Depression years of the 1930s to the late 1940s, there was an important softening of the hostility against the reformist, democratic, and labor-based left. This occurred both within most of the countries of Latin America as well as within the United States and, to some extent, in its foreign policy. One brazen exception was Roosevelt's complicity in undermining and defeating the Republican forces and ensuring the victories of the fascist- and Nazi-backed Franco-led militaries in the Spanish Civil War of 1936–9.[13] Aside from that exception, from the US angle, where supposed "communism" did not appear to loom large, at least to most people, this was about the crisis of the Great Depression. Roosevelt's New Deal politics were meant to resolve it, and his "good neighbor" policy toward Latin America was in that spirit. During the war up to mid-1943, it was all about the Grand Alliance of the liberal capitalist powers with the Soviet Union against fascism, a socioeconomic and political model that was dead set against independent labor and the left. Most of South America's governments signed on to the Grand Alliance between the United States and the Soviet Union against fascism. Out of that, the United States and the Soviet Union gained a lot of admiration. It was an unusual if not unique moment that saw labor and the left across the continent make serious gains. But it was a window that was now to be resoundingly shut with the advent of the new anti-Communism, led by the United States and enthusiastically embraced by landed oligarchs, industrialists, and conservatives in Latin America. A sign of the looming shift within the United States came in 1944, when the owner and publisher of the Chicago Tribune, Robert R. McCormick, wrote of the Democratic National Convention that was taking place in July in Chicago:

> They call it the Democratic National Convention but obviously, it is the CIO convention. Franklin D. Roosevelt is the candidate of the CIO and the Communists because they know if elected, he will continue to put the government of the United States at their service, at home and abroad .... The CIO is in the saddle and the Democrat donkey, under whip and spur, is meekly taking the road to communism and atheism .... Everybody knows that Roosevelt is the Communist candidate, but even the Communists cannot be sure where their place will be if he wins. His purpose is to overthrow the Republic for his own selfish ambitions [but] it is the duty of every American to oppose The Great Deceiver [Roosevelt].[14]

This hyperbolic editorializing was pertinent to the situations in and relations between the Republic of Panama, the adjacent US-controlled Canal Zone, and the United States. The rightwing US view of the CIO, presented so vociferously in 1944 as a Communist union that had taken over the Roosevelt camp, typified the political sea change from anti-fascism to anti-"Communism" as it was occurring within the United States. But by the mid-to-late 1940s it crept its way into US foreign policy toward Latin America. In February 1949 the US Ambassador to Panama, Monnet B. Davis, wrote to Secretary of State Acheson that the "need for combating anti-American influences in Panama is acute because of the success of subversive elements in achieving a position of real power and because of the vital political and strategic interests of the United States in this country." There had been a recent defeat of a US effort to attain a defense agreement with the Republic of Panama, and the ambassador mainly blamed Communists for the setback. He wrote that the "political enemies of the United States, particularly the Communists, now organized as the 'Partido del Pueblo,' quickly adopted the program of protecting the territory and sovereignty of the fatherland as a popular means of assuming leadership and preventing normally good relations with the United States." Furthermore, "the Spanish Republican and other Communist-influenced leadership in the National University have left no stone unturned to appeal to youthful national pride, encourage self-pity, inflame race and class hatred and focus all the resultant resentment on the United States and the Canal Zone relationship."[15]

The story of the US mid-level labor organizer Max Brodsky in Panama leads toward a sharper as well as broadly representative look at the political change in the Americas, north and south, from anti-fascism to anti-leftism. In a 1949 British report from Panama City, Brodsky was described as a "Russian-born naturalized American regional director of the United Public Workers C.I.O., assigned to the Union's Canal Zone Local 713." No doubt, Brodsky's Russian background automatically put him in a suspicious light, particularly given his work as an organizer of the 713, the only non-white labor union within the strategically high value Panama Canal Zone at least since 1920. The United States had muscled into what became the Zone in 1904, established sovereignty over it, directed the building of the canal to its finish in 1914, and operated it for the following decades. The 713 was the local wing of the United Public Workers of America (UPWA), which was organized in 1946 as a unit within the CIO. The CIO had been established in the United States as a breakaway union from the AFL in 1935. It had significant Communist influences and policies, most notably in its insistence on fully integrating African Americans into the workforce. Under pressure especially from Southern Democrats, Republicans, and their racist labor counterparts, the CIO gradually backed away from its leftwing positions, though it agreed to the establishment of the UPWA within its organizational network. Yet, as a matter of the "social facts," however false they were, it also continued to get attacked as a "Communist" union by opponents of Roosevelt, including McCormick of the Chicago Tribune quoted above, who wrote that Roosevelt was "the Communist candidate."

Brodsky was in Panama to organize the diverse body of laborers within the Canal Zone, which meant an assortment of North Americans, South Americans and West Indians. But he was not allowed to live in the Zone because he was not an employee of the US government, or of the Panama Canal Railway Company. He had to live in the Republic of Panama that flanked the north and south sides of the Zone, where he was also said to be involved in organizing labor. Meanwhile, the Zone was also a site of serious cultural-political contestation. Partly through Brodsky's and his colleagues' work in the Zone and their communications with North America, but also through the wide ranging channels of the UWPA and its parent CIO, news of the labor issues in the Canal Zone had long reached concerned audiences in the United States. Most famously, these included two of the most towering, brilliant and radical figures in twentieth-century US history, the supremely talented singer, Paul Robeson, and the outstanding sociologist and civil rights activist, W. E. B. DuBois. In 1947 Brodsky and others invited Robeson to perform in Panama and possibly in the Canal Zone in May. Robeson agreed to appear in concert only in Panama City and Colón. He refused to perform in the Canal Zone, saying, "I would not have [sung] on the Canal Zone to the white people there, no matter what they offered. I never have [*sic*] and never will sing as long as I live in places where my people are segregated in the audience." He drew very large and enthusiastic crowds of workers to all his performances, but there were notable absences, too, including the high-up US political and military officials from the Canal Zone, who had accepted invitations, but reneged on them. There was also a larger scale boycott. At least according to the leftwing Panamanian *People's Voice*, "no time was lost by anti-labor factions in hinting that Robeson has been dubbed a Communist and that as such he could be the most dangerous man on earth against the welfare of the worker." As Katherine Zien, puts it, by "scripting blackness according to the models of respectability and uplift provided by Robeson ... concert organizers Local 713 and George Westerman affirmed both the transnational ties of West Indian Panamanians to the U.S. civil rights movement, and their contributive value as citizens of Panama." These politics were deliberate challenges to the system of racial and class injustice as specifically seen in Panama, the Canal Zone, and throughout the Americas. Prior to this, Robeson's sympathies with the Soviet Union were well known, but he had been tolerated, sometimes even celebrated, in his native United States, during the New Deal and Second World War years. The turn came precisely in these early Cold War years, when the FBI hounded him more aggressively, Truman self-righteously dismissed his personal, face-to-face call for a federal anti-lynching law, and he was subject to questioning by the House Un-American Activities Committee (HUAC), which he defied. Robeson performed a stunningly wide repertoire in Panama, ranging from Old English, German, French and Italian songs to classical operatic pieces to Negro spirituals, such as "Let My People Go." He sang his own dignified rendition of "Old Man River" that replaced the original that was laced with racial slurs. Some expected "propaganda" from the man, but in place of it got spiritually uplifting and politically inspiring songs of peace, equality, and justice.[16]

In the months following Robeson's visit to Panama, he, Dubois, and others in the United States established the Citizen's Committee to End Silver-Gold Jim Crow in Panama. The main long-standing labor issue in the Canal Zone had employers hiring skilled white North American laborers as "gold" and Black West Indians as "silver." As the tensions escalated over such blatant discrimination, Brodsky came under closer scrutiny by both the United States and the British. The British reported that he was "stated by the Panamanian Government to have Communist connections." It is very difficult to substantiate these allegations one way or another, but that may not be exactly pertinent. On March 10 the Panamanian minister of foreign relations notified him that he had "twenty-four hours to leave the Republic on pain of deportation." However, upon learning of the order to deport Brodsky, several hundred union members protested, which prompted the Panamanian foreign minister to allege that "the Government had information that Communist elements were agitating in the movement on behalf of Brodsky, and that foreigners who intervene in the country's domestic affairs were subject to summary deportation." The US governor of the Canal Zone stated that any Canal or Railroad employees that engage in "any conduct prejudicial to good order … will be summarily dismissed." The British report applauded the Panamanian president's "forthright action" and its approval in the country's press; he expressed assurance that "the Panamanian Government will fight Communism wherever it finds it." A protest meeting on March 17 said to number between three hundred and four hundred persons was neutralized: "the National Police were on guard with a force of two hundred heavily armed men equipped with tear gas, tommy guns and gas masks." Simultaneously, along the border inside the Canal Zone "a strong force of United States civil and military police was posted, which made it quite clear that any demonstrators attempting to enter the zone would be warmly received." Altogether, the British report presented it as an "admirable display of force."[17] Clearly—and fitting a vile traditional pattern—the self-satisfying animus against leftwing, organized labor was free flowing.

Contentious as the labor issues were in Panama and the Canal Zone, the United States and its local allies, mainly consisting of a decidedly anti-Communist mercantile oligarchy that dominated Panamanian politics, retained a firm grip on power. This was not so in Guatemala, where elite national and US interests saw the emergence of left-oriented democratic politics and deemed them unacceptable. The country had been under the harsh dictatorship of Jorge Ubico from 1931 to 1944, when it was overthrown by an internal mass uprising that supported a military coup. It was popularly discussed as the "Guatemalan Revolution." The military junta that emerged actually organized democratic elections that brought Juan José Arévalo to power in 1944. He was a liberal democratic anti-fascist who aimed to create a society modeled after the US New Deal.

He indeed helped to stabilize the new liberal democratic system, but he was also a strict anti-Communist. The few Communists that existed in the country at the time advocated for land reform, as did many others, including hundreds of thousands of *campesinos*. But Arévalo refused to touch the issue. When his term as president ended in 1950, his minister of defense, the highly capable and charismatic Jacobo Arbenz—whom the United States painted as "an opportunist whose politics are largely a matter of historical accident"—stepped up as a candidate and won the elections. Arbenz's determination to devise and implement genuine land reform and comprehensive infrastructure development was impressive by any standards. Piero Gleijeses wrote that "Arbenz presided over the most successful agrarian reform in the history of Central America."[18] Even some American State Department and CIA observers both understood the need for reform and recognized that Arbenz was implementing it systematically, intelligently, and fairly with regard to both owners and peasants, with results that were initially very positive. Of course, other US foreign policy figures had no sympathy with the reformism at all. The thing they did agree on was that Arbenz had significant Communist input vis-à-vis land reform, and they were right. Arbenz was not a Communist, but the problem for the US cold warriors was that he was also not an anti-Communist. He deeply and firmly believed that Guatemala needed land reform, and he had close, like-minded associates, some of whom were members of the Guatemalan Party of Labor, the *de facto* Communist party of the country. Four of them became ministers in his governing parliamentary bloc in 1953–4.

But already in the spring of 1952, when the land reform legislation was promulgated by the government, the CIA produced a "National Intelligence Estimate"—a highest level national security report—stating that the "Communists already exercise in Guatemala a political influence far out of proportion to their small numerical strength" and that the situation there "adversely affects US interests and constitutes a potential threat to US security." In a sense, this was true: the Guatemalan Party of Labor had a few hundred members, with a small percentage of them militants and an even smaller percentage of them not necessarily "militant," but definitely committed to land reform and working with Arbenz to that end. The "estimate" went on to argue that "Communists and fellow travelers … have been successful in infiltrating the Administration and the pro-Administration political parties and have gained control of organized labor upon which the Administration has become increasingly dependent." The opposition against the "Communist inspired Administration" was depicted as weak and unorganized, which was another way of saying it needed US support. Nothing was mentioned in the report about the courageous and complex effort to reform the systematically unjust structure of landowning in the country, only that Communists were present and had influence in Arbenz's political circles.

The CIA's and other US reports on Guatemala comprised a virtual declaration of war against the Arbenz government. In 1952, Truman authorized the first US-backed *coup* against Arbenz and on behalf of the interests of the US-incorporated United Fruit Company, which was the largest landowning entity in the country outside of the government itself. They rallied support from three of the dictatorial leaders and regimes in the region—Somoza of Nicaragua, Jiménez of Venezuela, and Trujillo of the Dominican Republic—that feared Guatemalan reformism would look far too good to their own peoples. But the plan was aborted because it was too loosely organized and deemed likely to fail. The second effort came just two years later under the administration of Eisenhower and the Dulles brothers, John Foster as Secretary of State and Allen as head of the CIA, both of whom had strong ties with United Fruit. According to the 1952 CIA report,

> United Fruit Company, which conducts extensive operations in nine Latin American countries, dominates Guatemalan banana production. The Company controls the only effective system of internal transportation, the International Railways of Central America. Through its merchant fleet the Company has a virtual monopoly of Guatemalan overseas shipping. It owns or leases large tracts of land in Guatemala and is second only to the Government as an employer of Guatemalan labor.

For the top and most of the middle-level players, including the US analysts and policy makers, it came down first to the United Fruit Company, whose business interests centered on undermining independent and organized labor, and second, the supposed prospect of the "Sovietization." Closely fitting the worldwide pattern, but with particular similarity to the then recent overthrow of the reformist Mossadeq government in Iran, which was also authorized, encouraged, and directed by Eisenhower and the Dulles brothers, the presence and suspected "influence" of Communists in Guatemala supposedly triggered fears of a Soviet take over. One must appreciate the flimsiness of the "Soviet threat." As much as one might prefer to do otherwise, it is difficult to conclude anything but that the key US players in the situation were just cynical. They were primarily looking after US business interests, but they could not admit this to the US electorate, no more than they could as they formulated the Truman Doctrine, or justified their coup against Mossadeq, or a long list of other interventions. It had to be cast in terms of the great battle of the "good" United States versus the "evil" Soviet Union. Nothing played better in the war for people's minds, at least within the United States, though of course it also worked in favor the United States' Latin American and other allies. Backed directly by US finance and supplies of war material, and indirectly by the nearby dictatorial regimes, Carlos Castillo Armas and his supporters inside and outside of Guatemala launched their *coup* in June 1954. Most essentially, the remaining and relatively loyal forces of the Guatemalan military declined to fight the US-backed factions. Arbenz resigned at the end of June.

Even the esteemed conservative anti-Communist historian John Lewis Gaddis asserts simply that Sovietization was not in the cards. He called the US-backed *coup* a "massive overreaction to a minor irritant," though, quite fatalistically, he suggests domestic forces would have overthrown Arbenz anyway, because he was making such enemies among the military and the big landowners. Gaddis may have missed the point, namely, that Guatemala showed again that US anti-Communism tended toward hysteria and irrationality, with extremely destructive consequences. For decades, from the *coup* onward, it gave license to Castillo Armas and his successors—the US-backed "strong men" in the country in league with their vicious frontline people—to commit endless crimes against hundreds of thousands of innocents. It was how all of the allies of the United States in Central America justified whatever they did to serve themselves as they violently undermined socioeconomic and political reform. Arbenz's valiant effort at land reform, of course, was quashed under Armas, and fierce repression of all opposition followed—just as it did in Iran under the US-backed regime of the Shah until the 1979 Iranian Revolution. Civil war raged in Guatemala off and on from 1960 to 1996, especially pitting landless indigenous Mayan peoples and Ladino peasants against rightwing military and paramilitary forces fighting for landed oligarchs, some middle-class anti-leftists, some higher-echelon Catholic clerics, and their US supporters. Anti-Communist and anti-leftist politics were rampant and phenomenally damaging in Central America, as it was across so much of the rest of the world. The situation shows, once again, that one cannot come to terms with the United States during the Cold war, or with so many other examples of anti-leftist politics examined here since the early nineteenth century, without acknowledging such destructive hysterics.

Out of the wide variety of efforts to create something called "socialism," some have survived, though they have been punished. Cuba presents one of the most important cases of all, mainly because it has defied anti-leftist aggressions from the inside and out. Though not unscathed, it has sustained significant successes beyond its basic survival as a state. Cuba has shown that the liberal capitalist metropole has been exceedingly powerful, yet has had its limits, as places outside of its immediate sphere—in this case, only 90 miles away—have had relative strengths. In terms of the effectiveness of anti-leftist hostility, Guatemala went to the US-backed dictatorial right in 1954 and Cuba to the radical socialist left by 1959, which means the island in the Caribbean so close to the United States needs some special attention.

Ernesto "Che" Guevara was 25 years old and in Guatemala City when the Arbenz government was overthrown. The Argentinian already considered himself a medical professional for the people, even something of a revolutionary internationalist, but the circumstances of the *coup* taught him that a one-man revolution was a nonstarter. He had to get involved with an organized network of like-minded activists if he were to have any realistic chance of realizing his vision of equality and justice, not just in public health but also in economics, politics, and culture, all of which he rightly saw as interdependent. He was an outstanding example of a highly deliberate opponent—and product—of the development of modern market liberalization and capitalism. From Guatemala, he fled to Mexico City, where he met Fidel Castro, the young Cuban who was already a veteran of organized leftwing rebel politics. Castro had been involved in the late 1940s with the Caribbean Legion, a loosely organized internationalist paramilitary group established by Guatemala's Arévalo in 1945. Its purpose was to topple the dictatorships of Central America and replace them with democratic governments. It was even mildly supported in its early years by the Truman administration, though this was mostly as a legacy of Roosevelt's greater commitment to democracy in the region. But again, the broad trend in Latin American-US relations in the late 1940s to the early 1950s clearly showed US policy shifting to the right. In 1950 the Caribbean Legion was disbanded; it had achieved an important victory in Costa Rica in 1948 but was poorly organized, failed in two efforts against Trujillo in Panama, and was now tracked by the United States as a leftwing menace. By the early 1950s it was precisely the League's targeted enemies—the dictators and their regimes near to Guatemala—that assisted the United States in its ouster of Arbenz.[19]

Castro then organized "The Movement" in 1952, a political-military group that, within a year, consisted of around 1,200 mostly poor and working-class radicals from Havana who aimed to overthrow the Batista government. They launched their first attack on July 26, 1953, against the Moncada barracks in the city of Santiago de Cuba, on the southeastern coast of the island, hoping to trigger off a popular democratic uprising. But the plan failed, and Castro and his surviving comrades were imprisoned. Due to popular pressure inside and outside of Cuba, they were released in less than a year. Fidel and his brother Raul traveled to Mexico City, where they met Che Guevara and established the 26th of July Movement. Together, they redoubled the efforts of the Caribbean Legion and the Movement, but with a tighter cell system of organization, and with one clear target, the regime under Colonel Batista. The colonel had previously somewhat indulged the Cuban left, including the few Communists, when he was president from 1940 to 1944. But once he got more ensnared with the mafia, and saw the US writing on the wall in the early 1950s, he decidedly turned anti-Communist as he seized power militarily and established his dictatorship, described as "disciplined democracy," in 1952.

The United States only recognized Batista after a conversation between the US Ambassador Beaulac and Cuba's foreign minister, Miguel Angel de la Campa. The Ambassador wrote that he "reminded Campa that General [*sic*] Batista used to have close relations with the Communists. I asked whether we might expect that these close relations would continue. Dr. Campa said that the Provisional Government and he himself would do what could be done under the law to eliminate the freedom and privileges which the Communists were now enjoying in Cuba." The footnote to this report in the State Department files records Ambassador Beaulac stating, "I consider that our conditions for recognition have been met by the new regime and that we should proceed to recognize."[20] Recognition by the United States under Truman and Secretary of State Acheson followed within three days.

Despite the potential and real instabilities they tracked within Batista's Cuba—little genuine popular support, labor and student unrest, desperate to find world export markets for sugar, including temptations to sell it to the Soviet Union—the US State Department and CIA observers repeatedly expressed confidence that the dictator had things under control. They had their strong man in Cuba, who had already done the dirty work of the *coup d'état*. But obviously in retrospect, and even at the time, there was a disjuncture between these reports and the reality on the ground. The overconfidence persisted for several years. A 1953 "Public Order Law" that outlawed Communism in Cuba put the United States further at ease, as did the fact that two attempts to spark popular leftwing uprisings were repelled, first the one against the Moncada Barracks, and a similar one in April 1956 against the Matanzas Barracks, close to Havana, that was carried out by a group sympathetic with the 26th of July Movement. US Ambassador to Havana from 1953 to 1957, Arthur Gardner, brought his pro-Batista stance to an extreme that unwittingly favored Castro's movement. Gardner blocked reports of Batista's weaknesses and ignored and denied reports of the growing strengths and popularity of the 26th of July Movement, steadily keeping the State Department singularly unapprised of the shifting balance of forces in the country. Realistically speaking, the Movement could hardly have hoped for a better enemy. However, Gardner was not quite alone in his assessments. The Assistant Secretary of State for Inter-American Affairs, Henry Holland, wrote in May that the "abortive armed civilian attack on Cuban Army barracks near Matanzas on April 29 culminated a series of events which have weakened the position of President Batista." However, the "President remains fully in control," and "he has been forced to adopt stern measures, including the suspension of constitutional guarantees for forty-five (days) and a sweeping reorganization of the armed forces from which he derives his major support." Perhaps fixating on the official enemies instead of more broadly on the non-Communist left that included Castro and his group, Holland wrote the Communists had tried unsuccessfully to take advantage of the instability, "except for some infiltration in the ranks of the students" about which he showed no concern.[21] Castro had been getting wildly popular in Cuba at least since 1954, when he declared he had every intention of continuing the Cuban revolution, yet Gardner did not pass this information on to his superiors. Perhaps he had a knack for loyalty, but not for strategic assessment. The disconnect between the faltering-Batista-versus-rising-Castro drama, and Gardner's and Holland's reports on it, continued until it was too late for US interests. No doubt, Batista did the same, but, given his immediate personal stake in the matter, this was to be expected. This is not to overstress the importance of muddled US reports on Cuba at the time, but they were among numerous precipitating factors in play during a crucial and open-ended historical moment.

Gardner was dismissed from his post in June 1957. It had become clear to his superiors that his pro-Batista style was to block information that was either critical of the regime or that showed its relative weaknesses. His replacement was Earl E. T. Smith, an elite New York City investment broker who had headed the War Production Board under Roosevelt during the Second World War and spoke no Spanish. While it may have been too late for remedies, he tried to make up for lost time, traveling the country and offering a clear-eyed view of Batista's vulnerability vis-à-vis Castro's rising strengths. In September he reported to the State Department "that the Cuban Government has been unable to liquidate the Sierra Maestra rebellion; that there is little possibility that it can do so in the near future, and that the operation will continue to plague Cuban armed forces, with possibly serious effects on their morale."[22] Smith seems to have been correct and prescient in his observations, yet strikingly, he was also either neutral or trying to create a position for himself to put maximum pressure upon Batista to commit to a return to constitutional and democratic politics. In that case, at this point, he was just overly optimistic, if not naive. Castro and the 26th of July Movement had the overwhelming initiative over Batista, which made the US options extremely limited. In extremely negative terms, a report from US Consulate in Santiago de Cuba, written by Oscar H. Guerra, strongly suggested a similar trend:

Fidel Castro and his 26 July Movement appear to have grown from an annoying thorn in the side of the Batista Government to a slowly spreading cancerous tumor. Through persistence and the benevolent attitude of several American reporters and the American press, this man and his movement have managed to become sentimental favorites in the United States to such an extent that the Batista Government is now on the defensive.[23]

The Batista regime was indeed a problem with prominent figures in the US press and in Congress, while there was excitement about Castro's Movement, and what at least appeared to many, as his authentically democratic character. Castro made his way into US politics and the media far more than Ho Chi Minh ever did, yet the two had similar relations with the great power United States. Both wanted national independence and dignity for their peoples. Ho appealed to President Wilson in 1919 and again to Truman in 1945, clearly registering his admiration and respect for the American Revolution and its constitution, and asking for US support for Vietnamese independence from the French empire. But, both times, which also happened to be during the immediate aftermaths of the two world wars, he was roundly and contemptuously dismissed. Also both times, Ho resorted to the next best chance for national independence—first the French Communist Party, which he helped establish, then the Comintern, and, in 1945, the decision to go to war against the French empire that was backed by the United States. Soon it would be Castro's turn to appeal to the liberal capitalist superpower.

By early 1958, the 26th of July Movement became a mass, interclass movement, strong in the cities and the countryside. It was loosely organized, yet advantageously so. It was similar to the mainly Communist-led Popular Front anti-fascist movements of the 1930s and the Second World War, but without the tight organizational character that was a mark of the Communist parties of the time. Such a stamp on the movement would have easily drawn fire from the United States and bolstered Batista. Instead, the July 26 leaders and their popular movement captured the imaginations even of many in the United States, which itself was haltingly, but significantly, catching the *zeitgeist* of liberation from arbitrary rule, whether colonial, dictatorial, or authoritarian of any sort. Not coincidentally, it was the beginning of the latest wave of civil rights politics in the United States, and shortly followed the Hungarian Revolution of 1956, both of which were influenced by the even greater waves of Third World national liberation politics.

The Cuban revolutionary drama peaked in 1958–9. Batista was corrupt, embedded with the US mafia that had made Havana their playground. He was not seriously willing to risk free elections and civil rights; his social base was ever shrinking, now reduced mainly to only some segments of the military. The status of Castro was rising internationally and domestically, as his social base was ever expanding. In a rare move that reflected the infectious momentum of Castro's movement, the United States imposed an arms embargo on the Batista regime in the spring of 1958, pulling away a major prop at a critical time. The 26th of July Movement's momentum accelerated, as did the colonel's desperation. In December 1958 Batista ordered a full-scale attack on Castro's strongholds in the Sierra Maestra. He declared wage hikes and plans for free and fair elections. But it was all too late: "He did not fool the public, and government forces melted away when confronted with withering guerrilla attacks. When it became clear that the war was lost, Batista and his high command fled the island with as much cash as they could scrape together."[24] One week later, Castro's military forces entered

Havana unopposed and in fact welcomed by throngs of relieved and enthusiastic supporters.

The Cold War world of the time allowed for precious little that was extracurricular, but the Cuban situation was already remarkable for the fact of Castro's victory, for which the United States' indirect and tacit support was a contributing factor. From that point onward, Castro joined the ranks with Tito, Nasser, and others in the Non-Aligned Movement (NAM). A potential "third way" was contained in the politics leading up to the revolution, in which the United States gambled on a Castro victory, while Castro at least hoped for some degree of US support. At the peak of his revolutionary action, he was not a Communist, yet also not an anti-Communist. That seems to be why the United States was sufficiently willing to gamble on him—as opposed to the obviously corrupt public relations disaster, Batista. But the fundamentals of the situation would put Castro, the United States, and NAM to the test. The clash between the political economy of the Cuban-US relationship versus the goals of social and economic justice that Castro had long promised to his growing constituency made the bipolarization of Cuban-US relations after the revolution very likely. In 1959, 65 percent of Cuba's exports went to the United States, while 75 percent of imports came from the United States. Cuban dependency on the US economy was overwhelming. Most of the land in Cuba producing sugarcane (the main export commodity was sugar) was under foreign ownership, mostly US, but also French, Spanish and British. The United Fruit Company, International Telephone and Telegraph, Standard Oil, and other US corporations had operations in Cuba valued at the time in the billions of dollars, but most of the profits were funneled back into the United States. Cuba was one of the premier examples of what the contemporary Argentinian economist Raul Prebisch called an economically "dependent" state in the "periphery" of the world capitalist economy dominated by the "core" states, especially the United States, and particularly in its dominance over the Caribbean and Latin America. Castro came out of that world as a radical reformist— again, not a Communist—whose only real chance of success was in advancing his program in practice, despite any and all risks involved.

It was at this point, in April 1959, as the undisputed revolutionary leader of Cuba, that Castro visited New York City amid great fanfare—"Fidelmania." He appeared with the evening TV variety show host, Ed Sullivan, who seemed to be enamored with him and his gun-toting guerilla entourage—though he asked for confirmation that Castro was a Catholic, which he got to his satisfaction. For his part, President Eisenhower arranged to play golf, leaving his vice president, Richard Nixon, to engage with Castro. The two did not like one another. Nixon attempted to instruct the Cuban revolutionary socialist and anti-imperialist leader in the ways and interests of the US systems of private property, free enterprise, and worldwide free trade. For Castro, if anything, the conversation backfired. Back in Cuba, Castro began the process of nationalizing virtually all US and other foreign corporate property holdings in his new revolutionary state. Between the US economic behemoth and the small and apparently weak Caribbean island state, the war over property and resources was on, but, to a great extent based on its experiences in Guatemala and Iran, the United States was overconfident in victory in Cuba.

In June a CIA "National Intelligence Estimate" raised numerous alarms about the position of Communists within the new Cuban administration, as well as within the labor movement and the armed forces. The report stated that there "are a number of Communists or Communist sympathizers in the military forces, some of whom hold key spots. Castro's brother Raul, who is strongly sympathetic to communism, commands the armed forces. Major Ernesto 'Che' Guevara Serna, a key figure in the revolution who now commands Havana's most important military installation, has consistently furthered Communist interests." Fidel Castro was presented as a dictator and an administrative neophyte that was losing the support of the Catholic Church, the middle classes, and even from laborers—all of which had supported him up to the revolution. The document was license for an aggressive move against the regime at any time in the near future. In the spring of 1960, Eisenhower authorized the creation of an anti-revolutionary interventionist force in Central America, including preparations for an attack on Cuba. President Kennedy finally launched this Bay of Pigs operation in April 1961, but it was an embarrassing fiasco for him and the United States. Unlike the ease with which the CIA organized a group of less than 150 counterrevolutionaries to successfully oust Arbenz from Guatemala, the US-backed forces faced highly prepared and overwhelming opposition. The Cuban leaders had studied the Guatemalan scenario and learned from it. Meanwhile, the United States imposed a series of trade embargos on Cuba, a partial one in October 1960 and, under Kennedy, a full one in February 1962. By this point, Castro had decided to accept economic and political support from the Soviet Union. In October of the same year, US spy planes detected nuclear missiles on the ground in Cuba pointed at the United States. The ensuing Cuban Missile Crisis brought the world as close as it had ever been to nuclear self-incineration. The Castro brothers' and Che Guevara's defiance of the United States inspired many millions across Latin America and the rest of the world, while anti-Communists across the world redoubled their efforts. The Miami Cubans, so many of them exiles from Batista's Cuba, locked onto their mission to overthrow Castro and his government, which they saw as nothing but a vicious dictatorship, and somehow turn it into a liberal capitalist democratic society and state. In the words of Pepita Riera, a leading media voice of the Miami based anti-"Castro-Communists," "Cuba is a school for training in sabotage, red propaganda, terrorism and guerilla war for all countries of Latin America." And "as long as Fidel Castro and his regime exist, the Americas, peace, world stability and Christian civilization will all be endangered."[25] Her book purports to document Cuban Communist subversion in every country of Latin America and parts of the Caribbean.

During and after the dramatic events of 1959–62—the Cuban Revolution, the Bay of Pigs fiasco, and the Missile Crisis—the United States reached back into its increasingly thick Monroe Doctrine file and declared its intent to take the lead throughout Latin America on matters of socioeconomic development and military security. The Cuban Revolution clearly constituted a serious threat in and of itself, but also by example; the Bay of Pigs disaster suggested US military weakness in the face of that threat, while the Cuban Missile Crisis was partly resolved by the United States agreeing to not invade Cuba. In other words, the United States agreed to make no more military efforts to eliminate what was now a Soviet allied state very close to its own shores. If it did, it would risk nuclear war with its rival superpower, which now—legacies of the Monroe Doctrine notwithstanding—had a foothold in the western hemisphere.

Before the Kennedy administration had reached that point vis-à-vis Latin America, it launched the Alliance for Progress, a ten-year plan based on a liberal capitalist developmental vision that was intended to enhance economic development and promote liberal democracy and justice throughout the region. In terms of its goals, it was touted as a Marshall Plan for Latin America, aiming to promote economic development, and reestablish secure, liberal democratic governance. It was a liberal US version of the era's "liberationist" *zeitgeist*. In the words of Lincoln Gordon, US ambassador to Brazil (1961–6) and prominent member of Kennedy's Task Force on Latin America, "We should embark on a decade of democratic progress, to demonstrate in this Hemisphere that economic growth, social equity, and the democratic development of societies can proceed hand-in-hand."[26] The actual achievement of such development in Latin America would have been impressive, but there were several theoretical and practical obstacles. The vision was informed by Walt Rostow's "modernization theory" of economic growth that was laid out in his 1960 book *The Stages of Growth: A Non-Communist Manifesto*. The politics of the title—"*Non*" instead of "*Anti*"—were surely deliberate as a means of exuding a kind of "third way" confidence in the applicability of the supposed universal principles of liberal capitalist growth. But the confidence in its applicability was unfounded. The underlying assumptions of the theory were untenable given the political realities of landed oligarchical power throughout most of the region combined with the pressures of the Cold War. This "first world" economic vision had its radical "third world" rivals, including the Argentinian Prebisch's work on economics mentioned above, that helped make the case for political breakaway movements from the world economy as the only progressive solution for the world's poorer countries. The immediate situational politics across Latin America then involved the variations on the tensions between those pushing for structural changes, and those blocking them. "Third way" noncommunist leftism that Castro rode to power in Cuba, which even seemed to persuade liberal leftists, for example, in Kennedy's Alliance for Progress, was not long for that world. The Alliance made a great initial propaganda splash, but the Bay of Pigs and the Cuban Missile Crisis rendered the developmental side of it dead in the water.

The only major political will to enact the fundamental structural and political changes needed to realize the vision of the Alliance for Progress in Latin America was on the left. But from the early 1960s well into the late 1970s, especially under US President Lyndon Johnson, followed by Nixon and his secretary of state, Henry Kissinger, practically anything serious on the left got forced into the category of Communist subversion. As Thomas McCormick put it, for Johnson, Nixon and Kissinger, and their Latin American allies, "the only good revolution was a dead revolution." However, if serious ventures into socioeconomic development were too risky politically, US-directed military security and police operations were another matter. The default—one included in the blueprint for the Alliance for Progress—was systematic support for political-military firepower, intelligence, surveillance, as well as training for police and military officers from across South America at the School of the Americas in Panama. Eventually, all these default options were coordinated by the United States and its Latin American anti-leftist security allies, and folded into the notorious and deadly "Operation Condor" in the Southern Cone of Latin America. Tens of thousands of leftists were killed, tortured, and "disappeared," especially in Argentina, Chile, Paraguay, Uruguay, Bolivia, and Brazil, but also in Peru, Colombia, and Venezuela, as the operation peaked in the mid-1970s. In addition to US reactions against the Arbenz government and Castro's Cuba, its support for the overthrow of the democratically elected and seriously reformist governments in the Dominican Republic in 1963 and Brazil in 1964 (where the once high-minded Lincoln Gordon was US ambassador) contributed to the trend that got horribly intensified.[27] However, because Operation Condor should also be seen as a distinctive escalation of US anti-leftist politics in Latin America in the 1970s, it is necessary to first have a closer look at the United States, both at home and abroad, in the 1960s and early 1970s.

The Course and Character of Anti-Leftist Politics in the United States to the 1970s

McCarthyism was a serious and damaging force in US politics, until its main extremist and opportunistic author overplayed his hand, accused upper-echelon figures in the US military of being Communists, and hit the political wall. He was censured by the US Senate in December 1954 and ended up occupying a largely, but not completely, ignominious position in the lore of American politics. A few always insisted he was right; they argued he was unjustly proscribed from the body politic. The Senate vote to censure him was 67 to 22. But, given the legacies of anti-leftist politics in the United States at least since the 1860s–70s, plus what was going on around him at the time—Churchill's warnings about Soviet tyranny, Kennan's dark assessments of Soviet intentions, the HUAC inquisitions that had already begun in the late 1930s, and so forth—one must conclude that McCarthy simply did not go far beyond the pale of American anti-"red" politics. The grounds for what he did were well cultivated and fertile. McCarthyism destroyed the careers of some higher-end professionals—some lawyers, State Department officials, and university professors. It is estimated that ten thousand people lost their jobs.[28] But prior to, during, and after his approximately four-year run, anti-leftist politics that included anti-Communism—regardless of McCarthy—constantly took their political-cultural toll on the popular, progressive, and creative tendencies of modern liberal America, which tends to mean liberal-left New Deal America. In some cases, the liberal anti-Communists that were included in the "liberal consensus," who would later be subjected to the broader sweep of anti-leftist politics, were the worst offenders, particularly with regard to the crucial politics of labor unionization. In short, McCarthy's dramatic personal-political decline clearly did not mean the decline of more comprehensive anti-leftist politics that, on a scale broader and deeper than what McCarthy and his enablers had done, were soon unleashed against the elite figures and followers of the many civil rights and anti-war movements of the 1950s–70s, and perpetrated upon American society in the form of early neoliberalism.

It was, no doubt, stunning and frightening the extent to which anti-Communism permeated all spheres of public and private policy and behavior during McCarthy's 1950s heyday. It was the remobilization and re-weaponization of the antipathies against the left of the early to mid-nineteenth century, but into an entire cultural and ideological system. For many it became an identity, inseparable from xenophobic American nationalism that thrived on seeing threatening "foreign" forces everywhere. Beginning in early-nineteenth-century Europe, it appeared in the United States by the 1860s–70s, spread worldwide through imperialism and colonialism, took its extreme tolls in the period of fascism, Nazism and the Second World War, and was then taken up by the United States and its allies as the dominant ideology domestically and internationally in the Cold War. It followed in the tracks of capitalist industrialization and liberalized markets as they spread, extremely unevenly, lurching from crisis to crisis across the world. Its "made in the USA" character during the Cold War easily lent itself to well-deserved caricature, yet one should not lose sight of its longer-term material and ideological-cultural origins. This was liberal bourgeois civilization, now distinctly Americanized.

After the Great Depression, followed by the abyss of the Second World War and the Holocaust, that civilization was regenerating materially through US-led capitalist expansion. That period is widely referred to as the "golden age" of capitalism. The years 1945–70 saw the most rapid economic growth in modern history to date, in which the countries of the Organization for Economic Cooperation and Development (OECD), including the United States, on average grew 4–5 percent per year. As the expansion required more laborers, women and minorities got more jobs—proving themselves as capable as anyone. That structural tendency was also reinforced by serious political activism, but it was a slow and uneven process that, for those women and minorities more than others, was tenuous. The added problem was that, for far too many middle- and working-class white people, a more inclusive society with civil rights and liberties for all was alien and threatening, or was at least presented that way by political opportunists. Politics in the country meant sowing racist divisions and, in effect, if not by intent, a system of divide and rule. Racism, misogyny, homophobia, war mongering, anti-feminism, and more were all justified in the name of anti-Communism; all signs of social and democratic progress were smeared as "un-American" and "Communist." Black Americans and anyone encouraging and helping them to organize for their civil rights were targeted as "Communists," whether they were or not. In 1963 there were approximately seven thousand Communist Party, USA (CPUSA) members, after a peak of fifty-five thousand in 1940 and ten thousand in 1957. Of course, seven thousand CPUSA members within reach of the levers of power in the United States would have been something, but this was not the case. Those that stayed with the party remained largely in the intellectual and labor circles where they had been since the 1930s, and they were marginalized. But that did not dispel the fears or the opportunistic impulses in political and surveillance circles to invoke the Communist threat. It was a tried and true mobilizing force against the left, at least ever since the anti-bolshevism of the era of fascism and dictatorship of the interwar years.

Moves and pressures from the FBI and top political players, including John and Robert Kennedy, against Martin Luther King and his inner circle of friends, colleagues and confidants, got focused into the extensive FBI surveillance operation known as COINTELPRO (acronym for Counter Intelligence Program). As insidious and damaging as the operations were, a look at them and their targets is a window into both the agonies and inspirations in American politics up to the early 1970s. Take Jack O'Dell, raised in Detroit in the 1920s–30s by his grandfather, who was a janitor, and his grandmother, a music teacher. To join the anti-Nazi war, he quit his university studies and joined the Merchant Marines in 1942. Soon he also joined the National Maritime Union, whose distinction was its interracial egalitarianism, which he wholly embraced. In the 1950s he joined the CPUSA, but the Maritime Union, which buckled under pressure to go anti-Communist, expelled him for doing so. He did political work for the CPUSA in the south, but became alienated from the party and quit it later in the decade. He then gravitated toward the Southern Christian Leadership Conference (SCLC) and its nonviolent tactics, and became a trusted adviser to Martin Luther King. But the FBI hounded him. In late 1962 O'Dell resigned from the SCLC under pressure that was passed through King from the Kennedys and J. Edgar Hoover. King rejected the allegations against O'Dell but explained that "in order to avoid embarrassment to the SCLC, he has tendered his resignation."[29] Around the same time, King believed his movement was "on the verge of a major breakthrough in democratic advancement." He saw the violent attacks on activists who advocated for voter registration for Black people, even including the burnings of churches, as signs of strength, showing "the growing Negro vote is the strongest organized movement for the establishment and defense of Civil Liberties as well as of Civil Rights in the south."[30] He surely believed the same about the direct political attacks on his movement and its leadership. Amid the onslaught, this was a tragic truth. In early November 1962, the *New Orleans Times Picayune* newspaper reported that O'Dell was "active as a Communist organizer prior to 1958" and emphasized, first, that he took the 5th amendment against self-incrimination when interrogated by Congress and, second, that King insisted he never knew of anything of it. The innuendo was definitely meant to damage. It was characteristic of the political hits of the era, and it quickly made its way from the New Orleans office of the FBI, to Hoover, to Attorney General Robert Kennedy, and to the president. The pressure came down hard on King to dismiss O'Dell, who was demoted, but kept on as an advisor, until more pressure came the following year. O'Dell stated in a 1993 interview,

> We may have been out from under McCarthyism by the 60s but we were not out from under the official ideology of anti-Communism. President Kennedy on June the 23rd of 1963, had a meeting at the White House with the civil rights leadership because he had introduced the civil rights bill. He took Martin out on the White House lawn and told him that his relations with Jack O'Dell were jeopardizing the passage of the civil rights bill. He told Martin that I was the number four Communist in the United States. Martin said, "Well, I want to see the documentation of that?" He said, "Okay. We'll set up for you to see it." This is what Martin reported to us. Kennedy's rationale was that Strom Thurman and some of the southern Democrats were getting ready to make an issue of who Martin's connections were that they considered communists, Jack O'Dell being on the staff

and Stanley Levison as a confidant. Kennedy said to Martin, according to Martin, that if they made that a public issue he, Kennedy, would not support the civil rights bill. So Martin has a choice, in effect, coming out of that conversation, to sever these ties and salvage Kennedy's support for the civil rights bill or stay with his friends and have an attack come from Strom Thurman. Unless you sacrificed your principles you couldn't escape the anti-Communism. They had no reason to Red bait him but it went on anyway. I'm just saying that the anti-Communism had become institutionalized as an effective weapon in intimidating and preventing the movement from developing. And of course, it had succeeded in some instances and failed also because movement was developing anyway.[31]

One of Hoover's next targets was Stanley Levison, a progressive entrepreneur and committed civil rights activist from New York City that had been under FBI scrutiny and surveillance in the early 1950s. In December 1962 Hoover described developments on the political-cultural front that to him constituted enemy activity—it was none other than a fundraising affair in White Plains, New York, for the SCLC, featuring the celebrities of the "rat pack," Sammy Davis Jr. and Peter Lawford. But Hoover's eye was on Levison, one of the main organizers of the event. Shortly following the 1955–6 Montgomery Bus Boycott, Levison had been in consultation with King about strategic matters. King was then just 27 years old and Levison 44; they developed a close and vital political friendship, though one always challenged by the multipronged reactions against them. Levison had been affiliated with the CPUSA until 1954; the FBI had determined as much and had stopped investigating him shortly afterward. But now, with King's status and prestige growing on the national scene, the stakes were higher. Something was afoot, and Hoover went for the smear: "Levison, who recently organized the Gandhi Society for Human Rights in King's name, has been described by an informant who has furnished reliable information in the past as a secret member of the Communist Party." This was the message that was repeated to the Attorney General and the President for the next several months, until the moment on the lawn of the White House recollected above by O'Dell, when JFK warned he would not support the civil rights bill that was being promulgated unless O'Dell and Levison were completely removed from King's circle. O'Dell distanced himself further from King, while Levison insisted on stepping away, but, to the consternation of Hoover, the Kennedys, and President Johnson, both maintained intermittent contact with King, much of it detailed in FBI files from those years, until his death. Fortunately, at least, the contact was not enough for JFK to abandon his cooperation on civil rights legislation.

The next King confidant to get attacked was Bayard Rustin, whose commitment to civil rights for all was astonishing and deserves elaboration. His grandparents raised him as a Quaker. His grandmother was a member of the National Association for the Advancement of Colored People (NAACP), who hosted visits from prominent activists and intellectuals, such W. E. B. Dubois, when Bayard was a boy. Taking those influences to heart, he became a tireless civil rights activist. In 1936, he joined the Young Communist League (YCL) of the CPUSA because it was the premier political organization advocating and organizing for civil rights for all Americans. But he gradually grew disillusioned with the party and finally left it in June 1941, after the Nazi invasion of the Soviet Union, when the Comintern deprioritized civil rights and called for all Communist parties worldwide to support the Allied anti-Nazi war effort. Rustin had already developed ties with democratic socialist A. Philip Randolph, head of the Brotherhood of Sleeping Car Porters, who was strategizing for a civil rights march on Washington, as well as the socialist-pacifist A. J. Muste. Once Rustin quit the YCL, the three of them informed Roosevelt that they were prepared to organize a march on Washington in favor of two things: racially fair employment in the defense industries and the desegregation of the military. The threat of the strike succeeded in getting an executive order from Roosevelt for the Fair Employment Act on June 25, and the march was cancelled.[32] Discriminatory hiring practices in defense and government sectors were steadily lessened from that point on, though the desegregation of the military only happened under Truman in 1948. Rustin traveled to California and advocated on behalf of the Japanese Americans interned in prison camps. He spent two years in jail for his pacifism, there organizing for full civil rights for all inmates. Rustin traveled to India in 1948 for a close look at the ways of Ghandian nonviolence; he traveled to Africa for close-up observations of the continent's national liberation movements. He met Martin Luther King in Alabama in 1955 after the successful Montgomery Bus Boycott and advised him on nonviolent protest strategies that became the trademark of King's SCLC. He helped organize the Freedom Rides in 1961 that challenged the South's refusal to enforce Supreme Court decisions that interstate segregated busing was unconstitutional; and he was a key figure in the organization of the March on Washington in 1963. In the run up to the march, the notoriously racist senator from South Carolina, Strom Thurmond, accused Rustin of "being a communist, a draft dodger and a homosexual." In fact, he was a committed civil rights leftist, a pacifist, and a homosexual. Because of the latter, he tried to keep a low profile in King's circle in order to draw minimal negative attention, if possible. The prevailing view in intelligence and surveillance circles at the time was that homosexuality, which they totally stigmatized on its own, was also a red flag for susceptibility to Communist influence. But Rustin's organizing skills were so vital to the success of the massive public event that it was hard for him to avoid the limelight. He and A. Philip Randolph appeared on the cover of *Life Magazine* in September 1963 as the "leaders" of the March on Washington. Hoover's mission was faltering. Short of declaring them dead, there was perhaps nothing that he and the demographic he represented desired more than to be able to declare that King and his cohort were Communist.[33] In fact, that is what they did, with great disregard for the evidence, until April 1968, when King was assassinated.[34]

In late October 1963, FBI chief Hoover wrote to the attorney general of the United States, Robert F. Kennedy, regarding "the Communist Party USA, the Negro Question, Communist Influence in Racial Matters and Internal Security." This was specifically about Bayard Rustin, whose suspect attributes included "Deputy Director of the August 28th, 1963 March on Washington." Hoover stated that confidential and reliable sources reported that Benjamin Davis, national secretary of the CPUSA was "maintaining liaison with Rustin." The same source reportedly told Hoover that "the Negroes are now willing to know what the Communist Party has to say and to welcome whatever support the communists can give 'in this new stage, which is how to break the resistance of the Dixiecrats and how to stop the McCarran Act.'" The request was approved. It is pertinent here that the Kennedys were very friendly with McCarthy before his fall, of course also during Hoover's seemingly interminable tenure as head of the FBI. Their anti-Communist reflexes were lively. The attorney general's office agreed "to place a technical surveillance" on Rustin's present and any future residence. Yet it was to no particular avail, at least with regard to the landmark civil rights legislation that was in the works. After JFK's assassination, Johnson fought successfully to get the Civil Rights Act passed in 1964, thus outlawing discrimination based on race, color, sex, or national origin. The Voting Rights Act of 1965 outlawed discrimination in voting rights, especially the "literacy tests" that disenfranchised many African American and other minority and immigrant voters. As Jack O'Dell put it in his 1993 interview quoted above, "I'm just saying that the anti-Communism had become institutionalized as an effective weapon in intimidating and preventing the movement from developing. And of course, it had succeeded in some instances and failed also because the movement was developing anyway."

The anti-leftist tendencies characteristic of the predominant politics in the United States, so interwoven with racism as they were on the elite and popular levels, still could not completely stop the momentums of the King-led civil rights movement, or the slightly later phases of the Chicano and Native American movements. The Black nationalist-separatist politics of Malcolm X, while they lasted, had less momentum; they did not have great practical viability, while his intensive and extensive peregrinations, and finally the fact that he was assassinated in 1965 at age 39, lent themselves far more to his powerful legacy than to his 1960s movement and moment. US anti-leftist politics and racism, as well as those of the French, British, Dutch, and Portuguese on the world stage, were also not enough to shut down the movements for national liberation from colonial rule that inspired and undergirded civil rights politics in the United States. But the countervailing US anti-leftist and racist rhetoric that convinced too many ordinary Americans, especially those with white skin that, counter to the spirit of individual liberty and national liberation from colonial rule that tended to be so celebrated, year after year, from the American Revolution of 1776 onward, it was necessary to oppose civil rights for all in the United States, defeat Communists in Indochina and everywhere else, and infect politics worldwide to the point where they ultimately threaten to devour the best of the original vision of the American republic—this was and is nothing but real and potentially further betrayal and tragedy. Such politics obviously stunted and stymied leftwing movements, resulted in the deadly targeting of leading individuals, such as Patrice Lumumba, Martin Luther King, and Che Guevara, and virtually guaranteed, for the foreseeable future, that the predominant power system in the United States would remain one of unrelenting racial, social and economic injustice.

Malcolm X and King, despite their strategic and tactical differences, which lessened considerably in 1964–5, were wise to such politics and abhorred them. But also, in the last years of their lives, 1964–5 and 1967–8, respectively, each one experienced some combination of radicalization and transformation. Malcolm X embraced the politics of Third World national liberation, particularly through an Islamic notion of the brotherhood of man—and "man" it was; most unfortunately, neither he nor King ever got beyond patriarchy.[35] King also shifted toward a deep appreciation of the problem of economic inequality and developed the conviction that without economic equality, there would never be a sufficient breakdown of racial inequality in the United States or anywhere else. Neither figure had any trouble spelling out the problems of capitalism, colonialism, and imperialism that virtually necessitated liberationist politics. Both were highly religious. Malcolm X had embraced Islam in prison in the early 1950s and stayed with it through his many changes until the end of his life; King was a Baptist minister and social gospel leftist, painfully aware of the need for socioeconomic transformation, if not social revolution. While they still diverged on the tactical question of violence—nonviolence for King, violence in self-defense for Malcolm X—neither believed there would be any real human progress without a grand exit from capitalism, colonialism, imperialism, and racism.

Also in their final years, each one was a relatively solitary figure. After quitting the Nation of Islam in March 1964, Malcolm X spent several months in Egypt, Kenya, and Ghana, meeting with anti-colonialist leaders and Black American expatriates. He went to Saudi Arabia for the traditional *hajj* to Mecca. Though the FBI had their eyes on Malcolm at least since 1953 for being a "militant," they later tracked his travels in Africa closely and were particularly attentive to his meeting with Chinese embassy officials in Accra, Ghana. While these experiences amounted to a large personal revelation for him, allowing him to expand his horizons dramatically, he paid the ultimate price for it. In the end, the FBI forced him into a "Communist" or "fellow traveler" category. He was assassinated on February 21, 1965, at the Audubon Ballroom in Manhattan, as he was preparing to give a speech on pan-African unity. It has never been settled as to whether people in the Nation of Islam or in US intelligence services, or both together, killed him.[36]

King followed his conscience and gambled strategically as he came out against the US war in Vietnam. In his "Beyond Vietnam" speech of April 4, 1967, he expressed grave concern that the anti-poverty program launched by Johnson in early 1964, which he already believed was flawed because it was not coordinated and comprehensive, was "broken and eviscerated, as if it were some idle political plaything of a society gone mad on war." King "knew that America would never invest the necessary funds or energies in rehabilitation of its poor so long as adventures like Vietnam continued to draw men and skills and money like some demonic destructive suction tube." He "was increasingly compelled to see the war as an enemy of the poor and to attack it as such." Further addressing the war and its impact on the poor in the United States, he said,

It [the US] was sending their sons and their brothers and their husbands to fight and to die in extraordinarily high proportions relative to the rest of the population. We were taking the black young men who had been crippled by our society and sending them eight thousand miles away to guarantee liberties in Southeast Asia which they had not found in southwest Georgia and East Harlem. And so we have been repeatedly faced with the cruel irony of watching Negro and white boys on TV screens as they kill and die together for a nation that has been unable to seat them together in the same schools. And so we watch them in brutal solidarity burning the huts of a poor village, but we realize that they would hardly live on the same block in Chicago. I could not be silent in the face of such cruel manipulation of the poor.[37]

The speech in its entirety was a blistering, cogent, and comprehensive critique of the US war in Vietnam, while it also presented practical proposals for bringing it to an end. Based on ignorance and misinformation, a majority of Americans at the time supported the war, which was prosecuted with repeated escalations by President Johnson, a man terrified of being labeled "soft on Communism." After working closely with King on civil rights legislation, Johnson felt betrayed by him because of his anti-war stance. Even some close to King worried he was undermining the civil rights movement. King had tremendous frustrations, yet with his moral compass, he overcame them to the end. Of course, he had been a target of Hoover's and the FBI's for years, but the political moves that he made in the last year of his life arguably turned him from a fictional to a real threat to the American power structure. It was not just his hard-fought, yet nonviolent and successful, campaign for civil rights, which drew intense animosity from conservative Americans; he now came out against the US war in Vietnam and in favor of economic equality. Both directly and indirectly, he went after four of the practical and ideological pillars of the American power structure: racism, the foreign policy establishment, the economic system of capitalism, and the whole political-cultural edifice of anti-Communism. The fact that he was eloquent, that he a had large and diverse audience, that his tactics had proven effective, and that he raised and addressed these issues as interdependent parts of the same system of cruel injustice made him into one of America's and the world's best hopes, but the American power establishment's worst enemy.

In typical form, the FBI stepped up surveillance on him and launched a stealth campaign of falsehoods. The agency hatched a plan in March 1967 to "to furnish a suggested list of questions to a friendly news source to be used in interviewing Martin Luther King, Jr.," who, according to their sources, was inclined "to direct his entire efforts in opposition to the war in Vietnam." In California on February 2, for example, King "attacked the war," while "at one point he made a statement that might be considered revolutionary." He stated in part, "We have got to get out and demonstrate and protest until it rocks the very foundations of the Nation." The FBI memo also referred to some points on which he felt he had failed and was therefore personally vulnerable, such as a "voter registration drive in Chicago" that "failed miserably," and that he was "sensitive about allegations his personal appeal to the ghetto Negro is wanting." Further, the newly established Spring Mobilization Committee to End the War in Vietnam was recently appointed an executive director, Reverend James Bevel, whose "wife traveled to Hanoi, North Vietnam, in 1966." Hypothetically, the "friendly news source," equipped with the FBI's questions, could arrange for an interview about a book King was writing but then launch into the smear questions. King's reorientations toward full-time opposition against the war could be contrasted with other civil rights leaders who were not straying from the undoubtedly noble, but narrower, cause; "this then could be linked to show that King's current policies remarkably parallel communist efforts. Further, it is felt that since the position and paths taken by King and his group closely parallel that advocated by the Communist Party, this fact should be made known to the public." Hoover and several of his underlings signed off on the proposal.[38]

The key moment when King came out publicly against the US war in Vietnam was in New York City on April 4, 1967, during an evening speech at the Riverside Church in the Morningside neighborhood of Manhattan. Some of the details found in the FBI memos—entitled "Communist Infiltration of the...SCLC"—suggest in tragicomic detail the extent to which they had their eyes on him and his colleagues. During the day, "special agents of the FBI ... observed the following activities at the hotel .... Martin Luther King, Harry Wachtel and an unknown Negro male walked into the lobby at 10:55 a.m. and took the elevator that serviced the 15th floor; at 11:05 a.m. Andrew Young entered the lobby and took the same elevator, and at 11:12 a.m. Stanley Levison came into the hotel and took the same elevator." The FBI's default position on Wachtel and Levison at this point was that they were Communists, since they had past connections with the party and with leftwing and labor causes. But, regarding the speech that evening, which was "to an overflow crowd of more than 3,000 persons at the Riverside Church," the FBI highlighted several of its salient points, all of which demonstrated that King was a threat: first, he appealed to "Negroes and 'all white people of good will'" to boycott the Vietnam War; second, he portrayed "the American Government as 'the greatest purveyor of violence in the world today'"; third, "the United States was on the wrong side of a world revolution and [he] urged that the United States leaders admit 'that we have been wrong from the beginning of our adventure in Vietnam'"; fourth, King offered viable, constructive proposals for ending the war, though the FBI's only response to them was that "they were similar to Hanoi's demands" and "parallel the Communist Party line."[39]

A little over a week after the April 4 speech, the FBI zeroed in further on fundraising efforts by King, Wachtel, Levison, and others, who had attracted New York's Governor Nelson Rockefeller's interest in contributing a substantial contribution to the SCLC. Rockefeller hesitated because of King's recent public turn against the US role in Vietnam. Rockefeller was a member of the Republican Party and an anti-Communist but took a modern liberal stance on civil rights, and he was outspoken in his support for King. Grandson of John D. Rockefeller of Standard Oil fame, he had major wealth, including substantial investments in Latin American mining enterprises, as well as obvious influence in its politics. The FBI was concerned that he was actually susceptible to King's supposed Communist advisors, who argued that Latin America was about to become another Vietnam for the United States. As the memo put it, "King has clearly become merely a puppet in the hands of Levison and Wachtel." They were molding him to become not just the leader of "22 million Negroes, but now the accepted leader of the vast anti-war effort in the country." The same memo said that the recent Riverside Church speech "shows how much of a communist puppet he has become and illustrates the danger he represents in the hands of the scheming communists." Wachtel and Levison, the memo argued, "represent two of the most dedicated and dangerous communists in the country."[40] The agency believed "too much is at stake," that Rockefeller had to be discreetly advised that King was a Communist puppet. The governor later became vice president under Gerald Ford and was wide open to political advice from Henry Kissinger on the threat of "Communism" in Latin America. It is just that he supported King's civil rights movement; by no means did he see it as a threat to the United States, let alone a delivery system for Communism. In a book that King wrote shortly before he was assassinated, he stated that "Communism is a judgment on our failure to make democracy real and to follow through on the revolutions that we initiated. Our only hope today lies in our ability to recapture the revolutionary spirit and go out into a sometimes hostile world declaring eternal opposition to poverty, racism and militarism."[41] As he had been doing for years, in spite of the US intelligence services aggressively alleging otherwise, King once again dismissed the value of "Communism," yet by that point he had adopted a multipronged program of structural reform for the United States that was nothing less than revolutionary. From China to Kenya to Iran, Algeria, Guatemala, Cuba, the United States, and elsewhere, including so many countries in the preceding period, reform was tantamount to revolution. The injustices were that extreme and the responses to the politics that opposed them were that vicious and cynical.

King was assassinated on April 4, 1968, in Memphis, Tennessee, the day after he had given one of the most forceful and visionary speeches of his career to striking sanitation workers. The speech was a vision of human progress that used the allegory of the Hebrew flight from captivity in Egypt to present the vicissitudes of the struggle of African Americans from slavery, to emancipation, to the Jim Crow South, to the present moment in Memphis—"I have been to the mountaintop," he exclaimed, and nothing scared him any more. The following day, a white racist-nationalist, James Earl Ray, shot and killed him outside of his hotel room. His wife, Coretta Scott King, along with other colleagues, such as Ralph Abernathy, Jesse Jackson, Andrew Young, and committed followers, immediately tried to carry on his legacy by advancing the Poor People's Campaign. But on the larger societal level, where, to say the least, there had been a great deal of unease about King, as well as plenty of horrible hatred of him, there began the effort to sanitize his legacy: the creation of the lightweight sentimental myth of the civil rights "idealist." The extent to which he was integrated into the predominating American historical memory was the extent to which his real message of the need for an end to the combined abuses of racism, militarism, and capitalism was suppressed, even though a critical minority of people understood it and have tried to keep it alive and active. In the United States, the current "Poor People's Campaign," led by William Barber and Elizabeth Theoharis, is a vital example of that effort, as is the Black Lives Matter Movement.

As such dramatic events played themselves out on the national stage, COINTELPRO was also busy since 1956 across the country at the more local level, snooping, smearing, assassinating, dividing, and ruling. Its original target was the CPUSA, but by the mid-1960s, it was going after all groups deemed to be "leftist"—which they were—including feminists, native American activists, anti-war activists, Students for a Democratic Society (SDS), civil rights leaders, and Black Panther Party (BPP) members. Most infamously, they targeted the Chicago-based head of the Illinois chapter of the BPP, Fred Hampton, as a dangerous radical. Hampton was a socialist, internationalist, and community organizer whose political message was about interracial solidarity and class-consciousness. He created a "rainbow coalition" in Chicago that brought together not just a number of smaller political groups but also a number of rival street gangs.

For that kind of activity, on December 1969, in an operation spearheaded by the FBI, but also involving local Chicago police forces, Hampton and one of his colleagues were assassinated in their apartment in the middle of the night; several others were injured.

Less famously, but no less typically, figures in the New Left, the BPP, and SDS in Milwaukee, Wisconsin, all got the treatment and were set against one another. Infiltrators in the various groups planted accusations that the other groups were actually not in serious solidarity with them, that they could care less about them. The details of who was doing what to whom on behalf of the FBI are sketchy, because such information is heavily redacted from the declassified files. However, there is enough to show that the SDS was said by FBI infiltrators in the BPP to be nothing but self-centered white kids that were not inclined to share anything of value with the Panthers. The San Francisco office of the FBI planted a letter in September 1969 to a Bay area BPP newspaper, saying, with deliberate misspellings, "What's with this SDS out fit? I'll tell you what they has finally showed there true color WHITE. They are just like the commies and all the other white radical groups that suck up to the blacks and use us."[42] According to James Kirkpatrick Davis, "Hoover was nearly obsessed with the potential of an SDS/Black Panther Partnership." To a frightening extent, the FBI director and his minions got what they wanted. COINTELPRO infiltrated, wielded divide and rule tactics, and killed when deemed necessary, from New Jersey and New York City, to Baltimore, Chicago, Milwaukee, San Francisco, Oakland, and Los Angeles. With some success, the FBI managed to foment conflict within the ranks of the Black Panthers, effectively dividing them against one another. In a 2014 interview, Eddie Conway, a former BPP figure in Baltimore, who had just been released from nearly forty-four years in prison for allegedly killing a police officer in 1971, suggested the Black Panthers were targeted by law enforcement at all levels because they were socialists, not because they were armed and Black.[43]

Conflicting Global Currents: Leftist Upsurge, Economic Downturn, and the Shift to Neo-Liberalism

The year 1968 saw the convergence of all the worldwide currents of leftwing politics; in some places—Paris above all—they proliferated exponentially. Everything and everyone had to be liberated: nations, peoples, individuals, women, men, libidos, students, artists, musicians, architects, and youth. But where the stakes were highest, where they involved the very lives of hundreds of thousands of people, Vietnam was getting worse, militarily and politically, for the United States and their South Vietnamese allies. The Vietcong were being hit very hard, yet showed steady resolve against the world's premier superpower. The Tet Offensive against the South that was launched in January caught opposing forces completely off guard and instilled doubts in expanding portions of the American public about the justifications for and prospects of the war. Since 1966, even the US defense secretary, Robert McNamara, had his private doubts about the war's efficacy, though he kept quiet as the death tolls of American troops and Vietnamese soldiers and civilians climbed. Domestic US support for the war dropped as dramatically as protests against it rose. Anti-war currents swelled across Western Europe, the UK, and Latin America, propelled by King's and others' critiques of militarism generally, but also by the news of the carnage in Vietnam. Johnson was growing uncertain about the war, but he also felt betrayed by King, with whom he had collaborated in civil rights battles, because of King's increasingly vocal and public opposition to the war. But the problem for Johnson was not just King. Due to numerous pressures—the military failures, the rising oppositions, the dim prospects for the United States in Vietnam, as well as the sheer financial costs of the war and their likely ruination of his Great Society program—Johnson announced at the end of March that he would not seek reelection to the presidency. King was murdered several days later. It was an incalculable loss, but the anti-war and equality messages that he and others expressed were alive, spreading, and lasting.

Currents of liberationist politics in Paris during the spring of 1968 became nothing less than incendiary; they appeared, at least, to be bringing the society to the brink of revolution. The radical politics were in solidarity with the movements for national liberation from colonial power across the world, but they also translated into a radical critique of domestic power. Beginning with university student groups, there emerged a political and intellectual ferment that expanded spectacularly in scale to include most of France's working classes and intellectuals. Student discussions of the problems of exclusivist and elitist educational policies turned into larger critiques of the oppressive character of French societal power, including critiques of gender and cultural repression, and the dehumanizing effects of the burgeoning consumer and technological culture that they saw overtaking their society. One group at the University of Nanterre in Paris occupied rooms at the university to conduct their investigations, which prompted the administrative authorities to discipline them, even threatening to expel them. Sympathy came quickly and strongly from other students as well as faculty, who joined in protests and street demonstrations. The police attacked them brutally, which only increased their numbers, diversity, and solidarity. The major labor unions of the country voiced support for the students. By the end of May, millions of workers, students, intellectuals, and sympathizers from the broader society flooded into the streets. Charles de Gaulle fled to West Germany, recalling the attempted and ultimately disastrous flight from Paris to Varennes by King Louis XVI during the revolution in 1791. But de Gaulle was on a better track. Within a couple of days, he regrouped, returned to France, dissolved parliament, called for new national elections, pressured French industrialists to provide their workers with higher wages and better benefits, and called for his supporters to march on Paris. Outmaneuvering the groundswell of the left, the Gaullists came out stronger than ever—not just upwards of one million in the streets of Paris on May 30 but also a victory at the polls in June for a revived Gaullist government. Politically for the left, it was the revolution that wasn't, yet it gave way to a wide array of much needed change and reform. It may have been de Gaulle and the industrialists who finally decided upon a more favorable approach to French workers, but it was the vast protests that virtually forced them to do so. In the universities, long overdue reforms were enacted, including expanded educational opportunities for the underprivileged, and freedom for students to question professors openly in class. It also created a surge of artistic, intellectual, and political production, much of it under the loose moniker of the "post-modern." Nominally, the Gaullists' moves against the left were victorious, but they were also forced into a new social contract with the left, including labor, and with the majority of the French people. It was nearly a political revolution. The fact that French conservatives outmaneuvered it is something to reckon with, painful as that may be for some, but it was still a social and cultural rebellion that was significantly and lastingly transformative for French society.[44]

Although divisions within the left are mostly not a part of the scope of this study, the situation in Czechoslovakia in 1968 was such a critical development in the short and longer run for Eastern Europe and Soviet power that it warrants attention. Simply put, the terms of politics within Eastern Europe had to do very much with left versus rightwing socialism, with the latter recognizable as authoritarian statism. This was true in Hungary of 1956, Czechoslovakia in 1968, and Poland in the 1980s. In that setting, the reform socialist Alexander Dubcek was appointed in January 1968 by the Soviets as the general secretary of the Czechoslovakian Communist Party. But, apparently to the surprise of his overlords, Dubcek stuck to his reformism. He pushed for political and economic decentralization, which was popular among most Czechoslovaks. He took to heart (as did the young Mikhail Gorbachev) Nikita Khrushchev's 1956 denunciation of Stalin and call for systemic and political "de-Stalinization." But Dubcek's actual pursuit of reform alarmed the Soviet leaders and their allies throughout Eastern Europe, while it also generated major popular enthusiasm in and outside of Czechoslovakia, therefore looming large as a threat to Soviet power. As things seemed to be getting out of hand, Warsaw Pact tanks and troops were sent into Prague in August, crushing the Prague Spring and its "socialism with a human face."[45]

The Czechoslovak situation was part of the complex pattern of the leftwing rebellion in 1968 that was evident worldwide, in the United States, Eastern and Western Europe, Japan, Australia, Mexico, and the rest of Latin America. But because of the importance of the United States as the lead force against such politics—countless reactionary political-military forces took their cues from US leaders in this era—it is necessary to continue to track top-level American political as well as economic developments and show their worldwide effects. While leftwing rebellion continued worldwide, the potentials for political reaction against it led by the United States were facilitated by two things combined: first, Johnson's refusal to run for a second term; second, division within the ranks of the Democratic Party that, in principle, could have come up with a viable anti-war and social justice candidate. This opportunity was presented to the Republican candidate, Richard Nixon, to launch a "law and order" campaign on the domestic front and, in foreign policy, a promise to put the Vietnam War into the hands of the South Vietnamese, while winding down the US military presence. Nixon won the November elections by a small margin, but with Henry Kissinger as his Secretary of State, he did nothing but expand and escalate the US war. The carpet bombing of Vietnam's neighbors, Laos and Cambodia, which was meant to break any and all support lines for the Vietcong, caused hundreds of thousands of deaths of innocents. These were people guilty of fighting for their national independence, but facing untold misery, as well as incalculable environmental and physical devastation. It also provoked an ever-greater intensity of anti-war resistance across the United

States, largely centered on student activism, from Columbia University in New York City, to Madison, Wisconsin, to Berkeley, California. The National Guard's killings of four student anti-war protesters at Kent State University on May 4, 1970, and the police killings of two students at Jackson State College eleven days later were some of the most difficult events of those times within the United States. But the Vietnamese government's official estimation of lives lost in their wars with France and the United States from 1954 to 1975 is 2 million civilians and 1.1 million North Vietnamese and Viet Cong fighters. The death toll for US forces is 47,434 "hostile deaths" and 52,880 including "non-hostile" deaths.[46]

All of the above spelled to many that there was a reckoning in the works, with lessons learned and the promise of a turn toward a more progressive future. Indeed, there were cultural advances in the First World that included liberal civil rights for minorities of all sorts, as well as women, accompanied by the great movements for national liberation across much of the Third World. But on the economic level, the beginnings of a historic shift were taking place that would challenge, stunt, or even threaten to eliminate those gains. Beginning in the late 1960s, quarterly reports from US corporations showed striking decreases in profits. They were not mere blips. By the early 1970s it was clear they were the prevailing US economic trend. Following upon the boom years of the US-led "golden age of capitalism" since the end of the Second World War, this was the beginning of the long-term downturn in the world capitalist economy that persists well into the twenty-first century. It brought with it a whole slew of economic, financial, and political changes, most important of which is the political economy of neoliberal economic globalization. The change was brought on by the interactions of the very competitiveness of the economic system of capitalism, along with a series of contingent developments, beginning with the aftermath of the Second World War.[47] For this study, the relevance of these changes is in the deliberate, profound, and worldwide anti-"socialist" thrust of neoliberal economic and financial policies and politics.

Following the war, the United States invested tremendous resources into the economies of Western Europe but put a major focus on the buildup of West Germany and Japan—both defeated Axis states. The motive was to build up anti-Communist bulwarks, east and west, and create markets for American exports. Both countries had preestablished powerhouse capitalist structures that had enabled them to launch their delusional war efforts in the first place but were now physically devastated. However, as *strategic* investment propositions, they were second to none. They could be rebuilt and regenerated to become reliable anti-Communist, US-allied states with sustained economic dynamics. Politically, the strategy largely succeeded, but economically there were consequences that were not favorable for the United States. Japanese and German manufacturing benefitted dramatically from US financial and technical support for the rebuilding of their economies, but their successes posed competitive challenges to US production and pricing, which were exactly what showed up in the troubling economic news of the late 1960s–early 1970s. West Germany and Japan, with their newer and more technologically advanced plant and equipment, were able to produce big-ticket items, such as automobiles, more efficiently and cheaply than could producers in the United States, where infrastructure, factories, and technology were now relatively outdated. German and Japanese cars gained US market share, especially after another problem hit the world economy, namely, the decision by the Arab oil-producing states to cut oil production and raise prices on it as a protest against the Israeli occupations of Palestinian, Syrian, and Egyptian lands after the two Arab-Israeli wars of 1967 and 1973. The price was hiked from $3 to $12 per barrel in a matter of a few months; the US and European allies of Israel initially got no oil from the Arab states. Inflation socked the international economy, which, for the advanced capitalist states, particularly the United States, only exacerbated the preexisting problems of the competition between the leading liberal capitalist states that was driving down US corporate profits. But, just in terms of the markets for automobiles worldwide, the Germans and Japanese now had another competitive edge—fuel-efficient cars that had obvious appeal over the US "gas guzzlers."

One of the earliest and most important strategic responses to the problem of declining American corporate profits came from Lewis F. Powell Jr, an associate member of the US Supreme Court from 1971 to 1987. Powell wrote his memo in August 1971, just before Nixon appointed him to the Supreme Court. It was entitled "Attack on American Free Enterprise System" and written for the Chairman of the Education Committee of the US Chamber of Commerce. Powell wrote that the attack's "sources are varied and diffused. They include, not unexpectedly, the Communists, New Leftists and other revolutionaries who would destroy the entire system, both political and economic." But these elements "remain a small minority" and are "not yet the principal cause for concern." He explains that "the most disquieting voices ... come from the college campus, the pulpit, the media, the intellectual and literary journals, the arts and sciences, and from politicians." The chief culprits may be small in number, but they are often "the most articulate, the most vocal, the most prolific in their writing and speaking." Showing a crypto-Marxist analytical tendency, Powell reflects on how "one of the bewildering paradoxes of our time is the extent to which the enterprise system tolerates, if not participates in, its own destruction." He laments that, while public education at all levels is made possible by tax revenues mainly stemming from American business, and the boards of trustees are composed of "leaders in the system," the big public universities contain some of the most aggressive "attackers." He laments that the media facilitate the attacks, yet they are corporations ostensibly seeking profit. He quotes journalist Stewart Alsop (an establishment figure that had close and cooperative ties with the CIA) on how Yale University was "graduating scores of bright young men who are practitioners of the 'politics of despair'" and whose heads were full of "mindless slogans."[48] He quotes conservative economist Milton Friedman favorably and the great consumer advocate, Ralph Nader, negatively. Business, he says, has largely responded to the attacks by "appeasement" and by "ignoring the problem."

Powell called for the Chamber of Commerce to recruit its own "staff of highly qualified scholars who do believe in the system" to fan out across the country to influence universities, media, and any civil society groups; they should form a "Speakers Bureau" to advance their cause, as well as "panels of independent scholars" to evaluate and ensure that high school textbooks are "balanced" in the ways they treat free enterprise and "democracy" in comparison with socialism, communism, and fascism. At least he included fascism in the threatening political forms.[49] He was

Figure 9 Italian Communist Party leader Palmiro Togliatti and labor leader Giuseppe Di Vittorio in the 1950s. Both were leading anti-fascist figures of the fascist and Stalinist era of the 1920s–50s. Date: 1950s. https://www.raicultura.it/dl/img/2019/04/12/155507151301 1_h_00574800.jpg.

Source: Author unknown. Public domain; commons.wikimedia.org.

a decorated Second World War veteran. The Powell Memo was a call to action for the American right, and it was effective. The Heritage Foundation and the American Legislative Exchange Council (ALEC) were both established in 1973 in response to Powell's war cry. Both were and are free-market maximalist and highly influential, with ALEC operating especially energetically at the local grassroots and state legislative levels. The group has been writing legislation for conservative politicians at the state levels for decades. They are nothing if not anti-"socialist," where socialism is anything that is not free-market extremism. The early phase of the economic downturn in which Powell penned his memo was just the beginning of a long battle to shore up the viability of US corporations and, by association, capitalism in general in the United States and worldwide. The inflation that hit the world economy due to the oil price hikes of the mid-1970s just made matters all the more urgent. Finally, the Memo has remained a foundational document for the American right for the past fifty years, with the exception that it contains a soft, but significant, warning against fascism. Tragically, in the meantime, that concern has evidently vanished for an overly large portion of the contemporary American right, including its president, from 2016 to 2020.[50]

Figure 10 Martin Luther King Jr. and fellow activists during the 1963 March on Washington for Jobs and Freedom. To King's left is Eugene Carson Blake; to his right is Mathew Ahman. Others unidentified. Photographer, Rowland Scherman, National Archives and Records Administration.

Source: Public domain; commons.wikimedia.org.

Notes

1. See characterizations of cooperative organizations and movements in Sweden, Norway, Denmark, Holland, Belgium France, Switzerland, Italy, Austria, and West Germany in CAB 21/2745, 1948.
2. February 19, 1948, PR 41, British Embassy, Washington, DC, W. P. N. Edwards to Christopher Warner, FO 1110/24.
3. Ibid. Bill Stone was the then current head of the US Office of Information and Education (OIE).
4. Ibid.
5. Donald Sassoon, *One Hundred Years of Socialism: The West European Left in the Twentieth Century* (New York: Norton, 1996), pp. 102–12.
6. Paul Ginsborg, *A History of Contemporary Italy: Society and Politics, 1943–1988* (New York: Penguin, 1990), pp. 112–20. See more documents from the FRUS file: "The Ambassador in Italy (Dunn) to the Secretary of State," April 7, 1948.
7. Particularly on the EU and NATO, see Perry Anderson, "Under the Sign of the Interim," in *The Question of Europe*, ed. Peter Gowan and Perry Anderson

Figure 11 American troops in the Long Khanh Province of South Vietnam look to the sky for a helicopter evacuation of their fallen comrade. The original caption reads, "SP4 Ruediger Richter (Columbus, Georgia), 4th Bn., 503 Inf., 173 Abn Bde (Separate), lifts his battle weary eyes to the heavens, as if to ask why? SGT. Daniel E. Spencer (Bend, Oregon) stares down at their fallen comrade. The day's battle ended, they silently await the helicopter which will evacuate their comrade from the jungle covered hills in Long Khanh Province." By Pfc. L. Paul Epley, 1966.

(New York: Verso, 1997), pp. 51–71. See also Bevin's reference to the "German problem": https://history.state.gov/historicaldocuments/frus1950v03/d338.

8. Antonio Cazorla, "Early Francoism, 1939–1957," in *Spanish History Since 1808*, ed. José Alvarez Junco and Adrian Shubert (London: Oxford University Press, 2000), pp. 259–60, 273–4, and *passim*.

9. See Luís Nuno Rodrigues, "The United States and Portuguese Decolonization," Portuguese Studies, vol. 29, no. 2 (2013), pp. 164–85.

10. Juliet Perry, "Tribunal Finds Indonesia Guilty of 1965 Genocide; US, UK Complicit," CNN, July 21, 2016. Available online: https://www.cnn.com/2016/07/21/asia/indonesia-genocide-panel/index.html. See also Scott Sidell, "The United States and Genocide in East Timor," Journal of Contemporary Asia, vol.11, no. 1 (1981), pp. 44–61. For the British stance on East Timor, see The National Security Archive at George Washington University, https://nsarchive2.gwu.edu/NSAEBB/NSAEBB174/indexuk.htm; there, see Hugh Dowson, "Declassified British Documents Reveal U.K. Support for Indonesian Invasion and Occupation of East Timor, Recognition of Denial of Self-Determination, 1975–1976."

11. He was the father of Andreas, the later socialist prime minister, and grandfather of George Jr., socialist prime minister from 2009 to 2011.

12. Maria Margaronis, "Greek Anti-Fascist Protesters 'Tortured by Police' after Golden Dawn Clash," *The Guardian*, October 9, 2012. Available online: https://www. theguardian.com/world/2012/oct/09/greek-antifascist-protesters-torture-police.

13. Douglas Little, *Malevolent Neutrality: The United States, Great Britain, and the Origins of the Spanish Civil War* (Ithaca, NY: Cornell University Press, 1985).

14. See Tracy B. Strong, *Learning One's Native Tongue: Citizenship, Contestation, and Conflict in America* (Chicago: University of Chicago Press, 2019), p. 236.

15. The Ambassador in Panama (Davis) to the Secretary of State, Panama, February 3, 1949. Available online: https://history.state.gov/historicaldocuments/frus1949v02/ d294. The "Spanish Republican" figures the ambassador refers to were political refugees from the Spanish Civil War.

16. George Westerman was a Panamanian-born journalist, diplomat, and a vigorous international activist against racial and class injustice. He was of West Indian heritage. See Katherine Zien, "Race and Politics in Concert: Paul Robeson and William Warfield in Panama, 1947–1953," The Global South, vol. 6, no. 2 (Fall 2012), pp. 107–29. Available online: https://www.jstor.org/stable/10.2979/globalsouth.6.2.107.

17. For the report on Brodsky, see FO 371/74121, from the Mr. Greenway of the British Legation in Panama to the Secretary of State for Foreign Affairs, March 18, 1949, item 0915.

18. Piero Gleijeses, "The Agrarian Reform of Jacobo Arbenz," Journal of Latin American Studies, vol. 21, no. 3 (October 1989), pp. 453–80. Available online: https://www.jstor. org/stable/156959 (accessed March 19, 2020).

19. Lawrence A. Clayton, Michael L. Conniff, and Susan M. Gauss, *A New History of Modern Latin America* (Berkeley: University of California Press, 2017), Chapter Three, "Caribbean Basin Countercurrents," pp. 496–505, and *passim*.

20. See Memorandum of Conversation by the Ambassador in Cuba (Beaulac), Havana, March 22, 1952. Available online: https://history.state.gov/historicaldocuments/ frus1952-54v04/d326.

21. Foreign Relations 1955–57, Vol VI. Available online: http://digicoll.library.wisc.edu.

22. *FRUS*, 1955–7, Vol. VI: Department of State, Despatch From the Ambassador in Cuba (Smith) to the Department of State, Habana, September 16, 1957, p. 847.

23. https://history.state.gov/historicaldocuments/frus1958-60v06/d18: Despatch from the Consulate at Santiago de Cuba to the Department of State, February 21, 1958, the "Fidel Castro, 26 of July Movement." Report from US Consul in Santiago de Cuba, Oscar H. Guerra, February 1, 1958.

24. See Clayton, Conniff, and Gauss, *A New History of Modern Latin America*, Chapter 22, "The Cuban Revolution and Its Aftermath," p. 520. Available online: https://www. jstor.org/stable/10.1525/j.ctv1xxxjt.31. See also Salim Lamrani, "Fidel Castro and the Triumph of the Cuban Revolution," in *The Economic War Against Cuba: A Historical and Legal Perspective on the U.S. Blockade* (New York: NYU Press, 2013). Available online: https://www.jstor.org/stable/j.ctt9qgg7f.6z.

25. Pepita Riera, *Servicio de Inteligencia de Cuba Comunista* (Miami, FL: Service Offset Printers, 1966), pp. ix, xi.

26. https://history.state.gov/historicaldocuments/frus1961-63v12/d5.

27. For a historical and historiographical look at the US-backed coup in Brazil of 1964, see Anthony W. Pereira, "The US Role in the 1964 Coup in Brazil: A Reassessment,"

Bulletin of Latin American Research, vol. 37, no. 1 (2018), pp. 5–17. Available online: https://onlinelibrary.wiley.com/doi/epdf/10.1111/blar.12518.

28. Ellen Schrecker, "The Legacy of McCarthyism," in *The Age of McCarthyism: A Brief History with Documents* (Boston: Bedford/St. Martins, 2002), p. 104.

29. https://archive.org/details/fbi_file_mlk/page/n15/mode/2up (see documents n13–n19).

30. Ibid. Within the same group of documents cited above, see November 1962 King letter, and November 20, 1962, message to Hoover from New Orleans FBI regional center.

31. Interviewed by Sam Sills, August 8, 1993; Available online: http://historymatters.gmu.edu/d/6925/.

32. John D'Emilio, *Lost Prophet: The Life and Times of Bayard Rustin* (New York: Free Press, 2003), p. 38.

33. Regarding the matter of how McCarthy and the intelligence establishment viewed homosexuality, but also how homophobia eventually backfired on McCarthy, see Andrea Friedman, "The Smearing of Joe McCarthy: The Lavender Scare, Gossip, and Cold War Politics," American Quarterly, vol. 57, No. 4 (December 2005), pp. 1105–29.

34. For an excellent historical account of King's political experience, see Michael K. Honey, *Going Down Jericho Road: The Memphis Strike, Martin Luther King's Last Campaign* (New York: Norton, 2007), especially p. 28 on the Highlander Folk School gathering of 1957. By the same author, see "The Memphis Strike: Martin Luther King's Last Campaign" in the online newsletter of the *PRRAC Poverty and Race Research Action Council* (March–April 2007), April 1, 2007.

35. Martha Lott, "The Relationship Between the 'Invisibility' of African American Women in the American Civil Rights Movement of the 1950s and 1960s and Their Portrayal in Modern Film," *Journal of Black Studies*, vol. 48, no. 4 (2017), pp. 331–54.

36. See article by Garret Felber, "Malcolm X Assassination: 50 Years on, Mystery Still Clouds Details of the Case," *The Guardian*, February 21, 2015. Available online: https://www.theguardian.com/us-news/2015/feb/21/malcolm-x-assassination-records-nypd-investigation. It was announced in February 2020 that the district attorney of Manhattan will conduct a reexamination of Malcolm X's assassination. See also the 2020 film documentary "Who Killed Malcolm X," directed by Rachel Dretzin and Phil Bertelsen, produced by Fusion and distributed by Netflix.

37. For the full text, go to https://www.americanrhetoric.com/speeches/mlkatimetobreaksilence.htm.

38. US Government Memorandum, from C. D. Brennan to Mr. Sullivan; Subject: Martin Luther King, Jr., Security Matter, March 8, 1967.

39. US Department of Justice, FBI, New York City, April 5, 1967. Subject: Martin Luther King Jr., Communist Infiltration of the (SCLC). File no. 100-0106670/100-438794, pp. 1–4. See also April 6 letter from C. D. Brennan to Sullivan, with the same title and file number.

40. FBI Memo, Brennan to Sullivan, April 14, 1967, in same series as above.

41. Martin Luther King Jr., *Where Do We Go From Here: Chaos or Community?* (Boston: Beacon Press, 1968), pp. 200–1.

42. For some of the operation's material on Milwaukee, see https://vault.fbi.gov/cointel-pro/new-left/cointel-pro-new-left-milwaukee-part-01-of-01/view. This includes material on the "underground" publications, *Kaleidoscope* (repeatedly described as "pornographic"), and its successor, *The Bugle American*. See also James Kirkpatrick

Davis, *Assault on the Left: The FBI and the Sixties Antiwar Movement* (Westport, CT: Praeger, 1997), pp. 150–3, 179.

43. Eddie Conway, "The State Targeted the Panthers because We Were Socialists, Not because We Were Armed," video interview, September 15, 2014, by Paul Jay, *The Real News Network*. Available online: https://truthout.org/video/eddie-conway-the-state-targeted-the-panthers-because-we-were-socialists-not-because-we-were-armed/.

44. For a very comprehensive perspective and analysis of the events of 1968, especially in Western Europe, see Sassoon, *One Hundred Years of Socialism*, pp. 383–406. For a skeptical look at the situation, see Agnès Poirier, "May 68 – What Legacy?," The Paris Review, May 1, 2018. Available online: https://www.theparisreview.org/blog/2018/05/01/may-68-what-legacy/.

45. See Hobsbawm, *The Age of Extremes*, pp. 397–400; John Merriman, *A History of Modern Europe: From the Renaissance to the Present* (New York: Norton, 1996), pp. 1353–60.

46. For the US toll, see the National Archives: *Vietnam War U.S. Military Fatal Casualty Statistics*, at https://www.archives.gov/research/military/vietnam-war/casualty-statistics#hostile. For Vietnam's official estimate, see the article by Ronald H. Spector, "Vietnam War, 1954–1975," *Encyclopaedia Britannica*. Available online: https://www.britannica.com/event/Vietnam-War (accessed June 11, 2020).

47. The following account of the development of the global capitalist economy from 1945, at least up to the 1990s, is very much drawn from the work of Robert Brenner, "The Economics of Global Turbulence," New Left Review (Special Issue), vol. 1, no. 229 (May/June 1998).

48. For historical angles on Stewart Alsop and his CIA connections, see David P. Hadley, *The Rising Clamor: The American Press, the Central Intelligence Agency and the Cold War* (Lexington: University Press of Kentucky, 2019).

49. Lewis F. Powell Jr., *The Memo*, "Attack on American Free Enterprise System," from Lewis F. Powell Jr. to Mr. Eugene B. Sydnor Jr., accessed from the Washington & Lee University School of Law Scholarly Commons. Available online: https://scholarlycommons.law.wlu.edu/powellmemo/.

50. The case that the United States in recent years is a variant of the classic model of fascism that came out of Germany and Italy in the interwar years is presented in the epilogue.

Part Three

The Neoliberal Solution

Introduction

The turn to neoliberalism beginning in the mid-1970s was an audacious maneuver. It was first forced upon Chile by the United States beginning in 1973, introduced to some extent in the United States under the Carter administration, then launched domestically and more internationally around 1980 by Margaret Thatcher in the UK and Ronald Reagan in the United States. While in its beginnings it was very much an immediate matter of improving corporate reports, it was also a long reach back, over the era of modern liberalism, into the eighteenth and early- to mid-nineteenth-century heyday of Adam Smith's *laissez-faire* economic theory, its promotion in liberal free trade media, and its imposition by liberal parliamentarians in Britain and eventually elsewhere. In addition to the creation of the "social problem" of the impoverished working classes, the potentially deadly callousness of this approach was realized during the Irish famine of the late 1840s, when the liberals in the British parliament deemed it was best to let "nature" take its course in Britain's oldest colony, which contributed substantially to the approximately one million deaths and the tremendous displacement of the country's population through desperate waves of emigration. Returning to the present, with neoliberalism having been on the march for nearly a half century, it is difficult not to see parallels between the classical British liberal approach to the famine 170 years ago and the situation, at least in the United States, where the presidential administration in 2020 resorted to a do-nothing "herd immunity" policy toward the COVID-19 pandemic. This was classic *laissez-faire* or "hands off" and free trade liberalism, combined with Social Darwinism, and updated as neoliberalism in a leading capitalist great power state that, as of late 2020, had only 4.25 percent of the world's population, yet close to 20 percent of the world's deaths from the virus. According to Dr. Deborah Birx, "who served as the White House coronavirus response coordinator under the Trump administration," at least tens of thousands of fatalities from the COVID-19 virus could have been prevented: "The first time we have an excuse ... there were about a hundred thousand deaths that came from that original surge. All of the rest of them, in my mind, could have been mitigated or decreased substantially."[1] Most definitely, the US-led global neoliberal turn from the 1970s to at least 2020 has been audacious, yet equally callous and anti-democratic, and, in the recent context of the pandemic under the Trump administration, it has been deadly.[2] There is reason to see Trump as a sociopathic individual, but he still cannot be abstracted out from his historical context and politics. He selected classic tactics of fascism and synthesized them with neoliberal extremism. Most interestingly for this study, the new presidential administration under Joe Biden has apparently broken from those politics and is showing serious signs of having more in common with Franklin Roosevelt and the New Deal politics of the 1930s than anything the United States has seen since, with the possible exception of the Johnson administration of 1963–9. A major historical shift may be taking place that could have global implications, but it is too soon to tell.

Neoliberal economic ideology gained ground in conservative academic and political circles in the United States during the early 1970s, but its actual and original implementation—in fact, a violent imposition—was in Chile under the military dictatorship of General Augusto Pinochet that was established in 1973 after the US-backed overthrow of the democratically elected socialist government of Salvador Allende. This was the use of the Chilean state, society, and people as mostly unwitting subjects of an experiment that was forced onto and integrated into the anti-socialist political-military and police terror that characterized the dictatorship. This was the first big shot at the *rollback*—here deliberately using the term straight out of the US strategic arsenal—of anything but free-market extremism. It even anticipated Ronald Reagan's resurrection of US rollback policy in the Korean War that he deployed against the left in Central America in the 1980s. For years, great power states had muscled in on weaker ones for purposes of what was described euphemistically as "opening up" their countries or territories economically. However, the violence, war, threats of war, the abuse of labor, death tolls, and refugee crises, all of which, in some combination, typically accompanied the openings, would only be discussed by critics—with good investigative journalists in the lead—distant from the levers of power and after the fact. At least since the era of the mid-nineteenth century, "opening up" various parts of the world to free trade was the central mission for the imperialist states in their strategic rivalries with one another. The Belgians "opened up" the Congo, the British did so in what later became India, Commodore Perry of the United States attempted to do so against Japan. Such messaging persists. It is hard to expect anything else out of a system that depends on the indefinite expansion of markets at all costs. Furthermore, with some exceptions, the tendency is to reproduce past inequalities, such as those that existed in the "new world" of the Americas, as well as much of the rest of the world, centuries ago. Those who were conquered within the Americas, or enslaved and brought to them, were incorporated into "markets" but with little to no prospect of a fair chance within them. Native and African Americans have had to fight uphill battles to get any favorable position on the "playing field," because it was such an unfair game to begin with, and there is no significant effort at the top of the power structure to make it anything approaching a fair game. Over hundreds of years, this is how racism and divide and rule, as well as extreme socioeconomic inequality generally, became endemic to the Americas and much of the rest of the world. Thomas Pikkety's research on the ways in which inequalities of wealth are reproduced and increased over the long run is consistent with and supportive of this perspective, even though his conceptual approach is otherwise distinct from what is found in this book.[3]

Since the late 1970s and into the 1980s, the International Monetary Fund (IMF), dominated by the US Treasury Department, became the cutting edge of the latest means of the advanced capitalist states dominating the rest. The IMF's annual reports from the late 1970s at least to 2016 consistently stress the necessities of "structural adjustment," which essentially means privatization and deregulation, in order to regenerate economic growth.[4] In other words, it is about "opening up" after the decades-long era of significant political intervention in economic activity on behalf of working people in precarious economic positions. The problem in the 1970s and early 1980s was "stagflation"—a combination of high inflation, unemployment, and stagnant productivity—which had become endemic in the world capitalist economy beginning in the late 1960s. This was a serious set of problems, especially for working people, that needed to be addressed, but what drove the neoliberal campaign were immediate CEO and investor concerns about profitability. An indicator of the benefits that accrued from neoliberalism in the United States starkly illustrates this reality: growth in CEO compensation from 1978 to 2018 was an astounding 940 percent, while that of average wage earners was a measly 11.9 percent.[5]

But it would never just be about big money or the lack of it, because extreme inequality in modern electoral democracies only comes with a plethora of associated problems. Here are seven of them, which in combination, go far in characterizing our times: first has been the steady lessening of the influence of organized labor in the political processes of the advanced capitalist states because of economic globalization. Manufacturing operations and jobs got sent to countries where labor was cheap and nonunionized; if they existed at all, unions were pressured to concede hard-earned gains in wages, worker protections, and health benefits. Labor had no choice but to concede; for the most part, they could not pack up and search elsewhere in the world for secure jobs. Capital, on the other hand, had the distinct option to relocate to other parts of the world, and they did. The screaming gap between CEO salaries and the average pay for working people in the advanced capitalist states, especially the United States, never would have happened without that historic policy turn. Given labor's weakened political clout in the United States, the Democratic Party turned away from its commitments sustained since the 1930s and toward the financial clout of Wall Street. A second and entirely related problem of this large-scale policy shift was the onset of a combination of plutocracy and oligarchy. As the rich got exponentially richer, their influence within politics worldwide also grew to the point where they could influence policy, politics, and the media, in vast disproportion to their actual numbers as individuals. Presently, there are just over two thousand billionaires in the world, many of whom make or lose in one day more than most people will make or lose in a lifetime. Meanwhile, they have succeeded in protecting their billions of dollars from the scrutiny of tax authorities—also a time-honored tradition, of course, but one now way off the old charts. Estimates of the total amounts in tax havens across the world, on Caribbean islands and beyond, run into the trillions.[6] A third problem that ties in with the above is the decimation of the middle classes in some of those societies that featured them from the late nineteenth to the late twentieth centuries. Again, the United States is a case in point, where the "middle classes" in popular discourse tend to also include the working classes. However, even from that income-based definition of middle class, the impact of economic globalization has been to render that class socially and politically insecure, economically stagnant, and with reduced political influence, especially relative to the emergent plutocracy. This situation led into a fourth fundamental problem, which is the lack of what had been a long period of "brick and mortar" investment and financing within the United States. Finance took on a relatively larger role in this setting but did so through various forms of trickery. The subprime mortgage lending, including the use of "credit default swaps," resulting in absurdly risky situations for borrowers and obscenely high profits for lenders, were the financial vehicles of choice that led the United States and the world economy into the Great Recession that began in 2008—the worst abrupt and long-term downturn in the world economy since the Great Depression of the 1930s.

This shift to the importance of financial "devices" in the countries in which actual industrial production had been centered for at least 150 years has led into a fifth and more obviously political problem of the postindustrial societies. The insecurities of the middle and lower middle classes in capitalist industrial societies have been rightfully seen as important variables in the development of fascism and Nazism. Suffice it to say that Germany and Italy in the pre–Second World War era featured very shaky middle- and lower-middle-class demographics, while France, Britain, and the United States featured strong ones.[7] From this angle, in conjunction especially with the wars and refugee crises in the Middle East, Africa, the Mediterranean, and the European Union (EU), and the flows of economic and political refugees seeking asylum in the United States, it is not surprising that neofascism and neo-Nazism, thriving on xenophobia, have emerged strongly in several western postindustrial states. In the United States, President Trump supported such politics from 2016 to 2020, which gave them a greater chance to take shape openly and gain greater support. Neofascist politics are unlikely to disappear in the near future.

In the meantime, the end of the Cold War between the United States and the Soviet Union in 1989–91 was a cause for self-congratulation and "neoliberal triumphalism" in certain circles within the capitalist states. However, the euphoria was blinding, which raises problem number six. The legacies of the dynamics of the Cold War as they played out in the Middle East and beyond combined with the triumphalism to create a particularly deceitful and belligerent example of an attempt to open up new markets in the Middle East, particularly in Iraq. Operating on the lies that Iraq was involved in the September 11 attacks by Al Qaeda on the United States, and that it possessed weapons of mass destruction, the country was subject to a devastating attack from the United States that splintered it along sectarian lines to the point of civil war, then set off a wave of Sunni Muslim revisionist aggression throughout much of the region, especially evident in the Syrian Civil War that began in 2011. The entire regional situation remains unresolved and wields a significant, problematic, and unpredictable global impact well into the future.

In clear connection with the theme of this book, neoliberalism has reproduced a certain dynamic that has been endemic to modern societies, always eventually sustained by capitalist productive power, since the early nineteenth century. Specifically, the conjoined forces of capitalism and political liberalism—in this argument, most importantly manifesting as market liberalization—have, once again, created their leftwing oppositions. They exist across the world, in response to the systemic and policy aggressions of their foes. But, just as in the past, they have had to be undermined, if not destroyed, whether they are real or not. Trump, representing a peak of anti-"socialist" pathology, has branded his entire opposition as "antifa scum" in his call to the neofascist militias that have wedded their cause to him. This particular instance of the problem of anti-leftist politics may or may not be ephemeral, but it does seem to show that, at this point, fascism is not an aberration in modern history but a recurrent and endemic problem that is part of a syndrome of political conflict characteristic of modern liberal capitalist society.

The seventh and final point is the largest, that the expansion of capitalist production and the "opening up of markets" across the world for at least the past two hundred years, which has mostly comprised the industrial era, has involved an assault on the natural environment that is showing its climatic repercussions in our times in the forms of more intense and deadly heat, megafires, rising sea levels, and more destructive hurricanes and tornadoes. Though it was the Industrial Revolution, brought on by capitalism, that set humanity on this precarious path, it must be said that the record of environmental degradation of the industrialized state socialist regimes of the twentieth century was also extremely negative. It is the major problem that humanity faces in our times. Efforts to conceptualize the problem have resorted to geology, specifically that we are living in the anthropocene period, in which humanity has created the currently troubled state of its own existence, and its prospects for survival depend, more than anything else and more obviously than ever, upon its own rational and self-protective decisions and actions. The combination of the above seven points sets the stage for the seventh and final chapter of this book.

Notes

1. Maeve Reston, "Birx Shares Her Chilling Conclusion as America Arrives at a Moment of Introspection on the Coronavirus," CNN, March 27, 2021. https://www.cnn.com/2021/03/27/politics/covid-war-deaths-preventable/index.html. Dr. Birx explained that her background in the military made it extremely difficult to mount any sustained objections to her Commander in Chief.

2. For a meticulous and scathing critique of the neoliberal United States amid the COVID-19 pandemic, see Robert Brenner, "Escalating Plunder," *New Left Review* 23 (May/June 2020), pp. 5–22.

3. Thomas Piketty, *Capital in the Twenty-First Century* (Cambridge: Belknap, 2014). With a wealth of data, he shows this problematic, though unsurprising, trend, along with its relative exceptions, such as the period of the 1930s–40s of the Great Depression and the Second World War.

4. The period around 2016 may have at long last been a turning point in the IMF's neoliberal calculus. See Jonathan D. Ostry, Prakash Loungani, and Davide Furceri, "Neoliberalism: Oversold?," *Finance and Development*, vol. 53, no. 2 (June 2016). Available online: https://www.imf.org/external/pubs/ft/fandd/2016/06/ostry.htm.

5. Lawrence Mishel and Julia Wolfe, "CEO Compensation Has Grown 940% since 1978; Typical Worker Compensation Has Risen only 12% during That Time," Economic

Policy Institute, August 13, 2019. Available online: https://www.epi.org/publication/ceo-compensation-2018/.

6. Nicholas Shaxson, "Tackling Tax Havens," *Finance and Development*, vol. 56, no. 3 (September 2019). Available online: https://www.imf.org/external/pubs/ft/fandd/2019/09/tackling-global-tax-havens-shaxon.htm.

7. Two prominent authors on fascism employ this angle on their political-historical analyses of fascism, though not exclusively. See Robert Paxton, *The Anatomy of Fascism* (New York: Vintage, 2004), pp. 19, 43–4; Ian Kershaw, *Hitler: A Biography* (New York: Norton, 1998), pp. 36–7. See also a note of caution on this question by Aristotle Kallis in his historiographical essay that introduces *The Fascism Reader* (London: Routledge, 2003), p. 12.

7

The Overkill

Neoliberal Rollback in Latin America: Operation Condor and the Contras

US-backed operations against the Latin American left always involved some degree of informal international cooperation, as seen in the 1954 overthrow of Guatemala's Arbenz government. Such cooperation and coordination continued well into the 1960s and early 1970s, so that any formalization, expansion, and intensification of anti-leftist operations in region would be no surprise. Operation Condor was formally established in 1975 as a secret operation of internationally coordinated anti-leftist intelligence gathering and vicious political repression. Its top state participants included the rightwing dictatorships in Argentina, Chile, Uruguay, Paraguay, Bolivia, Brazil, and later Ecuador and Peru. As shown very clearly and meticulously by J. Patrice McSherry, the US-backed operation in South America had its informal predecessors dating back at least to the late 1960s, if not much earlier. It was actually modeled partly after Operation Gladio, the secret and nefarious network of anti-leftist paramilitary and police forces operating within the NATO network in Western Europe from the 1950s to the 1980s. As put by McSherry, in Latin America, the "regimes hunted down dissidents and leftists, union and peasant leaders, priests and nuns, intellectuals, students and teachers as well as suspected guerillas." They cooperated in "disappearing" those who fled repression in other member countries "and subjected them to barbaric tortures and death." Her work leaves no doubt "that U.S. officials considered Condor a legitimate 'counterterror' organization and that Condor was assisted and encouraged by U.S. military and intelligence forces."[1]

It remains important to situate Condor in the context, not just of US foreign policy since 1945, but in a still-larger and more general context of the domestic and international anti-leftist politics of the interwar years and those dating back to the nineteenth century. This was a series of reconstitutions of the same set of things, with some important modifications: budding capitalist industrial societies and the market liberalizations that accompanied them, and formations of self-protective left-oriented political organizations and ideas within those societies, followed by extensive and intensive types of hostility against the left as industrial society developed more fully. The self-protective left also went on the offensive, as did Allende's Popular Unity coalition in Chile from 1970 to 1973; they challenged the power positions of traditional landed, corporate, and military elites, who, in league with the United States under Nixon and Kissinger, proceeded to do everything possible to destroy them. Sometimes such international anti-leftist collaborations succeeded in their aims, as they did in Chile, other times not, as in Cuba. There was always a complicated and potentially unruly dynamic. As presented in Chapter 4, in 1945 the United States took the lead of the anti-leftist drives of all of the rival non-Communist great power states, including Nazi Germany's, and advanced the crusade worldwide. The way this was conceptualized and presented in the US political-cultural context and in its rhetoric was that it was all about the fight of "democracy" against "totalitarianism" or "communism." As a propaganda matter, the message played sufficiently well within the United States, but the truth of it was another matter—as was the experience of it in Latin America, the Middle East, and elsewhere.

One of the most notorious precursors to Condor, if not one of its premier examples, was the US-backed overthrow of the democratically elected socialist Popular Unity government of Salvador Allende in Chile in 1973. Nixon hated Allende because he believed he was a Communist and anti-US; Kissinger compared Allende to Hitler. They decided to "give Allende the hook," as Nixon put it.[2] However, in addition to the political-military hook for Allende and so many of his supporters, for the people of Chile there was also the economic hook, namely, the imposition of a neoliberal economic and financial regime. The US leaders had their CIA rally local rightwing support for the *coup* and conduct selective manipulations that prepared other parts of the Chilean population for the overthrow. These approaches succeeded in violently robbing Chileans of their democracy and imposing the dictatorship in its place. But the novel approach of the interventionists came from the "Chicago Boys," the thirty economists and financial experts trained by Milton Friedman and Arnold Herberger at the Department of Economics, University of Chicago. They all championed capitalist free-market extremism—privatization and deregulation of everything possible—with Chile treated as a laboratory. It was the beginning of the political-economic corollary of the strategic "rollback" policy of the United States against Communism. Under the brutally "controlled conditions" of the dictatorship, Chile was subjected to the fantasy of a completely deregulated and privatized liberal capitalist economy. Variations on that fantasy were soon to be inflicted on the economy and people of the United States and other states and societies across the world. This had coercive effects on people's economic lives but was also sometimes accompanied by outright political repression and extreme violence. In Latin America, especially Chile and Argentina, Operation Condor and neoliberalism were joined at the hip and expanded aggressively, with dire consequences for most people and deadly ones for tens of thousands of the *desaparecidos*—the disappeared—estimated at well over a hundred thousand—that dared to oppose the regimes and their economic policies, or were simply accused of doing so.[3]

Economic globalization and neoliberal politics developed in force in the 1980s, when for most observers, the Cold War had no foreseeable end. While the Soviet invasion and occupation of Afghanistan was the final blow to the often-shaky stretches of *détente* since the Cuban Missile Crisis of 1963, officials in the Reagan administration that assumed power in January 1981 were concerned about a new "domino effect" of the sort that the United States feared, but which never played out, in Southeast Asia. The concern was now about South America, where, of course, Condor had already been launched under Nixon and Kissinger, but US sights were also set upon Central America. By 1985, the US response to the surge there of leftist politics, along with its response to the Soviet occupation of Afghanistan, specifically fed into the "Reagan Doctrine." It was boilerplate American anti-Communism, with its usual improvisational twists and turns, depending on the circumstances. In Latin America generally, but especially Central America and the Caribbean, it was a version of "rollback" as opposed to mere "containment," recalling the earlier era of the Cold War in East and Southeast Asia, especially Korea, where the more aggressive option was a murderous failure. US alarm in Central America was triggered particularly by the successes of the Nicaraguan Revolution in 1979 that toppled the dictatorship of Anastasio Somoza Debayle, whose family had been in power for most of the period since the US occupation of 1912–33. As with just about everything in the Americas, the larger contours of conflict went deeply into the conquest of the northern and southern portions of the continent by the few great power European states. For South and Central America, this meant the highly inequitable patterns of landholding largely transplanted from Spain, where the prevailing pattern featured large tracts of land held by the small warrior aristocracy that was formed during the "reconquest" of the Iberian peninsula from the Moors from the eighth to the fifteenth centuries. The pattern was then modified to try to control the indigenous peoples of the so-called new world. Eventually, the capitalist powerhouse to the north, the United States, put its stamp of approval on what can be called generally these latifundist regimes. They appeared to constitute viable systems of economic exploitation and social and political control and stability that presented business opportunities for the funneling of primary commodities—mainly coffee and fruit, but also minerals and metals such as copper—into US markets. Meanwhile, the United States specialized in manufactured items that Central American economic players could barely dream of producing. This kind of inequitable economic power relationship underpinned what became the classic "dependency" model, according to which economies that mainly produced primary products got trapped in extremely unequal terms of trade relationships with predominantly industrial economies, in this case, especially the United States.

However, a critical look through the lens of Operation Condor in South America, as well as Central America and the Caribbean in the 1950s, shows that these regimes tended to be anything but stable. Imperative as it was given the needs for capitalist expansion, "business" tended to be politically dicey, to say the least. The political economy of fruit production in Central America was a perfect example: both the exploitation of peasant labor and the ways landed interests and their political allies were so vested in that exploitation created the basic need for self-protective, radical reformist peasant politics. As explained in the previous chapter, the overthrow of the land-reforming Arbenz government in Guatemala in 1954 laid the grounds for a horrific civil war that periodically raged into the 1970s–90s, with a peace settlement only reached by 1996. Nicaragua in July 1979 saw the socialist Sandinista National Liberation Front (FSLN) led by Daniel Ortega—also committed to land reform—take the final steps toward overthrowing the Somoza regime. An American diplomatic observer based in Honduras issued a report in July 1979 about El Salvador and the entire region that showed US fears. Assistant Secretary Vaky wrote,

> The radical, revolutionary left grows in size and popularity, shows confidence, has the initiative, and clearly expects to be boosted (and materially helped) by what happened in Nicaragua and by Sandinista elements. Thus the initiative at the moment rests with them tasting blood, (and) the question arises as to whether even electoral reform and revival of the process will be able to head off their momentum which now turns on institutional change and 'revolution.'

Vaky summed up with the following:

> We have a situation characterized by: a political/human rights situation which over the years has polarized political life, radicalized social discontent, and converted opposition into a virtual push for 'revolution'; and (an) organized well-financed and Marxist-led extremist sector which has the momentum and initiative and has been able to legitimize itself through the government's lack of reforms."[4]

A colleague of Vaky's on the US National Security Council, Robert Pastor, shortly afterwards wrote to US Secretary of State Brzezinski, describing "an intelligence assessment of Cuba's strategy for promoting revolution in Guatemala, Honduras and El Salvador." Pastor wrote, "at this time, the Cubans are training some of the cadre and encouraging different groups to better coordinate their activities. The scenario is ominous ... . My guess is that Salvador is headed for a full-scale insurrection by perhaps as early as this Fall, and we need to do something rather dramatic now to get them to focus on the real nature of their problem and to do something that will give the non-Communists a chance."[5]

What Pastor meant by the "real nature of their problem" was not exactly clear, but there is no doubt it had to do with the 'Communist threat' from the outside and inside, together with the lack of a viable electoral democratic system of power transfer in El Salvador. He did not address the basic problem that Vaky did, albeit with a US-directed anti-leftist agenda in mind, which was the problem of extremely inequitable landholding and all the tension and conflict it generated. However, from the standpoints of the prevailing US economic, political, and media climate, what the Carter administration was doing, just about everywhere, was not sufficiently effective, not "tough" enough, against the left.

Several things combined at that point to favor Reagan over Carter in the 1980 US presidential elections: the momentum of leftist politics in Central America, the strategic concerns about them in US foreign policy circles that filtered their ways into campaign rhetoric; the Iranian Revolution and the crisis involving fifty-two American hostages held at the US embassy in Tehran; the Soviet invasion and occupation of Afghanistan, as well as a litany of economic problems under the heading of "stagflation." By November 1981, the new administration had fully committed to a redoubled and expanded effort begun under Carter against the Central American left, particularly through covert coordination of and support for *contras*, or counterrevolutionary forces, first and foremost against the Sandinista government of Nicaragua.[6] The comprehensive policy prescriptions and pressures from the rightwing Heritage Foundation, established in early 1973 during the early stage of the capitalist world's economic downturn and the 1971 Powell Memo's war cry for free markets, had a major impact on Reagan's policies for his entire tenure. Its particular point on foreign policy at the time, at least in conventional US foreign policy terms, was a shift to "rollback" as opposed to "containment." But it was time to take the offensive not just against Communism but against left in general and everywhere. As usual, the rhetoric and the realities of this shift contrasted sharply. Given the harsh and violent character of the US-backed anti-leftist operations entailed in this somewhat new phase of the history of the problem, the introductory language of the "National Security Directive on Cuba and Central America" was a classic piece of propaganda, perhaps also functioning to delude its authors:

> U.S. policy toward the Americas is characterized by strong support for those nations which embrace the principles of democracy and freedom for their people in a stable and peaceful environment. U.S. policy is therefore to assist in defeating the insurgency in El Salvador, and to oppose actions by Cuba, Nicaragua, or others to introduce into Central America heavy weapons, troops from outside the region, trained subversives, or arms and military supplies for insurgents.

The US encouraged consolidation of and funneled military hardware to rightwing guerilla groups operating out of Costa Rica and Honduras that aimed to subvert the leftist Nicaraguan regime. Their rank and file were composed mainly of the prior Somoza regime's National Guard, but according to CIA documents, from 1981 to 1983, it also included leading figures from Argentinian intelligence and anti-leftist counterinsurgency circles, who trained and led as many as five thousand contra guerillas against the Sandinistas.[7]

El Salvador in 1979 presented a show of agonizing continuity with radical peasant politics seeking land reform, at least since the early 1930s, that would bring on extremely violent and deadly responses from those in power. Against the landed oligarchs, a broad array of leftwing forces began to coalesce and rise up, first against the rightwing anti-leftist security state, then against the outright military dictatorship that was established through a *coup d'état* in October. The leftwing Farabundo Martí National Liberation Front (FMLN) coalition forces were officially established in 1980, as the country slid into revolutionary civil war. The United States provided heavy weaponry, financial aid, and military advisors to back up the regime of Napoleon Duarte against its leftwing guerilla opposition. US-trained Salvadoran military and paramilitaries adopted more and more aggressive tactics against any and all leftwing forces, both on the popular and elite levels. Only most famously, Archbishop Óscar Romero, who had recently become a vocal critic of the government and military because of their vicious attacks on reformist peasants, was assassinated in March 1980, as he said mass in a chapel in the city of San Salvador. All signs pointed to one or more members of US-backed paramilitary death squads as the perpetrators of the crime.[8] The following December, members of the Salvadoran National Guard raped and murdered four American Catholic missionaries, three of whom were nuns. The end of the decade saw the bloody murder by Salvadoran army soldiers of seven Jesuit priests and two others at their residence on a major university campus in San Salvador. With some pressure from the United States, which by then was clearly failing in its self-assigned anti-leftist mission in Central America, the ugliness of the 1989 rapes and murders actually helped drive representatives of the rightist dictatorial regime to the negotiating table with their leftwing rivals, so that a ceasefire and settlement was finally reached in 1992. But this was not before the deaths of tens of thousands of mostly left, left-leaning, or suspected leftists in the period since 1979.

In case there is any need for confirmation, the Contra-Argentine-US collaboration against the Sandinistas of Nicaragua showed the unmistakable international coordination of the campaign within the Americas. Operation Condor, in which Argentina was a key player, was clearly linked with the anti-leftist wars in Nicaragua and elsewhere in Central America in the early 1980s and beyond. But it did not stop there; it was a revived global campaign. Ronald Reagan's State of the Union speech of February 1985 is conventionally seen as a statement of the "Reagan Doctrine," but it was also classic anti-Communist propaganda and a brazen statement of arbitrary privilege:

> We must stand by all our democratic allies. And we must not break faith with those who are risking their lives—on every continent, from Afghanistan to Nicaragua— to defy Soviet-supported aggression and secure rights which have been ours from birth.[9]

Iran, Afghanistan, and the Coming "War on Terror"

While Latin America and the Middle East present tremendous historical contrasts spanning thousands of years, the decades after the Second World War saw both regions become major arenas of anti-leftist maneuvering, especially on the parts of the United States, Britain, and their allies across each region. The consequences have been dramatic and far-reaching in global politics and warfare, including the creation of refugee crises and xenophobia, to this day. Each region was full of Cold War hot spots—Cuba, the forces on Condor's hit list in South America, and the targets in Central America; in the Middle East, the examples include Nasser's Egypt, Iran under Mossadeq, then under the Shah, then under the Ayatollahs of the Islamic Revolution. The Soviet invasion of Afghanistan in 1979 and the US response, combined with the Islamist backlash in neighboring Iran, created widespread and complex waves of aggressive moves by initially small, but later larger and more widespread, Islamic fundamentalist groups. Of course, this political form reflected the predominantly Islamic Middle East versus the largely Catholic Latin America, which, for its part, produced a significant movement of radical left "liberation theology" adherents among lower clergy members and many of their lay followers. Such politics for the United States, however much they contrasted with one another strategically, tactically and culturally, represented threats to the access to primary commodities, transportation corridors, and markets. Given the historical thrust toward ultra-free market policies produced by the crisis of stagflation that got early neoliberalism off the ground in US conservative intellectual circles and in parts of Latin America, US aggression ultimately in favor of free markets everywhere advanced the pattern that guaranteed the conflict.

The combined US-British overthrow of the popular Mosaddeq government of Iran in 1953 was followed by the imposition of a monarchical and military dictatorship and an attempt at rapid modernization under the Shah, Mohammad Reza Pahlavi. With its police state apparatus—SAVAK—personally loyal to the Shah and ferociously repressive against all opposition, it created serious internal enemies and resentments, while being generously backed by successive US presidential administrations all the way up to that of Jimmy Carter, who was elected over Gerald Ford in 1976. Despite Carter's avowed commitment to human rights as the basis for his foreign policy, most people under the Shah did not see its benefits. The number of political prisoners held by the regime by Carter's time in office ranged anywhere from 3,500 to 125,000. In one particular display of horror, on September 8, 1978, the Shah's forces shot mercilessly into a crowd of several thousand unarmed, anti-Shah demonstrators, killing at least eighty of them. Carter phoned the Shah to reaffirm US support for his regime. Opposition elements included clerics, Marxists, and liberal secularists, but poorer parts of the population—peasants, urban workers, small businesspeople, and lower middle classes—who were suffering from inflation rates of 40–60 percent, were trending more and more toward support for the radical Islamic cleric, Ayatollah Ruhollah Khomeini. By early 1979, he was enjoying a great swell of support for his Islamic vision of pure and divine social justice politics, as opposed to those of "the Great Satan," that is, the United States. The movement became overwhelming, forcing the Shah to flee the country permanently, bringing down his regime and, not least, inspiring many Muslims across the Middle East and beyond that there was hope for an Islamic political solution to what they saw as the Christian religiosity of the great power state imperialism that had been dominating them for too long. The inspiration transcended the Sunni versus Shia divide and in that regard became major ideological fuel, especially for small, but highly organized and audacious, "jihadist" politics against all enemies.[10]

At the end of 1979, the Soviet Union invaded and occupied Afghanistan in a futile and bloody attempt to impose a reliable regime and take a step toward quieting the surge of Islamic radicalism immediately outside, and potentially inside, its borders. Quickly and lastingly, Afghanistan became a crucial focal point for jihadist politics, first of all directed against the Soviet occupiers. For their anti-Soviet resistance, the jihadists, or the *mujahideen*, got enthusiastic material, financial, and moral support from the United States. Carter's National Security Advisor, Zbigniew Brzezinski, met with several leaders of the Afghan fighters in early 1980, promising such support to them, saying, "Your cause is right and God is on your side."[11] He later added in an interview that the intent was to "make the Soviets bleed, as much and as long as possible." His "realist" view was that the Soviets were on the move to take over the Middle East and the United States had to do everything possible to stop them; the aim was to trap them in a quagmire that would match the one the United States experienced only several years earlier in Vietnam.

While Brzezinski exuded great confidence in the policy he was implementing, he did not grasp the fact that he was laying the groundwork for the United States' next war, the "war on terror." He did not see this any more than John Foster Dulles foresaw the "blowback" of the Islamic Revolution of 1978–9 against the US-British overthrow of Mossadeq in 1953. These inordinately powerful individuals played their cards, but they were also players in a larger system of international structural power that was constantly and deliberately reproduced, in this case on behalf of the interests of the United States and its allies worldwide, while neglecting the interests of vast swathes of humanity worldwide. It was abundantly clear that things could go deeply wrong with their plans and executions. In that respect, both the United States in Iran and the USSR in Afghanistan laid complex traps for themselves, while the story line common to each was the complexity of the Cold War—always fraught with risks. After its defeat in Vietnam and constrained by the "Vietnam syndrome," the United States under Carter and Brzezinski were gleeful about the likelihood that the Soviet Union would fail in its bid to control Afghanistan. Though these conflicts were not functions of two great power states on equal playing fields—the United States was clearly the stronger power with the greater reach—they still provided triggers and fuel for two major global developments. One was the emergence of Islamic radicalism across much of the Middle East and beyond; the other was the unraveling of Soviet power over Eastern Europe, as well as the actual collapse of the Soviet Union and the end of the Cold War. Looking at them with great and justifiable retrospective bias, it is clear that these were major historical transformations, which, among other things, established the precedents for the "war on terror."

The conflicts in Iran and Afghanistan had their definite geopolitical dimensions, both with long histories tied in with British versus Russian imperialist rivalries, dating back at least into the nineteenth century. The Bolshevik Revolution, the Balfour Declaration, the collapse of the Ottoman Empire, the spread of French, and especially British power in the region; the disruptions of the Second World War, the Cold War environment after 1945, and, last but not least, the domestic socioeconomic and political dynamics all have to be considered in a comprehensive treatment of the conflicts in both countries and their consequences regionally and globally. But the angle of anti-leftist politics on the conflicts, particularly on the part of the United States from the late 1940s onward, introduces a compelling specificity to what happened. A look at the intended and unintended consequences of the US anti-Communist and anti-reformist politics in Iran, and the anti-Soviet politics in Afghanistan, shows the deep risks that were taken that created virtually immeasurable "blowback" against the United States, its allies, and its proxies. Regarding Iran, such politics created at least four major consequences: first, in 1953, they undermined reasonable strides toward social reform and national economic development; second, they brought on twenty-six years of military dictatorship under the Shah until he was overthrown in the revolution of 1978–9; third, inseparably from that revolution, the politics made the resort to the Islamic solution, which was sometimes fanatical, very popular within Iran as an alternative to the politics of more secular socioeconomic reform that, based on the 1953 *coup*, seemed to be forbidden by the United States; fourth, in effect, they helped make the Islamic solution into an example for the entire Islamic world in a way that would only spell further trouble for the United States. In case this was all not enough, the US material support for the Afghan guerilla war against the Soviet occupation, which finally succeeded in driving the Soviets out in 1988–9, emboldened some factions of those guerillas, most notably Osama bin Laden's Al Qaeda, whose members were mostly of Saudi Arabian origin, to turn their sights on the United States, that is, the "other superpower" that was perceived and claimed to be the latest part of a long western civilizational tradition of violating societies, politics, sacred values, and sacred ground in the Islamic world.

The New Model in Full Force: Globalized Capitalist Production and Its Political Consequences

By the late 1970s, the particularities of the downturn in the global economy had produced "stagflation," meaning relatively high inflation and stagnant production. For conservatives such as Margaret Thatcher and her US counterpart Ronald Reagan, stagflation was caused by excessive government spending on social democracy and/or the welfare state's overly expensive public institutions such as public university systems, or, in Britain, nationalized rail and telecommunications systems, and labor unions that were too good at bargaining for their members' wages, benefits, and other protections. In 1979, Thatcher ran her campaign on behalf of the Conservative Party with the slogan "Labor is not working." Amid the problems of stagflation, high unemployment, and a lot of confusion, she generated attention and hope. The Conservative Party won the election, Thatcher became Prime Minister, and conservatives in the United States, including Ronald Reagan, were impressed. Reagan was an ex-actor, ex-head of the Screen Actors Guild in 1950s Hollywood, which he purged of real and alleged Communist sympathizers, and ex-Governor of California. He was a great fan of Senator Barry Goldwater, the influential conservative whose politics anticipated neoliberalism. While Jimmy Carter arguably began the top-level neoliberal trend within the United States by deregulating the airline and trucking industries, Ronald Reagan made it the centerpiece of his campaign platform of lower taxes, smaller government, states' rights, a stronger military, and conservative religiosity—the latter two tenets ensuring religious-nationalist support for bellicose politics on the world stage. Given the economic problems in the United States, and the fact that Iranians had been holding fifty-two Americans hostage in their embassy in Tehran for almost a year and a half, Carter was vulnerable. Reagan won resoundingly in November 1980, whereupon he and Thatcher quickly developed a strong ideological and programmatic bond. But the historical significance was twofold: first, what coalesced at this point was a conservative movement against the "modern liberal consensus," or the "social compact," that had prevailed, with some strains, since 1945; second, at the head of that movement, from the pinnacles of power in the United States and Britain, Thatcher and Reagan were able to champion neoliberalism and implement it internationally, just as economic globalization was taking place. It has been neoliberal economic globalization ever since, at least up to 2020. Both leaders declared loudly that "government" was the problem and set out to dismantle their domestic welfare programs. But also, especially through the financial leverage of the IMF and the World Bank, the mission was to dismantle, or at least minimize, any such public spending programs anywhere in the world. It was not a harangue from the sidelines by Goldwater in the mid-1960s or localized discussions of a memo by a US Supreme Court justice. This was the United States and Great Britain implementing policies worldwide that were inspired by the likes of Goldwater, Powell, Paul Weyrich of the Heritage Foundation, Milton Friedman, James M. Buchanan, and the Austrian neoliberal economist, Frederick Von Hayek.

Apparently not the slightest bit wary of how the very competitiveness of the international capitalist economy was creating a "race to the bottom" in the United States, Britain, and eventually elsewhere, Reagan and Thatcher proceeded to reveal their animus against labor unions.[12] Given the vicissitudes of capitalist competition, unions were too expensive. In 1981, Reagan fired over eleven thousand air traffic controllers, whose union had endorsed him as a candidate in 1980. They were striking mainly in favor of less stressful working conditions, which they believed were creating grave dangers to pilots, passengers, and people on the ground. However, in a show of force against unionism in general, Reagan fired them for violating their agreement as public employees not to strike. It was a message to employers anywhere and everywhere to defy the tactics and strategies of independent organized labor; it was old-fashioned anti-unionism but also a perfect expression of the hostility of neoliberalism to any sort of political regulation and intervention in economic or public activity. Thatcher had a rougher road at first, as she faced off against rioting unemployed youth in London, Manchester, and Liverpool in 1981–2, but with some economic improvements and a nationalist military victory over Argentina in the war over the Falkland Islands in mid-1982, she regained momentum and celebrated another victory in the elections of 1983. She then took the opportunity to attack organized labor in the miners' strike in Britain of 1984–5. The National Union of Mineworkers (NUM) opposed the closures and the removal of state subsidies from numerous collieries across Britain. Thatcher went on the offensive against the internally divided NUM, led by Arthur Scargill, and defeated them with police forces in a damaging blow to trade unionism in general in Britain. From then until the late 1980s, she enjoyed fairly robust popular support, as Reagan did for most of his two-term presidency that lasted until 1990.

The victories that Reagan and Thatcher won over labor, and the anti-labor momentum they helped to create, had underlying systemic and structural support from the processes of economic globalization. Those processes favored capital, especially CEOs of major corporations, whose salaries and stock options skyrocketed; they did not favor labor, whose wages declined in new service sector jobs or stagnated if they could stay in the shrinking manufacturing sector. The crucial shift toward economic globalization occurred in connection with the economic malaise that set in after the late 1960s, which led corporate CEOs to first send production operations from their original bases in the upper Midwestern cities in states such as Ohio, Michigan, and Wisconsin, to locations in the American South, where labor was cheaper, less unionized, and taxes were low. But this was not sufficient to keep US production viable in the hypercompetitive world economy. The next frontiers for production operations were outside of the United States, wherever cheap and nonunionized labor was available.

The consequences of the move have been historic and profound; they entailed the breakup of what had been the economic organization of societies and states for approximately one hundred years. The terminology of the change is instructive. "Internationalization" was highly appropriate for the economic era of the late nineteenth century to the late 1960s–early 1970s. The period featured advanced capitalist states that produced major manufactured items—textiles, iron and steel, machinery, chemicals, steamships, automobiles, and so forth—and engaged in high levels of international trade, mainly between the higher producing states, as well as an increase of international financial relationships across the world, including increased investments and lending. "Nations" produced products in their entireties. The city of Detroit, for example, in structural coordination with parts manufacturers in cities within a radius of a few hundred miles, produced automobiles, which were then sold domestically and internationally. However, the distinguishing feature of economic globalization was that there was no more "Detroit," no more "motor city," because the costs of producing automobiles there, and in the area, became prohibitively high relative to non-US competitors' costs. As noted above, production operations got sent to the US south, where wages and unionization were lower than in the north, but just not low enough. At a relatively rapid pace, US manufacturing operations, or different branches of them, were relocated to Mexico, Brazil, Taiwan, Singapore, China, Ireland—all places that either had cheap and nonunionized labor, or specializations in design or assembly that were a bargain for the automakers. Automobiles, in this case, went from being produced in single economies with complex, internal systems of vertical and horizontal integration, to multiple national economies across the world, with their structural complexities geographically far flung. This was no longer "internationalization"; a new term was needed to match the new reality. "Globalization" fit the bill, appearing more and more in popular discourse in the late 1980s and into the 1990s. This was a radical change in the actual constitution of the forces of production, as distinguished from those of exchange, distribution, and consumption. The world economy, really the history of capitalism as a system of production, was entering a new phase.

The change pulled the rug out from under organized labor, eventually across all of the advanced capitalist states. There is hardly a more effective threat against any pro-labor union politics in a competitive capitalist industrial society than that of closing down manufacturing operations and sending them off to another part of the world. Economic globalization also subjected labor in the Third World economies— now described in mainstream circles with the euphemism "emerging economies"— to extreme wage exploitation and dangerous work environments.[13] But, as a serious knock-on effect of the change, labor within the United States, for example, also lost the sort of political representation it had been able to rely upon relatively steadily since the beginning of the New Deal in the 1930s. Of course, organized labor is about jobs, job security, unemployment compensation, health care packages, retirement pensions, and more, but within any system of electorally representative politics, it must also be fairly represented. One of the premier arrangements of the advanced capitalist states, as well as many semi-peripheral ones, especially from 1945 to the 1970s, was known as the "social compact." In the United States it was described as an ongoing process of negotiation between business, government, and labor. This was the consensus that accompanied the "golden age of capitalism," and many would have been forgiven for thinking that the whole package was there to stay. It tended to be overly nationalistic; American laborers came out of the pressures of anti-Communism in the 1940s–1960s with highly nationalistic attitudes. Little else was acceptable. But its place in US society was a worthy achievement, one which began its unraveling in the 1970s and still, in 2020, longs for its former self. For the "labor" element and all that it had achieved, to lose out so significantly in absolute terms was enough in itself. But, again, to add insult to injury was the fact that the growth in CEO compensation from 1978 to 2018 was an astronomical 940 percent, while that of average wage earner was only 11.9 percent. The balances of the social compact, and its counterparts in the formal checks-and-balances political-constitutional system—in other words, American economic society and democracy—together got obscenely skewed in favor of the rich. Organized labor was diminished as a power and a voice on the American scene. The rich took advantage of this, because they could. The road to extreme inequality was opened wide by the response to the end of the "golden age" on the part of leading figures in the capitalist economy. But again, it was not just about extremely greedy CEOs; it was the very system of capitalist competition whose dynamics provided the opportunity structure for them to get that way. It was a new gilded age—even more extreme than the first one of the late nineteenth and early twentieth centuries.[14]

The Collapse of the Soviet Union

At least since the 1970s, the economies of the Soviet Union and the Eastern Bloc were either stagnant or declining. Perhaps surprisingly, this in itself gave rise to little speculation within the capitalist states about the demise of the Soviet system, since it was seen as simply monolithic and securely authoritarian. But within the system there were growing popular currents of disillusion and disappointment with their leadership. Industry was inefficient, there were few consumer products; welfare systems were weakening, long food lines became normal; alcoholism increased, life expectancies shortened. Environmentally, chemical runoff from the industrial sectors was extremely damaging. Popular morale was low. With rare exceptions, the gerontocracy of the Soviet and East European leadership tended to dig in their heels about the failures of the system. Ever since Khrushchev's denunciation of Stalin and his declared commitment to supplant the Stalinist model with a more flexible and efficient one, very little progress had actually been made; the notoriously rigid Stalinist bureaucracy largely remained intact. Yet there were signs of change in the Eastern bloc, especially in Poland, where the Solidarity movement under Lech Walesa drew in millions of supporters in the late 1970s–early 80s. In 1981 it called for free elections. While Brezhnev and the Polish leader Jaruzelski moved to ruthlessly repress Solidarity, it still managed to survive underground. Movements for "reform communism" appeared in Hungary and Czechoslovakia, recalling Dubcek's aspirations toward "socialism with a human face" in the late 1960s. In significant contrast to the 1950s–60s, some at the highest levels of power in the USSR, along with some that aspired to such power, saw these developments as signs that another, more serious attempt at change was necessary. Even members of the old guard appeared to be open to a more dramatic change than anything seen since the early 1920s. After the rapid succession of the deaths of Brezhnev, Andropov, and Chernyenko from 1982 to 1985, the Politburo appointed the young agricultural secretary, Mikhail Gorbachev, as Prime Minister. Andropov had taken on Gorbachev in that position very deliberately, giving the young reformer and believer a chance. Gorbachev had taken Khrushchev's commitment to de-Stalinization to heart. He explained that he wished to return the spirit of Soviet policy back to its Leninist origins—pre-Stalinist—which, in particular, meant going back to some version of Lenin's New Economic Policy of the early 1920s that was about a mixed economy, public and private, and which was showing signs of success before Lenin died in early 1924 and Stalin prevailed over Trotsky by the late 1920s. With the exception of the Soviet victories over Nazi Germany in the Second World War, when Stalin was in full nationalist mode, he mostly made a horribly grim mark on the Soviet Union. For Gorbachev and his supporters, it was imperative to fully renovate the Soviet state and society.

To the astonishment of western observers, soon after acceding to power, Gorbachev announced a radically new set of policies for the entire system, summed up as *glasnost*, meaning more open government and freer expression, and *perestroika*, meaning bureaucratic and economic reforms for a Soviet system more responsive to its citizens. In 1988 he declared that dissidents could be elected to the Soviet Congress. He aimed to end the Cold War with the United States, loosen ties with Eastern Europe, and democratize foreign policy. The East European countries broke away from the USSR in 1989, unopposed by the Kremlin, as Soviet forces also withdrew from Afghanistan. Though Gorbachev did not envision or desire the end of the USSR, it collapsed in 1991. The institutional legacies of Stalinism were rigid beyond hope. The radical reforms implemented by Gorbachev rendered them very brittle. The floodgates for dramatic change were wide open. Even to the surprise of the CIA, the Soviet bloc was no more; the Cold War was over. After seventy-four years of tremendous pressure and often-immeasurable hostility from the outside and, especially in wartime, pressure from the inside and out, the Soviet Union undid itself, unintentionally, from the inside. However, in terms of anti-leftist politics, the neoliberal triumphalists of the United States and its allies that took credit for the Soviet collapse were now fully poised for the overkill.

Post–Cold War US-led Political and Military Triumphalism

The end of the Cold War was celebrated in leading intellectual and political circles in the "victorious" states with an unabashed triumphalism, a neoliberal form of which was famously delivered by Francis Fukuyama. Going for Hegelian philosophical glory, he argued that "history," as the drama of grand-scale political-ideological conflict on the world stage, was at an end; the "liberal idea" of "individual liberty and free markets" had prevailed. What set in motion this ultimate triumph occurred nearly two centuries prior: the victory of Napoleon's new French liberal revolutionary army over the old monarchical Prussian forces at the Battle of Jena in 1806. But, in the following 185 years, the liberal idea had to withstand two other world-historical challenges, one from fascism and the other from communism. For Fukuyama, both were permanently vanquished. There would still be religious, political, cultural bickering and clashes, potentially very bloody ones, but the basic matters had been settled. There would be no more grand-scale fascism, no resurgence of communism or any sort of leftist societal model to challenge, let alone upend, the liberal idea. Clearly, the end of the Cold War was a prime historical moment for such thinking, if not an overly intoxicating one. Fukuyama in particular deserves great credit for the audacity of his argument and for recognizing the potentially seismic political character of the liberalizations and popular rumblings in Eastern Europe and the Soviet Union during the months and years prior to the fall of the Berlin Wall. His original article was published just a few months before the Wall fell in 1989.[15] But his longer-term analysis and prognosis were off the mark. This is no longer particularly controversial, but it is useful as an example of what, in some circles, was the blinding euphoria of the time, and as a springboard to offer another broad view of what was going on.

Instead of an end to history, the post–Cold War period has been one of the regeneration, expansion, and reconstitution of social-historical forces and patterns of conflict that have predominated since the early-to-mid nineteenth century—the time frame for this book and close to the one used by Fukuyama. But rather than the "liberal idea," the driving forces for historical change in the entire stretch from then to now are the class-based dynamics of capitalism and market liberalization. This is not simply what purports to be a more materialist historical proposition to counter an idealist one; it is about the systemic and political-ideological conflict— the stuff of history, even for Fukuyama—that is guaranteed by those driving forces. By definition, as long as capitalism exists, there exists the bourgeoisie—industrialists, corporate moguls, financiers, and upper-middle-class professionals—whether they are private, statist, or a combination of both. In the pursuit of their narrow self-interests, especially through the liberalization of markets, they tend to lay fertile grounds for varying degrees and kinds of leftwing political oppositions, which typically consist of collective action. They then must find ways to control, diminish, and outmaneuver such opposition by all means—social, economic, political, cultural, and ideological. Their tactics characteristically include systematic divide and rule along ethnic, religious, and racial lines, while minor or major threats of force, or the use of it, also always exist as options. There are exceptions to this pattern—considerate, benevolent, unselfish bosses; times of relative prosperity and political decency, for instance—but this is the overall sociological character of the leading social class in capitalist society. They simply cannot definitively triumph over the leftist oppositions that they systematically encourage as they pursue their perceived socioeconomic interests. They must keep creating them, though indirectly, and they then must them put them down, directly and indirectly. To think otherwise would be to dismiss some of the most important, dangerous, and destructive aspects of modern history and society completely, and substitute for them a chorus of utopian free market platitudes.

The bourgeoisie has so far managed to largely and repeatedly prevail over its leftist oppositions, from one phase to the next, in the history of capitalist production since the seventeenth century. They have not just remained intact but have clearly and by necessity expanded their operations and reach. In our present era, roughly since the 1990s, the bourgeoisie is arguably stronger than it has ever been; it is led by a handful of billionaires, over two thousand of them, 85 percent men, over half of them operating out of the United States and China, with phenomenal global reach.[16] They are the crowning achievement—some say failure—of the new, neoliberal model. As a group, the few superrich have benefitted from decades of neoliberal economic globalization, privatization, deregulation, and technological advancement, as the very same processes have dramatically weakened the economic position and political leverage of labor. The plutocrats and the oligarchs that have sprung from these grand-scale changes have been eroding liberal democratic politics, which is to say modern liberal democratic politics, which would not have come into form were it not for the efforts of leftwing activists and movements dating back to the early 1800s. But their gains have been pushed back. In the United States, the globally reconstituted bourgeoisie have out-gilded the gilded age robber barons in terms of the extreme disparities between their income and wealth versus that of the vast majority of Americans.[17] Since the Reagan era, most leading US politicians have backed the policies that have brought the world to this point—again, with the Democrats largely abandoning their labor constituency and identity along the way, at least up to early 2020.

For those ordinary working people, there has been a triple sequence of setbacks since the 1970s–80s, each one more abrupt than the former, each facilitated by the bourgeoisie in all its neoliberal extremism, and each creating a boost for what Fukuyama saw as versions of the two challengers to the "liberal idea"—which he believed had been permanently vanquished. The first setback involved the onset and initial phases of globalization, the terms of which only became recognized and explicit in popular discourse in the 1990s. "Outsourcing" became a prevalent term, though it did not capture the full realities; for Americans, for instance, it just meant that "foreigners" were getting "American" jobs. But this was also when the term "capitalism" entered common American political discourse, supplanting the favorite Cold War era term of "democracy," whose rhetorical opposite had been "Communism" or "totalitarianism." For decades, in the propaganda wars between the United States and the Soviet Union, in which both sides adopted the most negative views possible of each other's societies and the most positive ones of their own, there had been a strong disinclination in the US press to use the term "capitalism" to describe the American model. Soviet propaganda never missed a chance to criticize American "democracy" as a sham and to insist on the harsh realities of capitalism and racism as the central features of American society. Jumping ahead, we see that both "capitalism" and "racism" are now normal, yet highly contentious, within popular US discourse, sometimes analytically conjoined, with the clear meaning that they are systematically and politically harsh for many Americans, as well as undeniable global problems. The use of such terms shows hope that many people are increasingly interested in, and able to come to terms with, reality. They are far less subject to glossy and self-congratulatory Cold War–style political propaganda. This is a welcome political, if not generational, departure, yet it is nothing to be particularly comfortable about, because a very large swathe of people in the United States and elsewhere refuse to question capitalism and admit to problem of systemic racism, domestically and worldwide.

The second setback for ordinary working people was the Great Recession that began in 2008, which would not have happened as it did, and perhaps would not have happened at all, without economic globalization generally, but crucially combined with the financial deregulations of the 1990s. Most notorious among these in the United States was the repeal of the Glass-Steagall Act under Bill Clinton in 1999. The move approved by Clinton "tore down the wall" between investment and commercial banking that had been legislatively erected in 1933, precisely to prevent runaway, destabilizing financial trickery by investment bankers using commercial banking deposits and loans as collateral for their speculative operations. Glass Steagall was a popular, democratic response to one of the central reasons why the "roaring twenties" turned into the stock market crash of 1929 and the worldwide Great Depression that followed. There was practical wisdom in the Act, which was too late to mitigate the volatilities of the 1920s but enough to help stabilize the US-led post–Second World War world economic order—otherwise commonly known as the "golden age of capitalism." This modern liberal arrangement could just not withstand the force of the shortsighted, opportunistic, and mnemonically vacuous triumphalist neoliberal bourgeoisie of the 1990s.[18] The third setback, presently, is the COVID-19 pandemic, whose negative public health, economic, and political repercussions have only just begun. This will be discussed further in the epilogue to this book, but it is a worldwide problem, uneven in its effects both within and between societies and states. In line with the way the United States has been highlighted in the second half of this book because of its extremely powerful global role since the end of the Second World War, the country again shows an outstanding distinction, only this time at the top levels of political leadership, in its astonishingly willful denial of the danger of the COVID-19 virus. As mentioned above, with only 4.25 percent of the world's population, in November 2020, it had close to 20 percent of the world's deaths from the virus. If a hard look at the way the British liberals treated the people of Ireland during the famine years of the late 1840s smacks of sadism, the way the Trump administration treated the population of the United States during the COVID-19 pandemic smacks of sadomasochism. Both are politically pathological.

Though they took longer to develop, there were military corollaries to the neoliberal political and policy triumphalism. In launching the Gulf War of 1990–1 against Iraq, the United States began to pivot toward a fully triumphalist military drive. When the United States established a military base in Saudi Arabia during that war, it provided a pretext for its near future number one enemy to attack the United States. One of the top justifications Al Qaeda used for its attack on the United States on September 11, 2001, was that the United States had established a military base in Saudi Arabia and therefore defiled the two most sacred places in the Islamic world, Mecca and Medina. However, just several months after the Gulf War, which ended with Saddam Hussein degraded, but intact, the USSR collapsed. A spate of declarations of national independence across the former Soviet state followed, which had their external impacts, particularly on Yugoslavia, which was already showing serious signs of ethno-territorial fragmentation. These were exploited and encouraged from within by nationalistically minded sub-Yugoslav Serb, Croatian, Bosnian Moslem, Slovenian, Kosovar Albanian, and Slav Macedonian leaders. From the outside, the breakup was encouraged first by Germany but soon by the Clinton administration. For Clinton's team, the entire complex Yugoslav question was conveniently reduced to the problem of Slobodan Milošević, the aggressive Serbian nationalist leader. But the fact was that, if Serbia were to be severely weakened, which it was, Yugoslavia would no longer be a viable proposition. For the United States and its various sub-Yugoslav anti-Serbian allies, Milošević was a convenient target as the political-ideological lynchpin of the Yugoslav problem. In short, the independent multinational socialist state borne out of the Second World War was destroyed, from north to south, region by region, from 1991 to 2001.

If the Gulf War was a pivot for the United States toward an attempt to create a "new world order" in some anticipation of the end of the Cold War, the way the United States and NATO stepped up under Clinton to finish off Yugoslavia was at least a functional preparation for a new stage of brash political and military triumphalism. Two particular and mutually opposing groups appeared at the forefront of this tendency. One was the Project for the New American Century, whose grand policy statement was published in 2000. The Project was led by a group of leading neoconservatives, with William Kristol at the helm and supported by numerous prominent figures such as Paul Wolfowitz, whom the younger Bush appointed as Secretary of Defense in early 2001. Their urgent call was for expanded, restructured, and more efficient foreign and domestic military strength and readiness, all to preserve the "American peace." One of the premier principles, or at least sentiments, of the statement was that the "history of the 20th century should have taught us that it is important to shape circumstances before crises emerge, and to meet threats before they become dire." While the group was soon to be wildly influential on the foreign and domestic strategic and security fronts, its impact was not in line with its apparent hopes in 2000, further stated as follows:

This transformation mission is … as compelling as the need to maintain European stability in the Balkans, prepare for large, theater wars or any other of today's missions. This is an effort that involves more than new weaponry or technologies. It requires experimental units free to invent new concepts of operation, new doctrines, new tactics. It will require years, even decades, to fully grasp and implement such changes, and will surely involve mistakes and inefficiencies. Yet the maintenance of the American peace requires that American forces be preeminent when they are called upon to face very different adversaries in the future ….

We must restore the foundation of American security and the basis for U.S. military operations abroad by improving our homeland defenses. The current American peace will be short-lived if the United States becomes vulnerable to rogue powers with small, inexpensive arsenals of ballistic missiles and nuclear warheads or other weapons of mass destruction. We cannot allow North Korea, Iran, Iraq or similar states to undermine American leadership, intimidate American allies or threaten the American homeland itself. The blessings of the

American peace, purchased at fearful cost and a century of effort, should not be so trivially squandered.[19]

Before the "mistakes and inefficiencies" of the US military triumphalism compounded across the Middle East almost beyond imagination, at least from 2003 onwards, there was a plan of action in search of a pretext. The real thing came with the Al Qaeda terrorist attacks on New York City and Washington, DC, in September 2001. Up to that point, the new Bush administration was floundering, but it now had a new avowed purpose, as revealed simply and succinctly by the younger Bush just two days after the attack: "Now is an opportunity to do generations a favor, by coming together and whipping terrorism, hunting it down, finding it, and holding them accountable. The nation must understand – this is now the focus of my administration."[20] The problem was that, as mercury scatters into multiple beads after being struck by a hammer, the heavy-handed as well as opportunistic response—referring to Afghanistan, but most especially to Iraq—of the Bush administration to the 9/11 attacks ended up proliferating terrorist activity across parts of the Middle East, Europe, and potentially the United States and beyond.

The US wars in Afghanistan and Iraq had the unrelenting contradiction of being post–Cold War triumphalist, yet unwinnable. On the political and popular levels in the United States, including most of all through the mainstream media, they started with righteous flourish; nearly twenty years later, they have not ended. According to a 2019 Pew Research poll, "Among [US] veterans" of those wars,

> 64% say the war in Iraq was not worth fighting considering the costs versus the benefits to the United States, while 33% say it was. The general public's views are nearly identical: 62% of Americans overall say the Iraq War wasn't worth it and 32% say it was. Similarly, majorities of both veterans (58%) and the public (59%) say the war in Afghanistan was not worth fighting. About four-in-ten or fewer say it was worth fighting.[21]

The two targeted societies and states started out very differently from one another, with Afghanistan a much more traditional, socioeconomically, and politically underdeveloped tribal society that had been in varying states of civil war and foreign occupation since the 1979. When the United States invaded in late 2001, there was barely any institutionally viable opposition to the Taliban state apparatus that had arisen there since the Soviet withdrawal. The Taliban received strong support of neighboring Pakistan, which sought stability to its west. Without such a viable institutional opposition, the United States had very little to use to build up any systematic and reliable internal institutional leverage against the Taliban. What they did have was a loose grouping of non-Taliban tribal leaders such as Hamid Karzai, the man of the hour for the United States in late 2001. But these were not the makings of a new state system, especially a modern one. The Taliban had not been defeated and were gradually reasserting their influence and power, as Karzai and the Americans floundered. It was a recipe for prolonged and periodically bloody stalemate.

Iraq was a more modern society and a relatively stable, but an often vicious, authoritarian state with a minority Sunni population maintaining political power over the majority Shiites. If pressured, that division could become incendiary, as it did when the US occupation forces under the direction of L. Paul Bremer outlawed the ruling Sunni Ba'ath Party, thus fatally alienating the Sunni elites and opening the way for Shiite dominance. The American occupation policy knocked Iraq into civil war, yet on May 1, 2003, Bush declared from a US aircraft carrier parked off the coast of San Diego, California, that it was "mission accomplished" in Iraq for the United States. A few weeks later, and in line with the "liberal idea" of "opening up" markets everywhere— Bremer declared jubilantly that Iraq was "open for business." The following summer, while the sectarian civil war was intensifying and further complicating the war between the occupiers and the insurgents, Bremer helped introduce "Operation Adam Smith" to Baghdad. One of the chief spokespersons for the effort was Greg Wong, the US Department of Commerce's senior commercial officer in the city. "We can rebuild Iraq, one business at a time," said Wong, who showed up in Baghdad to coordinate the many organizations then trying to help Iraqi companies get established and grow. The largest organization of this sort was "the U.S. Army's Operation Adam Smith, a multimillion-dollar plan to revitalize Baghdad's commercial districts and eventually build a business incubator at Baghdad University." The US State and Commerce Departments were "trying to establish U.S.-style chambers of commerce, first in Baghdad and later around the country." Wong explained that there were "more than a dozen nongovernment organizations" in Iraq, "hoping to mentor entrepreneurs and distribute grants and loans." They were mostly funded by the US Agency for International Development; the amounts on offer ranged from $100 to $5 million. However, the CNN article goes on to explain that "unfortunately, for all the money and all the energetic, well-meaning Americans being thrown at the problem, their efforts so far have produced few success stories."[22] Bush kept spreading the gloss in a 2005 speech to troops at Fort Hood, Texas:

> Iraqis have laid the foundation of a free economy, with a new currency and independent central bank, new laws to encourage foreign investment, and thousands of small businesses established since liberation. The troops from Fort Hood have done their part. In Baghdad, soldiers of the 1st Cavalry Division launched Operation Adam Smith, and the new generation of Iraqi entrepreneurs you helped nurture will create jobs and opportunities for millions of their fellow citizens.[23]

The above situation laid the grounds for certain crucial realignments: first, a new bond between Shiite Iran and Iraq, whose states had been mortal enemies during the Iran–Iraq War of 1980–8. Second was a new bond between the deposed Sunnis of Iraq with those of the Islamic State of Iraq and the Levant (ISIL), which had been involved in the Iraqi insurgency against the occupation but which also pitted itself against the Syrian government, beginning in 2011. By 2014, ISIL had expanded dramatically. It seized control of parts of northern Iraq and Syria, declared itself a caliphate, therefore claiming status as the latest legitimate heir to the political-religious glory of the prophet Muhammad—a claim that had little broad appeal in the Muslim world—and inflicting systematic abuses against any and all that did not support them. A central goal of the group's declared mission was to reconstitute the borders of the Middle East that had been first drawn up in the secret Sykes-Picot agreement of 1916 between British and French imperialists, in some consultation with Russians and Italians. In all of its political-religious fanaticism, the damage ISIL wrought was severe and costly in terms of human suffering and lives; they appear to have flamed out and fell to defeat as a significant and centralized political-military force by 2019. But the consequences of their actions, combined with the rest of the extremely harsh realities of the Syrian, Iraq, and Afghan wars, produced flows of desperate refugees that began to flood into Turkey, with many soon reaching the borders of Southeastern Europe.

Given its geographical location, Greece was immediately strained by the refugee problem. When the original influxes occurred in 2014–15, the country was still reeling from the impacts of the Great Recession and the imposition by the "troika"—the IMF, the European Central Bank, and the EU—of extreme financial austerity. Though it was not the trauma of invasion, occupation, and civil war that was still shaking Syria, Iraq, and Afghanistan, it was still a major and continuing influx of refugees from largely American triumphalist wars, while Greece was also subjected to the harshest, externally imposed, financial austerity regime of any country in the world. The political dynamics of these combined problems in Greece warrant special attention in the conclusion of this chapter, since they are important in themselves as well as emblematic of the far broader problems of the combined interactions and consequences of the post–Cold War, US-led, political and military triumphalism.

The 2004 Olympic Games in Athens and its environs were a crowning achievement for Greece. The games were "home"' in the land where they had been invented some 2,500 years ago. Meanwhile, the country's modern history since its early nineteenth century independence had been rough. Economically and politically, it was a small and weak state that often fell victim to various foreign manipulations and interventions, the worst of which was the Axis occupation of 1941 to 1944 that set off the civil war of 1943–9. The country was devastated and politically fraught with a rightwing security state and police forces that routinely harassed leftists, and worse. This was all intensified under the military dictatorship of 1967–74 that was imposed out of "fear"— really, the expectation—that what for them was an overly left-oriented government had come to power that might undermine the privileges of those in the security state and in the economy and society that otherwise benefitted from the victory of the British and US-backed rightwing social and political forces in the civil war. They called it a "communist threat," rallied the United States to its cause, overthrew the center-left government, and established a military and police state that was systematically aggressive, vicious, and torturous. The greatest internal oppositional challenge to the regime came from a student uprising at the Athens Polytechnic University in November 1973. In the end it was crushed by the dictatorship, which proceeded to double down on repression, but it was seared into popular memory as a heroic collective act of anti-authoritarian resistance. The regime then essentially brought itself down in 1974 as it launched a disastrous effort to unify Cyprus with Greece, bringing Greece and Turkey to the brink of war, and giving Turkey the pretext to invade, occupy, and claim sovereignty over northern Cyprus. Though the claim has not been recognized internationally, in fact, Turkey controls it to this day. For the dictatorship, the fiasco was humiliating and fatal. Its main supporters, including the United States, backed a shift toward electoral democracy.

Greece's democratic turn was accompanied by somewhat steady economic development as well as much freer politics. In the meantime, the European Economic Community (EEC) was steadily consolidating and eyeing the periphery of Western Europe for expansion. Greece joined in 1981, more for the sake of maintaining European political stability rather than for economic reasons. The leading figures in the EEC recognized the importance of such strategic criteria for inclusion, since they were what drove its original inception in the 1950s, shortly after the catastrophe of the Second World War. By the 1980s, an essential two-party system had emerged on the scene, the center-left Panhellenic Socialist Party (PASOK) under Andreas Papandreou and the center-right New Democracy (ND) party under Konstantine Mitsotakis.

Greece had its ups and downs economically but managed to stabilize from 1995 to 2005 and was widely recognized as having developed a fairly affluent society.[24] In early 2001, the country was admitted into the Eurozone, which in part meant that it was subject to financial monitoring by the European Central Bank (ECB), which was mostly under the influence of Germany, "the great European financial disciplinarian."[25] But this new step for Greece turned out to be just one of a series of developments that comprised the difficult side, not just of the country's upcoming Olympic moment, but also of the condition of its entire society. Unavoidably, Greece borrowed heavily in the period prior to summer, 2004, in order to finance the logistical and infrastructural preparations for the games. No matter what, this was going to worsen its debt-to-gross domestic product (GDP) ratio in the short run, but to make matters even more challenging, the news broke toward the end of the games that the numbers Greece had presented to the Eurozone officials in 2000–1 as its budget deficits and debt-to-GDP ratios were substantially lower than the real numbers. With expert assistance from New York's Goldman Sachs Financial Group, Greek officials had seriously misrepresented their data in order to enter the Eurozone.[26] In 2005, as Greece's deficit reached new heights, Greece and Goldman Sachs arranged for more ways of concealing the real data; the trickery worked sufficiently in the past and perhaps could do so again. For Goldman Sachs from 2000 to 2005 this was all a highly lucrative operation, worth at least $500 million. But in the meantime, the news revelations continued, and Greek deficits and debts expanded dramatically, which triggered a series of audits by the EU that confirmed both the deceptions and the stark realities of the Greek-Goldman Sachs scheme. This was bad enough financially and politically, but next up was the worst global financial crisis since the Great Depression.

The financial, economic, political, and social impact on Greece of the Great Recession that began in 2007–8 was extreme. Financially, the increase in the cost of borrowing became too steep for Greece to pay its debts, which just kept increasing. Its debt-to-GDP ratio increased from approximately 105 percent in 2008 to 170 percent in 2011 and 177 percent in 2015; unemployment rose to 26 percent generally, but by 2013 it reached a staggering 60 percent for younger people. GDP dropped by approximately 25 percent from 2010 to 2015. During the same period, the social toll was overwhelming. Many ordinary Greeks saw no way out; depression became endemic, and suicide rates, which had never been high in the country despite all of its past agonies, increased by 40 percent. Politically, the crisis shattered the credibility of the two major political parties, PASOK and New Democracy. By 2014–15, the financial and economic crisis combined with the stresses of the refugee crisis due to the wars in the Middle East to create fertile ground for neofascism in the form of the Golden Dawn party, which went from a peripheral criminal tendency lurking on the far-right political scene since 1980 to the third-largest political party in the Greek parliament, receiving 7 percent of the vote in the 2015 national elections. It trafficked in extreme xenophobia and wrapped itself in Greek flag as well as its own flag, which was strikingly reminiscent of the Nazi flag.

But the big winner of the January 2015 elections appeared to be the Syriza party under the leadership of Alexis Tsipras, which had been formed out of a coalition of smaller leftwing parties. Syriza gained the largest portion of the vote, over 36 percent, while center-right the New Democracy party came in second. Support

Figure 12 President Salvador Allende of Chile and his security and political entourage in Valparaiso, Chile, during the early 1970s. Allende was a democratically elected radical reformist who provoked the antipathies of Nixon and Kissinger in the United States, as well as those of the Chilean oligarchy. He was violently overthrown by them and their agents in a military coup on September 11, 1973, which was followed by the imposition of the dictatorship of General Pinochet.

Source: https://www.bcn.cl/historiapolitica/resenas_parlamentarias/wiki/Salvador_Allende_Gossens; public domain, commons.wikimedia.org.

Figure 13 Manolis Glezos (1922–2020) speaking in Omonia Square in Athens, 2015. Glezos was famous for tearing down the Nazi swastika from the Acropolis of Athens in the middle of the night of May 30, 1941, with his friend, Lakis Santas. This was part of a lifelong and tireless commitment to everything that it takes to achieve social and political justice for all individuals and peoples.

Source: Public domain; commons.wikimedia.org.

for Syriza was most definitely based on its avowed commitment against the austerity regime that had been imposed upon Greece by the IMF, ECB, and the EU since 2010, and which was clearly taking an extreme toll on Greece's well-being. Syriza's victory and its anti-austerity stance was hopeful for many Greeks, as well as others around the world who opposed the callousness of neoliberal austerity, and particularly the extent to which it was being imposed upon Greece, from the outside, in such an anti-democratic manner. The July 5, 2015, referendum on the question of yes or no to austerity produced a resounding 60 percent no vote against it. But, Syriza was not the actual winner. Greek democracy and Syriza got neutralized: hostile politics emanating from within Greece and Europe, and most importantly, the rule of global finance—systemically anti-leftist—amid the Great Recession, revealed one of the most effective weapons in the arsenal of capitalism and market liberalization within and between societies and states: big money firmly in the hands of the very few. It was an unfortunately fitting and representative update of the long history of injustice, tension, and conflict in the modern world.

Notes

1. J. Patrice McSherry, "Tracking the Origins of a State Terror Network: Operation Condor," *Latin American Perspectives*, vol. 29, no. 1 (January 2002), pp. 38–60. Available online: https://www.jstor.org/stable/3185071 (accessed September 6, 2020); McSherry, "Operation Condor: Clandestine Inter-American System," *Social Justice*, vol. 26, no. 4 (Winter 1999), pp. 144–74. Available online: https://www.jstor.org/stable/29767180 (accessed September 6, 2020).
2. See http://nixontapes.org/chile.html.
3. Kirsten Weld, "Because They Were Taken Alive: Forced Disappearance in Latin America," *ReVista, Harvard Review of Latin America*, Fall 2013. Availble online: https://revista.drclas.harvard.edu/book/discovering-dominga.
4. "Telegram from the Embassy in Honduras to the Department of State; Tegucigalpa, July 26, 1979, 1704Z 4063. For the Deputy Secretary from Assistant Secretary Vaky. Subject: El Salvador: A First Step. Doc. 376," *FRUS 1977–1980*, 15; Central America, 1977–1980. Available online: https://history.state.gov/historicaldocuments/frus1977-80v15/d376.
5. Ibid., doc. 377, Pastor to Brzezinski, August 1, 1979.
6. https://fas.org/irp/offdocs/nsdd/nsdd-17.pdf. This document is dated January 4, 1982, but the policy statement was signed by Reagan on November 23, 1981.
7. https://www.cia.gov/library/readingroom/docs/CIA-RDP90-00965R000504130057-0.pdf. This link is to a lengthy *Los Angeles Times* article by Doyle McManus and Robert Toth from March 4, 1985, entitled "The Contras: How the US got Entangled."
8. There has been some progress in the effort to find those responsible for the murder of Romero. At least it is clear that it was not about a "lone gunman": https://www.theguardian.com/theguardian/2000/mar/23/features11.g21; see also https://www.laprensagrafica.com/elsalvador/Declara-la-abogada-Almudena-Bernabeu-contra-Alvaro-Saravia-unico-acusado-del-magnicidio-de-San-Romero-20200304-0050.html.
9. https://2001-2009.state.gov/r/pa/ho/time/rd/17741.htm.
10. See Nikki R. Keddie's article on the Islamic Revolution in Iran, "Can Revolutions Be Predicted? Understood?," in *Debating Revolutions* (New York: New York University Press, 1995), pp. 3–26; also see Hobsbawm, *The Age of Extremes: A History of the World, 1914–1991* (New York: Vintage, 1996), pp. 453–55; Thomas J. McCormick, *America's Half Century: United States Foreign Policy in the Cold War and After* (Baltimore, MD: Johns Hopkins University Press, 1995), pp. 207–8.
11. CNN Documentary Series (released in 1998), *Cold War*, Episode 20, "Soldiers of God."
12. For a close analysis of how the "race to the bottom" has played out in the Eurozone, see Costas Lapavitsas et al., *Crisis in the Eurozone* (New York: Verso, 2012), pp. 22–3, and *passim*.
13. For a serious call to correct and expand the critical perspectives on neoliberalism to include those more from the global south with those of the global north, which tend to predominate, see Raewyn Connell and Nour Dados, "Where in the World does Neoliberalism Come from? The Market Agenda in Southern Perspective," *Theory and Society*, vol. 43, no. 2 (March 2014), pp. 117–38. Available online: https://www.jstor.org/stable/43694712.

14. Again, Piketty's *Capital in the 21st Century* demonstrates this same history. On the extreme gaps between CEO and labor compensation, see https://www.epi.org/publication/ceo-compensation-2018/.

15. Francis Fukuyama, "The End of History?" *The National Interest*, 1989.

16. https://www.forbes.com/billionaires/ (accessed August 9, 2020). These are numbers as reported in March 2020.

17. https://inequality.org/great-divide/america-2018-more-gilded-america-1918/ (accessed August 12, 2020).

18. Nomi Prins, *Collusion: How Central Bankers Rigged the World* (New York: Nation Books, 2018), pp. 8–11.

19. "Rebuilding America's Defenses: Strategy, Forces and Resources for a New Century," A Report of The Project for the New American Century, September 2000, p. 75. Available online: https://archive.org/details/RebuildingAmericasDefenses/page/n7/mode/2up.

20. "Emotional President Bush," September 13, 2001, on C-Span 2. See https://www.youtube.com/watch?v=0JOpGFjJg8A.

21. Ruth Igielnik and Kim Parker, "Majorities of U.S. Veterans, Public Say the Wars in Iraq and Afghanistan Were not Worth Fighting," Pew Research Center, July 10, 2019. https://www.pewresearch.org/fact-tank/2019/07/10/majorities-of-u-s-veterans-public-say-the-wars-in-iraq-and-afghanistan-were-not-worth-fighting/. (The numbers for the war in Syria are similar.)

22. Arlyn Tobias Gajilan, "Entrepreneurs in Iraq Tangle in U.S. Red Tape. American Agencies and Nonprofits Are Streaming into Baghdad to Spur the Country's Small Companies. But Do Lessons in Writing Business Plans really Help?," CNN Money, November 1, 2004. Available online: https://money.cnn.com/magazines/fsb/fsb_archive/2004/11/01/8190934/index.htm.

23. "Terrorism and Iraq," President George W. Bush Remarks to Troops at Fort Hood, Texas, US Department of State Archive, April 12, 2005. Available online: https://2001-2009.state.gov/p/nea/rls/rm/44533.htm.

24. https://data.worldbank.org/indicator/NY.GDP.MKTP.KD.ZG?locations=GR.

25. Allan Little, "How 'Magic' Made Greek Debt Disappear before It Joined the Euro," BBC News, February 3, 2012. Available online: https://www.bbc.com/news/world-europe-16834815.

26. For some of the earliest reporting on this matter, see Nick Dunbar, "Revealed: Goldman Sachs' Mega-Deal for Greece; Greece Uses Swaps to Hit EU Debt Ratios," Risk Magazine, July 1, 2003. Available online: https://www.risk.net/derivatives/structured-products/1498135/revealed-goldman-sachs-mega-deal-greece.

Summary and Conclusion

Systemic and political hostility against the left ranks and intertwines with the main critical issues of modern history, including capitalism, imperialism and colonialism, xenophobic nationalism, ideological conflict, patriarchy, and racism. Such hostility is embedded in the dynamics of class conflict between capital and labor, but also has a certain autonomy. The focus of this study has been more on the rhetorical, political, and physical hostility that is expressed and deployed from within the complex worlds of capital against the changing leftwing political spectrum of labor. While the hostility has its broad social parameters, it does not necessarily have any rational or controllable limits. In that sense, it shows pathological tendencies. It is a distinct, often unruly, and unpredictable force that grew out of and combined with the wider array of forces that have shaped the modern world from the onset of industrial capitalist society all the way to the current conflicts over neoliberalism, racism, plutocracy, gender, the COVID-19 pandemic and environmental catastrophe. At the very least, this book is a cautionary history of anti-"socialist" politics—a warning that they become unhinged and indiscriminately destructive.

The problem has been evident since the earliest stages of liberal capitalist industrial society in England and the liberal revolution and market liberalization in France. It was in both societies, with their varying contours, that various forms of socialism first emerged as intellectual and practical responses to liberalism, liberalized markets, and capitalist production. These latter forces created what in popular discourse was termed the "social problem" of the new, impoverished, and insecure laboring classes, especially that demographic found living in dark, dank, and crowded households close to factories, where men, women, and children were worked into chronic states of exhaustion. Early socialists such as Robert Owen and Saint-Simon argued that subjecting people to such agonizing labor regimes was not just immoral and unethical, but also, on the practical level, unnecessary. More humane means of producing commodities were within reach, as Owen demonstrated, even turning a reasonable profit on his enterprise at New Lanark, Scotland. But he and his French counterparts were targets of scathing attacks that often smacked of hysteria.

For many of the new liberal establishment's policy and cultural figures, the early socialists personified everything evil. As quoted at the beginning of this book, they were "God-hating, law abandoning, rulers despising, authority condemning, virtue-destroying, vice advancing, youth corrupting, polygamy-encouraging, adultery-enforcing, accountability refuting, conscience stifling, murder cloaking."[1] The new organization of production featured the antagonism between capital and labor, especially in the early days of no factory regulations, no protections for laborers, and no right to unionize. All these things exhibited liberalism's original and extremely callous disregard for the fact that labor was, day by day, overloaded with harsh and unjust realities. Those realities were often denied; in effect, they were also defended under the cover of wild anti-socialist rhetorical assaults. How critics of socialist ideas at the time could maintain such denial while virulently attacking their new socialist enemies should beggar the imagination. But it was such a predominant pattern of politics at the time, and it anticipated far worse things to come, that it warrants methodological treatment as a real, operative, contradictory pathology that was just in its early stages.

As capitalist industrial society expanded and its cyclical boom and bust character became fully evident, the economic downturn of the mid-to-late 1840s put the whole complex of labor, capital, and state forces to the test, particularly in France. Given the virulence of the anti-socialist rhetoric of recent years, as well as the practical matters at stake, how would the more privileged sections of the Parisian population and the French government deal with unemployment at 40 percent? For several months, there was some mercy through the establishment of the National Workshops modeled somewhat after the ideas of the socialistic Louis Blanc. But the sympathy ran out. While the economy was not recovering by mid-1848, French employers got impatient and rallied to convince the government to close the workshops. It was early June and getting food on the table for large sections of the workforce in Paris was suddenly extremely difficult. They took to the streets, demanding that the workshops be reopened. For that, some four thousand laborers were massacred, and thousands more were imprisoned and exiled, all for seeking something akin to what was later known as "unemployment compensation."

A pattern of intensifying antagonism was emerging on the political as well as the political-intellectual levels in the late 1830s and into the 1840s. The radical left intellectual ferment was most giving in France, with Pierre Proudhon's proto-anarchist salvo that "property is theft"—by which he meant big property—and Auguste Blanqui advocating a seizure of state power for the sake of a vaguely defined equality and justice. Most importantly in the long run was Marx, in Paris, exiled from the German Confederation, whose *Communist Manifesto* was published too late to have any impact on the broad European Revolutions of 1848. But his ideas may have seeped into the workers who rose up later during the "June Days" in Paris, only to meet their very grim fate. The liberals' abandonment of their working-class allies in Paris fitted the larger pattern of the Revolutions of 1848–9 across Europe, offering the opportunity for the political reaction that followed. Following upon this temporary and vicious chastening of labor, liberal, and liberal nationalist demands across Europe, the economy began an upturn, which quieted things on the domestic fronts until the strategic rumblings of the 1850–60s that involved the moves toward Italian and German unification. In that period, the bourgeoisie, big and small, which in 1848 still had radical elements seeking greater electoral political representation, turned fully conservative, choosing to protect their gains against the threat of the new working classes, many of whom were gravitating toward one or another form of leftwing politics.

But the relative stability was short-lived, if not illusory. The long history of European great power state rivalry was entering a new phase, intensified by the competitive dynamics of capitalist productivity, or the lack of it, and the ways that capacity endowed certain states, and not others, to rise to international imperial glory. The German Confederation had a long way to go if it were to advance to great power status on par with Britain and France, which both already had the major makings of far-flung colonial empires. Under Chancellor Bismarck, the Prussian monarchy made a series of moves to establish itself as effectively as possible as a top competitor, at least on the European stage. The Franco-Prussian War of 1870–1 was the final, victorious step in the unification of Germany and a highly destabilizing defeat for France. With Paris under Prussian occupation, the city's elites fled to their country homes, leaving the poorer populations of the city to their own devices. As a matter of self-protection, and as an expression of the fertile political culture of the Parisian left, the Paris Commune took shape as history's first socialist revolution. Its leadership and popular base included representatives of all of the left-leaning political tendencies of city that had been crystallizing at least since 1789. However, once the French state and Parisian political and governmental elites began to regroup, they attacked the Communards viciously, executing twenty thousand to twenty-five thousand of them. It was fully evident that the Parisian and French power elites' fears and hatred of the leftwing politics of their fellow citizens surpassed any problem they had with the remaining Prussian military occupiers of the city. This was the first of a series of international wars that triggered off domestic social revolutions, whose leaders and supporters—even merely suspected ones—tended to get punished severely. Of course, they were not always defeated, as in Russia of 1917, but they would still be subjected to harsh punishment from the outside and severe challenges from the inside, just as they would also resort to harsh measures against their perceived internal enemies.

Anti-leftist politics were central to the dynamics of the age of empire that ultimately exploded in the First World War, which became the "big bang" of sorts for the rest of modern history. They became an even stronger and direct force in the interwar era of fascism and appeasement that, in the end, guaranteed another world war. At that point, from the late 1930s onward, the potential became one for utter self-destruction. That has been averted and might still not happen, that is, if sanity prevails and there are no thermonuclear accidents. But, aside from the question of total self-annihilation and the death toll of millions from poverty, famine, and malnutrition, the wars of the past century annihilated upward of one hundred million people. Those wars in which they died, including the Second World War, the Cold War and its proxy wars, and the US-led wars in the Middle East since the end of the Cold War, cannot be understood without a close look at the animus against the left that is systemically and politically evident in capitalist production, market liberalization, and their loosely allied religious, cultural, intellectual, military, and police supports.

The example of the Second World War warrants reemphasis. The worst war in human history was, at least in principle, actually avoidable until at least the spring of 1939; it could be argued that it was even avoidable two weeks before it started in the west with the Nazi invasion of Poland in early September 1939. If the British had been willing to join in a "collective security" pact with the Soviet Union against

Nazism and fascism, Hitler most likely would have dropped his reckless quest for world domination, at least for the time being, and perhaps with finality. But the British remained fundamentally anti-Soviet at the time, even then, in mid-August 1939, when they believed they could not escape war with Nazi Germany. The fact was they still had a chance to avoid war but either could not see it or, instead, chose war. This is a blaring instance of what this book argues is the problem of anti-"socialist" politics, in this case a specific refusal to work with the Soviet Union against fascism and world war. It was about avoiding "socialism" at all costs; in this case, it would have just been a pragmatic alliance with the USSR to put Nazi Germany in check before it was too late. But it was exactly at that point, in mid-August 1939, that Stalin gave up on his three-year effort to get Britain to agree on collective security. Instead, he turned to Hitler and agreed to the Non-Aggression Pact with Germany, which gave Hitler a free hand to attack northwestern Europe and Britain, while it gave Stalin and the USSR time to prepare for what they saw as the inevitable Nazi invasion of their state. One would be hard put to view Britain's refusal to work with the USSR against Hitler's Germany as rational. One might fall back on the position that they just made a grave mistake, given their incomplete knowledge at the time. This study shows it to have been most definitely a "mistake," but more deeply, one that is explained as a tragic instance of a long cultivated pattern and pathology of hostility against the left that only got further amplified after the 1917 Bolshevik Revolution. Hitler was actually a creature of a broadly similar anti-leftist hostility, though in a different setting and on a different trajectory, distinctively mixed with his virulent racism and anti-Semitism, and directed against the domestic left—against socialists, anarchists, communists, and "Jewish bolsheviks." Ultimately, Hitler's version of the pathology was channeled against the Soviet Union as a state and society, and in the Holocaust against the Jews, the Romani people, homosexuals, transsexuals, and the infirm—all as supposed genetic inferiors. This was, and remains, an overwhelming trauma.

This study has been divided into chapters representing several successive phases of this expansion and the ostensible "solutions" to the "social problem" in modern world history, that is, the problem of the existence and plight of the working classes in capitalist societies. The classical liberal solution was to stick to liberal theory and ideology, which meant not intervening in new markets for any reason, therefore leaving everything up to "nature." The gap between the classical liberal policy position and the realities of most workers' lives, as well as those of others, was vast, yet it was presented by the liberals as the best that could be done. The narrowly self-serving and callous character of their stance was truly astonishing. Of course, the nasty rhetorical attacks on leftists and socialists for their supposed atheism, or at least their supposed heresies, just compounded the problem and the challenge to understand it. Saint-Simon got excommunicated from the Catholic Church for advocating a "New Christianity" that prioritized the needs of the poorest people in society.

The supposed "imperial solution" to the social problem explored in Chapter 1 was conjoined with an extreme nationalist solution. Together they promised increased domestic income along with popular political glory and pride. There may have been some modest income gains for the working classes in the European imperialist states, along the lines of what Cecil Rhodes argued would "avoid civil war in Britain," though it is not clear that this was the case. The extreme nationalism that was aroused within the imperialist states also provided satisfaction to ordinary people that they were part of something larger on the world stage, in particular a national and supposed civilizing mission for the "uncivilized" peoples under their states' colonial domination. Meanwhile, the German government under Bismarck took the lead on establishing a variety of state unemployment, injury, and retirement programs for labor. As much as he detested the German Social Democrats (SPD), as shown in the anti-socialist laws he promulgated in the 1870s–80s, he clearly recognized the threat they posed to the old guard Prussians and the need to outmaneuver them. Despite the Chancellor's efforts, the SPD continued its rise through parliament in which it became the largest party from the 1890s up to the First World War and beyond. France and Britain followed suit on the welfare front, though not as systematically, while the United States lagged behind until the Great Depression of the 1930s. Meanwhile, considerable segments of the European social democratic movements and parties in the great power states were persuaded by the argument about the "civilizing mission." In turn, this made them more amenable to nationalist rhetoric and politics, thus setting them up for the total collapse of their fundamental political commitments, as their party leaders in 1914 voted to go to war against one other. Imperialism and xenophobic nationalism were fraught with a savagery that saw particular genocidal expression on the part of imperialists in the Belgian Congo and in German Southwest Africa, but another sort of savagery then within and between the opposing trenches of the "home fronts" of the Great War, with imperialist-nationalist generals sending their troops to slaughter by the hundreds of thousands.

Increased critical awareness of the futile and wanton carnage of the war, and the nationalist deceptions and delusions that brought it on in the first place, fed the surge of socialist politics in the latter part of the war. These matters are addressed in Chapter 2, carrying the study through the interwar years to 1939. Clearly, socialism now had a specific revolutionary variant established in Russia, which was a source of deadly controversies within the broad spectrum of the left worldwide. Yet for those inclined against the left, any idea that a spectrum even existed tended to wither away— conveniently enough, they were all "bolsheviks." British foreign policy makers even slipped into this mode of thinking when it suited them, as it did in their approach to the Spanish Civil War. This was often just a matter of political opportunism on the part of fascists, quasi-fascists, liberals, and conservatives, and it was very effective and deadly. The Second World War then unleashed more of the fallout from the explosive "contradictions" that led to the First World War, including the racism, Social Darwinism, and anti-Semitism that fueled the Holocaust as well as so much of the rest of the war. Politically, the war opened the way for a victorious leftwing revolution in Yugoslavia under Tito. It also opened the way for a Communist-led, anti-fascist resistance movement in Greece, which was indeterminate in its ultimate political aims, yet was, in any case, the target of subversion and destruction by the British, their Greek nationalist anti-leftist allies, and the United States. The Second World War also played to the strategic advantages of the Chinese Communists, which had a great deal to do with Chiang Kai Shek's fundamental anti-Communist obsessions. Recalling similar anti-leftist politics in Yugoslavia and Greece, or even the Parisian elites during the

Franco-Prussian War, Chiang feared the leftists in his own country more than he did the ruthless Japanese invaders. Ho Chi Minh and the Vietminh resistance organization he led in Indochina indirectly benefitted from Chiang's anti-Communist priorities; they benefitted the Chinese Communists that supported the Vietminh in their role against Japan and later for independence from the French. On a grander level, there is a remarkable irony in this view of the Second World War and its aftermath; to a great extent, it was brought on by a complex convergence of anti-leftist currents, yet it gave rise to, or tended to favor, a whole slew of left-oriented resistance and national liberation movements across the colonized and Axis-occupied worlds.

Consequently, for the post–Second World War period, covered in the three chapters of Part II, the leftist targets were more numerous than ever. For the new cold warriors of the United States, it was time to launch the largest political crusade in human history—global anti-Communism—with very mixed and troubling results. The treatment of the Cold War in this book is inevitably selective but hopefully representative of the character of the period. First of all, in terms of sheer survival, there is the obvious positive that the world was not obliterated in nuclear war. But in terms of the specificities, the anti-leftist war in Greece, which could have been avoided, was victorious. In very different circumstances, the anti-leftist war was a failure in China, where the Communists under Mao Zedong defeated the "nationalists" under Chiang Kai Shek by 1949. At that point in East Asia, the stakes were extremely high, but the carnage of the warfare that overlapped and followed in Korea and Indochina, perpetrated more by the United States and its allies than by the Soviet, Chinese, Korean, or Indochinese Communists, was deeply chilling. This author cannot escape the impression that a great deal of it was vengeful and gratuitous—MacArthur, Ridgway, and Donald Nichols played their parts and, in some circles, became folk heroes for doing so.[2] That kind of behavior cannot be separated from the historical and pathological antipathy against the left covered throughout this book. There is obviously a deep pool of capacities within human beings for very constructive and destructive behavior, but it is the contours and dynamic of history and society that bring them out and shape them. Of course, the French were bent upon aggression against the Vietminh in their US-backed war in Indochina. The Americans displayed it again as they tried, against French advice—which was based on hard lessons—to militarily defeat the Vietnamese leftwing nationalists. Where the French failed, so did the Americans.

The study moves on in Chapter 5 to sub-Saharan Africa, North Africa, and the Middle East, where the human carnage was almost nothing compared to the horrific extent of it on the Korean peninsula and Indochina, but the damage was serious and long-lasting in people's lives throughout those regions and in the imperialist societies and states. A number of developments compounded the bitter legacies of the longer history of imperialism, such as British colonial authorities' harsh treatments of the Mau Mau rebels and Jomo Kenyatta under false pretenses, leading to the relinquishment of the Kenya colony; as well as the French war against the Algerian rebels and its longer-term consequences in France. Also, in the longer term, was the reaction of the Iranians against the arbitrary anti-"communist" interventions of the United States and Britain that brought their country under the repressive and violent modernization regime of the Shah. The reactions against the Shah from within Iran eventually led to the Islamic

Revolution under the Ayatollah Khomeini and contributed strongly to the dramatic surge in Islamic fundamentalist politics across the Middle East and elsewhere.

Following along with the "mixed results," if not the largely negative US-led anti-Communist crusade of the post–Second World War era, Chapter 6 gets to Western Europe, Latin America, and the United States up to the 1970s. It is a disparate grouping perhaps on the face of it, but all three were places where robust and widely varied forms of leftist politics emerged, only to be undermined and subjected to extreme hostility followed by neoliberal austerity. Leftist and left-leaning movements and organizations in Spain and Greece fell to defeat in the 1930s and 1940s, respectively, but did not die out; in Portugal, leftwing resistance against Salazar and his successor, Caetano, grew. In the 1970s, the dictatorships fell, and South and Southwestern Europe more or less joined ranks with their Northwest European counterparts as social democrats. This was an important stretch for West Europeans in terms of the quality of life, but it was not to be a permanent state of affairs. This was because monetarism, privatization, and full-force neoliberalism, mainly emanating from the United States, but channeled through the European Commission, were on the move. In Latin America, one leftwing target got hit very violently—Guatemala under Arbenz—while Cuba got away but has faced multipronged hostility from the United States since 1960. The rest of Latin America was, meanwhile, being softened up for another wave of attacks on the left, under the direction of the United States, but in collaboration with the landed oligarchies and their police and paramilitary forces across the region, many of them trained by US experts.

Part III of this book is short, though the lone chapter within it deals with several far-flung topics. The idea is that we are in the middle of a relatively incomplete phase of the history of anti-"socialist" politics. The title of the lone chapter in the section is "The Overkill," which is meant to convey three things: first, the extreme beatdown inflicted upon any and all government interventions in the economy that were, from the public and societal standpoints, established to move toward greater equality for all people to enjoy the fruits of the amazingly productive economic system of capitalism. These were put in place in the United States during the Great Depression and the Cold War, partly to prove that the United States had something to counter the USSR's claims of government for the people. The end of the Cold War in 1991 leads into the second suggestion of the title, that the wars in the Middle East since the 1990s should be seen as neoliberal triumphalist in character, driven by hubris, by a false, dangerous, and destructive pride that has destroyed societies and hundreds of thousands of lives across the region. It has also had a grim effect upon society and politics in Europe and the United States. Third, the title is meant to specifically highlight the assault on government regulations intended to protect the natural environment. The *rollback* of such regulations, especially under the most recent presidential administration of Donald Trump in the United States, but also against the more general backdrop if decades of deregulation, constitute the weaponization of the myopia as well as the flimsiness of the Paris Accords of 2015, which were just half-measures, but at least in the right direction. These problems constitute the weaponization of the myopia of capitalist profitability, which in itself has a systematic anti-leftist thrust.

This book has aimed to demonstrate that there is a certain insanity, even a license for it, in the political and coercive dynamics of class conflict within and between capitalist

Figure 14 One of the mass graves of Spanish republicans discovered in an excavation from July to August 2014 at Estépar, in the province of Burgos. Dating from the start of the Spanish Civil War, the grave contains twenty-six republicans who were killed by nationalists in August–September 1936.

societies and states, as well as in parts of the world that are subjected to their power and influence. In the past two hundred years, this dynamic expanded from a small part of Europe to envelop most of the world. Its anti-socialist political pathology, by which it systematically and politically creates "socialist" oppositions of all sorts, which it then must try to destroy for the sake of its survival, has been repeatedly abusive and inimical to societal decency and environmental health. It continues to involve a distinctive historical syndrome of tension, conflict, and warfare that would be far better as a thing of the past, as a memory of how abusive it *used* to be.

Notes

1. See the beginning of the Introduction of this book.
2. Blaine Harden, "How One Man Helped Burn Down North Korea: The Story of One of the Most Effective and Brutal Spymasters in U.S. History, and the Beginning of an Infamous Love Affair with Napalm." Politico Magazine, October 2, 2017. https://www.politico.com/magazine/story/2017/10/02/donald-nichols-book-north-korea-215665

Epilogue: The Pathology, the Pandemic, and the Prospects

The world since the 1970s has experienced a series of big and small breakups and remakes—systemic, political, financial, cultural, technological, and more. This may be nothing new. Looking from the 1970s back to the Second World War, or from then to the pre–First World War era, or, indeed, from then to the mid- and early nineteenth centuries—which was very close to the Liberal and Industrial Revolutions—changes, breakups, reconstitutions, and surprises have kept coming. It clearly was and is not just the two original revolutionary "events" that mattered; it was that they introduced a dynamic of constant and dramatic change, for better or for worse. The changes featured increasingly profound and unequal power relationships on an expanding scale, from the local to the regional to the global. In terms of the structures of world power and the conflicts they generated, it was very much about the uneven development of capitalism within and between societies, states, and the colonies of some of those states. This has been a constant and mostly unforgiving problem, yet not one always so easy to see clearly. But most recently, despite its deadly character, the COVID-19 pandemic has starkly revealed the destructive character of the neoliberal juggernaut that took off in the 1970s.

The focus of this book has been on how the system of capitalism and market liberalization constantly, and with a crucial degree of necessity, has created the grounds for oppositions against it that have then had to be undermined. In the move to do so, there is a discernable pattern of blindness, hysteria, and irrationality. While that dynamic has been operative for at least the past two hundred years, it has had specific characteristics and has been fraught with particular dangers in each era of its existence. From the 1970s to the present, the worldwide neoliberal political-economic campaign has probably outdone what preceded and overlapped with it, the US-led campaign against Communism from the Second World War to 1991. But the two campaigns were also strategically consonant with one another in a way that suggests neoliberalism to be a continuation of the anti-Communist campaign, but with modified means, and an even more extensive geographical scope. Most importantly for this study, the neoliberal campaign has had an expanded political target—"socialism," which, for those that use that term pejoratively, evidently means anything that is *not* maximally free market capitalist. That is its absurdity and pathology, yet also its inner logic and reality. From a fairly conventional standpoint, capitalism in its various political forms, including its neoliberal form, can be seen as systemically and politically anti-"socialist." But the argument here is that the historic constitutions and reconstitutions of capitalism in its varying political forms have always created what they are against. They have laid the grounds for socialisms of all sorts, and when they take shape, they get attacked, often with pathological fervor. Capitalism and market liberalization are, therefore, repeatedly caught in a syndrome of their own making, the reality of which their supporters tend to remain in denial.

At the beginning of the third decade of the twenty-first century, it is too early to say that the neoliberal era has run its course. But there are signs that it has, some of which are on the level of politics and political conflict. One way or another, they are responses to the consequences of the neoliberal capitalist globalization, including the triumphalist wars addressed in the last chapter and the conclusion of this book. This epilogue will examine just a few of the political and economic changes that have occurred worldwide, more or less since 2016. This will include some of the ways in which the crisis of the COVID-19 pandemic has laid bare, magnified, and exacerbated the problems of capitalism in general, but especially its neoliberal form. The section will end with a large historical perspective on capitalism, market liberalization, and anti-leftist politics.

The breakups and breakdowns in politics and society in recent decades, or at least the marked tendencies in those directions, have included economic and political-institutional structures, some of which had prevailed since the late nineteenth century. Production was concentrated in just a few places but then spread across the globe; fissures appeared within the European Union (EU), including the fact of Brexit and the recent possibility of the Greek exit from the EU; major strains also appeared within the EU over how to handle refugees from wars in the Middle East and from poverty in Africa. Ecosystems, long under strain, are now breaking under the extreme pressure of the anthropocene. Many of the major political parties of the post–Second World War era electoral democracies are shrinking dramatically relative to new far-rightwing xenophobic nationalist parties, such as the Bharatiya Janata Party (BJP) under Narendra Modi in India and the fledgling Alliance for Brazil under Jair Bolsonaro. The worldwide rise of rightwing authoritarian racist, xenophobic, misogynistic, and virulently anti-leftist politics would seem to have little to do with "free markets and the liberal idea" trumpeted by the leading conservative and liberal triumphalists of the 1990s and since, but this needs to be considered beyond appearances.

Bolsonaro in Brazil, Duterte in the Philippines, Erdogan in Turkey and his foreign policy aggressions, Modi in India, Orban in Hungary, and Trump in the United States are all rightwing populists, if not fascists; they deploy vicious racist, xenophobic, hypermasculinist politics, hostility against the left, and disdain for anything resembling real democracy. They consistently put private corporate interests over labor and environmental concerns, if the latter exist at all. Taken to their logical ends, the serious fits and starts these leaders have made toward authoritarianism would suggest a certain degree of convergence with what has shaped up as the Chinese model in the past three decades—capitalist production based on a thoroughly maltreated working class within an authoritarian political mold. Of course, that kind of political-economic arrangement finds itself within a version of the same syndrome in which the other capitalist economies exist. However, given China's political intellectual heritage steeped in Maoism and Marxist-Leninism, there must be a relatively acute awareness among both the dominant and subordinate classes in the country that the potentials for upheaval, whether liberal, socialist, or some combination of the two, are very strong. In a way that exudes irony, yet which is dwarfed by its historical gravity, the Chinese Communist state is constantly deploying surveillance domestically and worldwide for any signs of what could only be construed as a liberal-left or socialist organization emerging against its power.[1]

In the United States, the Republican Party was quite possibly rescued from a slide into dissolution by Donald Trump in 2016 but turned into a party of enablers for tax cuts for the rich and extra-constitutional authoritarian assaults on liberal electoral democracy. The separation of powers and the right to peaceably assemble and protest came under severe threat; calls were issued to arrest journalists for doing their work; the office of the presidency was used by Trump's family members for personal, commercial and material gain, and a major effort was launched to disenfranchise millions of Americans that voted against Trump. Most recently, on January 6, 2021, an insurrectionary, Trump-inspired mob stormed the nation's Capitol Building in a violent and failed effort to disrupt the proceedings that would finally and officially usher in a new presidency under Joe Biden. The insurrectionists justified their actions with obvious lies and conspiracy theories repeated endlessly by Trump: that the elections were stolen from him. These are just a few of the problems of "trumpworld." India, Brazil, and the United States show similar syntheses of neoliberalism with neofascism, some of whose central tenets are extreme nationalism and racism. Modi is the neoliberal super-Hindu, going after the Muslims of India; Bolsonaro is the hypermasculine super-exploiter, going after the indigenous peoples of the Amazon rain forest in order to reap super-profits from the destruction of those forests. Trump has gone after Mexicans, Muslims, Blacks, Central Americans, Chinese, and immigrants and refugees of all sorts—at one point or another he has gone after just about everyone except the white people in his "base." The social compact of labor, business, and government, including a general commitment, feigned or not, to progressive reforms in race relations, is in tatters. Likewise with the common commitment to scientific knowledge, even to rationality itself. It is too expensive. In the world's bastion of free-market capitalism, there is a turn on the part of a large portion of the population toward greater madness that, given the pathologies of anti-leftist politics expanding on the world stage for the past two hundred years, is probably what should be expected. But it is both unacceptable and unnecessary.

Politics of late in the United States have been described as the most explosive since the eve of country's civil war of 1861–5. There has been a near collapse into acrimony and seemingly unbridgeable division. While police forces seemed to just melt away when the hundreds of overwhelmingly white insurrectionists stormed the capitol building in Washington, DC—with Trump apparently enjoying the show—decisions about policing and security earlier in 2020 were in stark contrast. Police and US Marshalls went rogue against demonstrators for social justice and against police brutality and the militarization of police forces across the United States. The protests were triggered by the murder—really a public execution on the streets, in plain sight—of George Floyd, a Black man, in Minneapolis, Minnesota, by a white policeman and his partners, on May

25, 2020. The protests spread countrywide and worldwide. Within the United States, it was especially in Portland, Oregon, where things went extra-constitutional. The police and US Marshalls removed their identity tags, attacked demonstrators indiscriminately with truncheons, tear gas, and rubber bullets, drove around in unmarked rented vans, from which they ambushed suspected demonstrators, put hoods over their heads, and took them into detention. Trump and his minions, many of them neofascist vigilantes that got to dress up and join with the rogue officers, called all the protesters "antifa."

Here was an example for the ages of the phantom politics that Marx famously referred to in the *Communist Manifesto* of 1848, when "a specter" was "haunting Europe." "Antifa" barely exists. It is nothing compared to the demonical image of it peddled by Trump and his supporters. It's 99 percent a bogeyman, yet its alleged existence and actions fueled, or at least justified, the fascist-style actions of the aspiring "law and order" candidacy of Trump for his attempted 2020 run for a second and final term in office. "Antifa" is short for "anti-fascist," which is rooted in the interwar and Second World War–era struggle and war against fascism and Nazism—against Mussolini, Franco, Hitler, and the Japanese regime, which eventually Britain, the United States, and the Soviet Union together defeated militarily.[2] So, if there is anything but a loose electoral gamble on the part of Trump to use such a term to cover those that oppose him within the United States, one can easily construe his accusations to mean that he, his base, and his thugs are, indeed, fascists. At the same time, all who oppose him are anti-fascists and, of course, "socialists" because they are not free-market extremists. Based on this rhetoric and its attendant actions, it is no leap to say that it suggests that Trump the fascist declared war on the socialist antifa and pro–Black Lives Matter (BLM) majority of Americans but was defeated by them at the polls. That's a fortunate victory for electoral democracy. But, the mob that attacked the Capitol Building, and the people they represent, do not believe their leader was defeated. They believe that the "socialists," Joe Biden and Kamala Harris, stole the elections, because their leaders and his allies in the rightwing media have told them so. At least sixty cases of alleged electoral fraud presented to the courts by Trump and his supporters were struck down as having no evidentiary merit.[3] No such case was accepted. Unfortunately, these politics will not disappear from the US scene during the foreseeable future.

Another rhetorical twist came from Trump in a July 3 US Independence Day speech to a large grouping of his supporters in front of a famous monument to four American presidents, Washington, Jefferson, Lincoln, and Theodore Roosevelt, at Mount Rushmore, in the state of South Dakota. To his mostly white audience, he said,

> In our schools, our newsrooms, even our corporate boardrooms, there is a new far-left fascism that demands absolute allegiance. If you do not speak its language, perform its rituals, recite its mantras and follow its commandments, then you will be censored, banished, blacklisted, persecuted and punished.

Rousing his crowd further, he said, "Not going to happen to us!" And, "Make no mistake, this leftwing cultural revolution is designed to overthrow the American revolution!" When Trump went on to say he was sending in federal officers to protect monuments and arrest and prosecute those who took them down, the crowd's passions overflowed and they started chanting "USA! USA!"[4] Finally, in an attack on sports professionals such as the American football player Colin Kaepernick and the basketball great, Lebron James, who had the courage to take a knee or speak out against police brutality and racial injustice—their audiences reach into the millions—Trump said, "We stand tall, we stand proud and we only kneel before almighty God."[5] Though this is sheer hypocrisy coming from Trump, it is also a tap into the deep well of American racist and religious nationalism.

A little elaboration is in order to begin to grasp how the fascist option and synthesis took shape in the United States under Trump. Though the synthesis has its distinctive features, it also has fundamentals in common with the classic model of fascism that came out of interwar Europe. Racism has its long and horrible history in the United States, where it has tied in with extreme nationalism again and again against "others" both domestically and abroad. There has also been an anti-labor thrust in the country that famously exploded against the Great Railway Strike of 1877. However, nearly a century later, that hostility reared its head in another manner under Ronald Reagan. His attack on independent labor unions began with firing of the employees of the Professional Air Traffic Controllers Organization (PATCO) in 1981. The Republican Party supported this with ease, but also, with the onset of globalization and the more general undermining of labor, the Democratic Party became complicit in the tendency. Such hostility against independent, organized labor, with the right to collectively bargain with their employers, is a central feature of classic fascism. It ties in with corporatism, in which economic corporations collaborate with the state to completely control labor, the result being a "corporatist state." Another aspect of the classic model is paramilitary violence against all opposition, as is a mass fascist movement and party. Trump has neofascist paramilitaries in his base—Proud Boys, Three Percenters, Oath Keepers, and others—while the Republican Party, the way it submitted itself to Trump and enabled his fascist politics, earned it that special modern historical categorization of a "fascist party and movement." Yet another matter is the "führer principle," according to which the leader is the lightning rod for the nation and the one-party state. Trump and his fervent followers together fit this category, though he did not, and does not, appear to have the strategic mind, sufficient support, or the surrounding institutional type of crisis to advance a fascist takeover of the state. He and his supporters apparently tried and failed to do this, and they may try again. The fact that voter suppression is underway with a vengeance in several states in the United States after the recent federal elections suggests a similar fascist trajectory and another feature distinctive to the American institutional setting. However, considering the record for Trump and his supporters on the electoral and judicial fronts, there is an institutionally based reason for some confidence that the effort to create an authoritarian, white supremacist state will not succeed.

On the foreign policy front, Trump is a "revisionist," as were Hitler and Mussolini. They all scrapped and defied treaties and conventions with the aim of pleasing their bases and asserting and consolidating their power. But the differentiating matters of context were crucial. Even the different contexts in which Mussolini and Hitler's regimes took shape were almost endlessly crucial, yet they still shared the common crises of the interwar years in Europe, as well as several common features of their regimes. Between them and Trump, in appearance and substance, there is an even more vast set of contrasts. Yet the main distinction featured in the United States, even aside from the wide gap between the changes in the global settings, is that Trump already presided over an empire, whereas Hitler and Mussolini's revisionisms involved militarily aggressive efforts to establish empires, nearly from square one. That meant war, which did not happen under Trump, because the aggressive territorial expansionism had already happened. He just maintained the American political-military presence in Europe, Africa, the Middle East, parts of Latin America, and East Asia, and nearly got the United States into war with Iran and North Korea. He did oversee the reduction in the numbers of US fatalities in Iraq and Afghanistan. As important as this is, for many American voters, this seems to be the only thing that counts on the foreign war front. The Trump administration's support for Saudi Arabia's vicious and catastrophic war in Yemen, for example, got very little attention from most American voters.[6] All in all, the fascist synthesis in the United States under Trump contained several of the main characteristics of the interwar year model but added to them two things not present in that model, Christian evangelical religiosity and neoliberalism.[7]

The second half of this book has placed a great emphasis on the United States, both internationally and domestically. There is probably some ethnocentrism involved here, mainly because of the nationality of the author, but there are two main justifications for it: first, the paramount role the United States has played in world history, especially since the Second World War; second, there are signs that US society is in a state of deterioration and in significant relative decline as a power on the world scene. This has major, though unpredictable, implications for precisely the problem of anti-leftist politics, and more. The history of the United States up to the present fits very importantly into this historical perspective on the modern world and deserves the otherwise inordinate attention that it gets in the book.

Aiming for a comprehensive perspective on the problem of anti-socialist politics in modern history, including an attempt to account for the trend toward rightwing authoritarianism, it is very helpful to begin with one of the most outstanding historians of the modern era since the French Revolution, the late Eric Hobsbawm. His book on the pre–First World War era, the *The Age of Empire, 1875–1914*, argued that "liberal bourgeois society" and civilization were loaded with contradictions that were ultimately and spectacularly self-destructive. To name a few of them, elitist liberal democracy gave way to mass politics of a sort that sidelined liberals to an extent to which they were unaccustomed; the world of competitive, family-owned liberal capitalist enterprises gave way to large-scale joint stock corporations that had strong monopolistic tendencies; colonial rule over countless millions of people and their territories across the world brought on anti-colonial wars of revolutionary national liberation that spanned decades; finally, unparalleled peace gave way to unparalleled warfare and slaughter—the First and Second World Wars and more. This argument is breathtaking and persuasive, yet he drops it in his next book, *The Age of Extremes*, which covers what he and others call the "short 20th century" from 1914 to 1991 and the end of the Cold War. In that book, neither the bourgeoisie nor its contradictions have any centrality. It is not clear why Hobsbawm did this, but it stands out. Here I would like to pick up on his analysis from *The Age of Empire*, apply it to the rest of modern history to date, and consider its relationship with the lines and legacies of anti-leftist politics presented in this book.

The structure and the content of Hobsbawm's argument in the *Age of Empire* is dialectical and historical. This means that one historical "moment" generated its opposite, its antithesis; those two moments then combined as a particular "synthesis" of the two. Liberal capitalist society was the thesis, the original moment. He presented it in his book very deftly as a rich and complex ensemble of societal and international forces, yet he still treated it as a unitary historical "moment." Its antithesis was a combination of mass politics, warfare, revolution, and anti-colonialist rebellion that lasted for decades, as it seriously challenged, and in some ways undermined, the original bourgeois capitalist society. The interactions and antagonisms between those two "moments," or sets of contradictory and conflicting historical forces, was what comprised most of the twentieth century, including the Second World War, the Cold War, and much more. But again, Hobsbawm did not sustain this sort of analysis about the twentieth century, so one has to surmise the implications of his argument about the few decades before the First World War in order to see if they have any value for most of the rest of the twentieth century and possibly up to the present. The question is what the synthesis was between those extremely conflicted moments that were the opposite sides of the contradictions of the age of empire, and how that synthesis might have become the basis for the resumption of another round of conflicts on an expanded scale.

Theoretically, at least, according to Hegel and Marx, such a resolution of the contradictions would occur at a higher and enlarged level. They were both Enlightenment optimists that believed historical change was ultimately progressive. Hobsbawm does state this exact belief, but perhaps because of what he had seen and experienced in the twentieth century, he was cautious. The dialectic is not necessarily progressive, even though it could be. It would just have to unfold and develop, for better or for worse. In this case, the resolution of the thesis versus the antithesis of the age of empire would also necessarily feature either the bourgeoisie in some expanded form or a social force that replaced it as the leading social class that pursues its interests and generates its own contradictions. On that point, the bourgeoisie by no means perished in the First World War. Between the 1920s and 1970s, it is true, as Hobsbawm argued, that it was relatively less prominent than it was in the pre–First World War era. But if we go to the crucial political-economic change and process that happened from the 1970s to the present—the combination of the internationalization of capitalist production with the launching of the neoliberal global campaign—we see that the synthesis was neoliberal capitalism. The bourgeoisie was back with a vengeance. This was an expanded and reconstituted model for the world economy and a new defining force for world history, replacing the old model and its forces that had their beginnings in the age of empire and whose contradictions peaked in the 1960s.

Again, the old model involved industrial production within a few powerful states, which were then enmeshed with one another through international trade and financial relationships. That was sustained into the late 1960s. However, as explained in the last chapter of this book, and thanks to the work of Robert Brenner who demonstrated it, it was then that US rates of corporate profit began to show sharp declines. In order to stay competitive, American corporations then led the way to the new model—outsourced industrial production to plants established abroad—to Mexico, Taiwan, Burma, eventually China and elsewhere, where labor was cheap and nonunionized. The other advanced capitalist countries soon also transferred operations overseas. Symbolic of the change was that, in the span of about twenty years, Detroit, Michigan, went from the thriving hub of US automobile production to an empty shell of its former self. But the social and economic damage to the American working classes, which were then described by most American observers to be "middle class" because their income and economic security were at relatively high levels, was unmistakable. They were decimated. As Trump repeatedly says he wants to "make America great again," he is trafficking upon the emotions, nostalgia, and memories of the white male Americans and their families who benefitted the most from what is commonly referred to as the "golden age of capitalism." But those glory days were conditional, obviously not permanent. Further, with no shortage of irony, they were unthinkable without the New Deal policies of the Roosevelt administration of the Depression and war years—decried by the right as "socialism"—that actually persisted at least into the 1960s–70s. Trump and many others fail to realize that it is exactly the highly celebrated competitive character of capitalist production that has led to the drive to deregulate and privatize, which, in turn, creates the race to the bottom. That is the high cost of low prices that capitalist producers are compelled to achieve and offer to undercut their competitors. The US economy had its moment of global dominance, when the rest of the potential competitors of the United States were devastated by the Second World War. Once they recovered—especially West Germany and Japan—with US assistance, the United States started to fall behind. By the 1970s, to remain competitive internationally, American corporations had to resort to cheaper labor outside of the United States.

Liberal bourgeois capitalist society definitely created and then destroyed itself in the age of empire, but only in one particular form. The bourgeoisie as a central, highly self-conscious and deliberate socioeconomic class did not end up entirely on the sidelines, let alone vanish. It vigorously led the fictitious economic dynamism of the late 1920s; it was devastated, but not destroyed, by the Great Depression, and it was rejuvenated, reconstituted, and, in a functional sense, shifted to the United States by the Second World War. In terms of economic growth, the post–Second World War record in the advanced liberal capitalist states was the most spectacular to date compared to the late 1960s and early 1970s, when the downturn began in the United States and eventually spread elsewhere. The rise of Margaret Thatcher in Britain and Ronald Reagan in the United States was the turning point of the breakup and reconstitution of the old model on a grander scale, after its main challengers, in their main forms of fascism and socialism, were supposedly defeated. The unit of capitalist production went beyond the nation-state, to a grouping of nation-states, to the point where the "international" became the "global." Now, of course, we have other, associated terms that have entered reality-based popular discourse, such as plutocracy, oligarchy, and the 99 percent versus the 1 percent.

Some are shocked at the resurgence of some of the most pernicious politics and ideologies that were supposed to have been overcome. But this should surprise no one. World society remains on extremely treacherous territory, very much as it was in 1900, but now possibly more than ever. That remains to be seen. We are still experiencing the repercussions of the self-destruction of the age of empire, yet within a globalized neoliberal capitalist framework that has thrown up its own contradictions and fallout, very much like the old ensemble, but writ larger than ever on the world stage. One of those contradictions of the later, neoliberal wave of "free markets and the liberal idea" is the tendency toward "rightwing populism," or neofascism and neo-Nazism in some places, including the United States.

The nexus between the "liberal idea and free markets," as Fukuyama put it, and the triumphalist wars, the xenophobia, the breakups, and the trends toward authoritarianism is the drive to deregulate and privatize, which has been the mission of the US-led global bourgeoisie since the 1970s. It has involved an assault on the public sector, including the state, government, public service, public education, health, and more, to the point where those that control the state and the governments are increasingly inclined to treat their power as a private matter, as opposed to a matter of the common good. This is not exactly new, but it has seen a qualitative entrenchment. Political and financial players have gained power as oligarchs. They elevate themselves and their cronies; they make moves by legislation or by decree to enhance their opportunities to get richer and more powerful, thereby essentially privatizing the levers of power. It is the politics of not caring about anyone but your cronies and people who look like you, to the extent that you need them, because there is still a semblance of electoral politics and popularity that needs to be upheld. This is where neofascist tactics become prominent, which could easily also be sustained in the event of a shift to authoritarianism.

They all need a popular and potentially militant base, just to make sure no oppositional base builds up and tries to overthrow and punish them. Those that join the vigilantes and paramilitaries can be seen as people whom capitalist society has also failed, but they ended up getting *enlisted* into the racist, nationalist, fascist cause. As for leftwing politics and the multiple targets they would throw up, the potentials are enormous. But so is it likely that attacks against them from various sectors of the neoliberal-fascist right will increase. With the rise of this tendency, the "liberal idea" either seems quaint, or it has been retooled and weaponized, along with the myopias of profitability. In any case, at least up to the end of 2020, "free markets"—the extreme sort, as in, a free for all for the few—appear to be expanding.

The more any patently unjust advance of this sort occurs and becomes obvious, the more people tend to change their minds about it and incline toward opposing it. There was a lot of that up to 2019. But with the COVID-19 pandemic, the injustices are clearer than ever and generating more robust opposition against them. According to a recent report from the World Health Organization (WHO), the pandemic

has decimated jobs and placed millions of livelihoods at risk. As breadwinners lose jobs, fall ill and die, the food security and nutrition of millions of women and men are under threat, with those in low-income countries, particularly the most marginalized populations, which include small-scale farmers and indigenous peoples, being hardest hit.[8]

This global observation also needs to also be grasped on a country-by-country basis. The hard realities repeat themselves, with whatever variations, wherever one goes. Again, none of this is exactly new, but the problems are magnified and exacerbated to an extreme extent, which could also become far worse. The same WHO report highlighted the plight of "millions of agricultural workers – waged and self-employed who, while feeding the world, regularly face high levels of working poverty, malnutrition and poor health, and suffer from a lack of safety and labor protection as well as other types of abuse." They have low and unreliable incomes to begin with; they lack social support and are essentially forced by their circumstances to keep working in situations highly risky for themselves and their families. Migrant agricultural workers tend to be in the most marginal and precarious situations, because they have no stable and reliable infrastructural, public, or governmental supports. Neoliberalism has only worsened their problems in recent decades, with its assaults on public sectors worldwide. The report urges that "guaranteeing the safety and health of all agri-food workers … as well as better incomes and protection, will be critical to saving lives and protecting public health, people's livelihoods and food security." It must be emphasized that this is the WHO that the Trump administration in the United States scapegoated, vilified, and severed its relationship with in 2020, as the world pandemic was on the rise. Trump accused the WHO, in effect, of being a tool of the Chinese government, which supposedly had recklessly unleashed the COVID-19 virus on the rest of the world. It is clear that the administration's priorities were to somehow prioritize an "America first" agenda, which did not include "saving lives and protecting public health, (and) people's livelihoods." Any institutional voice that may have been louder or more persuasive than Trump's on these issues had to be quashed, at least as much as possible. It may not be a choir of angels, but the WHO is institutionally committed to caring about real people's lives across the world, especially those that are underprivileged and, in this case, getting hammered by the pandemic. The WHO deals with the "social problem" on the global scale, while the United States under Trump condemns and attacks it. This is an old story, expanded worldwide.

Continuing with their recommendations, the WHO report advises that

> adhering to workplace safety and health practices and ensuring access to decent work and the protection of labor rights in all industries will be crucial in addressing the human dimension of the crisis. Immediate and purposeful action to save lives and livelihoods should include extending social protection towards universal health coverage and income support for those most affected.

There could hardly be any other high-echelon policy statement in today's world that would fly so much in the face of the persistence of neoliberalism. While the United States has been the lead global force for neoliberal transformation, in the current circumstances of the pandemic, noted in Chapter 7, the United States has a little over 4 percent of the world's population and around 20 percent of its COVID-19 deaths. In line with the general observations of the WHO report, the most vulnerable populations in the United States to the COVID-19 virus are poor and minority frontline workers. They are the people that produce the food, so much of which is produced at factory farms that are hotbeds for new viruses, but which are also sites of high-density

COVID-19 social contagion among laborers. They deliver and sell the food, they are the frontline health care workers who are trying to stem the tide of mortality. These and many more comprise the world of labor that does so much to sustain the rest of the population, while it is largely taken for granted. They face the harshest working conditions; they are the least protected from the coronavirus; in "normal" times, they are the most exposed to chemical fertilizers, workplace accidents, lack of health care, and lack of opportunities for education. They are most likely to face prison time for petty crimes in the United States, when "white collar" financial trickery and criminality that destroys livelihoods by the hundreds of thousands gets essentially unpunished, if not rewarded. An update on the fortunes of the billionaires is as follows: "Amid Warnings of Surging Worldwide Poverty, Planet's 500 Richest People Added $1.8 Trillion to Combined Wealth in 2020."[9] This is not 1914, but it is a first-order global catastrophe, whose predictable and surprise repercussions are coming our way. Based on the patterns of the past two hundred years, attacks on the left and "socialism" are predictable, as are further assaults on the environment, unraveling liberal democracies and increasingly obscene levels of inequality and injustice. The surprises, hopefully and possibly for the better, remain to be seen.

On that somewhat hopeful note, and as a counterpoint to much of the above, there are other breakups that have been happening, as well as advances built on gains from the past, that have been very positive. These include the challenge to white male societal and global dominance, and to white privilege in general; the further breakdown

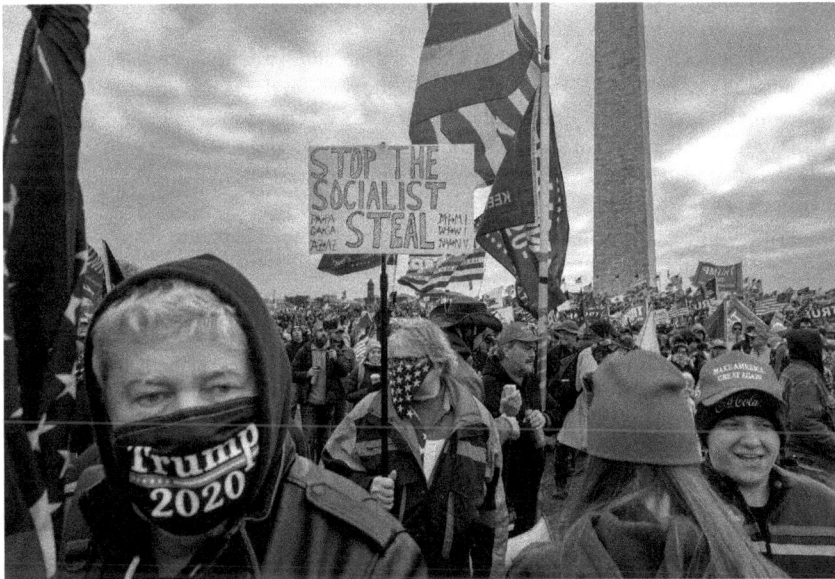

Figure 15 Supporters of Donald Trump in Washington, DC, on January 6, 2021, in their failed insurrectionary effort to overturn the legal and legitimate results of the November 2020 US presidential election.

Source: Getty images -1230733966–1.jpg.

of complacency and denial of systemic racism, of traditional gender categories and politics, of languages with restrictive gender grammars; the slow, uneven, but significant deterioration of patriarchy, even in the Muslim world; the spasms of defiance against the authoritarian hegemonies in the Arab world of 2012; the breakdown of complacency about the ways our civilization threatens the natural environment; the breakdown of silence from the professional sports world about the blaring injustices in our societies; and the breakdown for a large number of Americans of hostility against socialism, and the enthusiastic embrace of the democratic socialism of Senator Bernie Sanders. These particular breakups are promising on the world stage and have fed positively and promisingly into the politics of the present administration in the United States. These are powerful, hopeful, and necessary developments being pushed by serious, aware, and courageous people across the world. However, people still have to remember that we remain in that syndrome of an economic and political system that, by necessity, creates the grounds for opposition against it and, also by necessity, then maneuvers to undermine and sometimes destroy that opposition. As this book has hopefully demonstrated, this is an exceedingly treacherous dynamic of modern history.

Notes

1. See Perry Anderson's comparison of the Russian and Chinese Revolutions, in "Two Revolutions," *New Left Review*, no. 61 (2010), pp. 59–96; Joel Kotkin, "China's Looming Class Struggle," Quillette, October 18, 2019. Available online: https://quillette.com/2019/10/18/chinas-looming-class-struggle/.
2. This excludes Franco, who kept Spain officially out of the war but sent over forty thousand troops to the Eastern Front to join the Nazis in their anti-Soviet war.
3. See Jim Rutenberg, Nick Corasaniti, and Alan Feuer, "Trump's Fraud Claims Died in Court, but the Myth of Stolen Elections Lives On," *New York Times*, December 26, 2020, updated January 7, 2021. Available online: https://www.nytimes.com/2020/12/26/us/politics/republicans-voter-fraud.html.
4. The monuments being torn down are all to icons of American racism.
5. https://www.theguardian.com/us-news/2020/jul/04/. us-under-siege-from-far-left-fascism-says-trump-in-mount-rushmore-speech.
6. See Nicolas J. S. Davies and Medea Benjamin, "Trump's Endless Wars," *The Progressive*, October 7, 2020. Available online: https://progressive.org/magazine/trump-endless-wars-davies-benjamin/.
7. A very helpful article on these questions of fascism is Robert O. Paxton's "The Five Stages of Fascism," *Journal of Modern History*, vol. 70, no. 1 (March 1998), pp. 1–23. See also Aristotle A. Kallis, ed., *The Fascism Reader* (New York: Routledge, 2003), including the excellent "Introduction: Fascism in Historiography," pp. 1–41.
8. "Impact of COVID-19 on People's Livelihoods, Their Health and Our Food Systems: Joint Statement by ILO, FAO, IFAD and WHO," World Health Organization, October 13, 2020. Available online: https://www.who.int/news/item/13-10-2020-impact-of-covid-19-on-people%27s-livelihoods-their-health-and-our-food-systems.
9. See article of the same title by Julia Conley, *Common Dreams*, January 2, 2021. Available online: https://www.commondreams.org/news/2021/01/02/amid-warnings-surging-worldwide-poverty-planets-500-richest-people-added-18-trillion.

Bibliography

Primary Sources

Unpublished Documents

British National Archives, London. **K V2**/501, files on Grigori Zinoviev; **FO 608**/195/2 on the Russian Civil War, 1919; **CAB 1/27/4**, visit to England of Dr. Nair and Mr. Tilak, 1918; **CAB 23**/7/16, war matters in Europe and Colonial India, 1918; **CO 111**/594/37, on seditious newspapers linked with the *Ghadar* Rebellion and how to deal with them, 1914; **CAB 1**/27, on war policy, July 1918; **CO/111**/594, Arab Socialism, Nasser, Marxism-Leninism; **FO 1110**/1600, discussion of Marxism-Leninism vs other socialist approaches, 1956; **FO 371**/12777, discussions of Marxist theory in Moscow, 1955–7; **FCO 7**/125, anti-Communist law in Argentina, 1967; **FO 371**/179692, anti-communism in Paraguay, 1965; **WO 216**/968, on imperial counter-subversion against communism and nationalism in the colonies; **FO 1110**/24, Information Research Department (IRD) on US approaches to anti-communism, 1948; **FO 371**/26865, Portugal during the Second World War; **CO537**/6556, "anti-communist propaganda terminology," 1950; **FO 959**/41, anti-communist policy in East and Southeast Asia, 1949; **FO 371**/129370, on the Asian Peoples' Anti-Communist League, 1957; **FO 1110**/118, on Dutch Indonesia, 1948; **CO 537**/6567, "anti-communist measures in West Africa," 1950; **FO 371**/91177, Communism in the Middle East, 1951; **FO 371**/131867, anti-communism in Central and South America, 1958; **CAB 21**/2745, general anti-communist strategy, the vitality of the cooperative organizations in Western Europe, high value of Social Democracy in Britain, 1948; **CAB 21**/2746, anti-communism general; **FO 371**/74121, anti-communism in Panama, 1949; **CO 1027**/367, anti-communism through Catholic missions in Latin America, 1962; **FO 1110**/1760, anti-communism in Athens, 1964; **WO 208**/5008, "Communism in India," 1949–50; **FO 628**/31/343, India and Southeast Asia, late 1914; **CAB 301**/152, Communism in Kerala, India, 1958.

Published Documents (mostly available and accessed online)

Central Intelligence Agency (CIA): see the "Freedom of Information Act Reading Room" at cia.gov for materials on situations across the world during the Cold War.
Federal Bureau of Investigation (FBI): Freedom of Information Act materials on FBI surveillance of suspected subversives, 1950s–70s.
Foreign Relations of the United States (FRUS): online materials on US foreign policy worldwide.
National Security Agency (NSA): materials in this book tend to be found interspersed in the FRUS archives.

Newspapers (all accessed online)

Guardian, 1990–present
New York Times, 1871–present
Times of London, 1815–1921

Miscellaneous Published Documents

Lewis F. Powell Jr., "The Powell Memorandum; Attack on the Free Enterprise System,"
    August 23, 1971, Washington & Lee University School of Law Scholarly Commons.
    Available online: https://scholarlycommons.law.wlu.edu/powellmemo/1.
Manifesto of the International Socialist Congress at Basel. From: Sam Marcy, *The
    Bolsheviks and War*. Berlin: Vorwärts, 1912, pp. 23–7.
Manifesto of the International Socialist Congress at Basel. From: Sam Marcy, *The
    Bolsheviks and War*. Berlin: Vorwärts, 1912, pp. 23–7.
United States Department of Commerce. "Translations on International Communist
    Developments, No. 823," April 1966.
United States Government. History of the Joint Chiefs of Staff. *The Joint Chiefs of Staff and
    the First Indochina War, 1947–1954*. 2004.

Diaries and Memoirs

Churchill, Winston. *Diaries, 1941–1945*, edited by Martin Gilbert. New York: Rosetta
    Books, 2015.
Eden, Anthony. *The Memoirs of Anthony Eden*. Facing the Dictators.
    London: Cassell, 1962.
Hull, Cordell. *The Memoirs of Cordell Hull*, in two volumes. New York: Macmillan, 1948.
Maisky, Ivan. *The Maisky Diaries: Red Ambassador to the Court of St James's, 1932–1943*,
    edited by Gabriel Gorodetsky. New Haven, CT: Yale University Press, 2015.

Original Historical Documents

Modern History Sourcebook for materials on virtually all aspects of nineteenth-century
    Europe: https://sourcebooks.fordham.edu.
Peel, Robert, "The Tamworth Manifesto," December 1834. http://www.victorianweb.org/
    history/index.html.

Secondary Sources

Aidt, Toke S., and Raphaël Franck. "Democratization under the Threat of
    Revolution: Evidence from the Great Reform Act of 1832." *Econometrica* 83.2
    (2015): 505–47.
Alvarez Junco, José, and Adrian Shubert, eds. *Spanish History since 1808*. London: Oxford
    University Press, 2000.
Anderson, Benedict. *The Spectre of Comparisons: Nationalism, Southeast Asia, and the
    World*. New York: Verso, 1998.

Anderson, Perry. "After the Event." Symposium: Response. *New Left Review* 73 (2012): 49–61.

Anderson, Perry. "The Age of EJH." Review of *Interesting Times: A 20th-Century Life* by Eric Hobsbawm. *London Review of Books* 24.19 (2002).

Anderson, Perry. "Confronting Defeat: Perry Anderson Reflects on Eric Hobsbawm's Account of the Making of the Contemporary World." *London Review of Books* 24.20 (2002): 10–17.

Anderson, Perry. "Two Revolutions: Rough Notes." *New Left Review* 61 Jan/Feb (2010): 59–96.

Anderson, Perry. *The New Old World*. New York: Verso, 2011.

Anderson, Perry. "After the Event." Symposium: Response. New Left Review 73 (2012): 49–61

Anderson, Perry. "Gandhi Center Stage." *London Review of Books* 34.13 (2012).

Anderson, Perry. "Consilium." *New Left Review* 83 Sept/Oct (2013): 113–67.

Anderson, Perry. "Homeland." *New Left Review* 81 May/Jun (2013): 5–32.

Anderson, Perry. "Imperium." *New Left Review* 83 Sept/Oct (2013): 5–111.

Angenot, Marc. *Rhétorique de l'anti – socialisme: Essai d'histoire discursive 1830 – 1917*. Québec: Les Presses de l'Université Laval, 2004.

Ayusawa, Iwao F. *A History of Labor in Modern Japan, 1894–1966*. Honolulu: East- West Center Press, 1966.

Azimi, Fakhreddin. "The Overthrow of the Government of Mosaddeq Reconsidered." *Iranian Studies* 45.5 (2012): 693–712.

Azpuru, Dinorah, and Violeta Hernández. "Migration in Central America Magnitude, Causes and Proposed Solutions." In *Migration and Refugees*, edited by Gerhard Wahlers, 72–95. Konrad Adenauer Stiftung, 2015. Available online: https://www.jstor.org/stable/resrep10111.8.

Ball, Stephen J., and Richard Bowe. "The Neoliberalization of the State, the Processes of 'Fragmentation,' and Research Implications of the New Political Terrain of English Schooling." In *Knowledge, Policy and Practice in Education and the Struggle for Social Justice: Essays Inspired by the Work of Geoff Whitty*, edited by Andrew Brown and Emma Wisby, 97–114. London: UCL Press, 2020.

Barkaoui, Miloud. "Kennedy and the Cold War Imbroglio: The Case of Algeria's Independence." *Arab Studies Quarterly* 21.2 (1999): 31–45.

Batdorf, John W. *Anti-Socialism. A Plea to Patriotism. The Federal Constitution*. New York: Anti-Socialist Press, 1915.

Baxandall, Rosalyn. "Re-Visioning the Women's Liberation Movement's Narrative: Early Second Wave African American Feminists." *Feminist Studies* 27.1 (2001): 225–45.

Bayly, C. A. "Ireland, India and the Empire: 1780–1914." *Transactions of the Royal Historical Society* 10 (2000): 377–97.

Bennett, Gill. "Secret Intelligence and British Policy, 1909–45." *Secretintelligencefiles.com*. Files from World Wars to Cold War. Web.

Berend, Ivan T. *Decades of Crisis: Central and Eastern Europe before World War II*. Los Angeles: University of California Press, 1998.

Berend, Ivan T. *History Derailed: Central and Eastern Europe in the Long Nineteenth Century*. Berkeley: University of California Press, 2003.

Berger, Victor. *Victor Berger's Work in Congress: Voices of the Press*. Milwaukee: Social-Democratic Publishing, 1912.

Bethell, Leslie, and Ian Roxborough. "Latin America between the Second World War and the Cold War: Some Reflections on the 1945–8 Conjuncture." *Journal of Latin American Studies* 20.1 (1988): 167–89.

Bhupatiraju, Samyukta, and Rahul A. Sirohi. "From Neoliberalism to Post-Neoliberalism." *Social Scientist* 46.7–8 (2018): 41–54.

Biswas, Ajanta. "Sakharam Ganesh Deuskar and the Swadeshi Movement in Bengal: The Second Identity." *Social Scientist* 33.3–4 (2005): 66–73.

Blackburn, Robin. *Banking on Death – Or, Investing in Life: The History and Future of Pensions*. New York: Verso, 2002.

Bormann, Martin. "Minutes of a Meeting at Hitler's Headquarters" (July 16, 1941). *German History in Documents and Images, Volume 7. Nazi Germany, 1933–1945*. Online research base created by the German Historical Institute, Washington, DC. Available online: https://germanhistorydocs.ghi-dc.org/pdf/eng/English59.pdf.

Bosworth, R. J. B. *Mussolini's Italy: Life under the Fascist Dictatorship, 1915–1945*. New York: Penguin, 2005.

Bournazos, Stratis. "The Greek Anti-Communist Press, 1925–1967: An Initial Approach." *Archeio Takseio* 5 (2003): 52–63.

Brasted, Howard. "Indian Nationalist Development and the Influence of Irish Home Rule, 1870–1886." *Modern Asian Studies* 14.1 (1980): 37–63.

Brenner, Robert. "The Boom and the Bubble." *New Left Review*. 6 (2000): 5–43.

Brighi, Elisabetta. "Beyond Repression: Reflections on Phoebe Moore's Chapter." In *Digital Objects, Digital Subjects: Interdisciplinary Perspectives on Capitalism, Labour and Politics in the Age of Big Data*, edited by David Chandler and Christian Fuchs, 145–50. London: University of Westminster Press, 2019.

Brockett, Charles. "US Labour and Management Fight It Out in Post-1954 Guatemala." *Journal of Latin American Studies* 42.3 (2010): 517–49.

Brogi, Alessandro. "Ending Grand Alliance Politics in Western Europe: US Anti-communism in France and Italy, 1944–7." *Journal of Contemporary History* 53.1 (2018): 134–57.

Buchanan, James. "An Interview with James Buchanan." *Austrian Economics Newsletter* (1987). Mises Institute, 2017.

Buhle, Paul. "The Jack O'Dell Story. Review of *Climbin' Jacob's Ladder: The Freedom Movement: Writings of Jack O'Dell*, edited by Nikhil Pal Singh. Berkeley: University of California Press, 2010." *Monthly Review*, May 1, 2011. Available online: https://monthlyreview.org/2011/05/01/the-jack-odell-story/.

Burke, Edmund. *Reflections on the Revolution in France: A Critical Edition*. Edited by J. C. D. Clark. Palo Alto, CA: Stanford University Press, 2002.

Burton, Antoinette. "Tongues Untied: Lord Salisbury's 'Black Man' and the Boundaries of Imperial Democracy." *Comparative Studies in Society and History* 42.3 (2000): 632–61.

Bush, George W. "President Discusses the Future of Iraq." *The White House. President George W. Bush*. whitehouse.archives.gov/news/releases, February 26, 2003. Web.

Chandrasekhar, C. P. "Notes on Neoliberalism and the Future of the Left." *Social Scientist* 39.1–2 (2011): 20–34.

Chapman, Michael E. "Pro-Franco Anti-Communism: Ellery Sedgwick and the 'Atlantic Monthly.'" *Journal of Contemporary History* 41.4 (2006): 641–62.

Chattopadhyay, Paresh. "Indian Communists on the Crisis of Socialism." *Economic and Political Weekly* 25.38 (1990): 2119–21.

Chowdhuri, Satyabrata Rai. *Leftism in India, 1917–1947*. New York: Palgrave Macmillan, 2007.

Claeys, Gregory. *Imperial Skeptics: British Critics of Empire, 1850–1920.*
    Cambridge: Cambridge University Press, 2010.
Clapson, Mark. *The Blitz Companion: Aerial Warfare, Civilians and the City since 1911.*
    London: University of Westminster Press, 2019.
Clayton, Lawrence A., Michael L. Conniff, and Susan M. Gauss. *A New History of Modern
    Latin America.* Berkeley: University of California Press, 2017.
Cleary, A. S. "The Myth of Mau Mau in Its International Context." *African Affairs* 89.355
    (1990): 227–45.
Cogan, Charles G. *Charles de Gaulle: A Brief History with Documents.*
    Boston: Bedford, 1996.
Colhoun, Jack. *Gangsterismo: The United States, Cuba and the Mafia, 1933 to 1966.*
    New York: OR Books, 2013.
Connell, Raewyn, and Nour Dados. "Where in the World Does Neoliberalism Come
    from?: The Market Agenda in Southern Perspective." *Theory and Society* 43.2
    (2014): 117–38.
Cronin, Stephanie. "The Left in Iran: Illusion and Disillusion." *Middle Eastern Studies* 36.3
    (2000): 231–43.
Cumings, Bruce. "Political Participation in Liberated Korea: Mobilization and Revolt in
    the Kyŏngsang Province, 1945–1950." *Journal of Korean Studies* 1 (1979): 163–203.
Cumings, Bruce. "On the Strategy and Morality of American Nuclear Policy in Korea,
    1950 to the Present." *Social Science Japan Journal* 1.1 (1998): 57–70.
Davidson, Basil. "The Motives of Mau Mau": Review of *Unhappy Valley* by Bruce Berman
    and John Lonsdale. *London Review of Books* 16.4 (1994).
Davies, Norman. "Lloyd George and Poland, 1919–20." *Journal of Contemporary History*
    6.3 (1971): 132–154.
Dignan, Don. *The Indian Revolutionary Problem in British Diplomacy, 1914–1919.* New
    Delhi: Allied, 1983.
Dreifort, John, E. *Myopic Grandeur: The Ambivalence of French Foreign Policy toward the
    Far East, 1919–1945.* Kent, OH: Kent State University Press, 1991.
Dunscomb, Paul E. "'A Great Disobedience against the People': Popular Press Criticism of
    Japan's Siberian Intervention, 1918–22." *Journal of Japanese Studies* 32.1 (2006): 53–81.
Eichner, Carolyn J. *Surmounting the Barricades: Women in the Paris Commune.*
    Bloomington: Indiana University Press, 2004.
Eley, Geoffrey. *Forging Democracy, The History of the Left in Europe, 1850–2000.*
    New York: Oxford University Press, 2002.
Engels, Friedrich. *Socialism: Utopian and Scientific.* 1908. Translated by Edward Aveling.
    Atlanta, GA: Pathfinder, 1989.
Engels, Friedrich. *The Origin of the Family, Private Property and the State.* 1884.
    London: Penguin Classics, 2010.
Fanon, Frantz. *The Wretched of the Earth.* 1963. Translated by Richard Philcox.
    New York: Grove Press, 2004.
Fairclough, Adam. "Was Martin Luther King a Marxist?" *History Workshop* 15
    (1983): 117–25.
Fairbank, John K. "The Problem of Revolutionary Asia." *Foreign Affairs* 29.1
    (1950): 101–13.
Falzon, John. "A Community Perspective: The Human and Social Costs of Wage
    Stagnation." In *The Wages Crisis in Australia: What It Is and What to Do about It,*
    edited by Andrew Stewart, Jim Stanford, and Tess Hardy, 243–9. Adelaide: University
    of Adelaide Press, 2018.

Fforde, Matthew. *Conservatism and Collectivism, 1886–1914*. Edinburgh: Edinburgh University Press, 1990.

Fisk, Robert. "Iran: A Nation Still Haunted by its Bloody Past." *The Independent*, February 8, 2009.

Fisk, Robert. "With Sten Guns and Sovereigns Britain and US Saved Iran's Throne for the Shah." *The Independent*, October 23, 2011.

Folly, Martin H. "British Attempts to Forge a Political Partnership with the Kremlin, 1942–3." *Journal of Contemporary History* 53.1 (2018): 185–211.

Foner, Eric. *Give Me Liberty!: An American History*. 2005. New York: Norton, 2017.

Fried, Albert, and Ronald Sanders, eds. *Socialist Thought: A Documentary History*. New York: Doubleday Anchor, 1964.

Friedman, Andrea. "The Smearing of Joe McCarthy: The Lavender Scare, Gossip, and Cold War Politics." *American Quarterly* 57.4 (2005): 1105–29.

Furet, Francois. *The Passing of an Illusion: The Idea of Communism in the Twentieth Century*. Chicago: University of Chicago Press, 1999.

Gaddis, John Lewis. *We Now Know: Rethinking Cold War History*. New York: Oxford University Press, 1997.

García Ferreira, Roberto. "El derrocamiento de Jacobo Arbenz y la Guerra Fría en América Latina: Nuevas fuentes y perspectivas." *Revista de Historia de América* 149 (2013): 453–80.

Garrow, David J. "The FBI and Martin Luther King." *Atlantic Monthly*, July–August 2002.

Gleijeses, Piero. "The Agrarian Reform of Jacobo Arbenz." *Journal of Latin American Studies* 21.3 (1989): 453–80.

Gleijeses, Piero. Review of *The Caribbean Legion: Patriots, Politicians, Soldiers of Fortune, 1946–1950*, by Charles D. Ameringer. *Journal of American History* 83.4 (1997): 1482–3.

Gilbert, Martin. *The Roots of Appeasement*. 1966. New York: Rosetta Books, 2015.

Gilbert, Martin. *Winston S. Churchill*. Vol. 7: *Road to Victory, 1941–1945*. New York: Rosetta Books, 2015.

Ginger, Ann Fagan, and David Christiano, eds. *The Cold War against Labor*, vol. 1. Berkeley: Meiklejohn Civil Liberties Institute, 1987.

Ginger, Ann Fagan, and David Christiano, eds. *The Cold War against Labor*, vol. 2. Berkeley: Meiklejohn Civil Liberties Institute, 1987.

Ghods, Reza M. "The Iranian Communist Movement under Reza Shah." *Middle Eastern Studies* 26.4 (1990): 506–13.

Goswami, Manu. "From Swadeshi to Swaraj: Nation, Economy, Territory in Colonial South Asia, 1870 to 1907." *Comparative Studies in Society and History* 40.4 (1998): 609–36.

Gott, Richard. "Latin America as a White Settler Society." *Bulletin of Latin American Research* 26.2 (2007): 269–89.

Guevara, Ernesto Che. *The Motorcycle Diaries: Notes on a Latin American Journey*. Preface by Aleida Guevara March, Introduction by Cintio Vitier. Melbourne: Ocean Press, 2011.

Guins, George C. "The Siberian Intervention, 1918–1919." *Russian Review* 28.4 (1969): 428–40.

Hadley, David P. *The Rising Clamor: The American Press, the Central Intelligence Agency, and the Cold War*. Lexington: University Press of Kentucky, 2019.

Hajimu, Masuda. *Cold War Crucible: The Korean Conflict and the Postwar World*. Cambridge, MA: Harvard University Press, 2015.

Halliday, Fred. "Cold War in the Caribbean." *New Left Review* 1.141 (1983).

Hanley, Charles J., and Jae-Soon Chang. "U.S. Allowed Korean Massacre in 1950." Associated Press Report, July 5, 2008. CBS/AP.

Harrington, Michael. *Socialism*. New York: Bantam, 1972.

Hassan, Robert. *The Condition of Digitality: A Post-Modern Marxism for the Practice of Digital Life*. London: University of Westminster Press, 1989.

Heale, M. J. *American Anti-Communism: Combatting the Enemy Within, 1830–1970*. Baltimore, MD: Johns Hopkins University Press, 1990.

Heehs, Peter. "Foreign Influences on Bengali Revolutionary Terrorism 1902–1908." *Modern Asian Studies* 28.3 (1994): 533–56.

Herring, George C. "The Cold War and Vietnam." *OAH Magazine of History* 18.5 (2004): 18–21.

Hirschman, Albert O. *The Rhetoric of Reaction: Perversity, Futility, Jeopardy*. Cambridge, MA: Harvard Belknap, 1991.

Hobsbawm, Eric. *The Age of Empire: 1875–1914*. 1987. New York: Vintage, 1989.

Hobsbawm, Eric. *The Age of Extremes: A History of the World, 1914–1991*. New York: Vintage, 1996.

Hoeveler, David J. *Watch on the Right: Conservative Intellectuals in the Reagan Era*. Madison: University of Wisconsin Press, 1991.

Hofstadter, Richard. *The American Political Tradition and the Men Who Made It*. New York: Vintage, 1948.

Hofstadter, Richard. *The Paranoid Style in American Politics and Other Essays*. Cambridge, MA: Harvard University Press, 1952.

Honey, Michael. "The Memphis Strike: Martin Luther King's Last Campaign." *Poverty & Race Journal*. Civil Rights History. March–April 2007.

Horne, Gerald. "The United States to Seize Cuba to Prevent 'Africanization'? *Race to Revolution: The U.S. and Cuba during Slavery and Jim Crow*. New York: NYU Press, 2014.

Horne, Gerald. *White Supremacy Confronted: U.S. Imperialism and Anti-Communism vs. the Liberation of Southern Africa, from Rhodes to Mandela*. New York: International, 2019.

Hoston, Germaine A. *State, Identity, and the National Question in China and Japan*. Princeton, NJ: Princeton University Press, 1994.

Hucker, Daniel. *Public Opinion and the End of Appeasement in Britain and France*. London: Ashgate, 2011.

Iber, Patrick. "The Anti-Communist Left and the Cuban Revolution." In *Neither Peace nor Freedom: The Cultural Cold War in Latin America*, 116–44. Cambridge, MA: Harvard University Press, 2015.

Japan Times. "Purge of Communists." 1936. Reprint from *japantimes.com. jp*. ("75 Years Ago"), December 18, 2011.

Johnson, Chalmers. *Blowback: The Costs and Consequences of American Empire*. New York: Holt, 2000.

Johnson, Chalmers. *Nemesis: The Last Days of the American Republic*. New York: Holt, 2007.

Judge, Edward H., and John W. Langdon. *A Hard and Bitter Peace: A Global History of the Cold War*. Hoboken, NJ: Prentice Hall, 1996.

Judge, Edward H., and John W. Langdon, eds. *The Cold War: A History through Documents*. Upper Saddle River, NJ: Prentice Hall, 1999.

Judt, Tony. *Postwar: A History of Europe since 1945*. New York: Penguin, 2005.

Kallis, Aristotle, ed. *The Fascism Reader*. New York: Routledge, 2003.

Kaplan, Robert. "Was Democracy Just a Moment?" *Atlantic Monthly*, December 1997.

Keddie, Nikki R. *Debating Revolutions*. New York: New York University Press, 1995.

Keegan, John. *The Second World War*. New York: Penguin, 2005.

Kennedy, Paul. "The Costs and Benefits of British Imperialism 1846–1914." *Past & Present* 125 (1989): 186–92.

Kennedy, Paul. *The Rise and Fall of the Great Powers: Economic Change and Military Conflict from 1500 to 2000*. 1987. New York: Vintage, 1989.

Kershaw, Ian. *Hitler: A Biography*. New York: Norton, 2010.

Kim, Hakjoon. "The American Military Government in South Korea, 1945–1948: Its Formation, Policies, and Legacies." *Asian Perspective* 12.1 (1988): 51–83.

King, Martin Luther, Jr. *Where Do We Go from Here: Chaos or Community?* Boston: Beacon Press, 1968.

Kington, Tom. "Documents Reveal Italian Dictator Got Start in Politics in 1917 with Help of £100 Weekly Wage from MI5." *The Guardian*, October 13, 2009.

Koh, B. C. "The War's Impact on the Korean Peninsula." *Journal of American-East Asian Relations* 2.1, Special Issue: The Impact of the Korean War (1993): 57–76.

Lamrani, Salim. "Fidel Castro and the Triumph of the Cuban Revolution." In *The Economic War against Cuba: A Historical and Legal Perspective on the U.S. Blockade*, 17–22. New York: NYU Press, 2013.

Lapavitstas, Costas, Annina Kaltenbrunner , Duncan Lindo , J. Michell , Juan Pablo Painceira , Eugenia Pires , Jeff Powell , Alexis Stenfors, Nuno Teles, and L. Vatikiotis. *Crisis in the Eurozone*. New York: Verso, 2012.

Lawrence, Pieter. "Report on Mau Mau." July 1960. *Socialist Standard*. Public Domain: Marxists Internet Archive, 2016.

Levine, Yasha. "Michele Bachmann: Welfare Queen." *Truthdig*, December 22, 2009.

Lonsdale, John. "Mau Maus of the Mind: Making Mau Mau and Remaking Kenya." *Journal of African History* 31.3 (1990): 393–421.

Louro, Michele. "The Johnstone Affair and Anti-Communism in Interwar India." *Journal of Contemporary History* 53.1 (2018): 38–60.

Lu, David. *Japan: A Documentary History: The Late Tokugawa Period to the Present*. New York: Routledge, 2015.

Luff, Jennifer. "Labor Anticommunism in the United States of America and the United Kingdom, 1920–49." *Journal of Contemporary History* 53.1 (2018): 109–33.

Mansfield, Peter. *A History of the Middle East*, 2nd ed. London: Penguin Books, 2003.

Marcy, William L. "The End of Civil War, the Rise of Narcotrafficking and the Implementation of the Merida Initiative in Central America." *International Social Science Review* 89.1 (2014): 1–36.

Marx, Karl, and Friedrich Engels. *The Communist Manifesto*. 1848. New York: Penguin Classics, 2002.

Masri, Rania. "Post-War? Or New Phase of the War?" *International Socialist Review*, July–August 2003.

Massey, Douglas S., Jorge Durand, and Karen A. Pren. "Explaining Undocumented Migration to the U.S." *International Migration Review* 48.4 (2014): 1028–61.

McClain, James L. *Japan: A Modern History*. New York: Norton, 2002.

McCormick, Thomas J. *America's Half Century: United States Foreign Policy in the Cold War and After*. Baltimore, MD: Johns Hopkins University Press, 1995.

McCusker, Brent, and Alistair Fraser. "Land Reform in the Era of Neoliberalism: Case Studies from the Global South." *Geographical Review* 98.3 (2008): iii–vi.

McLeod, Mark W. "Indigenous Peoples and the Vietnamese Revolution, 1930–1975." *Journal of World History* 10.2 (1999): 353–89.

McSherry, J. Patrice. "Operation Condor: Clandestine Inter-American System." *Social Justice* 26.4 (1999): 144–74.

Merriman, John. *A History of Modern Europe: From the Renaissance to the Present.* New York: Norton, 1996.

Merriman, John. *Massacre: The Life and Death of the Paris Commune.* New York: Basic Books, 2014.

Milani, Abbas. *The Shah.* New York: Palgrave Macmillan, 2011.

Minehan, Philip. *Civil War and World War in Europe: Spain, Yugoslavia and Greece, 1936–1949.* New York: Palgrave Macmillan, 2006.

Moncada Barracks Museum. "Ofensiva final del Ejército Rebelde." Information board with map. Alamy Stock Photo.

Morales Domínguez, Esteban. "Cuba: Science and Race Fifty Years Later." In *Race in Cuba: Essays on the Revolution and Racial Inequality*, edited by Gary Prevost and August Nimtz, 145–62. New York: NYU Press, 2013.

Morgan, Nick. "The Antinomies of Identity Politics: Neoliberalism, Race and Political Participation in Colombia." In *Cultures of Anti-Racism in Latin America and the Caribbean*, edited by Peter Wade, James Scorer, and Ignacio Aguiló, 25–47. London: Institute of Latin American Studies, 2019.

Morgenfeld, Leandro. "Trump, nuestra América y la experiencia de Mar del Plata." In *Cuba: el legado revolucionario y los dilemas de la izquierda y las fuerzas progresistas en América Latina*, edited by César Bolaño, Mely del Rosario González Aróstegui, Julio Paltán López, Fernando Luis Rojas López, and Rafael Magdiel Sánchez Quiroz, 105–60. Paris: CLACSO, 2018.

Munck, Ronaldo. "The Labor Question and Dependent Capitalism: The Case of Latin America." In *The Social Question in the Twenty-First Century*, edited by Jan Breman, Kevan Harris, Ching Kwan Lee and Marcel van der Linden, 116–33. Oakland: University of California Press, 2019.

Naoroji, Dadabhai. *Poverty and Un-British Rule in India.* London: Swan and Schonnenschein, 1901.

Nuno Rodrigues, Luís. "The United States and Portuguese Decolonization." *Portuguese Studies* 29.2 (2013): 164–85.

Núñez Sarmiento, Marta. "U.S. Proposals for an Unwanted Transition in Cuba: A Critique." *Latin American Perspectives* 41.4: Cuba in Transition (2014): 147–63.

Olmsted, Kathryn. "British and US Anticommunism between the World Wars." *Journal of Contemporary History* 53.1 (2018): 89–108.

Olson, James S., and Randy Roberts. *My Lai: A Brief History with Documents.* Boston: Bedfor, 1998.

Paige, Jeffery M. *Agrarian Revolution: Social Movements and Export Agriculture in the Underdeveloped World.* New York: Free Press, 1975.

Parenti, Michael. *The Anti-Communist Impulse.* New York: Random House, 1970.

Parramore, Lynn. "Meet the Hidden Architect behind America's Racist Economics." *Institute for New Economic Thinking* 648 (2020).

Paxton, Robert O. *The Anatomy of Fascism.* New York: Vintage, 2004.

Perreault, Thomas, and Patricia Martin. "Geographies of Neoliberalism in Latin America." *Environment and Planning* 37 (2005): 191–201.

Petras, James, and Henry Veltmeyer. "Imperialism and Democracy: Convergence and Divergence." *Journal of Contemporary Asia* 42.2 (2012): 298–307.

Pinderhughes, Charles. "How 'Black Awakening in Capitalist America' Laid the
    Foundation for a New Internal Colonialism Theory." *Black Scholar* 40.2 (2010): 71–8.
Piketty, Thomas. "The Top 1 Percent in International and Historical Perspective." *Journal
    of Economic Perspectives* 27.3 (Summer 2013): 3–20.
Piketty, Thomas. "Putting Distribution Back at the Center of Economics: Reflections on
    'Capital in the Twenty-First Century.'" *Journal of Economic Perspectives* 29.1 (Winter
    2015): 67–88.
Pipes, Richard. *Property and Freedom*. New York: Vintage, 2000.
Polanyi, Karl. *The Great Transformation: The Political and Economic Origins of Our Time*.
    New York: Farrar and Rhinheart, 1944.
Popplewell, Richard J. *Intelligence and Imperial Defence: British Intelligence and the Defence
    of the Indian Empire 1904–1924*. Philadelphia: Routledge, 1995.
Poulantzas, Nicos. *Fascism and Dictatorship: The Third International and the Problem of
    Fascism*. Translated by Judith White. London: Verso, 1979.
Prashad, Vijay. *The Darker Nations: A People's History of the Third World*. New York:
    New Press, 2007.
Prins, Nomi. *Collusion: How the Central Bankers Rigged the World*. New York: Nation
    Books, 2018.
Raby, David. *Fascism and Resistance in Portugal: Communists, Liberals and Military
    Dissidents in the Opposition to Salazar, 1941–1974*. Manchester: Manchester University
    Press, 1988.
Ramnath, Maia. "Two Revolutions: The Ghadar Movement and India's Radical Diaspora,
    1913- 1918." *Radical History Review* 92 (2005): 7–30.
Ramnath, Maia. *Haj to Utopia: How the Ghadar Movement Charted Global Radicalism
    and Attempted to Overthrow the British Empire*. Los Angeles: University of California
    Press, 2011.
Reynaud, Paul. *The Foreign Policy of Charles de Gaulle*. New York: Odyssey Press, 1964.
Riera, Pepita. *Servicio de inteligencia de Cuba comunista*. Miami, FL: Service Offset
    Printers, 1966.
Rosenkranz, Susan A. "Breathing Disaffection: The Impact of Irish Nationalist Journalism
    on India's Native Press." *Southeast Review of Asian Studies* 27 (2006).
Saha, Poulomi. "Singing Bengal into a Nation: Tagore the Colonial Cosmopolitan?"
    Journal of Modern Literature 36.2: Aesthetic Politics—Revolutionary and Counter-
    Revolutionary (2013): 1–24.
Saull, Richard. "Social Conflict and the Global Cold War." *International Affairs* 87.5
    (2011): 1123–40.
Sassoon, Donald. *One Hundred Years of Socialism: The West European Left in the Twentieth
    Century*. New York: Norton, 1996.
Sayed-Ahmed, Mohamed Abd El-Wahab. "US-Egyptian Relations from the 1952
    Revolution to the Suez Crisis of 1956." PhD thesis. Department of Economic and
    Political Studies, School of Oriental and African Studies, University of London, 1987.
Schrecker, Ellen. *The Age of McCarthyism: A Brief History with Documents*. Boston:
    Bedford/St. Martin's, 2002.
Schulman, Bruce J. *Lyndon B. Johnson and American Liberalism: A Brief History with
    Documents*. Boston: Bedford, 1995.
Schwartz, Fred. *You Can Trust the Communists (to Be Communists)*. Englewood Cliffs:
    Prentice-Hall, 1960.

Scullin, Joshua. "The Mau Mau Insurrection: The Failed Rebellion that Freed Kenya." *History Undergraduate Theses*. 29. University of Washington Tacoma, 2017. Available online: https://digitalcommons.tacoma.uw.edu/history_theses/29.

Sehanavis, Chinmohan. "The Impact of Lenin on Bhagat Singh's Life." *Mainstream* 45.42 (2007).

Sheehan, Neil, Hedrick Smith, E. W. Kenworthy, and Fox Butterfield. *The Pentagon Papers: As Published by The New York Times*. Toronto: Bantam, 1971.

Sigelmann, Laura. "The Hidden Driver: Climate Change and Migration in Central America's Northern Triangle." *American Security Project*, 2019. JSTOR. https://www.americansecurityproject.org/wp-content/uploads/2019/09/Ref-0229-Climate-Change-Migration-Northern-Triangle.pdf.

Silver-Greenberg, Jessica, and Robert Gebeloff. "Arbitration Everywhere Stacking the Deck of Justice." *New York Times*, October, 2015.

Skaperdas, Stergios. "Policymaking in the Eurozone and the Core vs Periphery Problem," CESifo Forum, ISSN 2190-717X, ifo Institut - Leibniz-Institut für Wirtschaftsforschung an der Universität München, München 12.2 (2011): 12–18.

Skaperdas, Stergios. "Seven Myths about the Greek Debt Crisis," Department of Economics, University of California, Irvine, October 28, 2011 (unpublished paper).

Soviet Information Bureau. *Falsifiers of History (Historical Report)*. Edited by Joseph Stalin. Moscow: Foreign Languages Publishing House, 1948.

Stavrianos, Leften. *Lifelines from our Past: A New World History*. New York: M.E. Sharpe, 1992.

Stiglitz, Joseph E. "The End of Neoliberalism and the Rebirth of History." *Project Syndicate: The World Opinion Page*, November 4, 2019. Available online: https://socialeurope.eu/the-end-of-neoliberalism-and-the-rebirth-of-history.

Stone, Marla and Giuliana Chamedes. "Naming the Enemy: Anti-Communism in Transnational Perspective." *Journal of Contemporary History* 53.1 (2018): 4–11.

Stone, Richard. "Forensic Finds Add Substance to Claims of War Atrocities." *Science*, New Series 325.5939 (2009): 374–5.

Stoner, K. Lynn. "Recent Literature on Cuba and the United States." *Latin American Research Review*. 31.3 (1996): 235–47.

Storrs, Landon R. Y. "Attacking the Washington 'Femmocracy': Antifeminism in the Cold War Campaign against 'Communists in Government.'" *Feminist Studies* 33.1 (2007): 118–52.

Striffer, Steve. "The Cuban Revolution and the Cold War." *Solidarity: Latin America and the US Left in the Era of Human Rights*. London: Pluto Press, 2019.

Szulc, Tad. "Fidel Castro's Years as a Secret Communist." *New York Times Archive*, October 19, 1986.

Taba, Marius. "Antigypsyism in a Time of Neoliberalism: Challenging the Radical Right through Transformative Change." In *Romani Communities and Transformative Change: A New Social Europe*, edited by Andrew Ryder, Marius Taba, and Nidhi Trehan, 65–92. Bristol: Bristol University Press, 2021.

Terretta, Meredith. "'In the Colonies, Black Lives Don't Matter.' Legalism and Rights Claims across the French Empire." *Journal of Contemporary History* 53.1 (2018): 12–37.

Therborn, Göran. *Science, Class and Society: On the Formation of Sociology and Historical Materialism*. 1976. London: Verso, 1980.

Thomas, Martin. "France's North African Crisis, 1945–1955: Cold War and Colonial Imperatives." *History* 92.2 (2007): 207–34.

Thomas, Philip. "Neoliberal Governmentality, Austerity, and Psychopolitics." In *Psychology and Politics: Intersections of Science and Ideology in the History of Psy- Sciences*, edited by Anna Borgos, Ferenc Erős, and Júlia Gyimesi, 321–8. Budapest: Central European University Press, 2019.

Tønnesson, Stein. "The Longest Wars: Indochina 1945–75." *Journal of Peace Research* 22.1 (1985): 9–29.

Trotsky, Leon. "A Fresh Lesson on the Character of the Coming War." *New International* 4.12 (1938): 358–66.

Trotsky, Leon. "The Chinese Revolution." *Fourth International* (New York) 6.10 (1945): 312–16.

Urwin, J. W., and Anti-Socialist Union of Great Britain, Statistical Committee. *Socialism Exposed*. London: The Union, 1914.

Vasconi, Tomás A., Elina Peraza, and Fred Murphy. "Social Democracy and Latin America." *Latin American Perspectives* 20.1 (1993): 99–113.

Verdery, Katherine. *What Was Socialism, What Comes Next*. Princeton, NJ: Princeton University Press, 1996.

Von Kuehnelt-Leddihn, Erik. *Leftism Revisited: From de Sade and Marx to Hitler and Pol Pot*. Preface by William F. Buckley Jr. Washington, DC: Regnery Gateway, 1990.

Von Mises, Ludwig. *Socialism: An Economic and Sociological Analysis*. 1922. Translated by J. Kahane, Foreword by F. A. Hayek. Liberty Fund Library of the Works of Ludwig von Mises. OLL. Available online: https://oll.libertyfund.org/title/kahane-socialism-an-economic-and-sociological-analysis.

Wengraf, Lee. "Legacies of Colonialism in Africa: Imperialism, Dependence, and Development." *International Socialist Review* 103 (Winter 2016–17).

Westad, Odd Arne. *The Global Cold War: Third World Interventions and the Making of Our Times*. New York: Cambridge University Press, 2007.

White, Timothy J. "Cold War Historiography: New Evidence behind Traditional Typographies." *International Social Science Review* 75.3–4 (2000): 35–46.

Wiesen Cook, Blanche. "The Impact of Anti-Communism in American Life." *Science & Society* 53.4 (1989/1990).

Wilson, Edmund. *To the Finland Station: A Study in the Writing and Acting of History*. Garden City, NY: Doubleday, 1940.

Wolfe, Justin. "Conclusion: Exceptionalism and Nicaragua's Many Revolutions." In *A Nicaraguan Exceptionalism: Debating the Legacy of the Sandinista Revolution*, edited by Hilary Francis, 179–84. London: University of London Press, 2019.

Wolfe, Patrick. "History and Imperialism: A Century of Theory, from Marx to Postcolonialism." *American Historical Review* 102.2 (1997): 388–420.

Woods, Colleen. "Seditious Crimes and Rebellious Conspiracies: Anti-Communism and US Empire in the Philippines." *Journal of Contemporary History* 53.1 (2018): 61–88.

World Bank. "Republic of Iraq." In *Middle East and North Africa: Macro Poverty Outlook*, 14–15. Washington, DC: World Bank Group, 2020. Available online: https://pubdocs.worldbank.org/en/747731554825511209/mpo-mena.pdf.

X, Malcolm (1964). *The Autobiography of Malcolm X, as Told to Alex Haley*. New York: Ballantine, 2015.

Index

www.ingramcontent.com/pod-product-compliance
Lightning Source LLC
Chambersburg PA
CBHW050409280326
41932CB00013BA/1790